Omai, Pacific Envoy

I *Omai by Sir Joshua Reynolds, c. 1775*

OMAI
Pacific Envoy

E. H. McCormick

Auckland University Press
Oxford University Press

This volume includes quotations from *Boswell for the Defence* (1960), ed. W. K. Wimsatt and F. A. Pottle, and *Boswell: the Ominous Years* (1963), ed. C. Ryskamp and F. A. Pottle. Copyright Yale University. Used with permission of William Heinemann Ltd., London, and McGraw-Hill Book Company, New York.

Publication of this book has been assisted by a grant from the Minister of Internal Affairs.

First published 1977
Printed in New Zealand
from type set by Typocrafters
by the University of Auckland Bindery
Colour plates printed by Wilson and Horton Ltd.
Bound by L. D. Hanratty Ltd.
ISBN 0 19 647952 5

To
Keith Sinclair
and
Keith Sorrenson
Friends, Colleagues, Patrons

Preface and Acknowledgements

IN ORIGIN THIS BOOK IS THE BY-PRODUCT OF A STUDY, BEGUN SOME YEARS ago, of James Burney and his circle. After completing a first draft I realized that Omai had received undue emphasis in the early chapters, that he had in effect taken over the enterprise. So, setting aside the typescript (only temporarily, I trust), I decided to undertake a separate work devoted solely to Omai. My aim has been to put him in his setting of place and time, to relate such biographical details as could be ascertained or surmised, and to trace the course of his posthumous reputation both in his native islands and in Europe.

For a man of whose life only a little more than four years are recorded the scale of treatment may seem — may well be — somewhat disproportionate. But Omai was more than the first Polynesian to visit Britain, more than the amiable buffoon whose '*How do, King Tosh?*' and similar fatuities have been quoted in scores of books and articles. As I hope the following pages will show, he was a kind of catalyst, provoking discussion of many issues — moral, philosophical, religious — concerning eighteenth-century society. In his person, moreover, he dramatized dilemmas which still confront Europeans in their dealings with Pacific peoples. Whatever may be learned from Omai's example (and I have left readers to draw their own conclusions), the lessons still seem relevant. Indeed, I see his story re-enacted daily on the streets of Auckland — a spectacle that redeems the city from banality and makes it one of the most interesting in the world.

In compiling the book I have used much hitherto unpublished material drawn from libraries in England, Australia, New Zealand, and the United States. My chief sources, however, have been the late J. C. Beaglehole's magnificent edition of Captain Cook's journals and the *Endeavour* journal of Joseph Banks. One of Professor Beaglehole's characteristics as an historian — and one of his few weaknesses, it seems to me — was the intensity of his response to figures of the past. For Omai he apparently felt neither sympathy nor regard: 'he was really a very foolish inattentive fellow' ran a summing up in the introduction to volume iii of Cook's journals (p. lxxxviii); 'he was at bottom a foolish inattentive fellow' was again the verdict in *The Life of Captain James Cook* (p. 449). In the latter work, to my consternation and for reasons

I have failed to discover, the generally accepted *Mai* was rendered *Mae*.

Readers must again make up their own minds about Omai or Mai (as I shall continue to call him) from the abundant and often conflicting evidence assembled below. In my opinion, for what it is worth, he acted well in the testing situations into which circumstances and the whims of his patrons led him. And where his conduct was most severely censured by European observers (during the interlude at Tahiti, for example) it could be defended as in accordance with his inherited precepts and customs. One day I hope some writer, perhaps of Polynesian origin, will emulate the Abbé Baston and retell the story of Omai from his own point of view.

For a chronicler with no competence in any of the Polynesian tongues there have been some problems. Contrary to the advice of learned friends, in rendering native words I have omitted glottal stops, partly because they are unfamiliar to me, partly because they rarely appear in my sources. The form of personal names has presented further difficulties. Following the style which it seemed natural to adopt for Omai, I have called individuals by the designations used by eighteenth-century explorers and writers (Oberea, Ereti, Otoo) while indicating the probably 'correct' versions in the text. Geographical terms are normally given in their modern forms, though sometimes it seemed appropriate to employ such superseded place names as Van Diemen's Land and Batavia. The index with its cross-references should clear up any uncertainties. Quotations, it is hardly necessary to say, are rendered without alteration and, always subject to a small margin for human error, may be assumed to reproduce any peculiarities in the original texts or documents.

Obligations incurred at every stage of the work are many. It has been my good fortune to benefit from the labours not only of J. C. Beaglehole but of others who have contributed to what is surely the golden age of Pacific scholarship. Bernard Smith's *European Vision and the South Pacific* has again been a guide and inspiration, as it has been ever since I reviewed it for *Landfall* in March 1961. In dealing with the unfamiliar subject of French exploration I have largely relied on J.-E. Martin-Allanic's exhaustive study of Bougainville and J. Dunmore's more general survey. In the penultimate chapter I have used D. L. Oliver's *Ancient Tahitian Society* and, had it appeared earlier, would have drawn more often on that superb conspectus of a vanished culture. I have also relied heavily on recent bibliographers of the Pacific, especially P. O'Reilly and E. Reitman, Miss M. K. Beddie, Miss Phyllis Mander-Jones, ana R. E. Du Rietz.

The book was written while I was research fellow in Arts at the University of Auckland. I am deeply grateful to the University for awarding the fellowship and to the Department of History for hospitality and help during its tenure. A more specific and personal debt is indicated in the dedication. Particulars of the collections which have made manuscripts or pictorial material available will be found in the section on sources (pp. 337-8) and in the list of illustrations (pp. xiii-xviii). I wish to thank the institutions concerned and their staffs for meeting my often troublesome requests and gladly pay my customary tribute to long-suffering friends in the University Library, the Public Library, and the Museum Library, Auckland. Nor must I fail to record my appreciation of the encouragement given by Mr. E. W. Smith, Director of the Auckland City Art Gallery, and his staff in organizing the exhibition, 'The Two Worlds of Omai'.

Among other friends and colleagues I am specially indebted to Professor W. H. Pearson for sharing with me his unrivalled knowledge of Pacific literature and for his services in tracing the music for the pantomime *Omai*. Dr. Averil M. Lysaght, an equally generous scholar, has made available her Banks papers and has been tireless in seeking out elusive manuscripts on my behalf. For the rest I can only list those who have helped with criticism, with translation, and with advice or information on specialized subjects: Professor B. G. Biggs, Mr. E. Craig, Mrs. Jessie Harding, Dr. A. B. Hooper, Mrs. Robin Hooper, Professor K. J. Hollyman, Miss Anne Kirker, Dr. R. A. Lochore, Mrs. Phoebe Meikle, Dr. R. G. Phillips, Miss Una Platts, Mr. M. Shadbolt, Dr. Elizabeth Sheppard, Professor D. I. B. Smith, and Dr. Kathryn Smits. Regrettably the limitations of this book prevented my using a *trouvaille* which perhaps indicates some surviving memory of Omai in English or American folklore. According to my friend Mr. A. C. Stones, during his boyhood he saw a lavishly tattooed man exhibited under that name in Manchester. Further investigation proved him to have been 'The Great Omi', originally sponsored by Robert Ripley of 'Believe it or not' fame. Particulars of this celebrity will be found in Bob Considine's *Ripley, the Modern Marco Polo* (New York, 1961), pp. 143-4.

That was the situation when I handed over my typescript to the publishers and left for England in May 1976. Since then the score of obligations has lengthened in both hemispheres. Thanks are due to Mr. D. R. Thompson for the care he has shown in the setting of a complicated text; to Messrs. R. Dudding and K. Ireland for professional expertise in reading the proofs; to Mrs. Susan Stenderup and Mr. R. Ritchie for help in their specialized fields of illustration and design; to Messrs. M. Gill and J. F. Maynard for their efforts to re-enact the story of Omai on television; to Mr. R. D. McEldowney for innumerable services and his unfailing patience with a temperamental author; to his assistant, Mrs. Norma Jenkin, for many kindnesses; and for favours I need not specify to my sister, as always, and to Mr. B. W. Harley.

Auckland
March 1977   E.H.M.

Contents

Illustrations

Original titles, where known, are reproduced with minor typographical modifications.

Acknowledgements

The illustrations have been reproduced through the courtesy of the following: Alexander Turnbull Library, Wellington, 9, 66-68; Ashmolean Museum, Oxford, 28, 34, 37; Auckland Museum Library, 10, 20, 25, 31, 47, 51, 59; Auckland Public Library, 5-7, 14-18, 23, 24, 52, 54, 55, 58, 60; Auckland University Library, 1, 2, 57; Australian Historic Memorials Committee, Canberra, 19; British Library Board, London, 3, 4, 61, 69; British Museum Trustees, London, 11, 12, 30, 32, 39, 43, 56; Castle Howard Collection, York, I, IV; F. H. Haigh, Auckland, 44-46, 49, 50, 53, 70; Henry E. Huntington Library and Art Gallery, San Marino, California, 41; Kroepelien Collection, the Royal University Library, Oslo, 33, 71; National Library of Australia, Canberra, 48, 62-65; Parham Park Collection, Sussex, II; Public Archives of Canada, Ottawa, 29; Public Record Office, London (by permission of the Controller of H.M. Stationery Office), 21, 22, 42; R. E. Rathbone, Auckland, 13; Rex Nan Kivell Collection, National Library of Australia, Canberra, 26, 27, 40; Victoria and Albert Museum, London, 8, 35, 36; Westminster City Library Archives Department, London, 38; Yale University Art Gallery, III.

Photographic credits: Alexander Turnbull Library, Wellington, 9, 66-68; Ashmolean Museum, Oxford, 28, 34, 37; British Library, London, 3, 4, 61, 69; British Museum, London, 11, 12, 30, 32, 39, 43, 56; Coverdale and Fletcher, York, I, IV; J. S. Daley, Auckland, 1, 2, 5-7, 10, 14-18, 20, 23-25, 31, 44-47, 49-55, 57, 60, 70; W. Gardiner, Worthing, II; Henry E. Huntington Library and Art Gallery, San Marino, 41; A. Loot, Auckland, 13; J. Metcalfe, Auckland, 8, 35, 36, 38; National Library of Australia, Canberra, 19, 26, 27, 40, 48, 62-65; Public Archives of Canada, Ottawa, 29; Public Record Office, London, 21, 22, 42; Royal University Library, Oslo, 33, 71; Yale University Gallery, III.

In the preparation of sketch maps thanks are due to the Council of the Hakluyt Society for permission to use material in *The Journals of Captain James Cook*, ed. J. C. Beaglehole. Grateful acknowledgements for his services are also given to R. M. Harris, cartographer, Geology Department, University of Auckland.

1. Mai and the European Discovery of Tahiti

LITTLE CAN BE SAID WITH ASSURANCE ABOUT THE EARLY LIFE OF THE YOUNG Polynesian who came to be known as Omai. It is generally agreed that he was a native of Raiatea, an island of the Society Group to the northwest of Tahiti. There is less unanimity concerning his age, but he seems to have been born, by European reckoning, soon after the middle of the eighteenth century — about the year 1753 according to one reliable witness.[1] The rest can be pieced out from his own uncertain testimony or is to be inferred from the recorded customs of his people.[2]

Mai, as he was called by his family, was, it appears, a younger son and a member of the *raatira*, the second order of Raiatean society. Hence his birth would not have been celebrated with the observances that marked such an event in the superior class, the *arii*. Not for Mai the elaborate ceremonies attending the first public appearance of a future chief; and not for Mai the human sacrifice. Nevertheless, all unconsciously in earliest infancy he was introduced to those traditional rites that were to govern his actions throughout every stage of his future existence. With whatever trophies they could muster, his relatives gathered at their meeting place, the ancestral *marae*, to greet the newborn child. There in an atmosphere of high seriousness the religious offices were performed, perhaps by his father. The prescribed incantations were recited and a sacrifice was probably offered up in the form of a slaughtered pig. Then in the customary Polynesian manner followed speeches, feasting, the exchange of gifts.

After his ceremonial début Mai returned to his female kin, remaining in their indulgent care till he emerged from babyhood. They fed him with the best of food to make him fat, they bathed him in cold water to make him strong, they rubbed his body with scented oils, they pampered him, they petted him. Gradually he came to recognize their faces and in time learned to distinguish the names and features of the small group that assembled at the local *marae*. Precise relationships were at first obscure or may have seemed unimportant, since all were linked by ties of blood and joined in reverence for their common ancestors. Later, however, Mai was taught to differentiate carefully among his various kinsfolk and would have applied to each a special term indicating the place he or she held in the intricate network of family affinities.

1

From an early age the boy would have grown familiar with the bays and lagoons of his native island. He learned to swim almost as soon as he began to walk and even in childhood would have picked up fragments of traditional lore from the men and women thronging the palm-fringed beaches. The Raiateans were a great seafaring people, renowned fishermen and expert canoe-builders. Most revered of all their deities was Taaroa, god of the sea, and in common with other Polynesians they delighted in the legends of Maui, supreme angler of all creation. Mai heard of the hero's exploits as he played on the beach with his brothers or listened at night while members of his family diverted themselves with the telling of tales. In addition he heard and memorized practical hints thrown out by his elders — the best shells to use for making fish-hooks, the various methods of weaving nets, the techniques and ritual followed in fashioning a canoe.

1 Fishing by torchlight

His knowledge expanded when, perhaps in the company of a *taio* or special friend, he explored the fertile valleys and steep volcanic hills of the interior. Like Taruia and Vini of Tahitian legend, they scaled the heights in search of prized feather birds or with boyish abandon slid over slippery cascades into the pools below. But these expeditions were fraught with peril to the uninitiated. All Society Islanders and Tahitians venerated Raiatea as the most ancient of the group, the primal source of their being. The island abounded in burial sanctuaries and *marae*, one of which, Taputapuatea, was the most sacred in Polynesia. Mai and his companions learned that they must avoid such places in case they infringed the laws of *tapu* and incurred the fearful penalties imposed by gods and men.

The laws of *tapu*, the growing child soon realized, governed many of his actions. He must not approach the men working on a sacred canoe or the builders of a chieftain's *marae* — they were strictly *tapu*. He must not deface the great forest trees or hunt the rarer birds — they, too, were *tapu*. The crops of *taro* and breadfruit were *tapu* until ready for harvesting, and so were certain delicacies reserved for the chief. This and other prohibitions were formulated in the sayings Mai learned from his elders. 'These things which are *tapu* to the *arii* must not be eaten', they told him, specifying further: 'the turtle, the cavally, the chest and fillet of the hog, the first fruits of the land. All these are *tapu*.'[3]

Other precepts defined his duties to his birthplace, to the chiefly class, to his parents, to the members of his family:

To the land that bore you, all owe respect: it is the parent.

To the *arii*, to his children, to his family, all owe respect. The *arii* is sacred

2 A marae *in Tahiti*

as a god. He is the descendant of the gods.

To the blood of their parents, all owe respect. Beware that you do not sin against it.

To your relations by blood or adoption you must be faithful, and to your stock. Do not avert your eyes from the misfortune of your stock.

Others again prescribed the sacred laws of hospitality and laid down the rules covering property:

Let your eye not fall upon a man who passes your door without bidding him come in to eat. You must share your food with your neighbour.

Let your hands be always open. You must never refuse to give anything that is demanded from you.

Such guides to conduct were instilled into the boy or absorbed unconsciously when he was allowed to accompany his father to welcoming ceremonies for visitors and the annual festival of first-fruits. On that occasion vast quantities of breadfruit and pork were baked in ovens of heated stones covered with leaves and earth. After it was cooked the food was placed in gourds or wooden dishes and served in long sheds decorated with greenery and garlands of flowers. Strict protocol governed the placing of guests, and the women were housed apart from the men. When he was considered big enough to sit with his father and older brothers, Mai had left infancy behind him. At the age of ten or so he passed another milestone: he was taken to an expert in the art of *tatau* and received the first painful incisions of designs that would, in the coming decade, cover legs, thighs, and much of his body.

At about this time — or perhaps even before the ordeal of tattooing had begun — the boy was caught up in a disaster of which only the barest facts are known.[4] Warriors from the nearby island of Borabora, under their chief Puni, invaded Raiatea and overwhelmed the defenders. Mai lost his father in battle and fled with his surviving relatives to Tahiti, one hundred miles away. Apparently the dispossessed family settled at Haapape, a district in the north of Tahiti Nui, the larger of the island's two circular peninsulas. Other refugees, among them an *arii* and priest called Tupaia, sought asylum farther south at Papara, domain of the high chief Amo and his redoubtable wife Purea.

Haapape resembled Mai's old home in most respects. There was a similar setting of beach and lagoon backed by forest-clad hills; except for minor differences the language was the same; and in essentials the religion and social customs of the two places were identical. Tahitian children spun their tops and launched their toy canoes and played hide-and-seek just as Mai had done in Raiatea. The Tahitian people ranged themselves in the same immutable order — the *arii* at the top, the *raatira* in between, and beneath them the lowly and landless *manahune*. And, exactly as in Raiatea, the Tahitians assembled at their *marae* to minister to the gods and carry out their age-old observances. All this was only natural, for, as the Tahitians themselves acknowledged, Raiatea was their ancient parent, the revered Havaii of myth and legend.

Mai and his people were thus not strangers in completely alien sur-roundings. They came to Tahiti as honoured guests, greeted with all the consideration due to kinsmen in distress, even the most distant of kins-men. But nothing could alter the fact that, like the despised *manahune*, they were landless and, once the first lavish hospitality of their hosts was expended, must contrive a living wherever they could. More galling still, they were far removed from their own *marae* and must, in the manner of exiles, gather at the seashore to practise their devotions. There they may be pictured as they directed incantations at the heads of their conquerors or renewed their vows to avenge the dead and regain their lost homeland.

Mai spent the next few years in Tahiti, adding to his stores of know-ledge and experience while he passed from childhood to adolescence. It seems unlikely that he, an outsider, was admitted to the seminaries reserved for priestly initiates. But he may well have attended one of the secular houses of learning where pupils memorized the chants which preserved traditional lore — the names and movements of the stars, the divisions of time, the sequence of seasons, the ancient myths and genealogies. Whatever its source, his formal learning was supplemented, as in Raiatea, by practical lessons imparted by elders or picked up casually on beaches and plantations. Having outgrown childish games, he now competed with his friends in such manly sports as boxing, wrestling, and surf-riding; and in their company he watched the dances and dramatic spectacles performed by bands of roving entertainers, the *arioi*. Like youths in other ages and countries, Mai would have taken pride in his developing body and, more fortunate than many, would have learned to make love in the uncomplicated Tahitian fashion. He was approaching, or had already undergone, initiation into manhood — a solemn event marked by the rite of supercision — when, at about the age of fourteen, he was again overtaken by disaster. Mai was a victim in the Tahitians' last forlorn stand against intruders from Europe.[5]

THROUGHOUT THE FIRST FLEETING DECADE OF MAI'S EXISTENCE, distant rulers, geographers, and philosophers had been shaping the destiny of his people and his own future. In 1753, the probable year of his birth, Jean-Jacques Rousseau began the famous discourse where he attempted to answer questions posed by the Academy of Dijon concerning the origins of human inequality. Earlier he had shown to his satisfaction and apparently to the Academy's (since they awarded him their prize) that so far from purifying society the arts and sciences had corrupted it. Now he addressed himself to the new topic which, as he conceived it, called for an inquiry into the nature of man. 'For how', he asked, 'is it possible to know the Source of the Inequality among Men, without knowing Men themselves?'[6]

Rousseau gave a novel twist to an ancient debate by enlarging its scope and bringing to it the resources of a probing mind and imagination. He claimed that, unlike most of his predecessors, he was concerned not with Europeans alone and not only with his own time. His subject was the whole of human kind since its primeval beginnings. Accordingly he proceeded to trace stage by stage man's course through dark aeons of history to his present condition of wickedness and folly. Only one shaft of light relieved the sombre picture. It was Rousseau's far from idyllic evocation of 'the real Youth of the World' — that epoch when, after emerging at length from the primal state of nature, human beings lived in rustic cabins, dressed in animal skins, used feathers and shells as ornaments, and with sharp-edged stones scooped out little fishing-boats or fashioned clumsy instruments of music. Most savage nations

A

DISCOURSE

UPON THE

ORIGIN and the FOUNDATION

OF THE

Inequality among Mankind.

'TIS of Man I am to ſpeak; and the very Queſtion, in anſwer to which I am to ſpeak of him, ſufficiently informs me that I am going to ſpeak to Men; for to thoſe alone, who are not afraid of honouring Truth, it belongs to propoſe Diſ-

B 3   cuſſions

3 Opening page in the first English translation of Rousseau's Discourse on Inequality

had been found in this condition, he said, and, as their example showed, it could be sanguinary and cruel. Yet despite its imperfections it was, Rousseau held, the state best suited to men, the one in which they might have remained but for a fatal accident — the invention of metallurgy and agriculture. 'With the Poet, it is Gold and Silver,' he proclaimed, 'but with the Philosopher, it is Iron and Corn, which have civilized Men, and ruined Mankind.'[7]

The *Discourse on Inequality* was not merely a bleak essay in speculative reasoning. At each step of his argument, often in extended asides, Rousseau supplied examples drawn from diverse sources, ancient and modern, acknowledged or unacknowledged. When illustrating the probable attributes of primitive man he took from de Condillac details of the child who in 1694 had been discovered living among bears in the forests of Lithuania: 'He did not shew . . . the least Mark of Reason, walked upon Hands and Feet, had no Language but some uncouth

Page 342.

4
*The legendary Lithuanian
bear child*

Sounds, which had nothing common with those of other Men.' No authorities were cited, however, in a summary account of other Europeans on the border line between the human and the animal: the little Hanoverian recently befriended by the English royal family; the two wild creatures, resembling quadrupeds, found in the Pyrenees in 1719; and, more remotely in the fourteenth century, the infant who had been suckled by wolves and who 'used afterwards to say at the Court of Prince *Henry*, that had he his Choice, he would much rather take up with their Company again than live among Men.'[8]

Of human beings in the following era — or their modern and perhaps debased representatives — Rousseau spoke at greater length. Here he derived most of his facts from Peter Kolb, the German naturalist, from Father du Tertre, the missionary, and from the travellers represented in the Abbé Prévost's *Histoire Générale des Voyages*. All such witnesses, he held, agreed about the physical prowess of barbarous nations and the acuteness of their senses. The Hottentots, according to Kolb, were better fishermen than the Europeans at the Cape of Good Hope; in swimming nothing could compare with them; their nimbleness in running was altogether inconceivable; and they could distinguish with the naked eye ships which the Dutch saw only with the aid of glasses. Du Tertre said much the same of the West Indians, praising above all their skill at shooting with their arrows birds in flight or swimming fishes. The Americans were no less famous for strength and dexterity and had tracked down the Spaniards as exactly as the best dogs could have done. 'Give civilized Man but Time to gather about him all his Machines, and no doubt he will be an Overmatch for the Savage', Rousseau conceded, 'but if you have a mind to see a Contest still more unequal, place them naked and unarmed one opposite to the other . . . .'[9]

As for the supposed superiority of civilization in other respects, Rousseau was far from convinced. Europeans had toiled for years to make savages conform to their own manner of living, he observed, yet they had been unable to prevail, even with the aid of religion. Missionaries sometimes made Christians but never civilized men. If these poor creatures were as unhappy as some people would have, why did they so constantly refuse to be governed like ourselves or live among us? Further, he pointed out:

> Savages have been often brought to *Paris*, to *London*, and to other Places; and no Pains omitted to fill them with high Ideas of our Luxury, our Riches, and all our most useful and curious Arts; yet they were never seen to express more than a stupid Admiration at such Things, without the least Appearance of coveting them.

There was, for instance, the North American chief who had been presented to the English Court some thirty years before and offered a thousand gifts. He refused everything: our fire-arms seemed heavy and inconvenient; our shoes pinched his feet; our clothes encumbered his body. Again there were those young Greenlanders and Icelanders whom the Danes had tried to educate and who had only pined away with grief or perished in attempting to swim back to their own country. Finally there was the well-attested case of a Hottentot boy brought up a Christian by the Governor of the Cape, trained as a European, and sent to the Dutch Indies. Soon after returning, he visited his Hottentot relations, exchanged his European finery for a sheep's skin, rejected Christianity, and announced his firm resolution to live and die in the manner of his ancestors.[10]

How varied was the human species, Rousseau reflected: some black, some white, some red, some beardless, some covered with hair. There had been and might still be people of gigantic size; it was even said there were whole nations with tails like quadrupeds. Possibly, he speculated, the orang-outangs and similar creatures reported by European travellers were those very beings which the ancients exalted as divinities under the name of satyrs and fauns. Perhaps more exact inquiries would show them to be men. Rousseau, however, was no mere credulous theorist but a pioneer of the nascent science of anthropology. The accounts in

Prévost and similar collections, he complained, were gathered by
ignorant or prejudiced voyagers — sailors, merchants, soldiers, missionaries. Better qualified observers, he urged, should now undertake the
study of mankind:

. . . I am amazed that in an Age, in which Men so much affect useful and polite
Learning, there does not start up two Men perfectly united, and rich, one in
Money, the other in Genius, both Lovers of Glory, and studious of Immortality,
one of whom should be willing to sacrifice twenty thousand Crowns of his
Fortune, and the other ten Years of his Life to make such a serious Voyage
round the World, as would recommend their Names to the present and future
Generations; not to confine themselves to Plants and Stones, but for once study
Men and Manners . . . .[11]

Rousseau's plea, buried in a lengthy footnote, went unheeded at the
time. Nor did his pessimistic exercise meet with approval from the
academicians of Dijon, for on its appearance in 1755 they failed to
award him a further prize. A year later, however, Charles de Brosses,
one of Dijon's most eminent citizens and President of the Burgundian
Parliament, published a work that not only won acceptance in official
circles but directly influenced the course of Pacific history. In his *Histoire
des Navigations aux Terres Australes*, following the lead of his friend
Buffon, de Brosses issued a blue-print for the exploration of the unknown
south and, incidentally, used the term Polynesia to define the island-
studded Pacific.[12]

De Brosses went beyond most other geographers in thinking undiscovered land might lie in the southern ocean. He believed a great
continent — perhaps more than one — *must* exist in order to maintain
the equilibrium of the globe. Within easy reach of the French possessions
in India, he advised, a settlement should be established whence an
expedition could set out to explore these vast regions with their wealth
of spices, gold, and precious stones. Such treasure might be exchanged
for trifles or the iron for which islanders showed an insatiable desire.
But the aims, he emphasized, should not be purely commercial, while
the leader must be not only brave and capable but also humane. And
(here de Brosses was more lavish and more specific than Rousseau) he
should take with him cartographers, astronomers, botanists, painters,
and such men as might win the friendship of savages — physicians,
surgeons, even musicians. This, he proclaimed, was an enterprise
wherein the French monarch might win glory not through war (engulfing
his subjects and his neighbours in common misery), but through peaceful
exploration and settlement.[13]

The sequel to de Brosses's benign planning was the outbreak of a
bloody and protracted conflict that spread from Europe to the Indies
and the Americas. The Seven Years War, nevertheless, made its contribution to the grand design of Pacific discovery. Future explorers,
ranging through eastern waters and the Atlantic, acquired or perfected

the skills of seamanship until, with the coming of peace in 1763 (about the time Mai was expelled from his childhood Eden), the rival nations resumed their search for colonies and markets. In this new phase of the struggle the initiative was taken by the British who in the years immediately following the Peace of Paris sent three expeditions to the south and produced their own continental theorist, the Scottish-born Alexander Dalrymple.

A correspondent and admirer of de Brosses, Dalrymple printed in 1767 a small book, *Discoveries made in the South Pacifick Ocean*, wherein he presented his views on that vast area of the globe together with some personal details. Almost since infancy, he wrote, exploration had been 'the fond object of his attention'. Stirred by the example of Columbus and Magellan, he had been 'inflamed with the ambition to do *something* to promote the general benefit of mankind, at the same time that it should add to the glory and interest of his country.' His ambition focusing on the discovery of *Terra Australis*, this had become 'the great Passion of his life'. Not its discovery, he went on to correct himself, for since the continent had been seen by Abel Tasman and others, no one could possibly *discover* it. Such certitude would seem to have called for no support beyond the relevant voyage narratives which Dalrymple did in fact publish in this and a later more extensive compilation. But he also provided scientific proof along lines similar to that given by de Brosses. The continent, he argued, was essential in order to counterpoise the weight of land in the north and maintain the earth's equilibrium. He too urged the dispatch of an expedition to visit *Terra Australis*, there to open up 'a very beneficial commerce', and, again following de Brosses, set out the desirable qualities of its leader. 'Intrepidity' and 'every naval accomplishment' were required but also 'knowledge . . . of past discoverers', 'a philosophick idea of winds and seasons', 'freedom from prejudice', 'and, perhaps, not less than all, a consideration of the rights and value of man's life, to secure a patient abstinence from the use of fire-arms against the native Indians'.[14]

There can be no doubt that Dalrymple saw in himself the ideal leader but, as he was forced to acknowledge, he had been 'disappointed in his hopes' and compelled 'to forego all thoughts of being employed in the manner he wished'. When an expedition was dispatched in 1767 his claims were passed over by the Lords of the Admiralty. Nor in appointing commanders for its two forerunners had they shown much concern for the qualities advocated by successive writers. They chose veterans of the late war more renowned for martial prowess and navigational skill than scholarship or humanity. The Hon. John Byron's voyage in the *Dolphin* between 1764 and 1766 added little either to geographical knowledge or to history. But the next explorer, Samuel Wallis, while searching for the Southern Continent in the same vessel, lighted on Tahiti and so uncovered abundant material for poets and students of man.[15]

5 *Tahitians and British clash; Omai was wounded on One Tree Hill at extreme right*

LYRIC WRITERS AND HIGH-PRINCIPLED THEORISTS would have found nothing to inspire them in Wallis's account of that seminal event. Rousseau, on the other hand, might have drawn from it support for his views on the wickedness of civilized man. Within hours of sighting the main island on 19 June 1767 the captain was already exasperated with the light-fingered natives who climbed aboard from their thronging canoes. The same day he cleared the ship by firing over the heads of his troublesome visitors — the 'veriest Thieves I ever met' he characterized them. As he sailed northwards in search of shelter and refreshment for his scurvy-stricken crew, such incidents multiplied and grew more serious, reaching a climax when he took refuge in a bay at the north-western tip of the island.[16]

On 24 June, while the ship was being warped into the harbour, a large fleet, commanded by a man seated on the canopy of a double canoe, gathered round the *Dolphin* and at a signal from the leader repeatedly showered it with stones. Wallis retaliated by ordering the guns to fire, which they did with destructive and dramatic effect. Half an hour later not a canoe could be seen and the inhabitants had vanished. The following day an armed party went ashore to take formal possession of the country, naming it at Wallis's behest King George the Third's Island. The captain and his lieutenant were both ill, so the ceremony was performed by Second Lieutenant Tobias Furneaux.[17]

Since all seemed quiet on the 26th, men were sent to fill water-casks at a river mouth near the anchorage. They were still busy when Wallis observed two fleets converging on the *Dolphin* from opposite ends of the bay while numerous warriors made for the watering party. Thinking, he explained, 'it was necessary to conquer them in the beginning', he ordered the crew to fire at the approaching canoes and then turn their guns on the shore. Immediately the fleets withdrew and the warriors fled to a hill overlooking the bay where crowds of women and children had already gathered. To drive home his stern lesson, Wallis next directed the guns at the multitude on the hill. They fired four shots, inflicting many casualties on combatants and onlookers alike. Among the wounded was the youthful Mai.[18]

Wallis had succeeded in blasting his reluctant hosts into submission. On the afternoon of the final clash, when the ship's carpenters had destroyed every canoe they could find, abject envoys came to the watering-place bearing green emblems of peace together with gifts of food and cloth. The sick went ashore to recuperate and trading began for pork, poultry, fruit, and soon for sexual favours, purchased, like other commodities, with spikes and nails. Supplies were becoming scarce and prices dear when, on 13 July, Wallis was introduced to a 'well looking Woman about forty five years old', tall, and of 'very Majestic Mein'. He called her simply 'the Queen', but she was in reality Purea of Papara on a visit to her husband's northern kinsmen.[19] Then at the height of her power, she had evidently heard of the strangers and decided to inspect them in person.

'The Queen' dominated proceedings in the fortnight that remained of the *Dolphin's* stay. She entertained Wallis ashore, called on her maidens to massage him, and on their way back to the ship lifted him over every 'Slough' and stream with as much ease as he would have carried a child. She supplemented these and other courtesies with lavish gifts of food and scoured the countryside for further supplies. The captain was duly grateful. On 24 July, having informed his tearful hostess that he must soon leave, he consoled her with a tribute of truly regal proportions — 'two Turkeys Two Geese, three Guinea hens, a Cat big with Kitten' and in addition garden seeds, shirts, glass bottles, iron pots, cutlery. Three days later, while the men of the *Dolphin* were preparing to leave Port Royal Harbour (as Wallis named his anchorage), she came aboard, embraced her friends in the most affectionate manner, and, weeping bitterly, bade them farewell.[20]

Wallis was no naïve sentimentalist. In summing up his impressions of the islanders he wrote with candour: 'notwithstanding all their civility, I doubt not but it was more through fear than love that they respected us so much . . . .' His account of the country and its inhabitants, while appreciative, fell far short of ecstasy. They were, he observed, stout, clean-limbed, the men of a tawny colour, the women very handsome, some 'really great beauties' — yet they would prostitute themselves for a nail. He mentioned their walled enclosures decorated with 'uncouth' figures, praised their culinary practices, and with a professional sea-man's ardour supplied full details of their nautical accomplishments. The climate seemed very good, there were few 'Muskettoes' or 'Flyes' and no noxious reptiles. For the rest, the people drank no kind of liquor, used no sauce but salt water, and — an afterthought — all, both men and women, had their backsides marked black.[21]

The report made no mention of the islanders' language and said virtually nothing of their social customs or religion. Wallis might have added to his knowledge of such topics had he, like later explorers, carried away a native-born informant. During the visit there had, in fact, been talk of recruits joining the crew for the homeward voyage, but they were not at the anchorage when the ship finally sailed.[22] Nor was Mai one of their number; presumably the youth was still recovering from the wound inflicted when the *Dolphin* opened fire on 26 June.

MAI AND THE PEOPLE OF HAAPAPE were not directly involved in the next encounter with Europeans in the year following the *Dolphin's* departure. After sighting the island on 2 April 1768, Louis-Antoine de Bougainville took the same northerly course as Wallis but turned back before reaching Port Royal Harbour and finally brought his ships into a lagoon off the district of Hitiaa. A seasoned navigator might have sought a less exposed roadstead, so sparing himself future anxieties. Bougainville, however, was a soldier-diplomat by profession and a sailor only at the call of patriotism. He had served under Montcalm in Canada and, influenced by his friend de Brosses, had set out to restore France's honour by

6 *Captain Wallis in conversation with 'the Queen'*

extending its dominions to the south. Brave, accomplished, humane, he approached de Brosses's ideal of leadership, while his expedition fulfilled most of that theorist's requirements. The two ships, the *Boudeuse* and the *Étoile*, carried an astronomer, a naturalist (Philibert Commerson), doctors, and a number of privileged supernumeraries, of whom the most eminent was the Prince of Nassau-Siegen. Only amateur musicians were included and unfortunately there were no artists.[23]

The French met with the same thronging reception as Wallis and unknowingly benefited from his harsh example. On 5 April, while they were still seeking an anchorage, one 'savage', a man of chiefly bearing, boarded the *Étoile* from a double canoe and insisted on staying the night. He was decked out in European clothes, treated to a meal in the sailors' mess, and taken over the ship. At the sight of guns he grew pale, and he appeared to recognize muskets, for on seeing them in the great cabin he cried 'poux, poux', while gesturing to show that they caused death. Still dressed *à la française*, the same 'Indian' was one of the crowd that greeted Bougainville when he landed from the *Boudeuse* next morning. The leader and his party were received by a chief of even higher degree — Reti by name (or Ereti as it was rendered) — who guided them through a verdant landscape to his home where he entertained them with a simple meal of fruit and fish, served on the lawn outside the house and washed down with draughts of clear water. To Bougainville it seemed like a feast of the golden age in the company of people still living in that happy epoch. An idyllic episode came to a close as the visitors embarked to the 'anacreontic' strains of a native flute.[24]

Similar allusions would adorn the journals of Bougainville and his more erudite companions throughout the ensuing week. The tattooed warriors were compared with the painted Britons described by Julius Caesar, their more than compliant women were variously likened to the goddess Venus, Helen of Troy, Queen Dido, and Eve before the Fall. Once assured that the visit would be brief, these denizens of the antique world were lavish in their hospitality. Ereti provided an immense shed to house the sick, he brought badly needed supplies to the French, he supped with them, stayed overnight in their camp, and summoned one of his wives to sleep with the Prince of Nassau. His subjects followed suit, displaying only venial faults. They were, alas, 'the most dexterous thieves in the Universe', while their uninhibited curiosity could cause embarrassment or worse. They seemed to delight in witnessing the sexual act and one day, surrounding Commerson's valet, they made unmistakable signs that the pretended manservant was a woman. Their victim was saved from further indignities by an officer who warded off the assailants by flourishing his sword. More serious incidents occurred, some with fatal results. On the morning of 10 April a native was shot dead; on the 12th three more were bayoneted in a brawl. Bougainville ostentatiously put the suspects in irons, but Ereti fled with his household and was reconciled only through Nassau's patient diplomacy. 'Are *these*

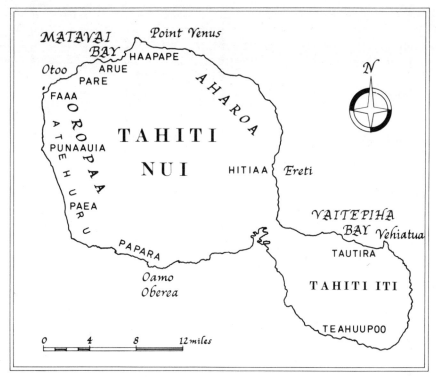

Tahiti, showing principal districts and chiefs

the savages?' asked one observer of the touching scene when the chief and his tearful wives made peace with the prince.[25]

These fatal clashes, combined with the onset of bad weather, convinced Bougainville it was time to leave. Accordingly he pressed on with the collection of supplies and drew up an Act of Possession naming the island New Cythera and the whole group the Bourbon Archipelago. As the *Boudeuse* unfurled its sails, Ereti arrived in a canoe, bringing not only his wives but a companion — none other than the *Étoile's* first intrepid visitor — who now wished to join the expedition. Since he thought the volunteer might be of great service to the nation, Bougainville explained, he gave his consent; further, he promised Ereti to restore Louis (as the man was known) to his home. Following an exchange of gifts and embraces, the French bade farewell to their weeping hosts and set off. The *Étoile* had already reached the open sea in safety, but the *Boudeuse* struck serious trouble and left behind two of its anchors. Altogether, lamented the commander, he had lost six in nine days.[26]

The anchorage had been 'detestable' wrote Bougainville, but no other complaints marred his recollections of the landfall as he voyaged westward. Nature (to summarize an extended rhapsody) had placed the

island in the world's loveliest climate, embellished it with the most
charming prospects, enriched it with every gift, peopled it with perhaps
the happiest nation on earth. Legislators and philosophers should, he
urged, go there to see as an established fact what they had not even
dreamed of — a thronging populace of handsome men and beautiful
women living together in health, plenty, and ordered amity. Not far
removed from the state of nature, they practised their simple arts, toiled
little, and enjoyed all the social pleasures of dancing, music, discourse,
love. The last, Bougainville truly believed, was the only god they
worshipped. Nor did they celebrate their devotions in solitude — the
lovers' transports were a public spectacle. Among other felicities, he
noted, nature had denied them anything that would excite European
cupidity and attract all the evils of the iron age. 'Farewell, wise and
happy people,' he ended, 'remain always as you are. I shall never
recall without pleasure the brief time I spent in your midst and as long
as I live I shall extol the happy isle of Cythera: it is the true Utopia.'[27]

Utopia, it soon appeared, was not exempt from civilized evils. By the
middle of May men on both ships were found to be afflicted with
venereal complaints. One of them was the native recruit who, though
badly infected, made light of the malady, indicating that his fellow
islanders treated it with herbs. While showing little aptitude for the
French tongue, he made it clear that his country was called Taiti, while
he himself was known as Ahutoru or, in the French rendering, Aoutourou.
This name ultimately replaced both Louis and Boutaveris, his version of
Bougainville which, following Tahitian custom, he adopted to honour
the commander. He was a chief but of uncertain antecedents. Apparently he was a kinsman of Ereti or, as some said, a brother; one chronicler,
on the other hand, held that his home was not Hitiaa but a different
part of the island.[28]

During his perilous course through the south-western Pacific, Bougainville
sometimes turned from more urgent concerns to contemplate his exotic
passenger. Though he made little headway with the French language,
Aoutourou did not lack intelligence. He showed detailed knowledge of
the stars and took a keen interest in the navigation of the ship. He was
evidently a man of delicate sensibilities, for he found the sight of routine
shipboard punishments a torture. Bougainville described him as timid
and sweet-natured. But he was not too timid to stand naked in defiance
of his Polynesian cousins (whose dialect he failed to comprehend). With
growing intimacy the commander picked up Tahitian words from his
charge and learned of Tahitian customs — that of human sacrifice, for
example. Aoutourou for his part displayed increasing admiration for
French ways while blushing for his own. He was much impressed by
his first glimpse of civilization, a small trading post in the Dutch East
Indies, and asked whether Paris was as beautiful. His enthusiasm for the
sights of Batavia had, in Bougainville's view, saved Aoutourou from
the effects of its pernicious climate, but he sickened before leaving the
port and called it 'the place that kills'. He is finally depicted at Mauritius

in the tantalizing phrase of Bernardin de Saint-Pierre — 'open, gay, a trifle dissolute'.[29]

Reaching Paris on 19 March 1769, Bougainville installed Aoutourou in his own home, but it was some weeks before he introduced him to his circle. The man had been unwell, he explained to his friends, the much travelled La Condamine and Pereire, the royal interpreter, who late in April scrutinized this novel specimen in two gruelling interviews. He was, they recorded, thirty years old, of average height, resembling in colour an East Indian or a Moor; his features were irregular but not deformed. The examination, interspersed with Bougainville's praise of New Cythera, covered many subjects but dwelt more especially on language. Following exhaustive tests, the experts found Aoutourou incapable of pronouncing certain French sounds, while his vocabulary disclosed scarcely a word from any known tongue — a fact which, in their opinion, argued the isolation of his people. They listened with interest to the anecdote of Commerson's valet and from it inferred that the natives' sense of smell was so acute that they could distinguish female odours from male. Adding a personal touch to their observations, they noted the navigator's solicitude for his charge and the affection each showed for the other. Soon after the second interview, on 30 April, Bougainville launched Aoutourou into society by presenting him to Louis XV and the young princes at Versailles. They displayed a gratifying curiosity but accounts of his response differ: according to one, he was dazzled by the regal spectacle; another states that the 'savage' expressed no emotion at all — not even, it seems, Rousseau's 'stupid Admiration'.[30]

Aoutourou was now *à la mode*, sought out by aristocrats and *savants*, welcomed into fashionable *salons* where the ideas of Rousseau had been simplified, sentimentalized, and associated with the ancient myth of a golden age. He was introduced to the Duke of Orleans and the young Duke of Chartres and the Prince of Conti; Mademoiselle de Lespinasse received him and the Duchess of Choiseul became both patroness and friend. At a dinner party given by Lacurne de Saint-Palaye of the French Academy, the President de Brosses saw his first Polynesian and, hearing the story of Commerson's pretended valet, learnedly discussed its implications. Buffon inspected the unique representative of Austral man in the royal gardens and, as he contemplated the exile in a similar setting, the Abbé Delille was moved to sentimental versification. Rousseau was not invited to study the uncorrupted descendant of natural man, but Diderot met him and wrote the probing and subversive *Supplément au Voyage de Bougainville* which he prudently refrained from publishing. Bougainville himself, who at first escorted Aoutourou everywhere, says little of his conduct in the polite world of the capital. He does, however, mention his protégé's pleasure in the opera, his passionate love of dancing, and his delight in the theatre where he was taken backstage and presented to the singer Sophie Arnould and the tragedienne Mademoiselle Clairon. In time he learned to find his own way to performances and, though he still had only a smattering of French, could take daily excursions alone and make purchases, rarely paying more than their worth.[31]

By December Bougainville decided it was time for Aoutourou to return. He could not support the man for ever and the fickle Parisians had lost interest in this living witness to his own discoveries. Moreover, his plans for founding a Pacific empire, with himself as governor, had come to nothing, frustrated by official indifference and an empty treasury. So, at heavy expense to himself, he arranged for his friend's passage to Mauritius, whence he would be transported to Tahiti. At the end of February 1770 the weeping Aoutourou embraced Bougainville for the last time and, bearing gifts from the Duchess of Choiseul to his distant countrymen, left for La Rochelle.[32] More than four years were to pass before a second Polynesian — in the person of Mai — would make his appearance in Europe.

WHILE AOUTOUROU WAS FÊTED AND EXAMINED IN PARIS, the district of Haapape had again been visited by the British. On 13 April 1769 Lieutenant James Cook, Dalrymple's successful rival, steered H.M.S. *Endeavour* into Port Royal Harbour and, escorted by an armed guard, went ashore with his party. The guard proved to be superfluous. It was less than two years since the *Dolphin*'s arrival and Wallis's forceful lesson had not been forgotten. 'No one of the Natives', wrote Cook, 'made the least opposission at our landing but came to us with all imaginable marks of friendship and submission.' The natives had little reason to fear, for the newcomers' aims were entirely peaceful. They came not to colonize or conquer but to observe the transit of Venus across the sun in the following June; and their choice of anchorage was due to a happy chance. Preparations for their voyage were already in train when Wallis returned to England and as a result of his report the newly discovered island was chosen as a base for their observations. The expedition was well qualified to carry out its mission. Cook, another veteran of the late war, was skilled in all the arts of navigation (among them astronomy), while one civilian member was Mr. Green, assistant to the Astronomer Royal. Of even greater moment for the future of learning (and the fortunes of Mai), the enterprise had been promoted by the Royal Society which had recommended the inclusion of one of its fellows, Mr. Banks, who had brought with him another fellow, Dr. Solander.[33]

Joseph Banks, wealthy patron of science, and Daniel Carl Solander, gifted pupil of Linnaeus, seem like the answer to Rousseau's plea for two enlightened men who would travel the world and study their own species. The resemblance is probably coincidental. In setting out for the Pacific, Banks was following his own inclinations rather than a philosopher's precepts. His first concern, moreover, was not mankind but inanimate nature. No mere moneyed dilettante, he had been an ardent botanist since boyhood and in the company of his like-minded friend Constantine Phipps had already journeyed far afield to Newfoundland and Labrador. When preparing for the present voyage he had spared neither trouble nor expense. At a cost of ten thousand pounds, Solander estimated, he had gathered a staff and supplied them with every possible facility. This was the best equipped expedition which had yet entered the Pacific and also the most accomplished. Besides Cook and Green there were navigators, map-makers, surgeons, and, in Banks's entourage, another Swedish naturalist, two artist-draughtsmen, and his own personal servants. Only musicians were lacking from the specifications of de Brosses whose two volumes were included in the ship's extensive library.[34]

To Banks, Port Royal seemed the 'picture of an arcadia' peopled by heroic figures on whom he conferred such names as Lycurgus, Hercules, and Ajax. Veterans of the *Dolphin*, on the other hand, noted the comparative fewness of inhabitants, the destruction of houses, and the scarcity of supplies. The position improved next day with the arrival of chiefs who led the British to the neighbouring district of Pare, about two miles to the west, and treated them with the hospitality shown to previous explorers. Banks, in the full vigour of early manhood, entered into the feasting and ceremonial with gusto. Forgetting his English fiancée and ignoring his obligations to a chief's wife, he was soon in pursuit of a pretty girl 'with a fire in her eyes'. On this happy occasion the natives fully sustained their reputation for generosity — but also for thievishness. Both Dr. Solander and the ship's surgeon had their pockets picked; still more disastrously a day later, a man was shot by over-zealous marines after snatching a musket. A loss that touched Banks more closely was the death on 17 April of his landscape-painter whose duties now fell on the accomplished botanical draughtsman, Sydney Parkinson.[35]

Haapape and the surrounding districts proved a paradise for Banks and his diminished staff. On the 18th he moved ashore to tents set up on the site of a fort then being built to serve as a depot and enclose the observatory. Soon he was immersed not only in botanical studies but in observations of this engaging if often exasperating people. He took charge of trade, he traversed the countryside with Cook and Solander, and indefatigably he probed into every aspect of island life. He acquired fresh informants with the arrival on the 28th of the *Dolphin*'s 'Queen', bringing in her train the Raiatean exile Tupaia whom he termed Tupia. The regal personage appeared in shipboard records as Oberea (or some similar variant), a form due to the mistaken fusion of the article 'o' with an English version of Purea. Other proper nouns (though not all) were likewise distorted, notably Otaheite which superseded Wallis's King George's Island on shipboard charts. Cook usually preferred local names to European and replaced Port Royal Harbour with his approximation to Matavai Bay; but he called the target of Wallis's final fusillade One Tree Hill, not Taharaa, as it was known to the Tahitians. The palisaded encampment, completed at the end of April, received the doubly appropriate designation of Fort Venus.[36]

Oberea's authority had visibly declined since the *Dolphin*'s departure.

She and her husband, it was gradually disclosed, had suffered defeat in
a factional war also involving the people of Haapape; hence the destruction noted by the *Endeavour*'s landing party. But she still retained some
influence and in her personal affairs seemed as exuberant as ever. The
day after she arrived Banks found her in bed with a 'lusty' young lover
and later, he implies, was invited to replace that 'gallant' — an offer he
evaded. An erotic note entered voyage journals in the carefree month
of May. Cook describes a fertilization ceremony performed before
Mr. Banks and a ritual act of copulation, apparently arranged by Oberea
and carried out near Fort Venus. Banks says nothing of the second
incident but coyly mentions his 'flame' and mildly censures Tupia for
providing himself with a 'bedfellow', 'tho', he adds, 'the gentleman
cannot be less than 45.' On his first appearance Banks characterized
Tupia as 'Obereas right hand man'. Soon the virile major-domo occupied
a similar place in his own circle, acting as his 'deputy' in the reception
of visitors or performing the roles of policeman and peace-maker in
successive contretemps with his incorrigibly thievish hosts. He escorted
Banks on several excursions but not when the botanist left with a party
for the nearby island of Moorea to watch the transit of Venus on 3 June.
It was a perfect day for observers both there and at Matavai Bay.[37]

Their official mission was completed, but Cook and his companions
stayed on for more than a month, constantly adding to their knowledge
of Tahitian customs. They witnessed a mourning ceremony in which
Banks, stripped of his clothes and blackened with charcoal, took a
leading part. They attended a performance given by the *arioi* who,
'like Homer of old', were poets as well as musicians and practised the
'devilish' crime of infanticide. They feasted on a 'most excellent dish' of
roast dog, prepared by the versatile Tupia. They met Oberea's husband
Oamo (more correctly Amo) with their young son, already betrothed
to a chieftainess ten years his senior. Further revelations followed
towards the end of the month when Cook and Banks made a circuit of
the island. At Hitiaa they spoke to Ereti and confirmed rumours that
two ships, supposedly Spanish, had called there and carried away his
'brother *Outorro*' (brother perhaps in the broad tribal sense). Crossing
to the smaller peninsula of Tahiti Iti, they reached Vaitepiha Bay in the
domain of a hereditary chief, the Vehiatua. In this district they saw a
grisly display of human jawbones and, more spoils of the recent fighting,
a goose and a turkey given by Wallis to Oberea. When they moved on
to the southern coast of Tahiti Nui, they were shown a 'singular curiosity',
the lofty basket-work image of *'Mauwe'* (the demigod Maui), ornamented
with feathers. But the supreme spectacle of the tour awaited them
farther along the coast at Papara. Here they found the 'masterpiece of
Indian architecture', an immense *marae* built by Oberea in overweening
pride to honour her son. And strewing the nearby coast lay 'numberless'
human bones, the remains of warriors slain by her jealous rivals.[38]

At the beginning of July they returned to Matavai Bay to prepare for
the voyage which, following Admiralty instructions, Cook would now

undertake in search of the Southern Continent. While the ship's gear was repaired and the fort dismantled, Banks continued to botanize and observe. He followed a river to its cascading headwaters, he planted citrus seeds brought from Brazil, he watched while a struggling girl was tattooed on the buttocks. The last days ashore were troubled by discord arising from the desertion of two love-stricken marines who were recovered after Oberea and others were held as hostages. Despite this indignity, the magnanimous woman was on the *Endeavour* when the ship weighed anchor on the 13th. She came to farewell not only her European friends but also Tupia. He had resolved to visit England, much to his own satisfaction, remarked Banks, for the Raiatean was 'a most proper man', well born, versed in the mysteries of his religion, and above all an experienced traveller. Since Cook refused responsibility for the recruit, Banks took him on his own account. 'Thank heaven', he exclaimed, 'I have a sufficiency and I do not know why I may not keep him as a curiosity, as well as my neighbours do lions and tygers . . . .' With Tupia went his servant, a boy aged about twelve, whom Banks called Tayeto.[39]

And what of Mai during this fresh incursion of European explorers? Facts again are few and often open to question. Now some sixteen years old, he was still living at Matavai Bay and, if one witness can be credited, was the pupil of a *tahua* or priestly expert. In that close-knit community he was certainly well aware of Cook, Banks, and Solander and knew them by their Tahitian names — Toote, Tapane, and Torano (alternatively Tolano). In spite of some vague evidence to the contrary, however, it is doubtful whether he was more to them than one of the anonymous crowd. He was too young, too lowly, too undistinguished to join the dignitaries who consorted with the visitors and figured in their journals. If he volunteered to sail with the expedition (and such offers, according to Cook, occurred daily), he could hardly have competed with the mature and accomplished Tupia. His own time was yet to come. Meanwhile, inspired by motives of revenge, he seems to have been meditating less extensive travels in the direction already taken by the *Endeavour*.[40]

Before they set out on their continental sweep, the navigators spent three agreeable weeks in the islands to the north-west of Tahiti. First sheltering in the small harbour of Fare on the coast of Huahine, they then crossed to Opoa in southern Raiatea (Ulhietea in Banks's rendering). Next they sailed past adjoining Tahaa and the forbidding, seemingly inaccessible Borabora (or Bolabola) to their final anchorage, Tupia's old home in the north of Raiatea. Cook took possession of the group in His Britannic Majesty's name and called them the Society Isles 'as they lay contiguous to one a nother'. In this excursion Tupia more than fulfilled Banks's expectation. He prayed for wind when the ship was becalmed and navigated it through perilous reefs; he conducted the rituals of greeting and propitiated local deities; he was guide, interpreter, adviser, easing the way everywhere for his grateful patrons. Neither of the two

main islands, they found, differed in essentials from Tahiti. Huahine,
under its benevolent 'King' Ori (Cook's Oree), was a scene of fruitful
harmony. In Raiatea, by contrast, displays of human jawbones were a
reminder that the place was in the hands of Boraboran conquerors. Yet
the people seemed carefree, diverting themselves with dramatic and
musical spectacles — *heiva* — to which the visitors were invited.
Towards the end of their stay they met Tupia's enemy, the renowned
Opoony (Puni) of Borabora, and found 'an old decrepid half blind man',
not the young warrior chief they had pictured. Laden with fresh produce,
they left on 9 August 'in search of what chance and Tupia might direct
us to', as Banks expressed it.[41]

Tupia disclaimed all knowledge of a continent in the surrounding
seas but named numerous islands of which the *Endeavour* sighted only
one in its southward course. For the rest, as week followed week, there
was nothing but a limitless expanse of ocean with lonely dolphins or
whales and a multitude of birds. Once they saw a waterspout and for
some nights watched a comet which in Tupia's view portended disaster
for his fellow Raiateans at the hands of their Boraboran masters. Lacking
other occupations, Banks worked to impose order on the notes and
impressions gathered in the four months since he had landed at Matavai
Bay. He left the natural history of the islands to be recorded in Parkinson's
drawings or in the specimens he and his assistants had gathered. But
man, more especially Tahitian man, he described in detail — his appearance and dress, his social customs and occupations, his diversions, his
religious beliefs, his language. For the first time Polynesians were presented without prejudice and in something of their complexity. Banks
occasionally erred or theorized from faulty evidence: European preconceptions led him to interpret Tahitian society in feudal terms, while he
accused their 'Spanish' forerunners of introducing venereal disease (his
contribution to an unending and necessarily inconclusive controversy).
Generally, however, he confined himself to the facts he had observed or,
on such esoteric subjects as cosmogony, derived from Tupia. His was a
major addition to the infant science of anthropology, precisely that
informed study of men and manners which Rousseau had called for.
And if his account failed to confirm either Rousseau's thesis or Bougainville's rhapsody, it celebrated the felicity of a people 'exempt from the
curse of our forefather' — one of the phrases Cook borrowed in his more
summary report.[42]

After fruitless searching in Pacific wastes, on 7 October they sighted
New Zealand, directed there not by chance or Tupia but by its Dutch
discoverer. Was this then the elusive continent, as Abel Tasman had
conjectured in the previous century? Banks thought so, but Cook proved
otherwise. As a result of six months' navigation he showed that the
country consisted of two large and many smaller islands. By a narrow
margin he forestalled another Frenchman, de Surville, less concerned
with exploration than commerce and notorious for kidnapping a chief,
Ranginui, who succumbed to scurvy during the passage to South America.

The British were responsible for more numerous and more violent deaths in the first unhappy clashes with a people not yet inured to naval discipline and, moreover, kidnappers on their own account (their intended victim being the boy Tayeto). The score of casualties might have been far higher but for Tupia's benign presence. He was, Cook acknowledged, of 'infinate service' in their dealings with these aggressive 'Indians' who, surprisingly, spoke a tongue like his own and who, to his horror, were cannibals. He comforted youthful captives, he preached moderation to defiant warriors, he intervened in the flogging of a thief — repeatedly, in short, he smoothed over difficulties with his kindly tact. He was present when the country was added to His Majesty's dominions at a ceremony in Queen Charlotte Sound, the spacious haven where the ship was overhauled before Cook made his circuit of the southern island and at the end of March 1770 left for New Holland. Tupia found little scope for his talents while the *Endeavour* pursued its hazardous course towards the Dutch East Indies. The naked inhabitants of New South Wales spoke an unknown language and were usually too shy to respond to his friendly approaches. And it was not Polynesian incantations but British skill that saved the ship from destruction in reef-strewn waters. To Banks's concern his protégé showed symptoms of

7
*Tayeto, Tupia's servant,
after Sydney Parkinson*

scurvy and was both dispirited and unwell when they reached Batavia early in October.[43]

The *Endeavour* was now in urgent need of repairs and, since their stay in the port would be lengthy, Banks rented a house where Tupia and his servant were also lodged. Tayeto, who was in the best of health, went 'almost mad' with excitement as he danced about the streets examining the 'numberless novelties'. The ailing Tupia responded more soberly but seemed to grow better and, dressed in Tahitian costume, walked through the city with his patron. On one outing a man stopped them to ask whether the 'Indian' had not been there before. So Banks learned the truth about the expedition of which he had heard at Hitiaa. It was, he discovered, not Spanish but French, under the command of Monsieur Bougainville, and had passed through Batavia eighteen months before with a native very like Tupia and a woman in men's clothes.[44]

Aoutourou had called Batavia 'the place that kills', and so it proved to his successors. By the end of October both were so ill with 'a putrid dysentery' that Banks took them back to the ship for a change of air before he himself sickened and left for the country. His charges at first showed some improvement but gradually declined under the compassionate eyes of Sydney Parkinson. Tupia 'gave himself up to grief', refused all medicines, and 'in the highest degree' regretted that he had ever left Tahiti. The more patient Tayeto was the first to succumb, on 17 December. Tupia was then 'quite inconsolable', frequently repeating the boy's name until he, too, died three days later. Cook thought his illness was due as much to dietary changes as to the unhealthiness of Batavia and characterized him as 'Shrewd Sensible, Ingenious . . . but proud and obstinate'.[45]

On Christmas Day they left the fatal port, bound for the Cape of Good Hope. Weakened by tropical heat and sickness, Banks and Solander barely survived the passage, but they were more fortunate than Green, Parkinson, and a score of others who died on the way. From French vessels at the Cape they learned that 'Otorroo' was then at Mauritius awaiting his return to Tahiti. Further details of Bougainville, picked up from the same source, prompted Banks to hope that, in order to forestall French claims, an account of the *Dolphin*'s and their own discoveries would be published without delay. He reached the Downs on 13 July 1771, and, disembarking with Cook and Solander, set out for London.[46]

2. Between Voyages

SINCE THE JOURNALS OF THE 'ENDEAVOUR' ENDED WITH DISEMBARKATION, the immediate sequel can only be surmised: the hire of chaise or express; the dash to London; and the formal call at the Admiralty where Banks's friend the Earl of Sandwich now presided as First Lord. There, one supposes, the trio parted to go their separate ways — Cook to his modest dwelling in Mile End Road and reunion with Mrs. Cook and their children; Solander to solitary bachelor quarters, perhaps in Bloomsbury; Banks to the house in New Burlington Street he seems to have shared with his sister Sarah Sophia. With the least possible delay, it can hardly be doubted, the returned voyager would have hastened to pay filial respects to the widowed Mrs. Banks at Paradise Row, Chelsea. And soon in all probability, by personal call or letter, he would have announced his arrival to members of his varied circle: 'Coz Bate' and his aristocratic connexions the Grenvilles; Constantine Phipps, companion on the Newfoundland journey, close friend since their years at Eton and Oxford; Sir John Pringle, President of the Royal Society, and Dr. Morton, Librarian of the British Museum, and John Ellis, the natural historian, and Mr. Lee, the nurseryman — these and numerous others. The pious Sarah Sophia spoke for family and friends when in one of her 'Memorandums' she offered up thanks for 'the wonderfull known miraculous & numberless unobserved Deliverances' her brother had experienced in the course of the expedition. 'How often', she exclaimed, 'have my Dear Mother & Self contemplated & admired the innumerable great dangers he hath escaped: & adored our Gracious GOD, for restoring him to us.'[1]

Private prayer was accompanied by public adulation. Since January brief messages from the *Endeavour* had been seeping into the press, but now the newspapers devoted paragraphs and columns to the exploits of Mr. Banks and Dr. Solander. These 'ingenious gentlemen', it was reported, had lately sailed round the world. They had spent four months at George's Land of whose language they had made themselves masters. They had touched at 'near forty other undiscovered Islands, not known to other Europeans' and gathered 'above a thousand different Species of Plants, none of which were ever known in Europe before'. They had brought with them two natives who were 'amazingly struck' by the sight of coaches and horses at Batavia but who, alas, had sickened and died.

'Mr. *Banks*, and Dr. *Solander*' had been absent three years, began 'An Authentic Account of the Natives of OTAHITTEE, or GEORGE'S ISLAND' presented in the form of a letter from a member of the *Endeavour*'s company to his friend in the country. These islanders, asserted the nameless correspondent, were very expert fishermen and 'the most dexterous thieves in the world'; their government was despotic, they acknowledged one Supreme Being, they built altars of very large stones. As for their women, they were of a copper colour, 'well made and well featured', they were 'extremely lascivious, and much injured with a certain disease', they followed one singular and *outré* custom — and that was 'painting their posteriors of a jet black'.[2]

The explorers' achievements were promptly acknowledged in the most exalted quarters. Early in August it was announced that Mr. Banks, 'one of the gentlemen who went to the South Seas to discover the transit of Venus', had been introduced to the King at St. James's and 'received very graciously'. Soon afterwards, accompanied by Dr. Solander and Sir John Pringle, he again conferred on the late voyage with His Majesty at Richmond. The curiosities brought home by Mr. Banks and Dr. Solander, ran a later notice, had already been seen by most of the nobility, and 'the most extraordinary Phaenomena' were shortly to be inspected at the Queen's Palace. Before the month was out news came that in the coming spring and under royal patronage the two gentlemen would set out on a second voyage. By September the proposed expedition had grown — on paper — to three ships under the command of 'the celebrated Mr. Banks' who, it was asserted, would found a colony in the South Seas. Meanwhile, in the middle of August, the less celebrated Lieutenant Cook had been presented at Court by Lord Sandwich. The officer formally handed over the *Endeavour*'s journals and charts to His Majesty, receiving in turn a commander's commission.[3]

The First Lord had apparently passed on news of these impending events to Banks who hastened to confide in his fellow voyager. 'Your very obliging letter', Cook replied, 'was the first Messenger that conveyed to me Lord Sandwich's intentions. Promotions unsolicited to a man of my station in life must convey a satisfaction to the mind that is better conceived than described'. What he did succeed in imparting was his indebtedness to Banks as a result of their association on the *Endeavour*. 'The reputation I may have acquired on this account', he continued, '. . . calls to my mind the very great assistance I received therein from you, which will ever be remembered with most gratefull Acknowledgments . . . .' Having dispatched these ponderous compliments, Cook turned to other duties which in mid-August included the disposal of assorted 'Curiosity's' — Tahitian cloth and breastplates, a carved box and 'Images' from New Zealand, 'Fish Gigs' from New Holland, a head ornament worn at 'Heavas' in Raiatea.[4]

Banks and Solander had been similarly employed with their own trophies. 'They are so very busy getting their things on shore, and seeing their friends, after an absence of three years,' wrote John Ellis, 'that

they have scarce time to tell us of any thing but the many narrow
escapes they have had from imminent danger.' Sometimes, however,
they left specimens and friends to unbend with other men of science or
to divert themselves in more frivolous company. They dined with members of the Royal Society Club, to which Banks had been elected in his
absence, and frequented royal and aristocratic circles. 'But the people
who are most talk'd of at present are Mr Banks and Dr Solander', wrote
Lady Mary Coke on 9 August. She had seen them at Court and afterwards at Lady Hertford's, she added, but had not heard the account of
their voyage round the world which, she was told, was 'very amusing'.[5]

All did not go well with Banks in that crowded summer of 1771. Soon
after his return he found himself involved in a tiresome controversy over
Sydney Parkinson's effects which would drag on for months and end
only at the cost of considerable ill-feeling and money.[6] Far more dis-
tressing to all concerned was the affair of his fiancée, Miss Harriet
Blosset. At some point in his travels — perhaps during the exhilarating
stay in Tahiti — he seems to have decided that the role of husband
was incompatible with his vocation as voyager-naturalist. The proper,
the manly course would have been to announce that decision to Miss
Blosset in the rural retreat where, said malicious gossip, she had spent
the past three years working waistcoats for her absent lover. But to the
surprise of disapproving friends and the diversion of prying society
Banks did nothing. It was left for Miss Blosset to make the journey to
London and demand an explanation. There were letters, there were
interviews (one lasting from ten at night till ten in the morning), there
was a brief reconciliation. Miss Blosset expostulated and swooned,
Mr. Banks pleaded and recanted, finally withdrawing from the engagement but not without some damage to honour and, it would seem, to
fortune.[7]

Early in September Banks left the scene of his triumphs and per-
plexities to rusticate with his fellow voyagers at Lord Sandwich's country
seat, Hinchingbrooke in Huntingdonshire. In spite of the disparity in
their ages (Banks was twenty-eight, Sandwich in his early fifties), the
two men had long been friends. As neighbours at Chelsea they had
fished and botanized together or joined in less innocent pursuits. A
common interest in mechanical experiment, combined with a penchant
for practical joking once, it is said, led them to devise an abortive
scheme for draining the Serpentine. Among the versatile First Lord's
other interests was music. Hinchingbrooke was the setting for entertainments where he would sometimes perform on the drums while singing
parts were taken by the talented Martha Ray. Sandwich had long been
separated from his wife and for the past decade this young woman had
lived openly with him and borne his children.[8]

Whether Miss Ray was hostess at the house party in September is not
recorded, but one of the guests was certainly another member of
Sandwich's musical circle. He was Dr. Charles Burney, well known in
London society as teacher, composer, and author. Entering her diary on

8 *Hinchingbrooke, Huntingdonshire*

the 15th of the month, his youthful daughter Fanny wrote that her father had lately spent a few days at Hinchingbrooke to meet Mr. Banks, Captain Cook, and Dr. Solander who, she said, had just made a voyage round the world and were soon to make another. Ever alert to promote the fortunes of his children, Dr. Burney took this opportunity to advance the career of his sailor son James. As Fanny expressed it in her somewhat tortured prose, 'My father, through his Lordship's means, made interest for James to go with them, and we have reason to hope he will have a prosperous and agreeable voyage.'[9]

Dr. Burney's kindly efforts were not confined to the members of his family. At an earlier meeting in Norfolk, Fanny relates, Lord Sandwich complained that the *Endeavour*'s papers in his possession were 'mere rough drafts' and asked someone to recommend 'a proper person to *write the Voyage*'. Thereupon Burney brought up the name of his old friend Dr. John Hawkesworth who met with the First Lord's approval and by October had been commissioned to prepare for publication not only the *Endeavour*'s journals but those of earlier circumnavigators.[10] For his labours, on the authority of that aristocratic gossip Horace Walpole, he received *'d'avance'* six thousand pounds from the booksellers and a thousand from 'the voyager' (meaning Banks).[11]

VOYAGE
AUTOUR
DU MONDE,
PAR LA FRÉGATE DU ROI
LA BOUDEUSE,
ET
LA FLÛTE L'ÉTOILE;
En 1766, 1767, 1768 & 1769.
SECONDE ÉDITION, AUGMENTÉE.

TOME PREMIER.

A PARIS,
Chez SAILLANT & NYON, Libraires, rue Saint-Jean-de-Beauvais.

M. DCC. LXXII.
AVEC APPROBATION ET PRIVILEGE DU ROI.

A
JOURNAL
OF A
VOYAGE round the WORLD,
In His Majesty's Ship ENDEAVOUR,

In the Years 1768, 1769, 1770, and 1771;

Undertaken in Pursuit of NATURAL KNOWLEDGE, at the Desire of the ROYAL SOCIETY:

CONTAINING

ALL the various OCCURRENCES of the VOYAGE,

WITH

DESCRIPTIONS of several new discovered Countries in the SOUTHERN HEMISPHERE; and Accounts of their Soil and Productions; and of many Singularities in the Structure, Apparel, Customs, Manners, Policy, Manufactures, &c. of their Inhabitants.

To which is added,

A Concise VOCABULARY of the Language of OTAHITEE.

Ornari res ipsa negat, contenta doceri. HOR.

LONDON,
Printed for T. BECKET and P. A. DE HONDT, in the Strand.
MDCCLXXI.

9 & 10 Bougainville's extended account of his voyage; the unauthorized narrative of the Endeavour *expedition*

BANKS THUS HAD SOME PART in launching the official narrative of his recent voyage, but it was too late to forestall the French, as he had hoped. Bougainville had published his *Voyage autour du Monde* in May, and — a fact probably known to Banks — an English translation had already been commissioned.[12] More vexing still, within weeks of his return the anonymous *Journal of a Voyage round the World, in His Majesty's Ship 'Endeavour'* was rushed into print and immediately became a centre of contention. Well aware of the ban on such unauthorized revelations, Thomas Becket, the co-publisher, introduced the book with a letter jointly addressed to the Lords of the Admiralty and to Mr. Banks and Dr. Solander. Nothing, he assured them, could have induced him to bring out the journal but a consciousness of its authenticity. He was further persuaded to do so, he said, from the agreeable manner in which it was written as well as from its honourable mention of 'those ingenious gentlemen, Mr. Banks and Dr. Solander'. He was convinced it was 'the production of a gentleman and a scholar' who had made the voyage.[13]

Becket went even farther in his calculated effrontery, according to the *Gentleman's Magazine*. When advertising the book he vouched for its genuineness by citing the letter he had himself composed. Official reaction, on the same authority, was swift and emphatic. Writing from the Admiralty Office on 27 September 1771, Banks and Solander publicly denied all knowledge of the journal but announced that a full and authoritative account of their voyage was then in preparation. The disclaimer had an immediate effect on Becket who promptly cancelled his prefatory letter and modified the advertisement. Having disclosed these circumstances, the *Gentleman's Magazine* refrained from reviewing the publication. It merely printed extracts and left readers to determine for themselves how far the journal was worthy of their attention.[14]

The extracts, presumably selected for their popular appeal, were in fact an edited paraphrase of the gentleman-scholar's remarks on 'Otahitee'. Here and elsewhere in his journal he was sparing of nautical particulars and virtually ignored natural history. In that field, he explained with a well-turned compliment, curiosity would thereafter be gratified by Mr. Banks and Dr. Solander, 'gentlemen of great erudition', who had been indefatigable in their researches. For his part he dwelt more especially on the island people, their appearance, their occupations, their customs, their amours. Some of what he disclosed was already known through newspaper reports but much was novel: the natives believed in a supreme god called 'Maw-we'; they thought the sun and moon generated stars; they supposed an eclipse was the time of celestial copulation; their sovereign had only one wife but many concubines; the men 'used' circumcision. His description of the Society Group (not given in the *Gentleman's Magazine*) was attributed to Tupia and reflected the exile's prejudices together with the author's preconceptions. Borabora was represented as a barren island without inhabitants until neighbouring sovereigns chose it for a penal settlement. When the population increased, the account went on, the criminals resorted to piracy, invaded Raiatea under their tyrant 'Opuna', and killed its sovereign whose youthful heir found refuge in Tahiti, living there in 'the manner of James II. while at St. Germains'. Tupia himself was depicted as Oberea's lover in a tale of 'amorous dalliance' and intrigue worthy of a Gothic novelist. Much space was given to the New Zealanders who, despite irrefutable evidence of their cannibalism, were admiringly characterized as 'of all mankind the most fearless and insensible of dangers'.[15]

The journal was diverting, suggestive, highly readable, and was soon reprinted in Paris, Dublin, and Berlin. The French rendering appeared twice in 1772, first independently and then in an edition brought out by Bougainville's publishers with the title, *Supplément au Voyage de M. de Bougainville: ou Journal d'un Voyage autour du Monde, Fait par MM. Banks & Solander, Anglois*. In spite of their exertions, the two ingenious gentlemen were indissolubly linked with this catch-penny enterprise.[16]

Meanwhile, in the late summer of 1771, a work of more limited extent but far larger implications had been issued by Alexander Dalrymple. Rousseau considered iron and corn to have been the ruin of mankind; Dalrymple evidently thought otherwise. Having failed in his bid to command the earlier expedition, he now proposed one whose purpose it would be 'to Convey the Conveniencies of Life, Domestic Animals, Corn, Iron, &c., to *New Zealand*'. The *Endeavour*, ran a preamble, had discovered that country to be two islands inhabited by a brave and generous race destitute of corn, fowls, and all quadrupeds except dogs. These circumstances being lately mentioned to certain men of liberal sentiments, they persuaded Mr. Dalrymple to offer himself as leader of a mission that would remedy the situation. The scheme had the support of Dr. Benjamin Franklin who, widening its scope to include other deprived countries, presented his views in a discourse that appealed both to humane feelings and self-interest. Britain, he pointed out, once in a similar condition, had derived vast advantages from the fruits, seeds, animals, and arts of other nations. Now the world's chief maritime power, she had the means and the men to visit distant people on the other side of the globe not to cheat them, not to seize their lands or enslave their persons, but merely to do them good. As a commercial nation, moreover, she should promote the civilization of mankind since trade prospered with people who had the arts and conveniences of life rather than with naked savages.[17] The British nation was in general unresponsive, but the appeal may have caught the eye and touched the conscience of Dalrymple's former rival, Captain James Cook.

That navigator was certainly aware of Bougainville's *Voyage* which, early in 1772, was brought to British readers in a version by John Reinhold Forster. The choice of translator was not altogether fortunate. A German expatriate, Forster possessed an imperfect command of both English and French; furthermore, he sought every opportunity of displaying his own erudition and his loyalty to Britain. As a result the book was spattered with ponderous footnotes questioning Bougainville's scholarship, veracity, and powers of observation. He had, alleged Forster, ignored an obscure predecessor in order to claim for himself the honour of being the first French circumnavigator. Elsewhere, citing the anonymous *Endeavour* journal, he denied one of Bougainville's tentative conclusions: 'The people of *Otahitee*, or as the author wrongly calls it, *Taiti*, are not idolators, according to the last published account . . . .' If the voyager had been longer in the island, Forster continued, if he had studied the language more thoroughly and observed with a less prejudiced eye, then his narrative would have contained fewer of the mistakes with which it now abounded. 'The English, more used to philosophical enquiries, will', he promised, 'give more faithful accounts in the work that is going to be published, of the great discoveries made by the British nation in those seas.'[18]

In the second French edition of his work Bougainville commented on his translator's jibes with urbane good manners tinged with irony. They were qualities that even Forster's graceless rendering did not wholly

efface. 'I am', he introduced himself, 'a voyager and a seaman; that is,
a liar and a stupid fellow, in the eyes of that class of indolent haughty
writers, who in their closets reason in *infinitum* on the world and its
inhabitants . . . .' The shaft was aimed at Rousseau or perhaps more
immediately at the sentimental disciples the explorer had encountered
in Parisian drawing-rooms. Since leaving Tahiti he had apparently
reconsidered his first impressions and while preparing his journal for
the press had dropped or modified some of his unrestrained tributes.
The edited account was more factual, more sober, far more critical than
the original. He gave some details of the island's vegetation (dismissed
by Forster for their superficiality); he ventured the opinion that the hills
contained no minerals since they were covered with trees (justly provoking Forster's derision); and at greater length he wrote of the skill and
ingenuity with which the islanders fashioned their canoes and fishing-
tackle. Where the idyllic flavour of his journal persisted most strongly
was in the scene of his reception by Ereti or in the description of his rural
walks when he felt himself 'transported into the garden of Eden'. And
intermittently he still saw the Tahitians as survivors from a golden age,
the women dedicated to the cult of love, the men fit models for paintings
of the ancient gods. But Cythera was now infected by the disease of
Venus. This was Eden after the Fall, a society disfigured by human
sacrifice, gross inequalities, and the cruelties of war.[19]

The revised view owed much to Aotourou (as the visitor's name was
now rendered). It was from this living source, Bougainville acknowledged,
that he drew most of his information on Tahitian religion, government,
and language. In answer to hostile critics he also felt compelled to clear
himself from blame for having carried the man away. The islander's
eagerness to follow them was unfeigned, Bougainville emphasized, and
his fellow countrymen seemed to applaud the project. As for himself, he
explained, since they were about to sail through an unknown ocean and
would depend on its people not only for subsistence but for life, he
thought it of great consequence to have with them someone of similar
customs and speech. Besides (here touching on his imperial ambitions)
how could France better cement an alliance with the island nation than
by sending back its representative well treated and enriched by useful
knowledge? In spite of his brave words, Bougainville's fears and scruples
were not wholly allayed. 'Would to God', he exclaimed, 'that the necessity and the zeal which inspired us, may not prove fatal to the bold
Aotourou!' And again, after recounting the events of his protégé's stay
in France and departure for Mauritius: 'O may Aotourou soon see his
countrymen again!'[20]

These sentiments did the 'Philosophical Commodore' great honour,
observed a writer in the *Gentleman's Magazine*, adding the hope that
English navigators would on their return bring news of the native's safe
arrival. The same periodical published no fewer than four articles on
the book during 1772. Two summarized the text, another dealt with
Aoutourou, and the fourth, a description of Tahitian canoes, inquired

in passing how, 'upon the Mosaical plan', islands a thousand miles distant from any continent first came to be peopled — a subject that was left for divines to reconcile. Bougainville's humanity and understanding were praised, while adverse comment was confined to Forster for his unsatisfactory translation and 'petulant' footnotes.[21]

The *Monthly Review: or Literary Journal* was more critical of the author. It censured him for diffuseness and, more severely, for his failure to supply the information required by philosophers in tracing mankind's progress 'between the age of the untutored savage, and that of the polished citizen'. Least defective in that respect was Bougainville's description of 'Otahitee, or George's Island' from which the writer went on to give extracts accompanied by his own comments. Successive quotations touched on diet, manufactures, government, and at greater length on the diverting subject of Tahitian women — their delicacy of feature, their coquettishness, their unashamed sensuality. Such details, noted the philosophical reviewer, had some bearing on questions of virtue and vice: 'In one country, chastity is disgraceful; in another it is meritorious.' 'We should beware, however,' he cautioned his readers, 'of judging of other ages and nations by the sentiments of our own.' On the subject of religion, as presented by Bougainville and Aoutourou, the writer was less satisfied. 'These extracts', he complained, 'furnish an example of that want of precision which we complain of in travellers. It is impossible certainly to conclude from them, whether idolatry, or impure theism, is the religion of this people.' Such lame and contradictory reports gave authority to opposite opinions and confounded the philosopher. 'But', he observed, 'in relation to the present case, as well as to others of still higher importance, it is with real pleasure we reflect that the public is soon to be enlightened by the discoveries and enquiries of Mr. Banks and Dr. Solander.'[22]

AN EAGER PUBLIC must of necessity curb its impatience for the present and make do with imperfect accounts of southern discoveries. Hawkesworth's compilation would not appear until 1773, while work on the natural history of the voyage, to which Banks and Solander were committed, seems to have suffered from their many other activities. His friends were 'so hurried with company' that they had no time for answering letters, wrote the apologetic Ellis to Linnaeus on 19 November. Earlier that month they were observed with other members of the Royal Society at a gathering to establish the height of St. Paul's. On the 21st they attended a ceremony at Oxford when the university conferred doctorates on its distinguished son and his Swedish companion. In the new year they were welcomed into one of London's most exclusive literary circles. At a function apparently arranged by Sir Joshua Reynolds towards the end of February, they discussed their experiences with Dr. Johnson. The great man was in benign mood the next day as he thanked the voyagers for the pleasure their conversation had given him, enclosed a Latin motto for the *Endeavour*'s goat, and wondered whether Mr. Banks might perhaps have an epic poem from some happier pen than that of his humble servant Sam. Johnson. A month later the inveterate hero-worshipper James Boswell dined with the 'famous' pair at Sir John Pringle's. He found Mr. Banks a genteel young man without affectation and decided that Dr. Solander, though a Swede, spoke English with more fluency and propriety than most natives.[23]

Such were among the duties and diversions of the inseparable friends in the winter of 1771-2. But their chief preoccupation since the house party at Hinchingbrooke had been the forthcoming voyage. Though rather more modest than some newspapers had announced, this expedition was to surpass all its forerunners in size and scope. As a precaution against the misadventures which had overtaken the solitary *Endeavour*, two vessels were to go, one under Cook, the other under Tobias Furneaux, veteran of the *Dolphin*. Cook would be in charge of the whole enterprise whose purpose it was not to found a Pacific colony, as earlier reported, but to prove once and for all the existence or non-existence of a southern continent. The general plan, later embodied in official instructions, was to explore Antarctic waters during the summer months and then carry on the search farther north. Though definite limits were not set, the voyage was expected to take at least three years. By the end of November two ships had been purchased and named the *Drake* and the *Raleigh*. At the King's request, in deference to the feelings of his brother monarch in Spain, they were soon rechristened the *Resolution* and the *Adventure*.[24]

There was no question of the 'celebrated' Mr. Banks leading the expedition, as had once been rumoured, but the First Lord formally asked him and Solander to take part and treated them with more consideration than was normally accorded naval supernumeraries. Early in December they were invited to discuss arrangements for the voyage with what was termed a 'private board' of Admiralty officials. It was perhaps as a result of this meeting that Solander dispatched by post-express a long, agitated letter to his friend Dr. James Lind of Edinburgh. Government, he announced, had resolved to send out two ships to the South Seas and he and Mr. Banks had leave to go in one. No expense whatsoever was to be spared, everything was to be made agreeable to those who went, and both the King and other great men in power desired the expedition to be as complete as possible. Would Dr. Lind, he asked, allow himself to be nominated as astronomer? The intention was, Solander explained, to leave in March, touch at Madeira, make for the Cape of Good Hope, proceed thence for a short stay in New Zealand, and 'afterwards set out upon Discoveries farther to the South than any European Navigator has been. In those high Latitudes spend two or three Summers & every Winter go up within the Tropics to compleat our former discoveries.' 'Good God,' he concluded, 'we shall do wonders if you only will come and assist us.'[25]

Dr. Lind was delighted to come, and his pleasure was doubtless enhanced when a generous parliament undertook to reward him with a grant of £4000. For the payment and equipment of his immediate

11
Captain
James Cook,
after
Nathaniel Dance

entourage Banks alone was responsible. After the indispensable Solander the foremost of his assistants was the Royal Academician John Zoffany who was engaged for a fee of £1000. In addition, chosen from his household or from a host of eager applicants, there was a retinue of draughtsmen, secretaries, servants, and musicians — thirteen in all. To meet their needs and his own, Banks gathered an immense and varied array of implements, instruments, scientific apparatus, and supplies — screw-drivers, axes, harpoons, French horns, artists' colours, drawing-tables, rat traps, wire catchers for insects and birds, magnifying glasses, microscopes, table delicacies, tents for shelter, arms for protection, with beads, combs, mirrors, feathers, fish-hooks for trade with the natives.[26]

The disposal of Banks's staff and their baggage posed serious problems for Cook and the navy officials concerned. One draughtsman and one

12 *The Earl of Sandwich, after John Zoffany*

secretary were to go on the *Adventure*, but the rest were assigned to
the *Resolution* with Banks himself and his chief lieutenants. Soon it
became obvious that, if the supernumeraries were to travel in becoming
privacy and carry out their duties in comfort, more room must be found.
So the requisite authority was obtained and major alterations undertaken. An additional upper deck was built, with a raised poop or 'round
house' for the use of Cook who generously gave up the 'great cabin' to
house his passengers. The work went on as the *Resolution* lay at Deptford,
often thronged by idle crowds of ladies and gentlemen curious to see the
vessel in which Mr. Banks would again sail round the world. One
regular visitor was the First Lord who followed proceedings with interest
and possibly some disquiet. As a result of the ship's reconstruction,
timetables had been upset and it was May before she was ready to leave
for Plymouth. The occasion was celebrated by an entertainment given
on board by Mr. Banks and graced by the presence of Lord Sandwich,
the French Ambassador, and other unspecified 'persons of distinction'.[27]

The *Resolution* had not sailed far when it was found to be dangerously
top-heavy — so 'crank', in nautical parlance, that the pilot refused to
venture beyond the Nore. The decision was accordingly taken, on Cook's
advice, to make for the dockyard at Sheerness and restore the ship to its
original state. The newly added superstructure would be removed and
the passengers housed in whatever space could be found or contrived
elsewhere. By 20 May Cook, who had been absent in London, reached
Sheerness to find the work 'in great forwardness' with the round house
and extra deck already taken away. On the 24th Banks and Solander,
who since the function at Deptford had also been ashore engaged in
last-minute preparations, visited the yard to inspect the retrimmed
Resolution. To say that Banks was outraged by the spectacle is an under-
statement; nor was he prepared to consider alternative plans for accommodation on the mutilated ship. Four days later his decision was recorded
in the laconic minute of some nameless official: 'Mr Banks does not
go . . . .' Not only Mr. Banks but Dr. Solander and Dr. Lind and
Mr. Zoffany and the train of musicians, draughtsmen, servants, and
secretaries with their baggage and equipment.[28]

Banks did not withdraw in dignified silence. He poured out his
grievances in a complaining, self-justifying, interminable letter to
Sandwich. He recalled the circumstances in which he had been invited
to join the expedition; he mentioned the pledges he had given to the
learned world of Europe; he described the preparations he had made to
meet those pledges — at a cost, he estimated, of above £5000; and he
dwelt on the most recent alterations to the *Resolution* which, he foretold, must infallibly condemn its packed crew to putrid distempers and
scurvy. Would the public, he inquired, expect him to go out in a ship
where his people would not have room to perform their duties? In a
ship that was, moreover, apparently unhealthy and probably unsafe?
Sandwich responded to the implied threat of publicity with a chilling
rebuke: If Mr. Banks gave himself time to think coolly, he would at once

see the impropriety of publishing his opinion that one of the King's ships was unfit to sail and would endanger the lives of her crew. Cook's loyalty in the unhappy quarrel was to the First Lord, but at the close of a punctilious report to Banks on the now unwanted baggage he made a gesture of reconciliation. He sent best respects to Dr. Solander and to Mr. Banks himself, since he would not have his company on the *Resolution*, sincere wishes for success in all 'exploring undertakens'.[29]

Displaying belated good sense, Banks decided not to pursue the controversy farther but instead to seek consolation in the undertakings mentioned by Cook. Since there seemed some hope that the East India Company might send him to the Pacific in the spring of 1773, he was unwilling to disband the staff gathered with so much effort and expense. But how could they be occupied in the meantime? The young magnate answered the question in his own lavish manner by deciding to transport his entourage and himself to Iceland. He had been thinking for some time of a voyage to Europe's northern waters, and Iceland, with its volcanoes, its relatively unexplored terrain, and its epic past, opened up attractive prospects for scientific and antiquarian study. So he chartered the *Sir Lawrence* at a cost of £100 a month and quickly completed preparations for the new venture. Mr. Zoffany had gone off to Italy, but Dr. Lind was willing to come and so, among less travelled volunteers, was Banks's companion on the *Endeavour*, Lieutenant John Gore, who had thrice circumnavigated the globe. Early in July the party, now numbering twenty-one, assembled in London and on the 12th left Gravesend.[30]

The following day, Monday 13 July 1772, the southern expedition sailed from Plymouth. In the weeks since Banks's departure, work on the *Resolution* had been completed and efforts made to replace the lost supernumeraries. As artist, instead of the mature Zoffany, went the young landscape painter William Hodges, assigned to Cook's special care with the direction that he be 'diligently' employed. On the scientific side Johann Reinhold Forster, Bougainville's translator, took over Dr. Lind's post and emoluments, while his son Johann Georg Adam travelled as assistant. Known at this period by anglicized versions of their names, they were experienced naturalists, if not wholly adequate substitutes for the illustrious Banks and Solander. In addition, two astronomers had been appointed long before Banks's defection — William Wales and William Bayly, both capable observers and mathematicians. With the exception of Bayly, all these men travelled on the *Resolution*. That ship also carried naval notabilities: not only Cook himself but the Pacific veterans, Charles Clerke and Richard Pickersgill, with two newcomers, Dr. Burney's son James and the youthful George Vancouver. Burney appeared on the muster-roll as an able seaman but was armed with a lieutenant's commission and the First Lord's promise of promotion. As he prepared to leave, his sister Fanny commented: 'I should prefer this voyage to any in the world if my ill stars had destined me a sailor.'[32]

3. The Voyage of H.M.S. *Adventure*

ECHOES OF THE CONTROVERSY WHICH HAD DELAYED THE EXPEDITION AND caused so much ill feeling continued to reverberate as the ships left England and made for the Cape of Good Hope. In the first scribbled entry of a letter-journal he was keeping for his family, James Burney mentioned 'the Dispute between Mr Banks & the Captain', referring his readers to the newspapers for fuller details. Cook himself gave a temperate version of the affair in his own journal but did not commit to that official record a curious sequel of which he learned at Madeira. Three days before they arrived, he wrote in a private letter on 1 August, a person going under the name of Burnett had taken ship after a stay of three months on the island. Reports were confused, but apparently the visitor had come with the intention of joining Mr. Banks on the *Resolution*. More startling still was the captain's next disclosure: 'Every part of Mr Burnetts behaviour and every action tended to prove that he was a Woman . . . .' Was Banks deliberately following the example of Philibert Commerson and his pretended valet? Cook made no reference to the earlier incident, though he probably knew of it from the English translation of Bougainville or from either Forster or Banks himself. He merely gave his unknown correspondent the facts and spoke briefly of the ships. So far the *Resolution* promised well, even better than the *Adventure*. With all their wine on board and fresh supplies of water, they would sail that evening.[1]

They continued on their way, called at the island of St. Jago in the middle of August, and then began the long haul off the western coast of Africa. In the weeks that followed, shipboard journalizers found little enough to chronicle beyond routine nautical particulars or details of wind and weather. George Forster deplored the 'wanton' destruction of monkeys bought at St. Jago as pets and thrown overboard, on Cook's orders, because they fouled the decks. Mr. Bayly on the *Adventure* described a brief, panic-stricken interval towards the end of August when the *Resolution* outsailed its consort and the ships lost touch. James Burney, no stranger to the ritual, mentioned the 'usual ceremony of ducking' after they crossed the Equator on 9 September. The commanders recorded successive fatalities — two hands lost overboard, two midshipmen laid low by a fever caught through imprudently bathing at

St. Jago. And as they sped through southern waters various observers noted the appearance of exotic creatures of sea and air — dolphins on 13 September, a pintado bird on 4 October, a whale on the 19th. By the end of the month they were anchored in Table Bay.[2]

At that cross-roads of shipping and centre of nautical gossip Cook picked up news of his French rivals. About eight months before, he learned, two ships from Mauritius had discovered land in the same meridian as that island but forty-eight degrees south. They sailed along the coast until a gale separated them and the commander (Kerguelen) was forced to return. Was this, then, a fresh clue to the existence of the elusive continent? Of even greater interest to shipboard readers of Bougainville's recent *Voyage* were reports of two more ships from Mauritius bound for the South Pacific. They had touched at the Cape and, as Cook observed, 'on board one of them was Aotourou, the man M. Bougainville brought from *Otahieta* and who died of the small Pox before the ships sailed from hence . . . .' This slightly garbled account referred to the ill-fated expedition of Marion du Fresne which had set out to restore Aoutourou to his people; and the unfortunate Tahitian had died the previous November off the coast of Madagascar, not at Cape Town as Cook then supposed. His own fear was that the man's death, following those of Tupia and Tayeto, would prejudice their countrymen against Europeans.[3]

The expedition spent three weeks at the Cape before setting out for the Antarctic. Cook lodged with the hospitable port commandant, Mr. Brand (or Brandt), while he supervised preparations and reorganized his slightly depleted crews. He enlisted a couple of new seamen and replaced the ailing first lieutenant of the *Adventure* who was allowed to return home. The vacant post was filled by promoting the second lieutenant, Arthur Kempe, and he in turn was succeeded by James Burney, transferred from the *Resolution*. So the First Lord's promise was fulfilled and Burney launched on his chequered career as a naval officer. In addition, the scientific staff was enlarged by the appointment of Anders Sparrman, a young Swedish naturalist and pupil of Linnaeus. He had been botanizing at the Cape and, with Cook's approval, joined the Forsters on the *Resolution*. A further group of supernumeraries, unlisted in journals or muster-rolls, was taken on at this stage. Both ships carried livestock — sheep, goats, pigs, poultry — not merely, as in the past, to supply fresh victuals but also for distribution in lands not endowed with such useful creatures. The two captains, moreover, had at their disposal quantities of corn and seeds to sow in suitable localities or bestow on the natives. Whether inspired by Dalrymple and Franklin or acting independently, Cook was about to begin his deliberate mission of introducing European benefits to the Pacific.[4]

As he approached the end of his stay, the conscientious commander reported to his naval superiors, wrote to a friend in Whitby, and composed a more difficult letter. Before setting out on his dangerous voyage he had evidently decided to make his peace with Mr. Banks. On 18

13 The Resolution *and the* Adventure *in the Antarctic, from a water-colour by Henry Roberts*

November he addressed his former companion and patron with manly
candour: 'Some Cross circumstances which happened at the latter part
of the equipment of the Resolution created, I have reason to think, a
coolness betwixt you and I, but I can by no means think it was sufficient
to me to break of all corrispondance with a Man I am under m[a]ny
obligations too'. Apologizing for the paucity of news, he went on to
assure Banks that both Mr. Forster and Mr. Brand had been gathering
specimens for his collections and touched briefly on his own plans. He
would be leaving in a day or two, well stored with every necessary
thing, but feared the French from Mauritius had got the start of him.
Here he discussed the two expeditions and mentioned Aoutourou's
death — a circumstance he was, he said, really sorry for. Finally, he
wished Mr. Banks all success with his intended South Seas venture and
sent respectful salutations.[5]

It was 23 November before Cook at last sailed in quest of the continent
and more specifically, as his instructions directed, for Cape Circumcision
which the pious Bouvet had discovered on New Year's Day 1739. A
further aim was to identify the more extensive coastline recently reported
by Kerguelen. Heading south from Table Bay, the ships soon met wintry
conditions, the more trying because of the pleasant weather they had

enjoyed at the Cape. For three weeks heavy seas swept over the decks, drenching the men and bringing destruction to the unfortunate livestock. Not a night passed without some dying, wrote Cook on 8 December; but they were not wholly lost, he added, 'for we eat them notwithstanding.' On the 9th seaweed was observed and two penguins — signs, it was hoped, that land was near. These expectations were apparently realized when the *Adventure* sighted what was taken for a headland but proved to be the first of innumerable 'Islands of Ice'. The intense cold increased the crews' suffering and caused more fatalities among the animals. On the 13th Lieutenant Pickersgill noted that most of the sheep brought from the Cape had died in the past twenty-four hours. 'Served fresh Mutton to ye People' was his next laconic comment. In spite of the hazards from floating bergs, increased by fog and snow, they pushed on until they were confronted on the 14th by an 'immence field of Ice' round which they worked for the next fortnight. A search to the west disclosed no sign of Cape Circumcision where Bouvet had placed it and, concluding on 3 January 1773 that it was 'nothing but Mountains of Ice', Cook turned back to the east.[6]

As they made towards their second objective, there was a gradual improvement in the weather and, to the wonderment of some observers, they enjoyed daylight 'the whole 24 hours round'. When water ran short early in January, attempts were made to replenish supplies by melting blocks of ice. The experiment was so successful that by the 12th both ships had filled all their casks and — a further source of wonderment — the water was not in the least salty. The same day, while the boats were out collecting ice, Mr. Forster shot an albatross. Cook recorded the fact without emotion but did remark that the birds had been following them since they fell in with the ice islands and, further, that some seamen called them quaker birds 'from their grave Colour'. They continued their eastward course and then penetrated so far south that on the 17th they crossed the Antarctic Circle, 'undoubtedly the first and only' ships to do so, wrote Cook with justifiable pride. Pack ice barring further progress, they again turned north and later east in the direction of Kerguelen's landfall. By the beginning of February they were somewhere near its reported position and found reassuring signs — seaweed with 'Divers' and terns, both birds usually met with near land. But the rumoured coastline proved as elusive as Cape Circumcision and, hampered by contrary winds, they searched the neighbouring seas without the least success. After a week Cook decided that if land did indeed exist it could be only an island of no great extent.[7]

At this discouraging stage of the voyage there was a further setback: on 8 February in fog and squally weather the ships lost touch with each other. Following Cook's instructions, Furneaux cruised three days in the vicinity, frequently firing guns, and, when the *Resolution* failed to appear, he set off for their agreed rendezvous in Queen Charlotte Sound, New Zealand. First, however, he made for Van Diemen's Land which, he wrote, had been discovered by Tasman in the previous cen-

tury and was 'supposed to join to New Holland'. Land was sighted on
9 March and the next day Second Lieutenant Burney was sent off in the
cutter to investigate. The results, duly recorded in his informal chronicle,
were disappointingly meagre. He could find no safe anchorage and no
inhabitants, only traces of their existence in heaps of scallop shells and
ashes from their fires. He did see a path leading through the woods but
before he could examine it the wind freshened, forcing him to return.
The natives again eluded the explorers in Adventure Bay, the sheltered
haven on the south-east coast where they landed to gather wood and
water. Furneaux described rough 'Wigwams or hutts' with other evidence of primitive human life — bags and nets made of grass, a crude
spear, a stone for striking fire, a tinder of bark. At the end of four days
he sailed north to discover whether in fact the country formed part of
New Holland and, after a somewhat cursory examination, inclined to
the view that it did. Eager to settle into winter quarters, on the 19th he
'stood away for Zealand'.[8]

After a stormy passage the *Adventure* anchored in Ship Cove, Queen
Charlotte Sound, on 7 April. Again sent ashore to reconnoitre, Burney
saw no sign of the *Resolution* but found a watering place evidently used
by the *Endeavour* since her men had cut their names on neighbouring
trees. In the busy days that followed, Mr. Bayly fixed his observatory
on a small fortified island, 'the Hippa', while the crew set up a depot
and tents for the sick on nearby Motuara Island. On the 9th natives
appeared under rather inauspicious circumstances. Coming alongside
in their canoes, they first inquired about Tupia. On learning he was
dead, they seemed most concerned and asked whether he had been
killed or died a natural death. Won over with presents, they came
aboard and seemed at ease until an officer spied a severed head in one of
the canoes, whereupon they left the ship and immediately rowed away.
They were not long in recovering from their shame or fear. The following day they returned in force and henceforward acted with great
friendliness, exchanging for nails and other trifles fish, curiosities, and
the services of their women. While this profitable commerce went on,
the crew planted gardens with vegetables and wheat, gathered wild
greens, and explored the upper reaches of the Sound. On the 25th they
moved the ship farther into the Cove in preparation for an overhaul,
leaving Mr. Bayly on his islet.[9]

They appeared to be settled for the winter when on 18 May shots were
heard from the astronomer's camp, signalling the *Resolution*'s arrival.
After they lost touch, Cook told Furneaux, he had made for Dusky Bay
in the south-western tip of New Zealand. There he spent six weeks and
then directed his course to the rendezvous. He had thought of next
visiting Van Diemen's Land to see if it joined New Holland, but since
Furneaux himself had cleared up that point 'in a great degree', he now
proposed fresh plans. Rather than idle away the whole winter in port,
they would explore the unknown parts of the Pacific to the east and
north, ending the cruise in Tahiti. As he hurried on preparations for the

new voyage in the next two weeks, Cook made his vigorous presence felt
in many directions. He scoured the countryside for wild celery and other
anti-scorbutics; he laid out gardens to supplement those planted by the
crew of the *Adventure*; and to the boar and sows already released by
Furneaux he added livestock from the *Resolution* — a ewe and a ram,
survivors of those brought from the Cape, two goats, and, as the sequel
shows, some poultry. In a couple of days, alas, the sheep died, probably
through eating a poisonous plant; 'thus', Cook lamented, 'all my fine
hopes of stocking this Country with a breed of Sheep were blasted in a
moment.' Still, with invincible optimism, he was confident the remaining
animals would be left alone to multiply, the goats in the mountains, the
pigs in the woods. The sceptical Burney was less certain: 'if the Zealanders
do not find them out & destroy them there may be a fine breed in a
Short time — but its ten to one if they are not hunted down soon after
we go away.'[10]

On 3 June, towards the end of this, his second visit to the Sound,
Cook committed to his journal recent events and a few general observations. Natives, he wrote, were now volunteering to go away on both
ships and some, it was rumoured, were offering their children for sale.
He strongly denied the charge, ascribing it to the ignorance of the
Adventure's men who were 'utter strangers' to local customs and language.
If children were not saleable commodities, New Zealand women certainly were, he was compelled to acknowledge. Up to this time he had
considered them chaster than 'the generality of Indian Women'. Now he
found them forced by their own men to prostitute themselves for a spike
or a nail. Such, he reflected, were the consequences of associating with
Europeans and, more shameful still, civilized Christians — to debauch
the morals of innocent people, to introduce among them wants and
diseases hitherto unknown, to disturb that happy tranquillity they and
their forefathers had enjoyed. 'If any one denies the truth of this assertion', he challenged, 'let him tell me what the Natives of the whole
extent of America have gained by the commerce they have had with
Europeans.' On this sombre note, more becoming to a follower of
Rousseau than to a sober English captain, he ended the account of his
stay. A southerly storm delayed them for some days but on 7 June they
left their comfortable haven for the open sea. They carried no native
passengers, for when it came to the point none of the volunteers were
prepared to embark.[11]

THEIR ROUTE, in a great arc that would carry them through another
unexplored tract of the Pacific, exposed them for the first six weeks to
familiar conditions — gales, contrary winds, a monotonous expanse of
ocean. Still, they did not suffer the intense cold of the Antarctic voyage.
On 22 July, while he noted the absence of birds for the first time since
leaving New Zealand, Cook also remarked that the weather was now so
warm they had to put on lighter clothes. Soon they were cheered by the

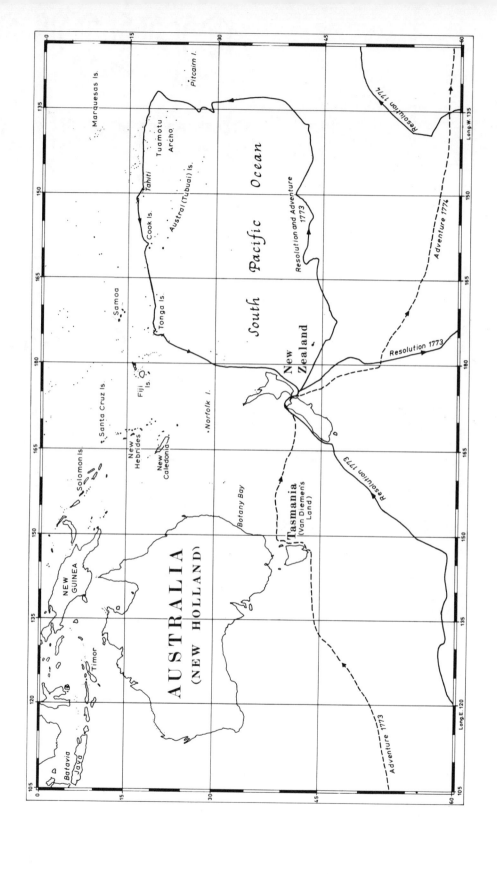

appearance of tropical birds but, on the other hand, alarmed by conditions on the *Adventure*. On the 23rd Furneaux recorded the death of his cook and on the 28th wrote that twenty of his men were stricken with 'the Scurvy & Flux'. Informed of these facts the next day, Cook sent a replacement for the galley together with dietary advice intended to stem the tide of sickness. By 2 August he was satisfied there was no continent in this area (and virtually certain none existed unless in polar regions). So, in view of the *Adventure*'s plight, he resolved to make with all speed for Tahiti. He was tempted to delay in order to fix the position of Pitcairn Island and again to identify an island supposedly discovered by Bougainville. But both times he pushed ahead, driven on, he explained, by the desperate state of the *Adventure* and the urgent need for fresh provisions. In the final week they threaded their way through the dangerous Tuamotu Archipelago and on the 17th narrowly escaped destruction on the reef outside Vaitepiha Bay on the northern coast of Tahiti Iti.[12]

During his tour with Banks in 1769 Cook had paid a brief visit to this bay and, in the interests of his scurvy-stricken consort, he now chose to

14
Tahiti from the Resolution,
after William Hodges

enter it rather than spend more time sailing north to his old anchorage. The people seemed as friendly as those at Matavai Bay, cruising round the ships with vociferous greetings and offering an abundance of tropical fruit in return for the usual trifles. But neither on board nor ashore could the visitors obtain the pigs and poultry they craved for after their almost unvaried diet of ship's victuals. The reply to their requests was always that such things belonged to the high chief, the Vehiatua, and could not be sold without his permission. That dignitary, however, failed to appear either on the afternoon of their arrival or the next day when Cook and Furneaux landed to inspect the watering place and 'sound the disposision of the Natives'. His absence was explained by reports of recent fighting picked up by the officers. Earlier that year the people of Tahiti Iti had defeated those of Tahiti Nui and, according to some informants, the Vehiatua had now fled to the mountains, fearing the British might seek to avenge their northern friends. Cook returned to the ship in a mood of frustration and, incensed by the pilfering of self-styled chiefs, cleared the decks. The pursuit of one marauder led to an ugly brawl in which the Tahitians hurled stones at the British who retaliated by firing a four-pounder and confiscating two canoes.[13]

With peace restored the next morning, the work of repair and recuperation went forward in an atmosphere of cautious sociability. Among the captains' first and most urgent concerns was the care of their sick. Since July there had been only one death, that of a consumptive marine the day after they arrived, but a third of the *Adventure*'s company were suffering from scurvy, some so badly they were unable to walk. Put ashore each day in charge of the surgeon's mate, the invalids soon responded to the change of air and diet. Parties also attempted to salvage anchors lost when the ships were entering the bay, but only one was recovered. Meanwhile Cook and other veterans of the *Endeavour* inquired about old acquaintances, while the Tahitians in their turn asked after absent members of the previous expedition, especially Mr. Banks. Nearly two days passed before they mentioned Tupia and then, to Cook's surprise and mild indignation, they displayed no uneasiness at his death and little interest in Aoutourou's. They did speak, however, of mysterious strangers who had come and gone since the *Endeavour*'s visit. From some reports it seemed they were French, from others Spanish, and two sailors claimed to have glimpsed a man of fair complexion — presumably a European deserter — before he fled into the woods.[14]

The days passed by uneventfully without sight of the Vehiatua and hence with no prospect of obtaining provisions except fruit and vegetables. Since the sick were now recovering, Cook decided the best course was to make north for Haapape and the familiar haven of Matavai Bay. He was awaiting a favourable wind to clear the dreaded reef when, on 22 August, a message came from the elusive 'King' or 'prince' (Cook used either term impartially), asking the commander to pay him a visit. At their meeting early on the 23rd the Vehiatua proved to be an amiable youth whom Banks had described on the previous voyage as a 'little olive liped boy'. He politely referred to that gentleman and in return for a sheet, an axe, looking glasses, and suchlike bestowed on his guest several hogs with the promise of more if only he would stay some months or even a few days longer. Cook had little faith in such assurances and set out on the 24th, leaving Mr. Pickersgill with the cutter to receive any supplies that might be forthcoming. The measure was justified and the Vehiatua's reputation enhanced when the officer caught up with the *Resolution* bearing a handsome tribute of hogs. On their way north Pickersgill and his men had spent the night at Hitiaa with the hospitable Ereti. Surprisingly, their host never once mentioned Aoutourou and took not the least notice when they did. Since he was the very chief who, Bougainville claimed, had presented Aoutourou to him, Cook found this 'extraordinary'.[15] (And still more extraordinary if, as Bougainville also claimed, the two were brothers.)

When the ships reached Matavai Bay on the afternoon of 26 August, many canoes came out to welcome them, while a great crowd, led by their 'King', lined the shore. Cook was on the point of leaving the

15
*Otoo,
after Hodges:
'a timerous Prince'*

Resolution to pay his respects when he learned that the monarch had taken fright and returned to his home at Pare. In the morning, after setting up a camp for the astronomers, the coopers, and the *Adventure's* sick, the two captains with other officers left for Pare to call on this man who since the *Endeavour's* visit seemed to have become the leading chief of Tahiti Nui. His name was Tu (or Otoo in Cook's version), and they found him seated in regal state, surrounded by his relatives and subjects, all with heads and shoulders bare. Cook, who had never seen him before, described him as between thirty and thirty-five years of age, over six feet tall, and 'as fine a person as one can see'. In return for the captain's gifts, Otoo offered a large quantity of cloth but Cook refused to accept it, explaining that what he had given 'was for Tiyo (friendship)'. Though he promised to supply hogs, the chief was unwilling to board the ship because, he said, the guns frightened him; 'indeed', Cook remarked, 'all his actions shew'd him to be a timerous Prince'.[16]

The following day Otoo overcame his fears sufficiently to visit the *Resolution*, bringing with him numerous followers with cloth, fruit, and fish but only one hog. These courtesies were returned and for several days friendly relations continued. During later excursions to Pare, Furneaux presented the chief with two of his remaining goats, a male and a female, while Cook, to Otoo's consternation, invested him with a broadsword which he hurriedly removed from his person. Both parties also provided entertainments. The Europeans diverted their guests with the music of bagpipes and the dancing of sailors; the Tahitians in return performed their own strangely contorted dances or staged dramatic spectacles, one of them partly topical in character since Cook heard his name repeated several times. This sociable interlude came to an abrupt end on the night of the 30th when, roused by the noise of brawling ashore, the commander sent off an armed party to arrest any sailors involved in the riot. A number were brought back and put in irons for their part in the disturbance which, Cook thought, 'was occasioned by their makeing too free with the Women'. Whatever its precise cause, the consequences of the affair were soon evident. When he landed in the morning, Cook found that Otoo and his subjects had fled from their homes. Seeking out the timid monarch, he allayed his fears and placated him with gifts that included three of the sheep brought from the Cape. They were of little value to anyone, Cook admitted, for they were in poor condition and all three wethers. He took this opportunity to fare-well Otoo who was 'moved' but not, it seems, deeply grieved. Most of the sick now being recovered and both ships repaired, the best course, he decided, was to sail on to the Society Islands where provisions might be more plentiful.[17]

The day they left for Huahine, 1 September, from a number of volunteers Cook selected a young man, Poreo by name, to go on the *Resolution*. He explained rather offhandedly that the native 'might be of service to us on some occasion'. The same afternoon Lieutenant Pickersgill returned from another foraging excursion which had taken him to Papara 'where the old Queen Oberea live'd'. She was, he briefly reported, very happy to see the boat's crew but too poor to give them any assistance. According to Burney, who apparently had the account from his fellow officer, she complained that she had 'not the least interest' with Otoo and when Mr. Pickersgill inquired why she did not come to Matavai Bay to see her old friends, 'She answerd she had no presents to bring & did not chuse to come empty handed, it lookd too much like begging'. Cook remarked that 'old *Obarea*' seemed poor, of little consequence, and much altered for the worse — a judgement he extended to her fellow countrymen when summing up impressions of his two weeks in Tahiti. Former navigators had found this 'fine Island' abounding in provisions of all kinds; now, despite a lavish expenditure of presents, he and his men had procured at both anchorages only a couple of dozen hogs and one solitary fowl. The scarcity he attributed to two causes — the destructive wars among the natives and the demands of European shipping. At Matavai Bay he had picked up further details of the mysterious vessel first reported on his arrival. It was about the same size as the *Resolution*, its commander was one, Opeppe, it had taken away four men, and it had left behind a new sickness which attacked the head, the throat, and the stomach, finally killing the victims. That old sickness, the venereal disease, Cook thought less serious in its effects than formerly, though some of his men claimed to have seen natives suffering from 'the Pox in a high degree'.[18]

After this visit Cook omitted any general survey of Tahitian life, explaining that one was supplied in the printed account of his former voyage. (Hawkesworth's compilation had in fact made a somewhat belated appearance in the previous June.) He did, however, include some remarks on Bougainville's description of island customs, beginning with the vexed question of human sacrifice. To clear up that point, while they were at Matavai Bay he and Captain Furneaux with one of their men who spoke Tahitian 'tolerable well' had inspected a *marae*. There they found a corpse and on questioning the natives learned that the practice certainly existed, though, Cook stressed, they were not sufficiently masters of the language to understand their informants fully. So far M. Bougainville was right, but he was wrong in saying that only 'Kings' were allowed to plant the willow tree or that 'Grandees' varied their servants' livery according to their own rank. And he was very much mistaken in asserting that there was no personal property on the island. These were not the only errors M. Bougainville had made; nor were they surprising since he had spent only ten days in Tahiti. The love of truth alone compelled him to mention these things, Cook emphasized, not any desire to find fault with M. Bougainville's book. On the contrary, he generously concluded, he thought it 'the most usefull as well as entertaining Voyage through these Seas yet published'.[19]

A HAPPIER NOTE marked Cook's account of their brief stay in Huahine; indeed he grew almost lyrical in describing the charms of this bounteous island. When they reached Fare on 3 September they received not only the thronging welcome they had experienced from the Tahitians but also an abundance of the pork and poultry so regrettably scarce among those war-torn people. The search for the two commodities had by this time become something of an obsession, natural enough in men who, Cook remarked, 'had been living Ten months on salt meat'. After giving the trading parties their instructions the next morning, he set off with Captain Furneaux and Mr. Forster to pay his respects to the principal chief, Oree, whose friendship he had won during the previous voyage. When the elaborate ritual of greeting was over, the old man fell on the captain's neck and embraced him, 'more like a son he had not seen these four years than a friend', as Cook wrote. The meeting ended with the traditional exchange of gifts, and all went well for some days until one of the visitors was attacked. On the 6th, to follow Cook's version of the incident, two men fell upon Mr. Sparrman, the naturalist, while he was botanizing alone. First they stripped the young Swede of everything but his trousers and then struck him with his sword, fortunately doing him no harm. Sparrman managed to ward off the assault and, with the help

16
Omai,
after Hodges:
'dark, ugly
and a downright
blackguard'

of a friendly native, reached the shore to report the 'outrage' to Cook.[20]

In the long run the affair merely served to enhance Oree's reputation for courage and honesty. On learning of the attack, he wept aloud from shame and forthwith, despite the pleas and protests of his subjects, set out with Cook in pursuit of the thieves. He failed to capture them but insisted on stepping into the boat to board the *Resolution*, once more in the face of opposition from his people who feared for his safety should he entrust himself to the Europeans. He dined on board and after returning to land was able to restore Mr. Sparrman's sword and part of his waistcoat. The following day, as the *Resolution* prepared to leave for Raiatea, he again appeared, this time with an invitation for the commander to land and either witness or himself administer punishment to the thieves who had now been taken. The *Adventure* had already cleared the harbour and Cook could not wait, but he took this as further proof of the chief's power over the islanders and friendship for himself. To the old man's wise guidance, he felt, were due the peace and prosperity which had long prevailed throughout his domain. The common people had frequently asked the visitors to attack their neighbours, the warriors of Borabora, but Oree gave his subjects no support and proclaimed his friendship for Opoony, the Boraboran leader. The 'Brave old Chief' was generous to the end, heaping lavish gifts on his guests as they departed. Altogether, Cook estimated, he had obtained some four hundred hogs on the island and about half as many fowls.[21]

The only rift in the parting was caused by a slight misapprehension. When Oree came on board, Cook understood him to ask for the restoration of four or five of his people who had been carried away in the *Adventure* without his permission. A boat was immediately dispatched with orders to bring them back, but it returned with only one. The facts were, Cook learned, that the solitary migrant had been on the ship since the first hour of its arrival and now left Huahine with the full knowledge of all the natives and with Captain Furneaux's approval. Since Oree had already disembarked and Furneaux wished to keep the man, Cook allowed him to stay on the *Resolution* while they sailed towards Raiatea. During the brief passage to that island, the newcomer made a bad impression on several observers. He was tall and slim with remarkably small hands, wrote the Forsters, but his features conveyed no idea of the beauty which characterized his fellow islanders: indeed, they had seen few so ill favoured; moreover, his colour was 'the darkest hue of the common class of people'.[22] Cook conveyed similar views more succinctly when he described him as 'dark, ugly and a downright blackguard'. In eighteenth-century terms, apparently, this only meant he was swarthy, plain, and of low birth — in which last respect, it may be remarked, he resembled the navigator himself. As for his appearance, the sketch made by William Hodges at this time or soon afterwards (and later engraved) shows a homely, irregular Polynesian countenance redeemed from the charge of ugliness by its good humour and vivacity; but one member of the expedition thought the likeness too complimentary — 'the only time I ever knew Hodges flatter in drawing'.[23]

With the arrival of the *Resolution* at Raiatea on 8 September, the unpromising recruit was sent back to the *Adventure* and the next day enrolled as a supernumerary under the name of Tetuby Homy. In these inauspicious circumstances, Mai — for he it was — began the protracted saga of his travels.[24]

Once the ships were safely moored, events followed the now customary pattern. Visits were exchanged between the captains and the leading chief, Orio, who, though a native of warlike Borabora, seemed almost as gentle and benign as his near namesake on Huahine. Similarly, in return for their beads and hatchets, the Europeans received gifts of local produce — here on so lavish a scale they were actually compelled to refuse some of the pork they were offered. This was Tupia's birthplace, and Cook was both touched and relieved when nearly everyone inquired after their countryman and, 'like true Philosophers', were perfectly satisfied to learn the manner of his death. There was also much talk of his foe Opoony, 'King' of Borabora and overlord of Raiatea and neighbouring Tahaa. The aged monarch, 'this great man, who has made all

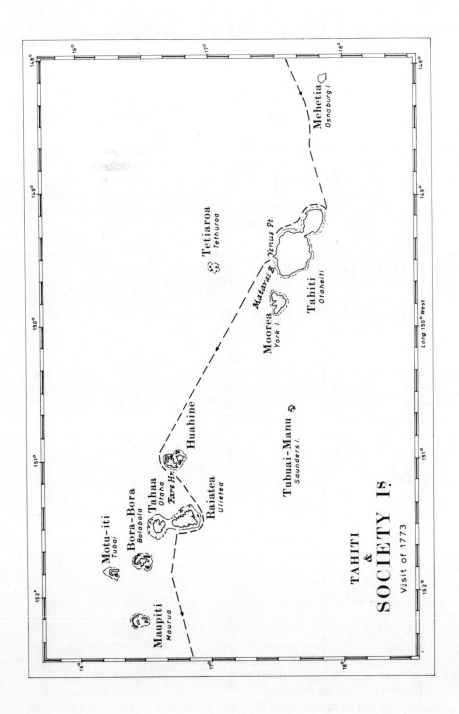

TAHITI
&
SOCIETY IS.
Visit of 1773

the Nations round him tremble' (as Cook described him), was absent at the time and now, they were told, was so decrepit he walked almost double, 'a very uncommon thing in these isles'. His daughter and presumed successor, a very handsome young woman, was said to receive the same outward respect as Otoo in Tahiti.[25]

As in 1769, the Raiateans excelled in 'Dramatick Heava', drama interspersed with dancing to the music of drums. The first such entertainment was given on the 10th and others followed nearly every day during the rest of the visit. The actors were usually men, the most talented of whom Burney nicknamed Garrick after his father's friend. Cook mentions that Orio's daughter took part in a play which, he observed, appeared to celebrate the local genius in the art of theft. Feasting or dining often followed the performances, and the women were as obliging as elsewhere in these hospitable islands. So the days passed in sociable harmony marred only rarely by some misunderstanding. Once, the Forsters related, they had just shot several kingfishers when they met the chief and his family strolling with Captain Cook. On seeing the birds the women grieved and Orio's 'fair daughter' fled away, lamenting the death of her 'eatua' or spirit. The chief himself said nothing until the naturalists were leaving for the ship when he earnestly desired them not to kill the kingfishers or herons on his island — for what reason the Forsters could never discover. Towards the end of the visit a more serious incident occurred, taking a familiar course — a clash between Europeans and natives followed by the withdrawal of the population in mingled guilt, resentment, and terror. Cook failed to discover what caused the flight but traced Orio to his refuge and in a tearfully emotional scene was able to dispel the chief's fears and effect a complete reconciliation.[26]

A further episode, potentially violent in its outcome, concerned the *Adventure*'s recruit. After spending one evening ashore, he arrived on the ship in the middle of the night, 'naked, leaving his Jacket & Trowsers behind him'. The reason for this sudden flight was a conspiracy which the intended victim later disclosed to Burney. A report had spread among the islanders (probably circulated by the man himself, Burney suspected) that he was 'going to *Britannia* to get poopooe's (guns) of the Aree' of that country in order to kill the people of Borabora. When they learned of his intentions, some Boraborans living on Raiatea resolved 'to prevent, or rather finish, his Travels'. Luckily for the young man, an acquaintance wakened him while he slept, told him of the plot, and advised him to get back to the ship as fast as he could; 'accordingly without regarding his Cloaths, he took to the water & Swam to a fishing Canoe who put him aboard'. Nor would he, wrote Burney, go ashore again during their stay on the island.[27]

Of the expedition's many chroniclers Burney alone seems to have mentioned the affair. Had it come to Cook's notice, he would certainly not have encouraged the volunteer in his plans for revenge. During this and the previous voyage he tried to avoid being drawn into local quarrels, always refusing to champion the cause of any one faction. As

17
Odiddy,
after Hodges:
'very handsome'

for the man's ambition to visit Britain, that again would have received little support from the prudent commander. In 1769 he had been reluctant to grant Tupia a passage and gave his consent only when Banks took full responsibility for the chief's future. True, at Tahiti he had already recruited one islander for the *Resolution*, but 'inticed away by a young Woman', Poreo deserted before the ships left Raiatea. From a number of eager aspirants he was replaced by a Boraboran called Hitihiti, or Odiddy, as his name was usually rendered on the *Resolution*. He was about seventeen or eighteen years old and 'very handsome' in the opinion of the Forsters who claimed to have introduced him to Cook and, on the basis of his fair complexion and fine clothes, assigned him to 'the better sort of people'. He was indeed of chiefly birth, professed kinship with the great Opoony, and, befitting his rank, embarked with a servant. He seemed far superior to the man on the *Adventure* but resembled him in one respect: several witnesses mentioned that he also wished to visit Britain. Cook failed to record the fact, if he knew it, merely remarking that the youth might be of use should they touch at any islands on their route to the west. Doubtless he assumed that both natives, if they survived, would be restored to their homes when the expedition returned here after its next cruise in southern waters. With stores replenished and crews refreshed, he had now decided to revisit the Antarctic by way of the Tongan Archipelago and New Zealand.[28]

The two ships finally sailed on 17 September. Of all their Pacific anchorages this island and neighbouring Huahine had come nearest to realizing the weary mariners' vision of an earthly paradise. In the next phase of the voyage, as he summed up his views and impressions, Cook wrote of the Raiateans that since their conquest by Opoony they had enjoyed all the blessings of peace. Now they seemed 'as happy as any people under Heaven', having 'all the necessaries and some of the luxuries of life in the greatest profusion'. In his present mood he was disposed to take a lenient view of their failings — or, rather, of their only failing, for he reflected benignly: 'One ought not to be too severe upon these people when they do commit a thieft since we can hardly charge them with any other Vice'. Passing on to consider their notorious laxity in sexual relations, he expressed an even more liberal attitude. Incontinency among the unmarried, in his opinion, could hardly be called a vice since neither the state nor individuals were in the least injured by it. And, though not prepared to concede a similar licence to the married, he thought wives here were perhaps as faithful as anywhere — at least he had not seen an instance to the contrary. Regarding the unchaste minority, they were, he held, no more typical of their sex and nation than were the women found in English naval ports or in the purlieus of Covent Garden and Drury Lane. In short, the more one was acquainted with these islanders the better one liked them; they were, indeed, the most obliging and benevolent people he had ever met with.[29]

WHILE THEY PURSUED THEIR WESTWARD COURSE past the Hervey Islands towards Tonga, the *Adventure*'s recruit was evidently both seasick and homesick. After some days he recovered, for on 27 September the kind Mr. Bayly noted that the 'Indian' from Huahine was now 'in high Spirits', being 'well of the Sea-sickness common at first going to sea' and having, moreover, 'forgot his country in some Measure'. His feelings when he found himself isolated in this alien shipboard world are also conveyed by rough jottings in Second Lieutenant Burney's informal journal where the young native is pictured:

keeping account of the number of Days with Chips — terribly frightend the 2d Day after leaving the Society Islands — it being Sunday the people were calld to Prayers — he seeing every body getting together, suspected it was to consult whether or not we should kill him — we were some time before we could learn the cause of his uneasiness & then it was with difficulty we were able to quiet his apprehensions —[30]

These were probably recollections set down later, not observations made at the time. In the early stages of the passage from Raiatea,

Burney seems to have taken little notice of the new arrival, mentioning
him in brief and impersonal terms as 'one of the Inhabitants' or 'the
Indian on board us'. It was only after a week or so that he singled out·
the supernumerary and set out to describe him for the entertainment of
his distant family:

The Indian who came on board us is named Omy, though we commonly call
him Jack — he is a fellow of quick parts — very intelligent, has a good memory &
takes great Notice of every thing he sees — he is possessed of many good qualities
— is Strong, Active, healthy & as likely to weather the hardships of a long
Voyage as any of us . . . .

The young officer's generous appreciation differed from Cook's curtly
disparaging dismissal, and there was a similar contrast in the two esti-
mates of Omy's social status. He was in this account the 'Second son of
an Independent man' or of chiefly rank in Burney's unduly simplified
version of island society. He was further dignified by having served as
'one of the under priests or assistants to the high priest of Huaheine' and
had been both warrior and traveller. From this versatile witness, Burney
acknowledged, he had acquired almost all his 'intelligence concerning
these Islands'. But further experience forced him to conclude that Omy
was 'not always to be credited', that he was in fact 'addicted to
romancing'.[31]
    Scattered references in the narrative throw a somewhat fitful light on
the young man's past. Nothing is said of his early life, but Burney states
quite explicitly that he was in Tahiti when the *Dolphin* was attacked
and 'got wounded in the Action'. Omy was able to supply a census of
the livestock which Captain Wallis left with Oberea, 'Queen of the
Island': '2 Geese — 3 Guinea Hens — a Turkey cock & Hen & a Cat'.
He likewise recounted the sad fate which had overtaken the 'unlucky'
queen's presents: '1 of the Geese died — the Guinea hens were Stole
from her & killed — the Turkey hen had 5 young ones but the Cat killd
them all.' And, final retribution and fatality, 'The Cat who was with
Kitten miscarried, was Stole & carried away to another Island & the
Turkey hen is since dead'.[32] He passed over the next episodes of Tahitian
history — Bougainville's brief visit, the *Endeavour*'s stay, the wars
between northern and southern rivals — but did speak of his travels and
of the adventures which seem to have befallen him when he left Tahiti
at some time after the *Endeavour*'s departure.
    Omy claimed to have visited most of the islands known to his people,
none of them equal in size to Tahiti or larger than Raiatea. At various
times, Burney related, they got him to make drawings of these places to
see whether the several versions agreed. On each occasion he put down
nearly the same number and gave the same names, 'but in respect of
situation they would not bear comparison', suggesting that he often
spoke from hearsay. He mentioned, for example, one group lying seven
or eight days' sail to the east. There a language quite different from his

own was spoken, while the inhabitants were tattooed in another fashion, the men 'with a Streak from the Corners of the mouth to their Ears', the women 'under the Neck from Ear to Ear'. The Society Islanders had but lately come to a knowledge of these people through an accident. Two canoes from the group were overtaken by a gale and driven to the north-west. They had been 'near a month at Sea when they saw Otaheite & Huaheine & made towards the latter, having had nothing to eat for the last 3 or 4 days'. When they at length reached the island, the chief 'entertained them in a friendly manner, but took away both their Canoes & gave them one of his own to return in'. Two of the voyagers, a man and a woman, had chosen to stay behind and, Omy reported, were then living at Huahine. On another island, called Oevah, dwelt men 'of a gigantic Size' who practised cannibalism. Omy himself had seen none of these anthropophagi, nor did he know 'how far or which way they lay'.[33]

In describing his martial adventures, Omy showed the Society Islands in a far less idyllic light than Cook; his narrative, indeed, suggested they were as beset by feuds and factions as Tahiti itself. During a war with Borabora he had fought in an engagement between two large canoes when four of his own relatives were killed along with Tereroa, chief of Huahine and brother of his successor, Oree. After the battle Omy and six others were captured by the victorious Boraborans and taken to their island where they were saved by the intervention of a woman who was an 'old Tio' of one of the captives; but 'this clemency occasioned great disputes, for these Islanders seldom shew any favour to their prisoners.' Not liking their 'precarious situation', the men from Huahine resolved to escape. On the second night of their captivity they crept out and found a canoe which they carried down to the water. Next they stole paddles from under a sleeping Boraboran, 'one softly lifting his head up while another drew out the paddles'. As they had 'a long way to go against the wind and no place where they durst stop', they could not leave 'without a stock of provisions, which they procured with equal dexterity — one of them got a Young Hog & to prevent his making a Noise, held him hard by the snout till he came to the water side, then plunged him in and kept him under till he was drownd'. They had barely cleared the island when they met a canoe whose Boraboran crew questioned them. Now the quick-witted Omy came to the rescue. He replied, imitating the speech and manner of the Boraborans, and, since it was dark, 'they passed on without suspicion & next night got to Huaheine'.[34]

This, Burney learned from Omy, was only one incident in a long-drawn and bloody struggle. Before the disastrous canoe battle, Huahine had been 'in a manner subjected' to Opoony and the Boraborans, a great many of whom settled on the island. Soon, having reason 'to be tired of their company', Tereroa, in Opoony's absence, summoned his allies from neighbouring Tahaa and together they fell on the Boraborans, slaughtering most of them while they slept. Opoony retaliated by killing Tereroa and had since attempted to regain his footing on Huahine, only to be foiled by Oree's 'bravery & conduct'. Tahaa and Raiatea, on the other hand, had been unable to withstand the Boraboran tyrant, and both islands were now under his authority.[35]

It might have been expected that Omy would have felt only hatred for the conqueror of his native island and the slayer of his kinsmen, but this was not at all the case. Opoony emerges from the young man's shipboard reminiscences as the greatest and most admired of island characters. He possessed two wives and three concubines and, such was the complexity of chiefly alliances, a former wife, now dead, had been the sister of his enemy Tereroa. He had but one living child, a girl, who if she survived would inherit his dominions, for he was unlikely to have any more off-spring, 'being now a very old man'. Yet he was 'Still greatly loved by his own subjects & feared by the other Islands'. One anecdote illustrated what Burney called his 'superiority' (meaning perhaps in local terms his *mana*). The Tahitians had 'made shift to purchase a large Anchor out of the ground that was left behind by Mons[r] Bougainville'. In doing so they broke one of the arms, but 'were foolish enough to carry the remainder about to the other Islands to be gazed at and admired.' Opoony 'saw & fell in love with it & they, *not out of fear* (so Omy says) but merely to oblige a man they wishd to the devil, made him a present of it'.[36]

Another side of the gifted leader appeared in Burney's summing up. Opoony, he observed,

in spite of old age & Blindness, (his Eyes being very bad) nevertheless retains all the Chearfullness & Merriment of a Young man, nor are his people ever happier than when in his Company — he is a great encourager of their Games & Revels . . . & has invented many new ones himself — I have given this Character of him from what Omy says, who stiles him a fighting man & man of Laughter — I never saw him —

Burney had not seen him because, Omy explained, on the expedition's arrival the chief had withdrawn to another island to avoid his old enemy Tupia whose cause he feared the visitors might espouse. Opoony was certainly 'a sensible, fine fellow', Burney wrote, and for his part he thought 'it would be a pity to assist any one against him' or the Bora-borans, a people, in his opinion, 'superior to the other Islanders'. One reason for their superiority, he learned from Omy, was that they alone killed none of their children. The consequence was that they were more numerous than the rest, and great numbers had 'found means to settle themselves on every one of the other Islands'.[37]

With the authority of a neophyte (aided no doubt by his talent for romancing), Omy spoke at some length of religion. Each island, he told Burney, had one or two high priests who were also the principal chiefs. In addition, there were inferior priests, a class to which he himself belonged. They worshiped a 'Being' called Maui (Moowe or Mowee in Burney's rendering) and made human sacrifices to him, not 'at any par-ticular Sett times' but when Mowee required it. The unwitting victim was killed and carried to the high priest who plucked out the eyes and offered them to Mowee. This being was consulted before anything extraordinary was undertaken and, if his reply was unfavourable, the enterprise was given up or deferred. Kingfishers were among the lesser deities, Omy stated, and the high priest understood what they said. On special occasions the people were assembled, the priests in the middle, the crowd in a ring surrounding them: 'Silence is then commanded & the high priest holding a small bunch of feathers in his hand, Speechifies — he then gives the feathers to one of the under priests who makes an Oration in his turn — thus they speak alternately, the feathers being held by the Speaker'. Omy would repeat the speeches — 'or rather songs' — which Oree and he had delivered. But what Burney found 'very extraordinary' was that preaching went on 'not in the common Language, but in a language, or Cant, invented purposely for this occasion'. Few or none of the audience understood it, and Burney doubted whether the priests did. When Omy was asked the meaning of any particular word or passage in a speech, he merely replied it was 'priest talk'. Perhaps, Burney surmised, 'he was not far enough advanced to be let into their Secrets . . . .'[38]

Omy proved to be a ready source of information on a variety of subjects. He possessed some astronomical knowledge, for he could distinguish planets from fixed stars and had studied the constellations. The two small stars close together in the Scorpion's tail he called the twins, the two brighter stars near them the mother and father — names which he explained by relating a story:

Mattibarie, a fisherman, had 2 Children (twins) a boy and a girl. by bad weather and worse luck he had lived several days on nothing but bread fruit — at last Luck changed and one night, after the children had been sent to rest, he brought home a great quantity of fish — he and his wife immediately drest some & made a very hearty meal the wife desired the children might be called to partake, but the greedy fisherman would by no means consent. The children happend to be awake all the time, but were afraid to speak and lay crying at their Fathers unkindness. Mowee took pity on them & sent down a Rope by which he hauld them up & placed them in the firmament. next morning the children were missing & the mother in despair was going to kill herself, when Mowee took her up & placed her by her Children. The fisherman repented of his unkindness & at length Mowee through the intreaties of his wife and Children was prevaild on to forgive him. accordingly the hauling line was sent down & he was hoisted up as high as the rest of his family —

All this, Omy said, had happened just before his grandfather was born; and, to prove the truth of his tale, there was still at Huahine a house called Mattibarie 'on the same spot that Mattibaries house formerly stood'. Among other scraps of esoteric information, Omy imparted his views on the relation between mind and body: the memory and understanding, he held, were 'lodged in the Belly'. 'The head', he affirmed, anticipating later prophets, 'is only an instrument — the head sees and speaks but the Belly dictates'.[39]

OMY AGAIN RECEDED INTO THE BACKGROUND when, at the beginning of October, the first Tongan landfall came into view. It was the island of Eua, called Middleburg by Tasman during his visit to the group in 1643. The people welcomed the navigators warmly, showing as little surprise or fear, Burney remarked, as if some other ship had just been there. Among the first to board the *Resolution* on the morning of the 2nd was a chief who with no less courtesy than his Tahitian cousins acted as host for the rest of the day. After escorting Cook and his party ashore, he led them to his house, delightfully situated in the shade of shaddock trees and bordered by plantations. Here the visitors were served with fruit and offered draughts of a liquor (*kava*) of which only Cook would partake. (His squeamish companions were put off because it was made by chewing a root that was then spat into a bowl of water.) In the afternoon the chief again regaled his guests, this time with stewed fruit and greens. They had already dined on board and ate little but, Cook noted in passing, Odiddy and the man from the *Adventure* 'did honour to the feast'. Musical compliments were paid on both sides. In return for a recital by the ships' pipers there was singing by three maidens followed by other women. Cook described the songs as 'noways harsh or disagreeable', words of mild praise he could have applied to both place and people. The inhabitants of this small island were consistently amiable, but they seemed unwilling to trade and were as reluctant as the Tahitians to part with fowls or pigs. The following day Cook gave the chief a gift of seeds and announced his departure. He had decided to make for Tongatapu, Tasman's Amsterdam Island, where that navigator had reported 'refreshments in plenty'.[40]

Even before they reached the island, the voyagers formed a highly favourable impression of Tongatapu. Less precipitous than Eua, it was of far greater extent, and every acre of land, they saw through their glasses, was laid out in plantations. Its people, too, showed no fear and were still more enthusiastic in their welcome than the neighbouring islanders. Many ran along the shore waving small white flags which Cook assumed were tokens of peace and acknowledged by hoisting a St. George's ensign. Venturesome canoes met the ships midway between the two islands, while others sailed out as they approached the anchorage on the north-west coast. One early visitor was a chief, or at any rate 'a man of some note', called Otago by Cook and apparently known to his countrymen as Ataongo. In the Tahitian fashion he exchanged names with the captain, accompanied him when he went ashore on the morning of the 4th, and for the rest of the brief visit served as a kind of major-domo. His efforts did something to compensate for the complete failure of Odiddy and Omy as interpreters. Both here and at Eua these ill-educated recruits could not understand 'a single sentence', Cook complained, and, greatly to their disadvantage, were compared with that

*18
Otago,
after Hodges:
'a man of
some note'*

scholar, gentleman, and seasoned traveller, Tupia.[41]

Each morning Otago arrived on the *Resolution* to guide Cook and Furneaux while they inspected cultivations or examined native dwellings and elaborately contrived burial places. He was often their go-between in trade and their intermediary in successive meetings with Tongan notabilities. One was a 'King' so impassive in his 'sullen and stupid gravity' that Cook first decided he must be an 'ideot'. Another was a bibulous high priest irreverently nicknamed 'Canterberry'. While the captains surveyed the sights and hobnobbed with the great, the Forsters botanized, Mr. Hodges sketched, and the sailors laboured or philandered. So the days passed in friendly accord sometimes broken here, as elsewhere, by 'incidents'. On the 5th a brawl at the landing place forced Cook to order out marines as protection for a trading party. The day before, with unparalleled audacity, marauders had made away with a grapnel weighing nearly a hundred pounds, and lesser thefts were of daily occurrence. Compared with its gains, however, the expedition's losses were trifling. Cook reckoned that he got 150 pigs on the island, double that number of fowls, and fruit in such quantities that it 'lumbered' the decks. He was duly grateful and distributed largesse with a liberal hand. Otago in particular was handsomely rewarded for his diplomatic services. Besides the customary nails and trinkets, he received a mixture of seeds — wheat, pease, beans — and, most precious of gifts, a dog from New Zealand and a bitch from the Society Islands. These animals were much coveted by the Tongans who seemed to have none of their own, though they knew them by the New Zealand name.[42]

The rediscovered islands and this novel branch of the Polynesians supplied shipboard theorists with further material for observation and debate. Burney admired the industry of the Tongans but decided the Society Islanders were more sociable. Cook was inclined to think otherwise and when he returned nine months later called the group the Friendly Archipelago or Isles 'from the extraordinary courteous and friendly disposition of their inhabitants'. Now he felt that bountiful nature had combined here with diligent man to achieve a state approaching perfection. 'I thought I was transported into one of the most fertile plains in Europe . . . .', he remarked of a walk through neatly fenced plantations along broad roads shaded by fruit trees. As for the inhabitants, 'joy and Contentment' were 'painted in every face', their 'whole behaviour' was 'mild and benevolent'. And in drawing the inevitable comparision with the Tahitians and their neighbours he concluded, 'when I consider their whole conduct towards us and the manner in which the few arts they have among them are executed I must allow them to be in a higher state of civilization.' Determined, as far as he could, to bar European evils from this island Elysium, he forbade women to board the ships and allowed his men ashore only if the surgeons considered them free of venereal disease. His tentative opinion was that Tongan women were less liberal with their favours than the Tahitians and their menfolk less addicted to thieving. In both respects he may have been misled by the warmth of the islanders' welcome and the brevity of a visit that lasted barely a week. It was an idyllic prelude to a further sojourn in the harsher latitudes of New Zealand and a summer in those far bleaker regions where he intended to complete his sweep of Antarctic seas.[43]

THE EXPLORERS CLEARED TONGATAPU on 8 October, setting out to complete the circular course they had begun five months before. Their experiences on the voyage southward were entirely predictable — gradually lowering temperatures, squalls, gales, the sighting of seaweed and birds — until, on the 21st, they saw the coast of New Zealand somewhere near Table Cape. Cook then steered for Cape Kidnappers (with its memories of poor Tayeto), seeking to dispose of the livestock and seeds he had carried from the fruitful north to bestow on these less favoured islands. The day afterwards a suitable recipient appeared in one of three canoes that visited the *Resolution*. He was a chief of commanding mien who benefited from the captain's bounty with a gift of boars, sows, cocks, hens, a profusion of seeds and roots. With this benevolent mission completed, the ships again headed south, passing Cape Turnagain on the

23rd on their way to the old anchorage in Queen Charlotte Sound. Their troubles began when, within sight of Cape Palliser, they struck a violent storm. Amid furious winds and mountainous seas the *Adventure*'s worthy astronomer could still spare a thought for 'Our Uaheine Man'. Omy, remarked Bayly, 'was much terified having never seen the like before'. But he was reassured by the vessel's seaworthiness and, Bayly continued, displaying his mastery of the Tahitian tongue, 'he cryed out with rapture (Pie Miti Middi-dehay am na Matti,) that is (it was a good Ship & the Sea could not sink her.)'. Brave words and prophetic, but not yet put to the final test. Baffled by contrary winds, they beat about the entrance to Cook Strait for almost a week, occasionally glimpsing the *Resolution* through the haze and spray. At the end of October they saw her for the last time; once more the men of the *Adventure* were alone.[44]

For the first few days of their solitary ordeal there was little relief, but on 4 November the storm died down and they managed to round Cape Palliser. They were now visited by canoes filled with natives — warriors and fishermen, it seemed — who traded weapons for a looking-glass and crayfish for pieces of Tahitian cloth. They also made long speeches but to what effect no one could tell — not even Omy who, Bayly reported, 'knew very little of the Matter'. The respite was brief and the calm deceptive. The same evening the wind sprang up with redoubled violence, blowing the *Adventure* back on its course and nearly driving it ashore. When the storm showed no signs of abating, Captain Furneaux confessed that he 'began to dispair of ever geting into Charlotte's Sound or joining the Resolution'. Bayly gives a graphic picture of the captain, a day or two later, coming 'down off the deck very much terrified to appearance', exclaiming 'he knew not what to do'. What he finally did was, in these critical circumstances, both sensible and prudent. He sped north from the ill-omened strait to find some safe anchorage where he might refill the almost empty water-casks and repair his ship, more severely damaged in the past fortnight than in all the preceding months of the voyage.[45]

The frustrated captain found a temporary haven in Tolaga Bay where the *Adventure* anchored on 9 November. The choice proved wholly fortunate. The bay was sheltered from the fierce westerlies and supplied plenty of wood and water, easy of access. The people, too, were friendly and with their cultivated plantations and stores of food seemed more settled than those of Queen Charlotte Sound. They exchanged their products for the customary trifling objects, though, in spite of their inordinate desire for iron, nothing would induce them to part with their stone adzes or the 'green Images hanging to their Necks'. Furneaux mentioned one slightly disturbing incident during the brief stay. As earlier in Queen Charlotte Sound, the visitors noticed in one of the canoes a severed head, apparently a woman's, decked out with feathers and ornaments. It 'had the appearance of being alive', Furneaux quaintly commented, but on closer inspection was found to be 'dry and preserved with every feature perfect, and kept as the Relict of some deceased relation'.[46]

19
Captain
Tobias
Furneaux

Having rested his storm-tossed crew and supplied their most urgent needs, Furneaux set out on the 12th for the southern rendezvous. But again he met contrary winds, this time from the eastern quarter, and was forced to put back into Tolaga Bay. Once more he expressed the fear that they would never catch up with the *Resolution* which he supposed was now in Queen Charlotte Sound and ready to resume the voyage. Hindered by the pounding surf, they took on fresh supplies and spent some days repairing the tattered rigging. At length, on the 16th, they got away and made fair progress as far as Cape Turnagain where bad weather blew up, bringing with it a repetition of the earlier experiences. For over a week they beat about Cape Palliser, barred from Cook

Strait by gales or, with the peculiar perversity of the elements, immobilized by calms. Finally, on the last day of November, they crept into the Sound and anchored at Ship Cove.[47]

Their forebodings, though not their worst fears, were soon confirmed. They saw no sign of the *Resolution* and 'began to doubt her safety' until the first boat's crew reached the watering-place. Here, carved on the root of a large tree, was the inscription, '"Look underneath"'. In obedience to these instructions they dug until they discovered a bottle containing a note from Cook. He had reached the Sound on 3 November, he wrote, and was leaving on the 24th. After waiting a few days for the *Adventure* at the entrance to the strait, he would make for the south and then eastwards. As he had not the least hope of again joining up with Captain Furneaux, he would not name a meeting-place. However, he might call at Easter Island in the coming March and would probably go on to Tahiti or one of the Society Islands; 'but this', he emphasized, 'will depend so much upon circumstances that nothing with any degree of certainty can be depended upon'. Given no precise instructions and no special rendezvous. Furneaux decided to get his own ship ready for sea as soon as possible and then follow Cook into the Antarctic.[48]

The day after they arrived, an encampment was set up to house the sick, the surgeon's mate, a cooper, sentries, and a few other men. Burney was in charge, accompanied by his new friend: 'Omy ashore with me at the Tent during our Stay here', he noted in one of his scribbled jottings. Mr. Bayly with his servant and his instruments occupied adjoining tents, and the routine work of replenishment and repair soon went forward. The discovery that much of the ship's bread needed rebaking added to the labours of the long-suffering crew who at this time showed some signs of insubordination. During their brief sojourn Burney twice recorded a punishment of twelve lashes for the crime of 'insolence', the first administered to a seaman by the name of Thomas Hill on 12 December. On the same date, in one of the cryptic entries of his narrative, he mentioned an excursion to neighbouring Shag Cove in the company of Lieutenant Kempe, Omy, and Jack Rowe, an able seaman recently promoted to master's mate. He concluded with the tantalizing words, 'Narrow Escape there', but failed to elaborate on the incident. Nor did he dwell on Omy's activities in the early days ashore beyond mentioning an unsuccessful attempt at self-education. The young man, he related, was present at the discovery of Cook's message and showed first 'disbelief' and then 'surprize' when the letter was deciphered. Indeed, so impressed was he by the power of words that he 'determined to learn to write & began with very good will, but so many people gave him paper, pens &c and set him copies & tasks that in a weeks time the poor fellow's head was bothered — too many Cooks spoilt the Broth'.[49]

Omy now dropped out of the record except for a brief reference in Burney's report on the two captains' experiments in acclimatization. Nothing, he wrote, was found of the hogs they had left — 'not so much as the least trace of them'. The fowls, on the other hand, though grown very shy, were 'in a fair way' of becoming a fine breed. He himself had found ten eggs under a hollow tree 'a good way up in the woods', while Omy spoke of seeing a hen with three young ones 'in his Rambles'. On being disturbed, the fowls had 'taken flight of about 100 yards without alighting'. As for the vegetable gardens, the 'Pease' had run wild, and, Burney suspected, the men of the *Resolution* had taken 'a good Share' before their departure.[50]

The inhabitants of Queen Charlotte Sound had by this time lost their novelty and were rarely mentioned by the busy mariners. Furneaux remarked that they still appeared very friendly and continued to supply fish and things of their own manufacture in return for nails, etcetera. But diarists of the shore party ignored their presence until forced to take note of it by two disturbing incidents. One night in the second week of their stay, Burney relates, the sentry caught sight of an 'Indian' near one of the tents and immediately gave the alarm. Thus members of the small contingent were on the alert when, an hour later, three fully manned canoes approached the encampment. Burney waited until they were within a ship's length of the beach before ordering one of his men to fire a musket over their heads; whereupon the would-be assailants consulted among themselves for at least five minutes and then paddled away. Some nights later, on 14 December, 'by the Negligence of the Centinel', Burney alleged, marauders broke into one of the tents and carried away their spoils to a canoe hidden among the rocks. This time it was Mr. Bayly who detected the thieves and fired on them as they fled into the woods, leaving their booty in the canoe. Two days later he packed up his gear to board the *Adventure* which was due to leave on the 18th. Amid the final preparations Burney was approached by some New Zealanders who had the effrontery to ask for the return of their canoe lost in the unsuccessful raid a couple nights before. As the ship was on the eve of sailing, he explained, he granted their request.[51]

On 17 December, when everything was ready for the voyage, Furneaux sent his large cutter to Grass Cove, in the eastern arm of the Sound, to gather a supply of the anti-scorbutic 'Cellery'. Ten men, led by Jack Rowe, left at dawn and were expected back by three in the afternoon at the latest. Since they failed to appear either that evening or the next morning, the worried captain ordered out the launch manned by an armed party of sailors and marines. Burney, who was in charge, was instructed to follow the eastern arm as far as Grass Cove and, if he saw

20 *The search party for the cutter's crew, led by James Burney*

no sign of the missing crew, to search along the western shore. The general belief was that the boat had gone adrift or run aground on the rocks. The 'melancholy news' brought back by Burney on his return towards midnight was far otherwise. At Grass Cove he discovered the remnants of clothing and the remains of men, with a crowd of vociferous natives replete after their cannibal feast. In his summary of the report Furneaux supplied a few grisly details:

they found the Relicks of several and the intrails of five men lying on the beach and in the Canoes they found several baskets of human flesh and five odd shoes new, as our people had been served Shoes a day or two before; they brought onboard several hands, two of which we knew, one belonged to Thomas Hill being marked on the Back T.H. another to Mr Rowe who had a wound on his fore finger not quite whole, and the Head, which was supposed was the head of my servant by the high forhead he being a Negroe, the Launch fired on them where they were assembled in great numbers on the top of a hill making all the signs of joy imaginable.[52]

In this crisis Furneaux obeyed the dictates of both prudence and humanity. While the *Adventure* awaited favourable conditions for sail-

A List of Men Slain by the Enemy in Queen Charlotte's Sound

Bounty paid	Nº	Entry	Year	Appearance	Absence and whether Preſt or not	Place and County where Born	Age at Time of Entry in this Ship	Nº and Letter of Tickets	MENS NAMES	Qualities	D.D. or R.	Time of Discharge
	2								Jab. Seb. Smelley	ab	DD	
	3								Thoˢ Woodhouse Janry 1773	Mid	DD	
	19								John Rowe	Mid	DD	
	26								Frasᵗ Murphy	DD		
	39								Michˡ Bell	ab	DD	
	49								Thoˢ Hill	ab	DD	18 Decᵗ
	90								John Cavanagh	ab	DD	
	100								James Jones	ab	DD	
	113								William Facey	ab	DD	
	115								William Milton	ab	DD	
									Tobˢ Furneaux	Captain		
									Peter Fannin	Master		
									Edward Jatins	Boatswain		

ing, he could, at some risk to boats and men, have sent avenging parties to the native settlements. He refrained from any such action and on 23 December left the accursed Sound. By that time the affair in Grass Cove had affected the lowliest of the ship's company. After his brief appearance in Burney's account of their stay ashore, Omy had ceased to figure in shipboard records — too insignificant perhaps for mention

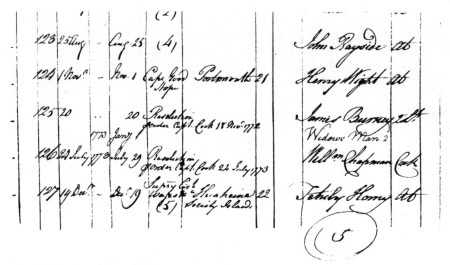

LEFT *21 The list of casualties*
ABOVE *22 Tetuby Homy becomes an able seaman*

even by the benevolent Mr. Bayly. On 19 December, however, presumably to fill one of the gaps left by the massacre, the supernumerary Tetuby Homy was entered on the muster-roll as an able seaman and thenceforward sank back into the anonymity of the lower deck. His feelings can only be guessed at when the ship, following the symmetrical pattern of this expedition, again headed towards the Antarctic. The feelings of more literate travellers are but sparsely recorded, though they are possibly implied by the *Adventure*'s course in the early months of 1774. The undeviating route in the latitudes south of Cape Horn suggests headlong, terrified flight: '*most extraordinary* infatuation', exclaimed Bayly, as he described the heedless rush that would have brought destruction had they encountered land. They met no land and nothing in the least novel (except to the hapless Omy): only again exposure to the intense cold and drenching seas; again the perils of fog and ice; again occasional birds and the lonely whale or seal. Early in March sickness among his men, combined with serious damage to the stores, compelled Furneaux to make for the Cape of Good Hope. He anchored in Table Bay on the 19th and had to spend almost a month in port resting his crew and refitting the ship. He set out once more and, after an absence of exactly two years, reached Spithead on 14 July.[53]

True to Burney's prediction, Omy had weathered the hardships of a long voyage and, despite all obstacles, had realized his own ambition to visit '*Britannia*'. The odds against him had certainly been heavy and the sequence of events leading to his arrival such as to suggest the force of some compelling destiny. If Oree's wishes had prevailed at Huahine, if the Boraboran conspirators had succeeded at Raiatea, he would never have set out on his travels. Had the *Adventure* not lost touch with the *Resolution*, in the course of time Cook would probably have restored him to Tahiti or the Society Islands. Even the tragedy at Grass Cove had conspired to further the appointed end: but for the loss of his men, Furneaux would almost certainly have delayed his return and made some attempt to link up with Cook in the Pacific. As it was, this unexceptional sample of Polynesian humanity — with no 'advantages of birth, or acquired rank' and none of 'shape, figure, or complexion', as Cook later expressed it — had been picked up almost at random and transported across the world. During the voyage he had, moreover, already sampled the diversions and hazards of European society under the guidance of a shipboard patron. After first granting him a passage, Furneaux seems to have shown little interest in Omy. But at the Cape of Good Hope, wrote the Forsters, reporting from hearsay, 'the captain dressed him in his own clothes, and introduced him in the best companies . . . .' And it was there, according to the same authorities (no friends of Omy), that he denied his lowly origins and assumed the fictitious character of 'a *hoa*, or attendant upon the king'.[54] Whatever its nature (and further details are regrettably lacking), the episode was a rehearsal for the more extended performance that opened when Furneaux escorted his protégé to the capital. Meanwhile, waiting somewhat dispiritedly in the wings, was a more influential patron whose recent activities must now be chronicled.

4. Mr. Banks, Lord Monboddo, Dr. Hawkesworth, and Others

IN THE TWO YEARS SINCE COOK'S DEPARTURE THERE HAD BEEN AMPLE TIME for Banks to regret his impetuous withdrawal. The northern expedition, intended as a prelude to his own Pacific voyage, had occupied the summer and autumn of 1772. After a leisurely passage in the *Sir Lawrence*, he and his party spent a fortnight in the Hebrides and by the end of August reached their chief objective, Iceland. On first landing, Banks, in the manner of southern navigators, wooed the somewhat timid fisher folk with gifts of ribbon and tobacco while Dr. Lind dispensed doses of physic and shocks from an electrical machine. Cordial relations were soon established and until late October the visitors toured the country-side, seeking out the natural wonders in which the island abounded. They examined lava fields and hot springs and spouting geysers, they climbed to the crater of Mount Hecla. And everywhere with customary zeal Banks collected mineral and botanic specimens, antiquities, books, manuscripts. Presents were exchanged and entertainments arranged on both sides. The Englishmen diverted their guests with the playing of French horns; the Icelanders sang their traditional songs, recited complimentary odes, and feasted the tourists on local delicacies — dried fish, sour butter, with whale and shark for dessert. To veterans of the *Endeavour* it was all faintly reminiscent of the Pacific. But they were of course half a world away from tropical Tahiti. As the northern winter impended, they loaded the *Sir Lawrence* with volcanic ballast, packed up their trophies, and made for home.[1]

Banks showed no urgent desire to reach London. He called at the Orkneys on the return voyage, may have visited the Highlands, and certainly stopped at Edinburgh. In that lively intellectual capital he and Solander met notabilities and discussed their travels, past and projected. One episode is recorded with tantalizing brevity in the journal of James Boswell: 'Went with Dr. Solander and breakfasted with Monboddo, who listened with avidity to the Doctor's description of the New Hollanders, almost brutes — but added with eagerness, "Have they tails, Dr. Solander?" "No, my Lord, they have not tails." '[2] Banks was also introduced to the erudite judge and may at this time have acquired *An Account of a Savage Girl, Caught Wild in the Woods of Champagne.* His copy of the pamphlet bears an inscription stating that Lord Monboddo had supervised the translation and 'chiefly' written the preface. The Savage Girl herself was one of those wild creatures so highly prized by eighteenth-century theorists. Commonly known as Mademoiselle Le Blanc, she had been found on the outskirts of the village of Songi in 1731. She was then about ten years old and wholly uncivilized in her behaviour — she ate raw flesh, climbed trees, swam like a fish, and could outrun hares and rabbits. She had since been weaned from her savage state and when Monboddo interviewed her in Paris was in corpulent middle age. In his opinion she was not, as the French supposed, of the Eskimo nation who were, he said, 'the ugliest of men . . . all covered with hair'. She was probably, he thought, a member of some fair-skinned race settled near Hudson Bay, whence she had been kidnapped by an unscrupulous sea captain. Her story, he held, supported his own belief that 'the *rational man*' had grown out of 'the mere *animal*'.[3]

With none of the fanfare which had marked his arrival from the Pacific, Banks was back in London late in November. Once the reunions and the greetings were over, his first care was for the spoils of his Icelandic tour. The manuscripts went into his library and ultimately to the British Museum; the natural history specimens and the geological samples were added to the collections at New Burlington Street; and the scoria used for ballast on the *Sir Lawrence* was divided between Chelsea and Kew. Since boyhood Banks had frequented the Apothecaries' Garden near his mother's home at Chelsea. Now he began his long association with the gardens at Kew and — perhaps on the gift of volcanic rock — laid the foundation of his friendship with their royal proprietor. At about this time he and Sir John Pringle persuaded George III to send one of Kew's under-gardeners, Francis Masson, to collect plants at the Cape of Good Hope. Royal patronage and public funds were not forthcoming, however, for a cause that touched Banks more closely. Before the end of winter he knew that his plans for a Pacific expedition — uncertain at best — would not be realized. Yet some prospect of distant travel still remained. There was a possibility that in the coming summer he might join Constantine Phipps in a search for the North-west Passage. Meanwhile in the company of another aristocratic friend, Charles Greville, he consoled himself with an excursion to Holland.[4]

The contrast with the volcanic mountains and thermal wonders of Iceland could scarcely have been more marked — unless in the tropical Pacific. Banks now found himself, as he wrote to Sarah Sophia, in a 'fenny muddy country' that reminded him of his native Lincolnshire. Equally striking was the contrast between the simple Icelandic community and the circles in which he and Greville moved in their progress through the Dutch cities. They paid their respects to the Prince of Orange at the Hague, they sampled the opera and other diversions at Amsterdam, they met scientific literati in Rotterdam, they sought out collections and called on dignitaries in Leyden, Haarlem, Utrecht. One link with the

north was a 'Levee' specially arranged so that Banks might meet Green-
land captains and pick up information for use in Constantine Phipps's
approaching Arctic expedition.[5]

He appreciated these and similar courtesies, he decided the Dutch had
been 'civiler' than he deserved, but his thoughts kept turning back to
the South Seas. In Amsterdam he discussed with a Mr. Bourse, 'advocate
to the East Indies Company', the *Endeavour*'s voyage, more particularly
its passage through the Dutch islands.[6] And 'to amuse the Princess of
Orange' he prepared a long discourse 'On the Manners of the Women of
Otaheite'. He was evidently in a relaxed mood at the time and wrote
with an enthusiasm recalling Bougainville's initial raptures rather than
the measured observations of his own voyage journal. In that island (to
summarize his often incoherent superlatives), Love was the Chief Occupation, the favourite, nay almost the Sole Luxury of the Inhabitants,
and both in body and soul the women were modelled with the utmost
perfection. European ladies might surpass them in complexion, Banks
conceded, but in all else they excelled — nowhere else had he seen their
equals. Forms like theirs existed here only in marble or on canvas, were
indeed such as might defy imitation by 'the Chizzel of a Phidias or the
Pencil of an Appeles'. Their figures were not squeezed by a cincture
'scarce less tenacious than Iron' nor swelled out below by 'a preposterous
mountain of hoops'. Their garments hung 'in folds of the most Elegant
& unartificial forms' like those seen on antique statues or on the angels
and goddesses of the best Italian painters. Their appearance, he went
on, was not a little aided by their freedom from European ideas of
propriety. A Tahitian maiden would by a motion of her dress disclose
an arm and half her breast, then a moment later bare the whole breast
— 'all this with as much innocence & genuine modesty as an English
woman can shew'. In this 'Land of Liberty' chastity was nevertheless
'Esteemd as a virtue' and women were no less 'inviolable in their
attachments' than in Europe. He absolved them from blame for the
practice of infanticide (which he ascribed to the selfishness of their men)
and in describing their domestic routine indulged in further superlatives.
In cleanliness, he held, these people excelled 'beyond all compare all
other nations', while the climate of their island he believed to be 'without
Exaggeration the best on the face of the Globe'.[7]

By the end of March Banks had returned home to face the inclemencies
of an English spring and, as the weeks passed by, must decide on the
goal of his now customary summer excursion. In the end he set off on a
botanizing trip to Wales with a party that included Solander and a new
friend, Dr. Charles Blagden of Edinburgh. He had toyed with the idea
of visiting the Mediterranean and given more serious thought to joining
Constantine Phipps in his northern voyage. In April he wrote with
proprietary air: 'we are employd in fitting out an expedition in order to
penetrate as near to the North Pole as Possible . . . .' A month or so later
he had decided not to accompany his friend, but for the benefit of Phipps
and his assistants supplied spirits, bottles, pins, snippers for the preserva-

tion of specimens, and special paper for the drying of plants. With elaborate instructions for their use he sent more general remarks. All kinds of northern animals would be curious, he observed, and, if it were possible to bring home a live white bear, he would be particularly glad. Likewise he much wished to see any seal differing from the common sort; the complete skin with the head and teeth should be procured. Since naturalists were almost totally unacquainted with whales, he went on, the foetuses of any species would be very acceptable. And so in similar strain for page upon page of admonition and advice covering the wide range of natural history. Early in June Phipps sailed in the *Racehorse*, while later in the month Banks departed on his more limited travels.[8] Though Arctic regions might be a promising field for scientific study, he had apparently concluded, they were not for him — and provided no substitute for the South Seas.

THE DENIZENS OF THE NORTH, if neither as ugly nor as hirsute as Monboddo claimed, could certainly not compare in comeliness or romantic appeal with the paragons of Tahiti. In December 1772 a party of Eskimos reached England, brought from Labrador by the fur trader and naturalist George Cartwright. Their leader was a priest, Attuiock by name, who had with him his wife and child, a younger brother Tooklavinia, and the latter's wife Caubvick. For a brief season the Eskimos were minor lions in learned and fashionable London. They dined with members of the Royal Society, they met the renowned anatomist John Hunter, they visited the opera and Drury Lane where they sat in the Royal Box, they watched the King review his troops in Hyde Park, and towards the end of their stay they were presented at Court. Interest in the visitors was not confined to such exalted circles. On landing at Westminster Bridge they were immediately surrounded by a curious crowd and so great was the press of people at their lodgings that Cartwright was forced to take a furnished house and limit callers to two days a week.[9]

The Eskimos' response to the sights of the capital disappointed Cartwright, though it might not have surprised Jean-Jacques Rousseau. They were astonished at the number of ships on the Thames but took little notice of London Bridge which they thought was a great rock extending across the river. Nor did they at first show any particular interest in St. Paul's, again supposing it to be a natural feature like the mountains of Labrador. A fortnight after their arrival Cartwright took Attuiock, disguised in European dress, for an excursion to the Tower and home by way of Westminster Bridge and Hyde Park Corner. On their return he expected the priest to speak of the wonders he had seen. Instead Attuiock sat down, fixed his eyes on the floor 'in a stupid stare', and at last soliloquized: '"Oh! I am tired; here are too many houses; too much smoke; too many people; Labrador is very good; seals are plentiful there; I wish I was back again."'[10]

Banks, who had seen nothing of the indigenous inhabitants during his visit to Labrador with Constantine Phipps, seized this opportunity of filling a gap in his knowledge. After his return from Iceland *Lloyd's Evening Post* reported that he and Dr. Solander had paid frequent visits to the Eskimos and expressed themselves 'extremely well satisfied with the observations and behaviour of those people'. The Eskimos in return showed great pleasure in seeing the gentlemen as they generally carried with them presents of beads, knives, or iron tools and behaved with politeness and respect. In moralizing strain the writer went on to draw a comparison with less enlightened callers:

These ingenious Gentlemen, who are inquisitive to mark the discriminations of the human character in every part of the world, could not help taking notice of the intelligent countenance and discourse of the Priest, and of the easy carriage and civility of manners of the whole family; while by too many of their numerous visitors they are held in contempt as Savages, because their heads have not undergone the operations of the Friseur, and gaped at as monsters, because their dress is not according to the *Bon-Ton*.[11]

Until he left for Holland Banks evidently continued to call on the Eskimos and commissioned a number of portraits, among them two fine pastel drawings by Nathaniel Dance showing Attuiock and Caubvick in their own costume. In February Cartwright took the family to his father's home in rural Nottinghamshire where they soon revived in health and spirits. The men marvelled at the flatness of the countryside and became keen fox-hunters, while the women, 'according to the universal disposition of the fair sex', enjoyed visiting and dancing. When they set out for Labrador early in May, Cartwright noted that they were well pleased in the expectation of soon seeing their native country, their relations, and their friends; he himself, he added, was very happy in the prospect of carrying them back, apparently in perfect health. His mood of self-congratulation was short lived. On the evening of their departure Caubvick complained of a sickness which was finally diagnosed as small-pox. The malady gradually spread to her companions, forcing Cartwright to delay the voyage and turn back to Plymouth. Thence early in June he left for a hurried visit to London, only to inform Banks on his return that the whole party, except for the younger woman, had now died. 'I last night ventured to tell Caubvick of the death of all the rest, having prepar'd her for it this week past,' he wrote, 'she was a good deal affected, but not so much as I expected.'[12]

The lesson of this tragic episode was not lost on Banks whose association with the Eskimos had already supplied the pretext for a long, flattering, consoling letter from a Scottish admirer met in Edinburgh during the return journey from Iceland. 'You will perceive, from the slight occasion on which I write to you, how desirous I am to revive a connection, the forming of which I shall ever reckon among the fortunate & agreeable circumstances of my life', began the eminent historian William Robertson. He had read in the papers of Mr. Banks's visit to the Labrador family, he explained, and now sought light on a question that perplexed him: Did the Eskimos, in common with all other natives of America, grow hair only on the head or were they, as rumour would have it, bearded like the inhabitants of northern Europe? He then expressed his concern over the projected (and apparently abandoned) southern expedition. 'I look with impatience into every News Paper to learn something about your future motions', he informed Banks. 'What a shame it is that the first literary & commercial nation in the world should hesitate a moment about encouraging the only voyage which in modern times, has no other object but the advancement of science.'[13]

News of literary Edinburgh followed, in particular the recent publication of 'a book on the origin & progress of language by Lord Monboddo, one of our Judges'. This work, as Robertson summarized it, held that men were originally quadrupeds; that several ages elapsed before they acquired the art of walking erect; that they were naturally without language; that the orang-outangs were men still in this state; that there were men with tails. 'Amidst all these oddities,' he commented, 'there are mingled ingenious & bold opinions; & the book is not destitute of considerable merit.' 'You are frequently mentioned in it & in a proper manner', he told Banks. The amiable Robertson ended with compliments to Solander and a reference to the approaching publication of Hawkesworth's narrative of their South Seas voyage: 'I long for the month of April when we are to be entertained & instructed. If you knew how many foolish & lying books of travel I have read, you would not wonder at my impatience.'[14]

HAWKESWORTH'S COMPILATION was in fact delayed until the summer, appearing only after Monboddo's speculative heresies had reached the London public. In its 'Catalogue of New Publications' for May 1773 the *Gentleman's Magazine* listed *Of the Origin and Progress of Language*, Volume I, published by Cadell and sold for six shillings. The magazine made no further reference to Monboddo's work, but for the benefit of its more studious subscribers the *Monthly Review* noticed it in two lengthy articles illustrated in the lavish eighteenth-century fashion with copious quotations. Though the book contained some fanciful and reprehensible ideas, remarked the anonymous reviewer, its author had read and thought much upon his subject. Few readers — indeed he ventured to say very few — would not find some things new and many others both entertaining and instructive. These would, in great measure, atone for its faults — and here he instanced the 'pompous and unnecessary display of metaphysical knowledge', the 'bigotted attachment to the Greek philosophy', and the account given of the orang-outangs. Upon the whole and in spite of such blemishes, he concluded (unconsciously echoing William Robertson), the work had 'a very considerable share of merit'.[15]

One of the book's incidental merits in the eyes of its first readers may have been a certain topicality. To supply a basis for his linguistic theories, Monboddo set out to define 'the *original* nature of man' and that, he asserted, would be found not in civilized nations but among barbarous peoples. A professed admirer of that 'author of so much genius', 'Mons. Rousseau', in describing primitive society he cited similar sources to those used two decades earlier in the *Discourse on Inequality* and often gave the same examples. With even greater diligence than his mentor he had combed through classical writers — Aristotle, Herodotus, Pausanius, and the obscure Diodorus Siculus, authority on the naked fish-eaters of Arabia. He had consulted later travellers for descriptions of the Hottentots and the orang-outangs whom, with more certainty than Rousseau, he classed as human beings. Again following the master, he listed European savages — the fourteenth-century child from Hesse-Cassel, the Lithuanian found in 1694, the Hanoverian brought to England in the time of George I, and one of particular interest to himself, the girl 'catched wild in the woods of Champaigne' and later known as Mademoiselle Le Blanc. He drew on missionary records for details of North American Indians and on a history of the Incas for his account of the aborigines of Peru. But, Monboddo pointed out, so great had been the changes since the time of Columbus it was not in the Americas that people living in the natural state must now be sought. It was in other regions as yet imperfectly discovered — 'the countries in the South sea, and such parts of the Atlantic ocean as have not been frequented by European ships'.[16]

What, then, was the nature of human society in this untouched quarter of the world? Monboddo's answer, based for the most part on the voyage narratives gathered by de Brosses, was scarcely reassuring to Utopia-seekers. William Dampier met in New Holland naked fishermen exactly like those described by Diodorus Siculus. Amerigo Vespucci lighted on a people living together in herds without government, religion, arts, or property. Jack the Hermit wrote that the Fuegians acted entirely like brutes with no regard for decency. Narbrough found cannibals, Le Maire savages who bit like dogs . . . . So, in anticipation of later armchair anthropologists, Monboddo assembled his highly selective, carefully documented evidence, culminating in the revelation that brought him lasting notoriety. He himself made no claim to have discovered men with tails. That, he observed, was a fact not only attested by Linnaeus and Buffon but (here again following Rousseau) one that was borne out by the satyrs of ancient mythology. His own modest contribution was to quote from Keoping, a Swedish traveller, who saw in Nicobar 'men with tails like those of cats'. As Monboddo emphasized, he accepted this 'extraordinary' assertion only after an exchange of letters with Linnaeus, and for the benefit of sceptical readers he quoted the correspondence in a footnote.[17]

Monboddo passed cursorily over recent Pacific voyages. He seems to have taken from Bougainville's published narrative some details of the Falkland Islands. The same source may have supported his view that a golden age, the 'poetical fiction' of the ancients, still existed in the South Seas. There was, however, no specific mention of New Cythera and

none of Aoutourou. Similarly — and despite William Robertson —
references to Banks were few and perfunctory. He and Solander were
credited with finding in New Zealand people who fed on human flesh
but who, far from being 'barbarous or inhuman', were 'brave and
generous'. Another passage, apparently inspired by a meeting with
Banks in Edinburgh, praised his enterprise and linguistic skill. But that
was all. When he brought this section of his work to a close, Monboddo
was in a mood of inquiring anticipation shared by other members of the
learned and literary world. Having summed up his findings on 'the
natural state of men' in southern regions, he went on: 'we have reason to
expect from those countries, in a short time, much greater and more
certain discoveries, such as I hope will improve and enlarge the knowledge of our own species as much as the natural history of other animals,
and of plants and minerals.'[18]

If the allusion was to Hawkesworth's narrative (and not to Cook's
latest voyage or to the abortive plans of Banks), it appeared not in the
spring of 1773, as Robertson had hoped, but in the following June. Even
so, its publication was a remarkable achievement on the part of those
concerned — printers, artists, draughtsmen, binders, and, above all
others, the compiler. Hawkesworth had fully justified Dr. Burney's
recommendation and carried out his commission with business-like effi-
ciency. From a mass of routine day-to-day records — not only Cook's
but those of his predecessors and their subordinates — he had selected
the more important and given them consecutive form. He had ingeniously combined the observations of Cook and Banks, acknowledging
the latter's help on the title-page and also in a preface. He had, according to his own testimony, consulted all the major contributors. And
within two years of the expedition's return he had completed *An Account
of the Voyages undertaken by the order of His Present Majesty for
making Discoveries in the Southern Hemisphere.* A dedication to the
monarch credited him with possessing 'the best fleet, and the bravest as
well as most able navigators in Europe'. It was further claimed that the
discoveries made under His Majesty's auspices were 'far greater than
those of all the navigators in the world collectively, from the expedition
of Columbus to the present time'. The work was presented in three
quarto volumes, the first describing the voyages of Byron, Wallis, and
Carteret, the second and third Cook's.[19]

When replying to his critics, Hawkesworth modestly claimed to have
been 'little more than an amanuensis for others'. He was of course something far different. He was a professional man of letters guided by his
own principles and the editorial conventions of his time. In working on
the voyages his object was to create a continuous narrative that would at
once record, instruct, and entertain. He relied on his sources for facts
and dates, but in other respects he felt himself at liberty to modify, add,
or omit as taste and literary considerations demanded. Hence he did not
hesitate to convert the language of untutored seamen into his own
measured prose nor to subject the journal of Banks to the same unifying

AN

ACCOUNT

OF THE

VOYAGES

UNDERTAKEN BY THE

ORDER OF HIS PRESENT MAJESTY

FOR MAKING

Difcoveries in the Southern Hemifphere,

And fucceffively performed by

COMMODORE BYRON, ‖ CAPTAIN CARTERET,
CAPTAIN WALLIS, ‖ And CAPTAIN COOK,

In the DOLPHIN, the SWALLOW, and the ENDEAVOUR:

DRAWN UP

From the JOURNALS which were kept by the feveral COMMANDERS,
And from the Papers of JOSEPH BANKS, Efq;

By JOHN HAWKESWORTH, LL.D.

IN THREE VOLUMES.

Illuftrated with CUTS, and a great Variety of CHARTS and MAPS relative to
Countries now firft difcovered, or hitherto but imperfectly known.

VOL. I.

LONDON:
Printed for W. STRAHAN; and T. CADELL in the Strand.
MDCCLXXIII.

23
*Hawkesworth's epic
of British
exploration*

process. A further device, also tending to unify, was discussed in his
introduction. To bring 'the Adventurer and the Reader nearer together'
and so, he explained, 'excite an interest, and . . . afford more entertainment', he had written not in the third person but in the first.[20] The result
was the creation of an Adventurer, brave and benign, persisting from
voyage to voyage and expressing himself in sub-Johnsonian English.
Moreover, since the author-compiler had felt himself free to introduce
his own ponderings and opinions, the Adventurer was endowed with
the gift of sententious utterance. This was the dominating figure in
Hawkesworth's epic of British enterprise in the South Seas.
    Like other epic heroes, the British Odysseus journeyed for a purpose.

But since the search for a southern continent had been fruitless (and was
in any case of little interest to Hawkesworth), this aim was relegated to
a minor place. With a certain inevitability and for a variety of reasons
— historical, geographical, literary — Tahiti became a focal point of
the narrative. In the opening volume, following Byron's unsuccessful
quest, Wallis in the guise of the Adventurer discovered the island, subdued its people, and won over its 'Queen' whose dramatic possibilities
Hawkesworth was quick to recognize and exploit. Then in the climactic
second volume came the protracted sojourn of Cook-Odysseus and his
companions, the reappearance of the Queen, now endowed with the
poetic name of Oberea, and the expedition's departure, bearing away
her favourite Tupia. In both episodes, but especially in the later one,
the attractions of Tahiti were thrown into relief by the prelude and the
sequel. Before reaching this haven of ease and plenty the navigators had
experienced the hazards and discomforts of a long voyage; on leaving it
they suffered even greater dangers and privations in the uncharted
waters of the Pacific. The contrast with exotic peoples encountered elsewhere was equally striking. Whatever their shortcomings, the Tahitians
seemed a world apart from the forlorn natives of South America or the
naked inhabitants of New Holland.[21]

Hawkesworth's picture of Tahiti was thus generally favourable. But
he gave no more support than Banks did to the view that the island was
a tropical paradise populated by survivors from a golden age. Indeed,
while retaining Banks's early impression of the 'Arcadian' appearance of
Matavai Bay, he dropped other more fanciful allusions: the classical
names originally conferred on local dignitaries, for example, or the comparison of wandering bards, the *arioi*, with Homer. Where he did not
hesitate to follow Banks, his chief source for the later expedition, was in
the emphasis given to erotic behaviour. The scene of the naturalist's
confrontation with Oberea and her lover was seized upon and filled out
with improbable details. (Banks was shown modestly withdrawing to
the adulterous queen's 'antichamber'.) An account of the fertilization
ceremony performed by young women was taken over from his journal
and, since he had made no mention of the public act of copulation witnessed near Fort Venus, a version of the incident was drawn from the
usually reticent Cook. So Hawkesworth provided diversion of a titillating
kind for his readers, but his aim was to instruct as well as entertain. In
the stern role of moralist he did not hesitate to condemn the islanders'
'dissolute sensuality' nor to hint darkly at vile customs which 'no imagination could possibly conceive'. Elsewhere he censured openly or by
implication their thievishness, their savagery in warfare, and the
inhuman practice of infanticide prevailing among their *arioi*.[22]

The mouthpiece for Hawkesworth's moralizing on the Tahitians was
the Adventurer represented by Cook who was shown holding himself
somewhat aloof from the spectacle of island life. He was leader, com-
mentator, dispenser of justice, and only to a limited degree an active
participant. The role of Banks was markedly different, the result partly

of the recorded facts, partly of their literary manipulation. Hawkesworth
was grateful to the botanist for so generously permitting the use of his
'accurate and circumstantial journal' and expressed his thanks in effusive
terms. On reading the document, however, he must have realized that
it sometimes disclosed the writer in an unflattering and even com-
promising posture. This scion of the landed gentry had mingled freely
with uncivilized natives; he had pried in most ungentlemanly fashion
into their customs; he had on one occasion shed his clothes and blackened
his person in the process; and he had, it was obvious, enjoyed the favours
of island women. How, then, should this potentially damaging material
be treated? Hawkesworth chose the path of discretion. He eliminated
explicit allusions to the young man's amours; he justified his undressing
and body-smearing on the grounds that 'he could be present upon no
other condition'; and he modified the account of his relations with
Oberea, omitting, for instance, all reference to her rejected overtures.
Nevertheless, in spite of Hawkesworth's efforts, the censored narrative
contained enough to establish Banks's reputation as an unconventional
and sometimes comic figure. He had begun his long career in the annals
of the expedition as a foil to the heroic and dignified Cook.[23]

Where Hawkesworth did less than justice to Banks and the other
ingenious gentleman was in the limited use he made of their contributions to natural history. In his final account of Tahiti he disposed of
animals, birds, and fishes in a few perfunctory lines. A further paragraph listed plants and trees, but there was no consistency in nomen-
clature and the catalogue was filled out with the misleading comment,
derived from Banks: 'the inhabitants . . . seem to be exempted from the
first general curse, that "man should eat his bread in the sweat of his
brow."'[24] Similarly a number of the plates tended to support an idyllic
conception of island life that Hawkesworth had been at pains to discount
in his narrative. Some illustrators confined themselves to representations
of native artifacts or straightforward landscapes based on the work of
Banks's lamented draughtsmen. Others drew to a greater or lesser
extent on the imagination: one engraver, Woollett, emphasized the
sombre and sometimes sinister atmosphere of Parkinson's sketches; a
second, Rooker by name, saw the Tahitians through a haze of Graeco-
Roman myth. But idealization in terms of the classical European past
was carried to an extreme by the artist Cipriani and his engraver
Bartolozzi in what purported to be the view of an interior in Raiatea.
Accompanied by the music of a nose-flute, lightly robed maidens danced
in a pillared *atrium* before an audience arrayed in the togas of ancient
Rome.[25]

This and a similar plate (showing the 'wretched' inhabitants of Tierra
del Fuego) moved the *Monthly Review* to mild protest. Truth and nature,
it complained, had been sacrificed to the painter's ideas of grace and
beauty. Cipriani's elegant pencil had depicted not South Sea Islanders
but figures which continually reminded the spectator of the antique or
productions of the Roman and Florentine schools. It was one of the few

adverse comments in a series of articles that ran through four numbers of the periodical late in 1773. The writer, on the evidence of his style and preoccupations, was probably that philsophical reviewer who in his notice of Bougainville had looked forward to the impending appearance of Hawkesworth's volumes. If so, his expectations were not disappointed. Ever since the discovery of America was completed, he remarked, there had been speculation on the state of 'that immense . . . part of the terraqueous globe' lying between the southern extremity of the new world and the Cape of Good Hope. The peculiar air of secrecy surrounding recent expeditions had excited new attention, while some imperfect and anonymous reports had served rather to provoke than satisfy the public's curiosity. Now they had the authentic account, abounding in curious information and, notwithstanding certain imperfections, adorned both in sentiment and diction by the editor's pen.[26]

The reviewer passed lightly over Hawkesworth's imperfections. He conscientiously surveyed each expedition, selecting for special attention those of Wallis and Cook; and from the immense expanse of the terraqueous globe he chose for extended treatment Tahiti and its unique inhabitants. Few nations (to summarize his scattered observations) had been discovered whose manners and customs carried such an air of singularity. Indeed, in government and habits they appeared to be nearly as much the antipodes of Europe as in their geographical situation. And nowhere was their conduct more truly paradoxical than in their attitude towards 'a certain appetite'. Among these people, both male and female, the very idea of chastity seemed unknown. Such were their enlarged notions that the gratification of bodily desires never gave rise to scandal. Nor was the act performed with any degree of secrecy — and here Banks's 'blundering' confrontation with Oberea and her youthful lover were cited: 'Our Otaheitean Princess appears to have been no more disconcerted . . . than if he had interrupted her at breakfast . . . .' The 'supposed sovereign', this lady *d'un certain age*', had obviously captured the writer's imagination. He had already expended pages in describing her relations with Wallis and in illustrating her dignity, her generosity, her extreme sensibility. She seemed to have had 'a most tender attachment to our adventurers', he noted, and to have been 'as susceptible as Queen Dido'.[27]

The comparison prompted melancholy ponderings on the recent history of these *'men of nature'* hitherto so widely severed from the rest of the world. Though Oberea's fate had been less tragical than the Carthaginian queen's, she too had suffered misfortune. On landing at Matavai Bay, Banks and his companions found that romantic spot a scene of devastation. After the *Dolphin's* departure, they soon learned, the island had been ravaged by a war which had dislodged Oberea and her consort from the seat of power. What, asked the philosophical reviewer, was the origin of this conflict? In seeking an answer he had recourse to the *Discourse on Inequality*:

The people of Otaheite, in the state in which they were found by our countrymen, present us with a picture of human society resembling, in more respects
than one, that which the ingenious but fanciful Rousseau has delineated, when
he exhibits a view of what he terms the *'real youth of the world:'* — a state
which he considers as the best for man; all the ulterior supposed improvements
of which 'have been so many steps tending, in appearance, towards the advantage of individuals, but in fact towards the deterioration of the species.' It is
'Iron and *Corn,'* our philosopher afterwards observes, 'that have civilized men,
and *ruined* mankind.'

Rousseau's thesis appeared to find some support in the pages of Hawkesworth. True, the Tahitians were already tolerably civilized and divided
into classes. But the introduction of European novelties, particularly
iron, had increased existing inequalities and sown the seeds of war.
Furthermore, this hitherto healthy race had been infected with 'a certain
loathsome disease' — not by the English but, according to Bougainville's
own testimony, by the French. On this reassuring note the reviewer left
Tahiti to dwell more summarily on the subsequent discoveries of Cook
and his 'philosophical adventurers'.[28]

The *Gentleman's Magazine* showed its approval of Hawkesworth's
compilation in its own lavish fashion. From June 1773 until March 1774
it issued a series of 'epitomes' so elaborate that a parsimonious reader
might have regarded them as a substitute for the published work and
saved himself an outlay of three guineas. Each of the expeditions was
described in detailed articles filled out with excerpts from the original.
Comparisons were sometimes made with other voyagers — Anson,
Alexander Selkirk, Bougainville — but editorial asides were infrequent
and critical comments even fewer. The anonymous writer found the
account of Oberea's parting with Wallis reminiscent of the scene between
Dido and Aeneas and suspected that Hawkesworth might have drawn
his tenderest strokes from Virgil. Citing both Wallis and Bougainville on
the vexed question of venereal disease, he positively asserted: 'the crew
of the Dolphin did not communicate it.' He lamented the death of
Tupia, 'perhaps, the most intelligent Indian' in the island, who, had he
survived, would 'probably have enlightened Europe with a new species
of learning'. Further, he regretted that Cook had not left the two
deserters at Tahiti to introduce civilized arts among the inhabitants and
give them 'higher notions of the Supreme Being'. Hawkesworth's narrative of the final expedition occupied at least half the reviewer's space
and inspired his highest praise. There was not, he claimed, 'in any
language, a voyage so full of variety, and so elegantly written.'[29]

An eager public evidently agreed with the reviewer's verdict. The
work was an immense popular success from the outset and soon ran into
a second edition. By the close of 1773 it had been separately published
in Dublin, and before another year was out versions had appeared in
New York, Berlin, Rotterdam, and Paris.[30]

READERS IN TWO CONTINENTS AND TWO HEMISPHERES might marvel at Dr. Hawkesworth's eloquent revelations, but the pundits of literary London were not impressed. The supreme pundit, indeed, condemned his old friend's work before it actually appeared. Boswell records this sparkling exchange in May 1773, prompted by a reference to the forthcoming publication:

JOHNSON: 'Sir, if you talk of it as a subject of commerce, it will be gainful; if as a book that is to increase human knowledge, I believe there will not be much of that. Hawkesworth can tell only what the voyagers have told him; and they have found very little, only one new animal, I think.' BOSWELL: 'But many insects, Sir.' JOHNSON: 'Why, Sir, as to insects, Ray reckons of British insects twenty thousand species. They might have staid at home and discovered enough in that way.'

Horace Walpole at least had the grace to read the book before belittling it with aristocratic disdain. The new *Voyages*, he remarked on 21 June, 'might make one a good first mate, but tell one nothing at all.' Dr. Hawkesworth, he went on, was still more provoking:

An old black gentlewoman of forty carries Captain Wallis across a river, when he was too weak to walk, and the man represents them as a new edition of Dido and Aeneas. Indeed, Dido the new does not even borrow the obscurity of a cave when she treats the travellers with the rites of love, as practised in Otaheite.

A fortnight later he had almost 'waded through' the three volumes to reach the conclusion: 'The entertaining matter would not fill half a volume; and at best is but an account of the fishermen on the coast of forty islands.'[31]

Published attacks were at once more specific and more forceful. A contributor to the *Gentleman's Magazine* severely censured the author-editor not only for his ignorance of the arts of navigation and astronomy but for failing to attribute the *Endeavour*'s survival on the coast of New Holland to God's special interposition. His heretical views on the nature of Divine Providence were again the target of an anonymous pamphleteer who asserted that by denying the possibility of such intervention Dr. Hawkesworth had lost 'his literary fame, and the esteem of mankind'.[32]

Most vehement of the critical pack, however, was Alexander Dalrymple. Still outraged that not he but the unlettered Lieutenant Cook had taken charge of the *Endeavour*, this contentious Scot set out to refute Hawkesworth's '*groundless* and *illiberal* Imputations' in a *Letter* littered with italic type and illustrated with voluminous excerpts from his previous writings and those of Pacific navigators. He demolished Hawkesworth's charge that he — Dalrymple — had misrepresented the records of Spanish and Dutch voyages in order to support his own conjectures; he disclosed discrepancies between the published charts and

A N

E P I S T L E

F R O M

OBEREA, QUEEN of OTAHEITE,

T O

JOSEPH BANKS, Esq.

Tranſlated by T. Q. Z. Eſq.

Profeſſor of the OTAHEITE Language in Dublin, and of all the Languages of the
undiſcovered Iſlands in the SOUTH SEA;

And enriched with HISTORICAL and EXPLANATORY NOTES.

The THIRD EDITION.

_____

L O N D O N:

Printed for J. ALMON, oppoſite BURLINGTON-HOUSE, in PICCADILLY.

MDCCLXXIV.

[Price One Shilling.]

25
The first in a
long series of
verse satires

corresponding sections of Hawkesworth's narrative; he denounced the
plates on both moral and artistic grounds; and he deplored those malign
influences in the Admiralty which had prevented him from commanding
the *Endeavour* and Mr. Banks from setting out in the *Resolution*.
Although four voyages had now been made, he pointed out in a 'Postscript to the Publick', it was not yet determined whether or not there
was a 'SOUTHERN CONTINENT'. '. . . I would *not have come back* in
Ignorance', he concluded.[33]
    In the preface to his second edition, Hawkesworth made some attempt
to answer Dalrymple, employing the basest of all controversial weapons,
ridicule. 'I am', he wrote, 'very sorry for the discontented state of this
good Gentleman's mind, and most sincerely wish that a southern continent may be found, as I am confident nothing else can make him
happy and good-humoured.' The irrepressible Dalrymple in his turn
replied in further *Observations* which he printed but did not publish

out of respect for his late opponent's memory. For Dr. Hawkesworth died in November 1773, the victim in Fanny Burney's opinion less of the 'lingering fever' to which his end was publicly attributed than of persecution from 'those envious and malignant Witlings' of the literary world.[34]

Dalrymple might fairly be described as envious but scarcely as malignant and certainly not as a witling. In all probability Miss Burney referred not to his ponderous diatribe but to a work that exploited the satiric and erotic possibilities of Hawkesworth's volumes. A pseudonymous writer, reputedly Major John Scott, seized upon two themes — the moral lapses of the voyagers (Banks in particular) and the licentious customs of Tahiti — which he elaborated in what proved to be the opening number of a verse cycle varied both in authorship and subject. *An Epistle from Oberea, Queen of Otaheite, to Joseph Banks, Esq.*, though dated 1774, appeared in the previous year, purporting to be a translation from the Tahitian language. Like reviewers and commentators before him, the writer saw Oberea as a Dido of the South Seas and shows her bereft of her lover Banks, known to her as Opano:

> Read, or oh! say does some more amorous fair
> Prevent *Opano*, and engage his care?
> I *Oberea*, from the Southern main,
> Of slighted vows, of injur'd faith complain.

Throughout the lament the author introduced references to practices and topics familiar to newspaper readers ever since the *Endeavour*'s return — the promiscuity of Tahitian women, their curious habit of tattooing the buttocks, the prevalence of venereal disease (inevitably attributed to French influence) — together with further customs and incidents described in the recently published narrative. The mock-heroic treatment was matched by a mock-scholastic apparatus of footnotes and references culled from both classical writers and Hawkesworth (whose 'pruriant imagination' was openly censured). In heavily facetious vein the author announced the early publication of a Tahitian grammar and dictionary uniform in format and price with Hawkesworth's *Voyages*.[35]

The effect of this usually good-humoured, if rather tasteless, exercise could scarcely have been lethal in itself, though it might have contributed to the anxieties that beset Dr. Hawkesworth towards the end of his life. His death wholly silenced the witlings, according to Fanny Burney, but not this versifier or (as the authorities assert) one of his imitators. Late in 1773 or early the next year there appeared *An Epistle from Mr. Banks, Voyager, Monster-hunter, and Amoroso, to Oberea, Queen of Otaheite.* An appropriately reflective note was sometimes introduced into the new monologue, as when Banks-Aeneas confessed that in seducing Oberea he was to blame, for in the other hemisphere European moral notions were either non-existent or completely reversed:

> Desire was mutual, but the fault was mine;
> For you, fond souls, who dwell beneath the line,

> In mutual dalliance hold perpetual play,
> The golden age repeating ev'ry day.
> What's vice in us, in you is virtue clear,
> Untaught in guilt, you cannot know to fear.

Such a passage is exceptional, however, and in general the mixture of satire and salacity is coarser than before, while criticism of Dr. Hawkesworth for the demoralizing nature of his work becomes even more explicit:

> One page of *Hawkesworth*, in the cool retreat,
> Fires the bright maid with more than mortal heat;
> She sinks at once into the lover's arms,
> Nor deems it vice to prostitute her charms;
> 'I'll do,' cries she, 'what Queens have done before;'
> And sinks, *from principle*, a common whore.[36]

The cycle plumbed new depths with the next contribution, '*An* Heroic Epistle *from the injured* Harriot, *Mistress to Mr.* Banks, to Oberea, *Queen of* Otaheite', published anonymously in the *Westminster Magazine* for January 1774. Banks's rejected fiancée, Harriet Blosset, was dragged from rural seclusion and endowed not only with the manners and vocabulary of a fishwife but with some classical erudition. Oberea is by turns 'savage Slut', 'wanton Gypsy', 'dirty Queen', 'Inveigling Harlot', 'royal bawd'. She is likened to 'a Gosport Jade' or 'lewd' Calypso and scorned for her presumptuousness in attempting to win back Banquo or Tolano (as Banks is indifferently termed):

> Think'st thou he'll leave my European grace
> For thy daub'd, yellow, dirty *tatoaw'd* face?
>
> Vain Oberea will in vain beseech,
> And to the bawdy winds betray her painted breech.

The jealous virago lampoons 'smug' Solander, ridicules Clerke for his 'choice of jades', and touches on the 'scenes obscene' described or hinted at by 'luscious' Hawkesworth. In a final burst of triumphant rhetoric she draws the stock comparison:

> Alas! these joys, like Dido, you have prov'd,
> Like her you've lost the godlike man belov'd . . . .[37]

Not all the verse inspired by Hawkesworth was satiric in conception. In the spring of 1774 there appeared the anonymous *Otaheite*, simply characterized as 'A Poem'. It was, in fact, an abbreviated version of that epic which Dr. Johnson had adumbrated after his first meeting with Banks. And though the botanist is not mentioned by name, his person

is faintly discernible in the abstract figures who move through the opening sections of the work. He is perhaps the 'sea-beat Wand'rer' restored
to his 'native Soil' after perilous travels through 'wide Limits of the
Southern World'; more certainly he is one of the 'Sons of Science' who
have sought out 'Tribes yet unknown . . . Wonders unexplor'd'; and
possibly he is the 'Sage' whose 'penetrating View' dares to pursue nature
to her 'inmost Depths'. After surveying regions 'Where Nations shiver
with Antarctic Frost', the Wand'rer reaches the poem's nominal subject,
'The CYPRUS of the SOUTH, the Land of Love'. Tahiti is first presented in
idyllic terms:

> Here, ceaseless, the returning Seasons wear
> Spring's verdant Robe, and smile throughout the Year;
> Refreshing Zephyrs cool the noon-tide Ray,
> And Plantane Groves imperious Shades display.

Tahitian love-making is touched on with only a hint of censure:

> Impetuous Wishes no Concealment know,
> As the Heart prompts, the melting Numbers flow:
> Each OBEREA feels the lawless Flame,
> Nor checks Desires she does not blush to name.[38]

But the author was no sentimental admirer of these people released by
nature from arduous labour and dedicated to a life of self-indulgence.
Comparing them with more virile nations, he comments disapprovingly:

> A Dream their Being, and their Life a Day.
> Unknown to these soft Tribes, with stubborn Toil
> And Arms robust to the cultur'd Soil;
>
> Unknown those Wants that prompt th' inventive Mind,
> And banish nerveless Sloth from Human-kind.

Yet passive indolence is among the least of Tahitian shortcomings; he
next summons up the spectre of infanticide, the more awful because of
the idyllic setting in which it is perpetrated:

> Does here MEDEA draw the vengeful Blade,
> And stain with filial Gore the blushing Shade;
> Here, where Arcadia should its Scenes unfold,
> And past'ral Love revive an Age of Gold!

The poet concludes by advocating that Christian morality and the truths
of revealed religion should be conveyed to these benighted islanders.

Prefiguring the course of future history, he urges his fellow countrymen

> To bid th' intemp'rate Reign of Sense expire,
> And quench th' unholy Flame of loose Desire;
> Teach them their Being's Date, its Use and End,
> And to immortal Life their Hopes extend . . . .[39]

ON THAT NOTE OF EARNEST EXHORTATION one phase in the record of British enterprise in the Pacific came to a close. Ever since the *Endeavour*'s return, less than three years before, accounts of the newly discovered region had been flowing from the press in a continuous stream. Newspaper reports, with their references to exotic places and people, had roused widespread curiosity which had been whetted rather than appeased by unauthorized revelations. Bougainville's narrative, in its English rendering, had excited further interest in New Cythera and its romantic inhabitants. The daring and often bizarre theories of Monboddo had imparted a philosophical flavour to the travellers' tales culled from de Brosses. Next had come Hawkesworth's three volumes where successive voyages had been placed in perspective and elevated to epic status. Following closely on Hawkesworth, Sydney Parkinson's brief *Journal* had added a pathetic footnote to the annals of the *Endeavour*.[40] Then there were verse publications — satiric or mildly salacious or meditative — with a spate of reviews, critical articles, and disputatious pamphlets. By the summer of 1774 the formerly meagre literature on the South Seas had swelled to considerable dimensions.

Banks's response to the recent accessions, wherein he had so prominent a part, remains a matter for conjecture. He could scarcely have been unaware of the *Epistle from Oberea* which soon ran into several editions (one ostensibly issued in his native Lincolnshire).[41] But with a dignified reticence he had not always displayed in his quarrel with the Admiralty he seems to have ignored the lampoon and its successors. On the subject of Hawkesworth's compilation, only obscure hints of his views survive in a letter from his colleague. Writing to Lord Hardwicke, Solander commented: 'Nothing can be more certain than that the Publication of the South Sea Voyages, at last became a *perfect Jobb*, which has been extreemly disagreable to Those who had in some measure a hand in it.' He hoped (but was not sure) that in their 'grand *Natural History Work*, Mr. Banks would, by way of preface, remedy Hawkesworth's omissions. That editor's few remarks on the customs, religion, and politics of the South Sea Islanders, he said, did 'no credit to the Work'. As for his lordship's observation upon the figures of Cipriani and Bartolozzi, it was, thought Solander, *'partly just'*: they had certainly made the people of Tierra del Fuego too handsome, but he was not sure they had exaggerated much in regard to the inhabitants of Raiatea and Huahine.[42]

Of the ingenious gentlemen's affairs in the period following their summer excursion to Wales again little can be said. In September 1773 they learned that Constantine Phipps had returned after his unsuccessful attempt on the North-west Passage, 'so', Banks wrote to Sarah Sophia, 'I am glad I was not one of the Party'. He may have been in a similar mood of self-congratulation the following month when news reached London of Marion du Fresne's awful end: in June 1772 Aoutourou's benefactor with more than a score of his men had been killed in New Zealand, 'and', as Solander surmised, 'in all probability afforded the inhabitants a good meal.' Banks might regret the lost delights of the south, but he was at least secure from its hazards while he laboured with Solander over the 'grand *Natural History Work*' or rusticated on his estate at Revesby Abbey or consulted with the King at Kew. He continued to win modest distinctions — election to both the Council of the Royal Society and the exclusive Society of Dilettanti. To his contemporaries, however, it might have seemed that after his brief hour of renown he had lapsed once more into relative obscurity. Horace Walpole was certainly of that opinion. On 10 July 1774 he wrote to Sir Horace Mann: 'Africa is, indeed, coming into fashion. There is just returned a Mr. Bruce, who has lived three years in the court of Abyssinia, and breakfasted every morning with the Maids of Honour on live oxen. Otaheite and Mr. Banks are quite forgotten.'[43]

Four days later Captain Furneaux reached Portsmouth with his living trophy from the Society Islands. A new chapter in the history of British relations with the South Seas was about to open and Mr. Banks was on the point of enjoying a fresh measure of fame.

5. The Advent of Omai

CAPTAIN FURNEAUX EVIDENTLY LOST NO TIME IN REPORTING TO HIS NAVAL superiors in the capital. Accompanied by his exotic companion, he travelled post-haste from Portsmouth to London and, if the newspapers are to be credited, arrived there on the night of 14 July, went into temporary lodgings, and the next morning called on Lord Sandwich at his house in the Admiralty.[1] The sequel is not wholly clear, but it seems that the First Lord then summoned Mr. Banks who with Dr. Solander hurried to greet Furneaux and the unexpected visitor from the South Seas. 'His name is *Omai*', wrote Solander in a description of the meeting; and as Omai — or one of its variants — he would henceforth be known. Now in his early twenties, he was still a boy when they were in Tahiti, observed the doctor, and not so 'remarkable' as to make them remember him. On this occasion he instantly recognized Banks but with Solander he had more difficulty. While he was talking to Furneaux, Solander related, the young native, who had been in the next room, ran in saying he heard the voice of Tolano (Solander's Tahitian name). After eyeing the doctor closely as he walked round him, Omai at last thought himself mistaken. 'He then', the account continues, 'desired Capt Furneaux to make me speake, which I had no sooner done than he cried out, he was sure I was Tolano, but much encreased in bulk.' Soon they were 'conversing pretty freely' with one another in the 'South Sea Language' which, happily for Omai, Solander, Banks, and his servant had not forgotten.[2]

Another witness of the reunion was Dr. Burney who also called at the Admiralty, probably to inquire after his son James (known to his family as Jem). What news their father picked up was quickly passed on by Fanny to her sister Susan. Captain Cook, she reported, was to stay at sea another year, but Captain Furneaux's ship had been so mauled in a storm and his crew so depleted by sickness and the loss of hands that he had been obliged to return to England without pursuing the original design. 'I am heartily glad that they *are* returned', Fanny went on, '& I hope that a Country so savage as New Zealand will never more be visited by my Brother.' She next turned to the man whom Captain Furneaux had brought with him and whom her father had enjoyed the satisfaction

94

of seeing. 'I found myself very curious to have the same sight', she remarked, continuing with a description of the 'Stranger':

He was dressed according to the fashion of his Country, & is a very good looking man — my Father says he has quite an *interesting* Countenance. He appeared to have uncommon spirits, & laughed very heartily many Times. he speaks few English words — & Capt. Furneaux a few Otaheite words. — they had got Mr Banks there, on purpose to speak with him — but Mr Banks has almost forgot what he knew of that language. But you must know we are very proud to hear that our *Jem* speaks more Otaheite than any of the Ship's *Crew*. — this Capt. F. told my Father, who was Introduced to this Stranger, as Jem's Father — he laughed, & shook hands very cordially, & repeated with great pleasure the name thus *Bunny*! O! Bunny! immediately knowing who was meant. & the Capt. Says that he is very fond of *Bunny*, who spent great part of his Time in Studying the Language with him.[3]

Following discussions with the First Lord and other officials, Banks carried off this heaven-sent replacement for the lamented Tupia, lodged him in his town house, and launched him on a meteoric social career. He escorted Omai to fashionable drawing-rooms, introduced him to such friends as Constantine Phipps, and on Sunday 17 July, only three days after the *Adventure* reached Portsmouth, presented him to the King and Queen at Kew. On the 21st he sent off a hurried note to his sister who was staying with their mother at Sunninghill in Berkshire. He had been so continually occupied these many days past that he had really had no time to answer her kind letters, he apologized. She would know by the papers that the *Adventure* had arrived, bringing an Indian from the South Sea Islands. The Admiralty had put the man under his care; '&', he explained, 'as I receivd so many marks of Freindship from His Countrymen I have taken the Charge'. That day they were to carry him to Baron Dimsdale for inoculation, after which he himself would be free and would wait upon Sarah Sophia and their mother at Sunning-hill. He sent dutiful respects to Mrs. Banks and, by way of postscript, a laconic item of news: 'ten of the Adventures people have been rosted & Eaten by our freinds in new Zeland'.[4]

In the next two years Omai was to fall under the scrutiny of varied and sometimes contradictory witnesses who communicated their impressions to an eager public or passed them on to less fortunate friends or consigned them to posterity in notebooks and journals. One such was Miss Banks who on the day her brother announced the Indian's arrival entered the earliest of a series of 'Memorandums' on the 'South Sea Islander' as she termed him at this time. He was, she asserted, 'a Priest in His own Country' and 'a native of Ulhietea' (one of many versions of the modern Raiatea). The information came not from her brother but more deviously from Dr. Mills, Dean of Exeter, who had it in turn from a letter written by Mr. Bates, Lord Sandwich's secretary, to a Mr. Desalis. From the same source emanated somewhat improbable details of the islander's conduct when he waited on the King the previous Sunday: 'he was much struck at first, and soon made a Speech to His Majesty to the following Effect. "Sir, You are King of England, Otaheite, Ulhietea, & Bola Bola: I am your Subject, & am come here for Gunpowder to destroy the Inhabitants of Bola Bola, who are our Enemies." '[5]

Hitherto the London newspapers had shown no particular interest in the premature appearance of Cook's escort. Several days after the event they duly noted the arrival of the *Adventure* (known to some bemused correspondents as the *Endeavour*).[6] They briefly reported the movements of Captain Furneaux (more often called Fonnereau).[7] And they casually mentioned that he had brought from the South Seas 'a native of those parts' or, alternatively, 'one of the Savages'.[8] Nothing more was heard of the Savage for nearly a week, but there was some news of the *Adventure*'s voyage. A glowing account from the ship's surgeon, Mr. Andrews, praised the exceeding fertility of the Bay of Plenty in New Zealand and recommended it as suitable for British settlement. A brief note stated that the ship's journals had been sent to the Admiralty, and from that office came a formal statement: Captain Furneaux had reached Spithead on the 14th instant, having circumnavigated the Globe and met with much ice but no land; he had parted company with the *Resolution* off the coast of New Zealand and did not expect her back that year.[9] There for the time being comment on the expedition ended as writers and correspondents turned to more diverting topics: the seventh marriage of Mr. Dickson, the Spitalfields weaver; the rebellious conduct of certain persons in the colony of Massachusetts; the return of Mr. Bruce from Abyssinia where the inhabitants ate meat taken from live animals and cut slices out of their captives till, 'piece-meal', they died.[10]

The emergence of a rival to Mr. Bruce was marked by a brief paragraph in the *Daily Advertiser* on 22 July. The native of Otaheite, it reported, had been presented to the King and was now with Mr. Banks, 'the gentleman who first projected the voyages to the South Seas for discoveries'. The native, 'a tall, genteel, well-made man', had known Mr. Banks in his own island and, on seeing him, 'immediately accosted him with the greatest seeming pleasure.'[11] Before appearing at Court, asserted the *London Chronicle* in a fuller account of the ceremony, the man had received instructions for his behaviour, but so great was his embarrassment as the King approached that he remembered only to kneel and when his sponsors urged him to speak could merely stretch out his hand and repeat the familiar, *'How do ye do?'* To which salutation His Majesty responded courteously by very freely shaking his hand. The nobles in attendance at the levee, the writer noted, displayed a good deal of mirth at the 'innocent native freedom of this Indian visitor' who, it was further stated, 'received invitations from many people of the first rank.'[12] In a contemporary print of the scene Omai, clad in a long white gown and holding a curious triangular hat or head-piece, is seen kneeling before the royal couple. Behind him stand Banks and

Solander, while the King steps forward to clasp the suppliant's hand.

Having belatedly discovered the celebrity in their midst, the newspapers now vied with one another to follow his every movement and, when their own resources failed them, copied their rivals, paraphrased them, or simply drew on the imagination. The *General Evening Post* reproduced the Court anecdote with minor changes, added its own quota of anecdote in successive issues, and recorded a notable social occasion. On Thursday 21 July, it announced, the native of Otaheite dined with the Duke of Gloucester, accompanied by Messrs. Banks and Solander, both of whom retained sufficient knowledge of his tongue to converse familiarly with 'this adventurer'. Also present at the function, according to a second announcement, was Mr. Bruce, 'lately returned from Abyssinia', who from the similarity of the Otaheitean to other languages was enabled to hold some conversation with his fellow guest. The native, ran a further paragraph, was to continue with Mr. Banks during his stay in England 'which it is presumed will be for some years, until he has acquired the English language, and a thorough knowledge of the customs of this country.' His introduction to one novel custom, already mentioned by Banks, was the subject of separate and conflicting accounts. In the first the native was reported to have been so alarmed by the apprehension of catching smallpox ('almost always fatal to the

OMIAH, the Indian from OTAHEITE, presented to their MAJESTIES at Kew, by M.ʳ Banks & D.ʳ Solander July 17, 1774.

people of his country') that on the advice of his medical friends he determined to be inoculated; accordingly he had left with Dr. Solander and
Mr. Banks for Hertford to consult Baron Dimsdale. The second version
credited the decision to the King who, on learning that the visitor had
not yet suffered from smallpox, 'said it would be extremely imprudent
to expose him to the crouds that curiosity would incline to see him,
before he was secure from that disease, so fatal to all his complexion.'
His Majesty therefore desired that the man might instantly be placed
under the care of Baron Dimsdale, 'at the same time declaring that he
would take him under his protection, and defray the expence that might
attend this and every other measure that might be for his advantage
or amusement while in England.'[13]

Late in July two correspondents in the *London Chronicle* used the
unsophisticated stranger to attack the evils of their age. The salutation
of the poor native of Otaheite to His Majesty, observed one anonymous
writer, would be pertinent if put to other European monarchs. The
'Semiramis of the North' would answer with difficulty if asked how she
did after breaking all her solemn engagements with the republic of
Poland. And if the 'great Machiavel of the North', guilty of so much
oppression and bloodshed, were similarly questioned, would it not
puzzle him to reply? 'In short,' this critic suggested, 'it might be very
well that all petitions and remonstrances for the future should conclude
with the famous question, How do you do?'[14]

The other letter was lengthier and more elaborate. Signing himself
Otaheite, the writer purported to be a native of the South Seas induced
to visit Europe by the 'beads, ribbands, and looking-glasses' which
navigators had bestowed on his people in return for their produce. Now
long resident in England, he read with interest that the *Adventure* had
arrived with 'one of the *Savages*' and asked what the term meant.
Savages, a learned friend replied, were 'all those barbarous nations that
are uncivilized, and that do not live in a regular manner or method of
policy or religion.' To which Otaheite in his turn retorted:

You had better have said, that all those who are not conversant with European
manners are Savages; for your definition, Sir, is as injurious as it is unjust. We
practise those virtues you only teach; are enemies to luxury, strangers to
adultery, constant to our wives beyond European example, . . . never go to war
but from a principle of self preservation or self defence, practise the virtues of
humanity and benevolence in a degree that would do honour to the noblest
Monarch in Europe; and whilst we entertain the most sublime ideas of an
Almighty Being, do not cut the throats of each other for differing in the manner
of worshipping him.

His fellow islanders, he went on, did not murder the innocent and help-
less indiscriminately; their men did not preach chastity to women while
taking every opportunity to violate it; nor did their women abandon
new-born children to the care of unfeeling nurses. 'Let me beg of you

for the future, Sir,' he urged, 'never to call us barbarous, you deserve the appellation yourself . . . .'[15]

Soon after, early in August, the *London Chronicle* returned to its anecdotal vein in a long article simultaneously published, with some additions, in the *St. James's Chronicle*. Everything relating to the native of Otaheite, ran an introductory note, engaged 'the Attention of Philosophers, as well as the commonly-curious'; these particulars were therefore laid before the public and could be depended on as authentic. The exceedingly miscellaneous particulars began with the 'Ranks of Distinction in Otaheite' which were three — 'Nobility, Gentry, and Mobility'. This native, the writer asserted, belonged to the last class, in person was rather taller than the middle size, tolerably well made, and 'so docile in his Memory' that he scarcely needed to be told the names and uses of things twice. He was first entertained in Lord Sandwich's drawing-room where he paid little attention to the company, 'being so taken up with admiring the Furniture, &c.' On meeting Dr. Solander (whom he knew in his own country), he ran up to him in the most cordial manner and embraced him so closely as to lift him off the ground. Being civilly reproved by the doctor and informed that a shake of the hand and the words 'How do you do?' were the usual salutation in this country, he repeated the greeting 'tolerably correct'. When taken to Court, he was 'as much dressed in the Habit of his Country as was consistent with Decency' and told he must kneel before the King and kiss his hand. Whereupon 'he replied, with some Emotion, "What, won't he *eat me* when he has got me down?"' Reassured, he knelt when the King approached and, remembering Dr. Solander's words, immediately repeated them, 'to the no small amusement of the whole Drawing-Room'. At a later function he greatly admired a watch which its owner, a nobleman, offered to him; 'but the other looking round the Room very carefully, said, "Won't these People think I stole it?"' He took this precaution, the writer assumed, because of the punishment his countrymen had received for thefts from visiting English sailors.[16]

Most of the remaining observations referred to the native's peculiarities and personal habits. When first desired to sit, he threw himself at full length on a sofa and only with difficulty learned the use of a chair. He dined principally on soups and partook 'promiscuously' of vegetables; he was rather fond of drinking and appeared to give the preference to Madeira. From the restlessness of his temper he seemed to want exercise which, according to report, he would shortly be indulged with in some of the private parks, 'after the manner of his own Country'. In respect to mental qualities, he apparently possessed scarcely any, for he sought 'immediate corporeal Gratifications', showing himself 'a *Sensationalist* of the first Kind'. He had never yet displayed 'any Inclination towards the English Ladies', though a Dutch lady at the Cape of Good Hope 'in some small Respects' attracted his regard but not his love. Finally, and perhaps through some association of ideas, the writer turned abruptly to 'Queen' Oberea. She was, he reported, 'retired to the Country' during

Captain Furneaux's stay and failed to visit him, explaining that she had neither hogs nor dogs to present him with. The real reason was: 'she highly resented the miserable and fatal Disease introduced by the European Sailors amongst her People, which had swept off almost all the Inhabitants of her Isle.'[17]

The rival *Evening Post* quickly published its own authentic particulars, supplying for the first time in the popular press a name for the visitor. The writer called him Omiah (to rhyme with Jeremiah?) and set out to defend him from his detractors. Omiah, he held, was far from displaying the simplicity and ignorance mentioned in some papers. On the contrary, his deportment was genteel, resembling that of well-bred people here — a fact that was the more extraordinary considering how short a time it was since he had left the South Sea Islands where manners, though by no means savage, were yet totally different from those of polished people in Europe. As for the report that he had feared the King might eat him when told he must kneel down to kiss His Majesty's hand, it contained more pertness and ill-nature than wit. That Court joke had not the least foundation in the usages of Omiah's country where the people were as far from being cannibals as the English; indeed, it confused their customs with those of the New Zealanders who inhabited an island very remote from Omiah's and who did actually eat *ten* of the expedition's men. Not to be outdone, in its next issue the *London Chronicle*, source of the ill-natured jest, calmly reproduced this and other portions of the article, adding its own self-righteous introduction: former accounts of Omiah were for the most part either false or a gross misrepresentation of the facts; it therefore presented a 'more just' version to the public.[18]

The new version made it clear that Omiah was a native not of 'Otaheitee', so well known through the voyages published by Dr. Hawkesworth, but of '*Ulatea*' whence he had been driven by the 'King of Bola-Bola'. Another refugee from the same place was Tupia who owned large possessions there and had become 'a person of great consideration' when Mr. Banks and Dr. Solander met him. Omiah likewise had some estate in his native island but, on becoming an exile, was at first obliged to take up fishing and similar employments to gain a livelihood. Being wounded in an unfortunate 'fray' with the British, he was thought entitled to some better provision and put under a priest 'to learn that kind of science which qualifies for the priestly profession'. He was in this situation when Mr. Banks and Dr. Solander visited the South Seas, and it was his acquaintance with them and other gentlemen of the *Endeavour* that probably disposed him to consent to coming with Captain Furneaux. In addition, it was said, a flatness in his nose, indicating Negro blood and making him 'less respectable', also induced him to undertake the voyage that he might gain 'personal consequence' and so compensate for this disadvantage. The article mentioned the death of the man brought to France by Mr. Bougainville and stated that another islander was on the *Resolution* which was expected to return the following year. If he arrived safely, the intention was to send out a ship, at government expense, to carry both men back to their country. For the present Omiah was at Hertford in the care of Baron Dimsdale. In submitting without hesitation to being inoculated, the writer observed, he showed the strongest instance of his implicit faith in Mr. Banks and Dr. Solander.[19]

HIS TWO PATRONS followed every stage of Omai's ordeal with close personal solicitude; it seems likely, in fact, that they rather than the King (as the *Evening Post* asserted) had proposed the measure in the first place. Only a year before they had witnessed the sad fate of the Eskimo family, almost wiped out by smallpox on the eve of their return to Labrador, and more recently, through the men of the *Adventure*, they may have learned of Aoutourou's death from the same fatal malady. Omai must therefore submit to inoculation, introduced from the Near East half a century before. And who better qualified to carry out the operation than its most eminent practitioner, a figure well known in the Banks circle? Six years earlier, on the recommendation of Solander's friend Dr. Fothergill, Dimsdale had travelled to Russia to inoculate the Empress Catherine and her son the Grand Duke Paul. His treatment had been an unqualified success, bringing the doctor both honours and wealth. The grateful Semiramis of the North had not only created him a baron but awarded him the magnificient fee of £10,000 together with an annuity of £500. Now he was established in the small county centre of Hertford, some thirty miles from London.[20]

The trio did not leave for Hertford on 21 July, as Banks had informed his sister. Perhaps their plans were upset by the invitation, or royal summons, to dine that evening with the Duke and Duchess of Gloucester. The next day they were still in London, for on 'Friday night, July 22' Solander began an apologetic letter to John Ellis in Hampstead. 'Nothing but the arrival of an Otaheite friend', he explained, 'could have made me so forgetful, in regard to you and many more of my English friends. But as I am one of the three that he can converse with, I have been obliged to give him almost all my time, in hopes that my other friends will forgive me.' He had waited upon Dr. Fothergill concerning the corals, he told Ellis, and had delivered the walnut twig to Mr. Fabricius. Then followed an account of Captain Furneaux's doings after he left England in 1772. Summing up the captain's exploits, Solander remarked: 'Notwithstanding he has not discovered any new lands, he has still made a glorious voyage; he has sailed round the globe, in a higher southern latitude than any ship before. He has proved that there is no large southern continent, and that the French pretended discoveries are small islands, instead of continents; or perhaps, as my friend Omai calls ice, things that the sun drives away, or causes to vanish.' He had been so long writing the letter, he went on, that Omai was almost asleep. His charge would visit Ellis at Hampstead as soon as he had recovered from smallpox; tomorrow they were to take him to Baron Dimsdale for the

operation which, with all his heart, Solander hoped might be 'attended
with success'. 'He is a well-behaved, intelligent man', the letter abruptly
ended.[21]

The proposed journey seems to have been made on the 23rd and four
days later Solander was back in London, again relating the details of
Furneaux's voyage to a colleague, this time Dr. Lind of Edinburgh, his
companion on the Iceland expedition. He said little of Omai but promised
in his next letter a full account of his 'South Sea friend' who, he said,
was 'now preparing for inoculation'.[22] During this interlude the young
man came under the scrutiny of a sympathetic observer, probably the
Revd. J. E. Gambier of Cookham. In the course of a visit to Hertford,
he reported to an unnamed correspondent, he had met Omiah through
Mr. Andrews, the *Adventure*'s former surgeon, who was acting as interpreter, and dined in their company. Omiah was fond of ham and all
animal food, but was very abstemious 'on an apprehension that such
viands are *un*-salutary.' No consideration could tempt him to eat a
morsel of chicken or a bit of pastry because he was shortly to be inoculated. 'How the strict & rational temperance of this *Savage*', the writer
moralized, 'ought to shame the Thousands among ourselves who prefer
gratification to *Health.*' Particulars of the man's appearance and build
were supplied. He was a little over five feet nine inches in height, and

lusty, strong made & active. broad chest & broad flat shoulders — legs very
well made — the calf muscular & large the ancles taper but strong. His Complexion much resembles that of an European, accustomed to hot climates: His
features are regular — his eyebrows large & dark — His Countenance is often
illuminated by a most unaffected Smile — His Hair black & dressed in the
english fashion. He was dressed in Pompadour — with white waistcoat, & he
seemed as easy in our habit, as if he had been born in Pall-Mall.

His hands were *'Tataowed'* according to the mode of his country where,
asserted this somewhat credulous witness, it was usual to mark the right
hand in a particular manner on marrying. Omiah was about thirty years
of age and bore nine such marks. Some of his wives, he said, he left on
account of their sterility, some he retained; and he bitterly regretted he
did not have his favourite wife with him in England.[23]

As regards language, Omiah pronounced with fluency a few common
expressions such as 'How do you do?' But as the whole island vocabulary
did not exceed a thousand words (according to this dogmatic authority),
he was at a loss for terms to express the new ideas with which his mind
had become stored since his arrival. For example, since these Southern
people had only two quadrupeds, the dog and the hog, he had no way
of describing a horse except as 'a great hog that carries people' and a
cow as 'a great hog that gives milk'. When introduced to Lord Sandwich,

. . . He first pointed to y[e] Butler — and said — (in his own language w[ch] was
interpreted by y[e] Surgeon of Cap[tn] Fourneauxs Ship —/ He is King of y[e] Bottles

— then pointed to Capt Fourneaux — said He is King of y^e *Ship* — But to Lord Sandwich he said — You are King of *all* Ships.

Further scraps of conversation and sundry anecdotes were adduced to illustrate other aspects of Omiah's character. His outlook was evidently utilitarian, for he said 'he would remove pretty trees that *bear no fruit* out of the shrubberys, & replace them with pretty trees that *bear sweet fruit.*' A man of delicate sensibilities, he was so affected by a funeral at Hertford that he was forced to leave: 'He wept plentifully with them that wept at the grave, & at length he went away from ye mournful Scene.' When told that people were buried in the local churchyard, he 'asked whether the Baron had not that place to put his patients in — and he Supposed that every person buried there had died under inoculation with the Baron.' Seeing some anglers near the town, he was curious to learn 'how they managed their Sport'. But as soon as he observed that they baited the hook with a living worm, he turned away with horror, saying he 'would never again taste fish caught with so much cruelty.' His compassion was matched by his courtesy. When he visited Gloucester House, Her Royal Highness, lacking a small gift for him, thought a pocket handkerchief, embellished with her coronet, might serve: 'She presented it to him — Omiah received it with reverence, and immed-diately Kissing the Coronet he Smiled & bowed profoundly to ye Duchess.' Bringing the letter to a close, the writer dwelt briefly on the islander's antecedents and singled out for praise two more characteristics:

He was intended for the honor of ye Priesthood — but he resolved to see ye Country of white men — & to trust white men because he Loved two white men — Banks & Solander (by ye way neither of y^m very white) and he was resolved to die or to know the truth of the white mens Story for himself.

All things considered — does the History of ye world produce a parallel instance of intrepidity & Curiosity? I think not[24]

By some means the letter came into the hands of a nameless but obviously well-informed writer who eliminated repetitions, phrased it more elegantly, and in other respects prepared it for publication. He correctly extended the list of quadrupeds known in the South Seas by including a third, the rat. To the account of Omiah's dietary habits he added that he handled knife and fork well and behaved at table 'with great decency, cleanliness, and void of any awkwardness'. For the benefit of students of Rousseau, he reported that while at first a house was 'matter of astonishment' to Omiah and horse-drawn carriages 'wonderful', he now accepted them 'without any marks of surprise'. He amplified some passages, excised others, and for the original naïve con-clusion substituted a suitably rotund piece of rhetoric:

Perhaps, if the history of his countrymen be considered, the doubts that must naturally be presented to him, and the circumstances of his independence, family, and popularity, there is not in any history of the world a much greater

OMIAH.

A Native of Otaheite, brought to England by Capt. Fourneaux.

27
*Probably the first
likeness of Omai
published in England*

instance of resolution, intrepidity, and curiosity, if a parallel, to what Omiah
has evinced.

The revised composition, entitled 'Genuine Account of Omiah' and
signed with the pseudonym Apyrexia, appeared in the August issue of
the *London Magazine*. A crude illustration showed the subject clad in
flowing gown and cloak, the right arm extended in a gesture of declamation, the left bearing a wooden stool, the hand plainly tattooed.
Copied by the newspapers, appropriated by other journals, this letter
was the most widely circulated of all contemporary reports of the intrepid
visitor.[25]

In the meantime he had again proved his heroic mettle. 'My Lord',
wrote Banks from New Burlington Street on 29 July, 'I have the honour
to acquaint your Lordship that this day Omai was inoculated in as good
spirits as possible'. Baron Dimsdale had delayed the operation, Lord
Sandwich was informed, partly in order to prepare his charge, partly
to obtain 'matter to his satisfaction for communicating the disease'. He

contrived to treat several children at the same time and showed Omai
'the person from whom the matter was taken'; she had 'a very favourable
Kind' and 'several large pustules on her face' — a source of gratification
both to his friends and to the patient who 'understood thoroughly the
disease he was to expect'. 'The regimen prescribed him by Baron Dimsdale
is rather strict but he has at all times conformed to it with the most
scrupulous exactness so that we have a most favourable opinion of him',
Banks reported, especially as in Russia, he went on inconsequently,
Dimsdale had treated with success a large number of Cossacks. With the
Baron's consent he had now brought the young man to town and would
keep him at New Burlington Street pending their return in a few days
to Hertford; there they would remain until the distemper was over. He
would then, Banks promised, bring Omai back to London and, as soon
as he was quite recovered, settle him in lodgings according to Lord
Sandwich's directions. 'I find him in all things', Banks ended, 'sensible
very docile & very gratefull for the favours receivd from your Lordship
who on all occasions he is told to look up to'.[26]

Banks duly left London on Thursday 4 August but first sent a brief
message to his sister. He found it necessary to go with his Otaheite friend
to Hertford, he told her, to be with him during his illness which was
expected to come on by the following Saturday. At this time Miss Banks
was pursuing her own inquiries into Omai's antecedents and present
condition. After all, she had learned from one of her brother's servants,
he was 'not a Priest of the Island he left but quite a common Man'. He
had quitted his home 'because his Countreymen teized him about his
Nose being flatter than other peoples'; further, they had warned him
that 'if he went with our people they would kill and eat him'. This conversation, she continued (giving her version of a story first recorded by
James Burney), recurred to Omai's memory the first time he was called
to prayers in the cabin, making him so afraid that he hastened on deck
and, as he later declared, would have jumped overboard had anyone
approached him with a knife. More snippets and anecdotes, culled from
various sources, added to the bulk of Sarah Sophia's 'Memorandums'.
Omai was 'overjoyed' at meeting Dr. Solander and her brother but had
not recognized the latter's servants. At Court he asked the King how
many children he had, kissed the Queen's hand, and altogether behaved
'very decently'. While visiting the Duke of Gloucester in the dress of his
own country, a 'great concourse' gathered about him, but no particular
notice was taken another time when, in English costume, he walked in
the park with Dr. Solander. Sometimes he inquired how many moons it
would be before he would return to the South Seas. Now, she reported,
he was under inoculation, had shown himself 'very tractable', and was
'perfectly sensible he was going to have an illness.'[27]

As he awaited the outcome of Baron Dimsdale's treatment during the
first week of August, Banks heard from Constantine Phipps. Since his
return from the Arctic in the previous autumn that industrious navigator
had been preparing an account of the voyage and only the day before,

he announced, had presented the published work to the King who received it 'very graciously'. He had ordered a copy with a set of prints for Banks and, if he should want more for any particular friends of his own, there were still a few in reserve. He was going into the country for the remainder of the summer, Phipps told Banks, and, in case there was anything to report or command, would be at Mulgrave, near Whitby, whence he would visit the York races. 'I beg you will remember me in Your best Otaheite to my worthy Friend *Omiha*', he asked, 'I am very Anxious to hear that he is past all Danger . . . .'[28]

Solander did not accompany Banks on 4 August and the next day drew up another of his accounts of the expedition. Writing from London to Lord Hardwicke, he described the *Adventure*'s voyage in detail but passed rather summarily over the 'young man' Captain Furneaux had picked up in the Society Islands. He knew those who had been with Captain Cook perfectly well, the doctor related, and it was pleasing to them that they 'had not forgot the South Sea Language', so they were able 'to converse with him without difficulty'. He was 'well behaved and intelligent' but 'not at all a handsome man, and rather browner than most of his countrymen, perhaps owing to his having been a fisherman.'[29] On the 10th, addressing his letter more specifically from New Burlington Street, Solander discussed with John Ellis the distribution of seeds brought to England by Captain Furneaux and Mr. Bayly. He had been to Hertford, he also informed Ellis, to attend his friend Omai during his 'confinement' and had left him the day before when he was declared to be out of danger: 'The small pox was come out, and seemed to be of a mild sort.' He had promised to go down again in a couple of days, Solander added, and would be with Omai until the following week.[30]

Once the medical crisis was over, Banks, who had remained at Hertford with the patient, was quick to announce the news. A message went to his sister and, dated 12 August, was duly entered among her jottings: 'he says "Our Indian is now in a fair way, he has indeed never been in any other: he is rather full than otherwise but a very distinct & good sort which I hope will turn on Thursday".'[31] Again on the 12th he wrote briefly to Dr. Charles Blagden, one of his companions during the tour of Wales a year before. 'Omai has now got through all Dangers from inoculation', Banks reported, adding mysterious details similar to those sent to Sarah Sophia: 'he is full but of a very distinct & good kind which we expect will turn tomorrow or next day'. As for the invalid's spirits: 'he has been Low these two days on account of pustules in his Throat which trouble him much but he fears nothing'. Otherwise they were all well, he assured Blagden; his one complaint was that the Dimsdales had shown no care of Omai and no civilities to themselves.[32]

The joyful tidings were also passed on to the First Lord who replied to Banks in an exceedingly amiable letter sent from Hinchingbrooke on 14 August. 'You have made me particularly happy in the account you have troubled yourself to give me of our friend Omai's being out of

II *Omai, Banks, and Solander by William Parry, c. 1776*

danger,' wrote Sandwich, 'pray make my compliments to him, & tell him how much pleasure I have recieved in this, as I shall in every thing else that can contribute to his well fare.' Following these courtesies he referred to more practical matters. The terms proposed for lodging and boarding Omai and Mr. Andrews — £160 a year — he considered perfectly reasonable, and the fact that the young man would be in Mr. Banks's neighbourhood, and consequently more under his inspection, would be 'a very great additional advantage'. He also thought twenty guineas a 'proper fee' for Baron Dimsdale and supposed the doctor would be perfectly satisfied with it. 'I am very happy to find that you intend to make me a visit', he went on; and if the guests would let him know when he might expect them, he would contrive to go to town when they were ready and bring them down to Hinchingbrooke in his coach.[33]

Five days later the saga of Omai's inoculation came to a voluminous end in the account Solander had promised his Scottish friend Lind towards the end of July. The visitor had now been in England more than a month, for most of that time in the company of his two patrons and Mr. Andrews, all three of whom had some knowledge of his language and had, presumably, shared his confidences and disclosures. Solander thus spoke with an authority equalled by none of the newspaper writers. Omai, he stated, was born in Raiatea where his father was 'a Man of considerable landed property' until, about twelve years before, he had been dispossessed and killed by Boraboran conquerors who still occupied his estates. With a few servants the boy took refuge in Tahiti and was there at the time of Captain Wallis's arrival. He was wounded in the side by a musket ball 'the famous day, when Capt Wallis fired upon the Otaheiteans on *One tree hill*'. The scar was still very visible, and so was another from a spear wound in the arm, received 'in one of their civil wars'. After the *Dolphin*'s departure, Omai, 'bound himself prentice to a Priest or Wise man' and was serving in that capacity during the *Endeavour*'s visit. Soon after, he left for Huahine where he was living 'as a private Gentleman of a small fortune' when Captains Cook and Furneaux reached the island. Becoming a favourite of the *Adventure*'s surgeon and its armourer, he resolved to go with them to Europe. His four servants all tried to dissuade him, as did his 'King', but Omai was resolute and parted from them in high spirits.[34]

Omai was 'not above 21 or 22 years old', Solander estimated, and had grown a little during the voyage. He was very brown, almost as brown as a mulatto, and not at all handsome but well made. His people, he said, laughed at him because of his 'flatish nose and dark hue' and this, Solander supposed, might explain his visit; for Omai hoped that when he returned and had 'so many fine things to talk of', he would be much respected. On his arrival he first lived at Mr. Banks's house and afterwards removed to Hertford where he had been inoculated by Baron Dimsdale. Now he was quite recovered and the next day they proposed going up to town for good. Mr. Banks and he, Solander reported, had been with Omai almost continuously, while Mr. Andrews, the *Adventure*'s surgeon, and Mr. Banks's servant had lived with him in the inoculation house the whole time. Luckily for them all, it happened that 'the blue Horse Guards' were quartered at Hertford and they had passed the weeks very agreeably in the society of the officers. The other day, he remarked, Lord Elibank, Governor George Johnstone, and Captain Blair had called on them, but poor Omai was then 'in his worst Pickle', so the visitors did not see him to great advantage.[35]

As yet Omai spoke no English, but Solander thought he would soon learn it, as he was desirous of doing so. He already knew several words and began to pronounce S 'tolerably well', though he could not manage R. He was well behaved, easy in his manners, and 'remarkably complaisant to the Ladies'. As only one of many instances of his 'Gallantry', Solander cited his kissing the Duchess of Gloucester's handkerchief. Omai was in sum a 'sensible communicative Man' and altogether a 'valuable acquisition'. He had pleased everyone, while he in turn was pleased by his reception. 'We *think* that the King has promised to send him back;' Solander went on. 'It is a thing so much wishd for, by us, I mean that an other S.S. Expedition should take place, that I have only said we *think* so . . . .' Lord Sandwich and Mr. Banks were now quite cordial again, he observed, and they were soon to go down to Hinchingbrooke. Solander apologized for continuing so long on one subject but explained that he could hardly get anything else in his head to write about, especially as his friend Omai was then sitting by his side, 'quite elevated by having been informed that he to morrow is to leave this place of confinement.'[36]

6. Omai in Society

VIGILANT OBSERVERS CONTINUED TO FOLLOW OMAI'S MOVEMENTS AND fortunes. 'We are informed', announced the *General Evening Post* on 25 August, 'that the native of Otaheite has undergone the operation of the small-pox much better than was expected, and will set out this week with Lord Sandwich and Mr. Banks on a tour into the West of England.'[1] The still nameless native, 'having recovered from the Small-pox', was next reported to have dined at Sir John Pringle's in Pall Mall on the 24th in the company of the Earl of Sandwich and several other noblemen. On the 25th, accompanied by Mr. Banks and Dr. Solander, he was observed at a Royal Society dinner held in the Mitre Tavern, Fleet Street.[2] Finally came the news that he had set out on the 27th with all three patrons, not for the west but for the First Lord's country seat at Hinchingbrooke. His lordship's band of musicians, the notice added, had received orders to hold themselves in readiness to assist at a grand oratorio to be given in compliment to the guests. The whole would be conducted by Signor Giardini.[3]

To members of the Burney family, then living in Queen Square, Bloomsbury, these events and persons were of more than passing interest. As sensitive to the fluctuations of social fashion as Horace Walpole himself, Fanny had now assessed the stranger's place in the current hierarchy. Entering her diary late in August, she wrote: 'The present *Lyon* of the times . . . is Omy, the native of Otaheite; and next to him, the present object is Mr. Bruce, a gentleman who has been abroad twelve years, and spent four of them in Abyssinia . . . .' Recently, she noted, Mr. Bruce had called at Queen Square with her friend Miss Strange and was 'almost gigantic!', the tallest man she had ever seen; but she could not say she was charmed with him — he seemed rather arrogant and had so good an opinion of himself that he had nothing left for the rest of the world but contempt. In her next entry, at the beginning of September, she turned to a more agreeable topic: 'My father received a note last week from Lord Sandwich, to invite him to meet Lord Orford and the Otaheitan at Hinchinbrook, and to pass a week with him there; and also to bring with him *his son, the Lieutenant.*' 'This', Fanny went on, 'has filled us with hope for some future good to my sailor-brother, who is the capital friend and favourite of Omai, or Omiah, or Omy, or Jack,

111

for my brother says he is called by all those names on board, but chiefly by the last appellation, *Jack!*[4]

Jack he might have been on the *Adventure* or yet another shipboard appellation missing from Fanny's list, Tetuby Homy, able seaman. Now he was an honoured visitor to country houses, a central figure in social functions, the guest and associate of noblemen. Early in the month the *General Evening Post* published an extract from a letter received from Huntingdon and dated Friday 2 September. Omai, it stated, accompanied by Mr. Banks and Dr. Solander, had spent the last week at Hinchingbrooke 'where Lord Sandwich has given them such a reception, that the stranger cannot but form a most favourable idea of his Lordship's hospitality.' Nor had the neighbourhood been less eager in showing their desire to please him, the correspondent reported: he had been entertained every day with new amusements. On Monday Lord Sandwich 'had a sailing party upon Whittle-Sea Meer, at which the Duke of Manchester, Lord Ludlow, Sir Robert Bickerton, and a great many of the Huntingdon gentlemen assisted.' On Wednesday a grand oratorio was performed at Hinchingbrooke. On Thursday the Duke of Manchester entertained the guests at Kimbolton and that morning, Friday, Lord Ludlow was giving a fox hunt. The next day they intended seeing Cambridge and on Monday, the letter ended, they proposed to set out for the north.[5]

Here and there the bare facts of the press report can be supplemented from more personal sources. At an early stage of the house party Banks sent an enthusiastic note to his sister which she dutifully copied:

Omai dressed three dishes for dinner yesterday, & so well was his Cookery liked that he is desired to Cook again to day not out of Curiosity but for the real desire of Eating meat so dress'd: he succeeds prodigiously: so much natural politeness I never saw in any Man: wherever he goes he makes Friends & has not I believe as yet one Foe.[6]

Omai's culinary talents, probably on the same occasion, are also referred to in the memoirs of Joseph Cradock, the musical impresario and minor man of letters. One day, he relates, Lord Sandwich 'proposed that Omai should dress a shoulder of mutton in his own manner', a suggestion that delighted the visitor, 'for he always wished to make himself useful.' A description of the procedure followed:

Having dug a deep hole in the ground, he placed fuel at the bottom of it, and then covered it with clean pebbles; when properly heated, he laid the mutton, neatly enveloped in leaves, at the top, and having closed the hole, walked constantly around it, very deliberately, observing the sun. The meat was afterwards brought to table, was much commended, and all the company partook of it.

'And', the writer admonished, 'let not the fastidious gourmand deride this simple method . . . .' Another anecdote, not certainly of this period

(Cradock is innocent of dates and erratic in sequence), describes Omai's response when offered 'stewed Morello cherries' at an 'elegant repast'. Instantly he jumped up, quitted the room, and, on being followed, informed his companions 'that he was no more accustomed to partake of human blood than they were.' He continued 'rather sulky' for some time and was induced to return to the table only when his fellow guests helped themselves to the dish. 'But', wrote Cradock, 'the most memorable circumstance, I recollect, relative to Omai, was when he was stung by a wasp.' While the company at Hinchingbrooke was breakfasting, he entered the room in great agony, his hand 'violently swelled', but was unable to explain the cause. At last, not knowing the word wasp, he made them understand that 'he had been wounded by a soldier bird' — a definition which, in Dr. Solander's opinion, could not have been excelled by a naturalist.[7]

A further contretemps appears to have marred the visit to Kimbolton, according to Miss Banks who had the news from a Miss King who, in turn from some nameless informant, 'heard when Omai was at the Duke of Manchesters he was Electrified which frightened him so much he ran out & would not come back till my Brother persuaded him he should have no more tricks played him . . . .' Sarah Sophia entered the item on 2 September with others she had gathered from her brother's housekeeper Mrs. Hawley. Omai, asserted that lady, had been strongly advised against leaving the South Seas with the English who, his 'King' warned, would certainly kill him, since Tupia, Tayeto, and 'likewise the man that went with Mr Bougainville never had returned to Otaheite.' (But, noted the well-informed Miss Banks, the first two died of a 'Distemper' and the third of 'small Pox'.) Mrs. Hawley was able to throw a little fresh light on the familiar subject of Omai's inoculation. He misunderstood what was told him, she claimed, and thought he was never to have the illness at all, 'in consequence of which when it came out he was very low spirited & said he should dye but was soon comforted by those about him . . . .' The most startling of Mrs. Hawley's revelations, however, combined the themes of revenge and romance: 'Omai says he wants to return with men & guns in a Ship to drive the Bola Bola Usurpers from his property that then he would place his Brothers there return himself to England where he proposed having a Wife. a young & handsome English Woman 15 years old.'[8]

While Miss Banks entered her devious jottings, Omai was on the eve of further social triumphs and more extensive travels through the English countryside. Early in September the Hinchingbrooke house party broke up and Solander returned to London, leaving Banks to head north with their protégé. 'Omai', he wrote to Charles Blagden, 'has now after having gone through all his Physickings absolutely recovered all the fasting &c. the consequence of the Distemper'. He himself would not be in London till the end of the month, Banks explained, for he was carrying Omai to the Leicester races and 'from thence to Ld Hinchinbrooks in Northamptonshire'; 'he is very much liked', he added, '& I do this to make him known agreeably without his becoming a shew'.[9] It was some measure of Banks's regard for the young man that he should have forgone his usual summer botanizing to undertake this excursion. He had hoped to spend some time in the company of Constantine Phipps at Mulgrave Hall in Yorkshire. But that versatile gentleman, now engaged in electioneering, wrote to say that, though he would have been very happy to see his 'Copper coloured friend, Omai', he had to visit Newcastle. He thanked his dear Banks for getting him out of 'the scrape' (through not presenting his book to the Queen, Banks noted), said that 'Election matters' were proceeding well, and expressed his pleasure that they would meet in town at the latter end of October.[10]

In the meantime Banks must content himself with less congenial companions and more frivolous diversions. Mr. Banks and Omai were amongst the noble and brilliant company at our annual music meeting this week, announced the *General Evening Post*'s Leicester correspondent on Saturday 24 September. They were at all the different entertainments, dined at the 'ordinary' on the previous Wednesday, 'likewise at the race ordinary', and at night attended the assembly. 'Omai, in particular,' the writer went on, 'is remarked to have behaved with great politeness, allowing for his short acquaintance with European manners; at church he saw a gentleman he had accidentally seen before at Buxton, and bowed to him with the address of a well bred European.' At all the public functions, moreover, 'he sat with ease, and conversed familiarly with his friends'; nor, it was said, was he 'insensible of the charms of beauty, every-where surrounding him.'[11]

The correspondent did less than justice to the musical proceedings. These included a rendering of Handel's *Jephtha* organized by Joseph Cradock who, it was claimed, had gathered for the occasion the greatest number of musicians hitherto assembled in England. The celebrated Giardini led the band, Mr. Commissioner Bates (Lord Sandwich's secretary), accompanied the choruses at the organ, while the First Lord, who had specially selected the oratorio, took the kettle-drums on both days. The self-styled dilettante, William Gardiner, witnessed the performance at the age of four and more than sixty years later still remembered the 'grandeur' of the sound created by the noble drummer and the display he made in flourishing his ruffles and drumsticks. 'I was riveted to the spot,' Gardiner recalled, 'and was so captivated with his Lordship's performance, that for a time I heard but little else.' He also recollected 'a tall black man in a singular dress'; it was 'the savage, Omai', 'brought down on purpose to see what effect this grand crash of musical sounds would have upon him.' His response was gratifyingly dramatic: 'He stood up all the time, in wild amazement at what was going on . . . .'[12]

Mr. Cradock himself noted that Omai 'attracted the eyes of the company more than any one' and supplied a further quota of somewhat banal anecdote. Banks evidently kept his charge under close supervision, for the morning after their arrival, Cradock relates, he was called up by a waiter very early and told that the 'stranger gentleman' had run away.

Whereupon, he wrote:

I hastily dressed myself, and endeavoured to pursue him as quick as possible.
All windows of the market-place were shut, but one gentleman was just opening
his door, to take his early walk, and to him I communicated my distress. 'You
need not be alarmed,' says he; 'for such a person as you describe I have just seen
from my chamber window, walking about very leisurely, and we can instantly
overtake him.' When we found him, Omai expressed no anxiety or surprise,
but returned with us with the utmost good humour and quietude. This was the
first time he seemed to have obtained his liberty, and he made the most of it.

'Omai was not averse from admiration,' Cradock continued, 'and he
soon gave me to understand how very happy he felt himself to be at
Leicester, for he was kindly received every where . . . .' He showed
marked aptitude for dancing, and a 'sprightly agreeable lady' who undertook his instruction said that in a week or two she would have taken the
floor with him at an assembly. In the tea-room he was 'the happiest
among the happy, very gallantly handing about cake and bread-and-
butter to the ladies'. He was, in short, 'naturally genteel and prepossess-
ing', yet not without vanity. He was 'attentive to dress' and at one
function expressed his anger to Cradock and Mr. Bates because his
clothes were not as good as those of the gentleman next to him: his own
suit was only of English velvet, while his neighbour's was 'from Genoa'.[13]
   Omai was something of a dandy but he was also an immortal soul,
the representative of a heathen and illiterate people. If Banks was indifferent to these facts or, amid the frivolities of Leicester, had overlooked
them, he was reminded of higher things by a letter received in late
September. The writer was one, Richard Stevens, who, addressing
Banks and Solander from the post office at Birmingham, explained that
he had heard 'Omiah the Otaheite' would shortly return to his native
country. 'Would it not', he urged, 'be a Laudable Undertaking to send
a Person, or Persons along with him to Convert if possible his Countrymen to the Christian Religion, & instruct them in some Branches of
usefull knowledge; such as, Reading, Writing, & Accots?' 'If such a Plan
shou'd be put in Execution,' he wrote, 'I make an Offer of myself to go.'
The two gentlemen would perhaps be surprised that a young man (for
he was only twenty-eight) should desire to banish himself to so remote
a country. The reason, Stevens frankly explained, was that for the past
seven years he had experienced nothing but the most severe misfortunes
and saw no probability of a change; hence he would go to any part of
the world if he could better his lot. 'I dare say', he ventured, 'if Government was to send a Person over, it wou'd be upon an eligible footing.'
His qualifications for this or some alternative post (such as companion
to a nobleman or gentleman, he suggested) were the mastery of 'a fine
Hand', and an understanding of the French language which he was
'allow'd to speak . . . with a pure Accent'. 'My Caracter', he finally
claimed, 'is irreproachable . . . .'[14]

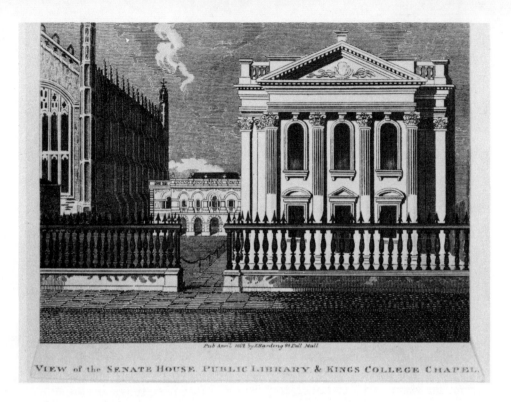

VIEW of the SENATE HOUSE PUBLIC LIBRARY & KINGS COLLEGE CHAPEL.

Higher matters were again in the ascendant when Omai paid a long-delayed visit to the University of Cambridge early in October. 'The Doctors and Professors struck him wonderfully,' reported a press correspondent, 'and he would fain have done homage to some, supposing them in a near relation to the Deity.' Indeed, by 'his superstitious dread of every thing which he looked upon as sacred', Omai displayed 'many marks of natural religion'. 'In his own country', the writer observed, 'he is himself in the Priesthood, which may be an additional reason for his attention to these things, and ought to be a motive with our Divines, to embrace this opportunity of enlightening his mind with the knowledge of true religion, and of sending amongst a nation of idolaters so able a missionary, and so likely to succeed.' Since coming to England, it was further noted, Omai had learned the use of firearms and was determined, he said, as soon as he returned, 'to shoot the King of Bolabola, who murdered his father.' The warrior-cleric was suitably arrayed in military uniform, 'his hair dressed and tied behind', and diverted the company with his naïve wit: 'Some one offered him a pinch of snuff, which he politely refused, saying, that his nose was not hungry.'[15]

Banks was not named in the press report, but his presence was mentioned by another observer, Richard Cumberland. Writing to his younger brother George on 10 October 'From My Cell in Maudlin', this slightly disgruntled candidate for holy orders censured the behaviour of the Cambridge election mob, 'as happy as the Juice of Malt coud make them', and described the visit he had paid to the Senate House that afternoon when the results were announced. He thought he had never seen the place so full before and singled out two notabilities for special mention:

Banks & Omiah were present the whole Time & the Latter was introduced to all the D^{rs}&c & behaved with wonderful ease & propriety — He is a stout well made Fellow: in Features & Complection something betwixt the Negro & Indian; was dress'd in a plain Suit with His Hair in the modern Style & seemd to talk & laugh much, tho I was not near enough to hear Him & in short gave great Satisfaction to all about Him — A rep[ly] made to one who offer'd Snuff was very good — No tank You, Sir, My Nose be no Hungry — a severe Satire on Snuff Takers. This is all I have heard or seen of Him.

George Cumberland, who, his brother discloses, was a follower of Rousseau, received the meagre impressions with enthusiasm: 'you cant conceive how you oblige me by your account of Omiah,' he wrote from London a week later, 'every little anecdote of a man born in full health and strength with all the Facultys of understanding (for such Omiah may be said to be, every thing he sees being new,) is well worth remarking; I hope you will be able to get yourself introduced to him before he quits Cambridge'.[16]

It seems unlikely that the obscure student was able to realize his brother's aspirations. The Cambridge visit was apparently quite short and towards the end of the month Banks and Omai were back in London. Their movements in the intervening fortnight remain a blank, unrecorded by their regular correspondents and unreported by the newspapers. Miss Banks did from time to time enter her jottings, but they were concerned less with Omai's current activities than with his past and his future. Her friend Miss Cox, she noted early in October, had heard from a nameless 'Lady' visiting Hertford at the time of Omai's inoculation how 'monstrously pleased' she was with the 'humanity of his Behaviour'; and she mentioned his grief while attending a funeral and his disgust at seeing anglers bait their hooks with live worms (two items Sarah Sophia could have drawn more directly from the newspapers). The next memorandum referred to practical and pecuniary matters. On meeting Dr. Solander, another friend of Miss Banks had asked who was paying Omai's expenses. The reply was that, while the visitor travelled with her brother, he bore them, except for clothes which the Admiralty furnished; but lodgings had now been taken for the *Adventure*'s surgeon and Omai who, nevertheless, Dr. Solander 'imagined', would be much more with her brother than anyone else, 'by way of going excursions with him &c.' The doctor also spoke of the King's promise to repatriate Omai and his countryman on the *Resolution*: the intention was not, he said, 'for the English to make by Force a settlement at Otaheite but by treating the Natives well & sending them home will we suppose make them our Friends in a much more humane & agreable manner.' Dr. Solander in person, Sarah Sophia recorded on 23 October, told her the *Resolution*

was not expected till 'the very latter end of next Summer'. Omai, he
informed her on the same occasion, was 'now perfectly contented with
staying as he considers the great pleasure he shall have in shewing Every
thing he has seen & Explaining to his Countreymen.'[17]

OMAI'S STAY IN LONDON at the end of October was a brief one. He and
Mr. Banks had returned from the country the day before, Solander told
Ellis on the 27th, and he would again go down to Hinchingbrooke
with Lord Sandwich on the 29th.[18] On the uncertain authority of Miss
Banks, it may have been during the three nights of this fleeting visit that
he was introduced to the English theatre. Sarah Sophia had taken
advantage of her brother's presence to ply him with questions concerning
his charge whom she now depicted in the most favourable light. Omai
was not only 'a Priest in his own Countrey', she was finally convinced,
but 'a well behaved quiet sensible Man desirous strongly of associating
with the best Company & behaving in a proper manner.' In general,
she believed, he disliked entering places of religious worship, 'saying till
I understand how to address myself in a proper manner to Your God I
dont think it right'. Surely he showed a proper humility, Miss Banks
commented, and she wondered whether this was why he had declined
to attend prayers on the *Adventure*, '& not from any fear of being eat.'
She spoke of his decorous behaviour at Court (that 'silly report' of his
fears that the King might eat him was 'intirely devoid of truth') and, to
illustrate his preference for the best people, went on to describe his
visits to the theatre with her brother:

At Sadlers Wells he was much pleased desired he might go the next night wch
my Brother complied with & carried him the 2d time he asked if Ld Sandwich
ever went? no I believe not: does any of the Nobility go? sometimes but seldom:
I will go no more says Omai Very well says my Brother I will carry you
tomorrow night to the Play where the Great People frequently amuse themselves.

Accordingly, Banks took him to a more fashionable theatre, with rather
disappointing results. While very attentive for the first two acts, Omai
was not much diverted and asked if people came there to have conversation; 'but some scenery towards the end & a Pantomime entertained him very well.'[19]
     With her brother's help Sarah Sophia amplified topics picked up from
other informants and learned of some that were novel. Omai, Banks
told her, was 'not so much delighted at the thought of seeing his Countrey-
man' on the *Resolution*, for he knew 'the person coming over to be a
Bola Bola Man'. From the same authoritative source she confirmed
accounts of Omai's grief on attending a funeral at Hertford; on the other
hand, his refusal to eat fish caught with live bait was not entirely because
of humane feelings but 'owing to a Religious Superstition wch prevails
in the S. Sea Islands in favour of worms.' On the important question

29 *Omai by Nathanial Dance, 1774*

OMAI a Native of UTAIETEA,

Brought into England in the Year 1774, by Tobias Furneaux Esq.r Commander of his Majesty's Sloop Adventure.

Humbly Inscribed to the Right Hon.ble JOHN EARL of SANDWICH, first Commissioner for executing
the OFFICE of Lord High Admiral of Great Britain and Ireland &c. &c.

By his Lordship's most devoted humble Servant

Fra.s Bartolozzi.

Published according to Act of Parl.t 25th Oct.r 1774.

30 *Bartolozzi's engraving of Dance, from a copy once owned by Banks*

of finance (so far as her microscopic script can be deciphered), Miss Banks understood that 'Government' had authorized her brother to incur whatever expenses he thought proper on Omai's behalf and to supply him with any pocket money required for use in public places. The authorities, she noted, had also fixed on someone whose name eluded her (in fact Mr. Andrews) 'to have the care of Omai' at a salary which would not begin until he returned from Hinchingbrooke where he was when she wrote towards the end of October. In her final entry, on 3 November, Sarah Sophia recorded without rancour a mild affront to her sex and nation: Omai did not like Englishwomen and therefore (contrary to her earlier statement) did 'not wish for a wife of this Country.'[20]

A week later, while the fastidious visitor was still rusticating with the First Lord (and also, presumably, with that accomplished Englishwoman Miss Martha Ray), his name cropped up in the correspondence of his friends. On the 10th Solander sent Banks a message to say that Bartolozzi had called that morning at New Burlington Street with some of 'Omais prints' and had, he believed, sent others with a framed copy to Lord Sandwich. But, Solander went on, he had observed that in the inscription Ulaietea was misspelt *Utaietea*. Luckily, not above seventy copies had been taken off and, if Banks wanted his own replaced by corrected ones, would he let Solander know? However, he pointed out, 'I think the error may pass as a proof of their being first Impressions'. He also discussed the absorbing subject of 'Electrical Eels' and promised his friend, apparently absent somewhere in the country, that the guns, which Greville expected before the end of the week, would be sent down as soon as they came; and if Banks's 'Russian Shoes' could be found they too would be sent.[21]

The engraving to which Solander referred was based on a small portrait by Nathaniel Dance probably commissioned by Banks. If less attractive than the pastels of the Eskimo family done by the same artist in the previous year, the pencil drawing seems to be a faithful likeness, wholly exempt from the charge of flattery levelled at the earlier head by Hodges. Omai is shown in voluminous robes of Tahitian cloth, a plaited bag and feather chaplet in the right hand, the left arm clasping a wooden stool. The hands are tattooed, the feet bare, and the shoulder-length hair falls in loose ringlets. The nose is certainly 'flatish' (but not exceptionally so for a Polynesian), the gaze steady, the expression impassive, with perhaps a hint of that 'sulkiness' to which the subject was occasionally liable. Bartolozzi in his turn had reproduced the drawing with the utmost fidelity — or at least the details of dress and accessories. With the head he was less successful: the face is thinner and longer than in the original drawing, the expression more animated, the hair more abundant, the nose even more negroid; altogether, his Omai, despite the nose, conjures up the Mediterranean rather than the Pacific.

Bartolozzi's engraving reached the print shops at a time when the subject of Tahiti was again entertaining fashionable readers. Silent since the publication of the 'Epistle from Harriot' earlier in the year, the witlings had lately renewed their satirical attacks in two works exploiting similar mildly salacious themes and following the same mock-heroic, mock-scholastic conventions. *An Epistle (Moral and Philosophical) from an Officer at Otaheite*, attributed to the politician John Courtenay, was addressed to a notorious *divorcée*, transparently veiled as Lady Gr*s**n*r. Apart from references in the opening invocation to 'circling arms', 'elastic hips', and 'ermin'd sages', little was said of the Grosvenor trial which had diverted society in 1772. The chief topics were those staples of Tahitian satire — sexual promiscuity, public copulation, infanticide, the tattooing of buttocks, the introduction of venereal disease — supported by quotations from Hawkesworth or the classics or, on one occasion, by a private letter from Dr. Solander. But Courtenay could discard his jocular and cynical manner to write with passion of 'lewd Kath'rine', comparing Russia and its 'dire Virago' with those 'southern isles' where 'Oberea's gentle virtues' prevailed. He celebrated the islanders' 'innocence' and, again drawing on Hawkesworth, praised their courage in the face of Wallis's attack:

> In their canoes, our floating forts defy,
> Nor from the thunder of our cannon fly.

Admiration, fear, and prayer were combined in the lines that followed:

> Beauty and Valour here have fix'd their throne,
> — Shall Europe's spoilers call this isle their own?
> May Heav'n and Britain shield the gen'rous race,
> Nor Tyranny their manly souls debase.[22]

The other work was more directly related to previous satires on Banks and the dead Hawkesworth; its authorship, indeed, is sometimes credited to Scott, the putative begetter of the Oberea cycle. With a sensitive nose for the topical, the versifier now brought Omai into the sequence, introducing him on the title-page as '*his Excellency Otaipairoo, Envoy Extraordinary and Plenipotentiary from the Queen of Otaheite, To the Court of Great Britain* and bearer of *A Second Letter from Oberea . . . to Joseph Banks, Esq*. His Excellency's unexpected arrival from 'so voluptuous a Court as that of Otaheite' had revived the spirits of 'every member of the fashionable societies in the neighbourhood of St. James's', ran an introduction which proceeded to give authentic particulars of 'this celebrated foreigner'. The particulars prove on examination to have been culled from newspaper articles, sometimes slightly altered or amplified. Befitting his new dignity, Omai-Otaipairoo had moved up a couple of rungs on the social ladder from 'mobility' to 'nobility'. At the Cape of Good Hope he was said to have been 'exceedingly pleased' with a Dutch lady, parted from her 'with some reluctance', and when returning on board 'ran back a considerable distance to salute her.' On the

A N

E P I S T L E

(MORAL AND PHILOSOPHICAL)

FROM AN

OFFICER AT OTAHEITE.

T O   L A D Y   GR*S**N*R.

WITH

NOTES, CRITICAL AND HISTORICAL.

BY THE AUTHOR OF THE RAPE OF POMONA.

————Lege ſub hac, Pomona fuit,
Grataque tenet tua munera dextra.   OVID.

L O N D O N:
PRINTED FOR T. EVANS, NEAR YORK-BUILDINGS, STRAND.
MDCCLXXIV.

31
A further addition
to the Oberea cycle

other hand, at the English Court he did not seem to take 'any extraordinary notice of the ladies'; 'probably', the author moralized, 'the
outre of their dress disgusted him as it really does *every* admirer of simple
nature.' However, it was 'a positive fact' that 'a lady on the first line of
nobility' (presumably the Duchess of Gloucester) had 'conceived a
particular *penchant* for this spirited adventurer' who would 'spend a few
weeks at her grace's villa.'[23]

Except for his prominent part in the introduction and his designation
as queen's courier on the title-page, Omai has no place in the satire itself
which reiterates the familiar themes of the series in monotonously
familiar measures. The bereft Oberea reproaches her absent Banks-
Opano for his desertion while proclaiming her continued loyalty to

A Love as true
As any Maid in any clime e'er knew.
Haply tho' now some fairer She you press,
You know not any more expert to bless.

Repetitiously and with a profusion of suggestive detail, she recalls the beginning of their liaison, its progress, and its consummation until she reaches the climax of her lament and introduces the one element of novelty — the announcement that after 'nine moons had gone their nightly round', the fruits of her union with Opano made their appearance:

> Two young *Opanos* grace the royal bed:
> Vig'rous the boys, and ah! so like the sire,
> They prove how warm, how pure was my desire . . . .

As the satire draws to a close, the twin princes unite their tears and lisping reproaches with Oberea's:

> E'en now, methinks, while dandling on my knee,
> In words half-form'd they strive to talk of thee;
> And, when they weep, I almost hear them say
> Why, cruel, went our Father far away;
> Why, curious, he, new herbs and roots to gain,
> Thus left us far amidst the Southern main . . . .[24]

BANKS'S RESPONSE to this and previous lampoons must remain a matter for conjecture. On the slight evidence of the letter Solander sent to him early in November he may have sought refuge from the knowing looks and malicious titters of London society on his Lincolnshire estate or elsewhere in the country; possibly his flight was so precipitate that he left behind indispensable fowling-pieces and cherished footwear. Whatever the facts, towards the end of the month he was back in town, again confronting the fashionable world and escorting Omai, who had returned from Hinchingbrooke, through a succession of social engagements. In one crowded week the young islander again visited the theatre, attended the House of Lords for the opening of parliament, heard the King deplore 'a most daring spirit of resistance' in the colony of Massachusetts, dined at least once with members of the Royal Society, and, most memorably, called on Dr. Burney and his family.[25]

The Burneys had recently established themselves in an historic house, once the home of Sir Isaac Newton, in St. Martin's Street, Leicester Square. Fanny found the street 'odious' after spacious Queen Square, but it was in the centre of the town and the locality was not lacking in congenial and accomplished neighbours. The studio of Sir Joshua Reynolds stood scarcely twenty yards away, while Mr. Strange, the well-known engraver, also lived near Newton House. There on the last day of November Dr. Burney entertained 'this *lyon* of *lyons*', as Fanny now termed Omai in her diary, or 'this great personage', the phrase used in an immensely long letter she sent the next day to her old friend Samuel Crisp at Chessington Hall in Surrey.[26]

The function, Fanny informed Mr. Crisp, was the outcome of a chance meeting of her brother Jem's at a performance of the play

Isabella at Drury Lane. Spying Mr. Banks and Omai from his upper box, he approached them to talk. Omai welcomed his shipboard friend 'with a hearty Shake of the Hand' and made room for him by his side. Jem then invited both men to dine at his father's, but Mr. Banks was unable to accept: 'he believed he was engaged every Day till the holy days, which he was to spend at Hinchinbrooke.' Very late the following night Jem received this note (presumably in the hand of an amanuensis):

Omai presents his Comp^ts to Mr Burney. & if it is agreeable & Convenient to him, he will do himself the Honour of Dining with Mr Burney to morrow. but if it is not so, omai will wait upon Mr Burney some other Time that shall suit him better. omai begs to have an answer, & that if he is to come, begs Mr Burney will fetch him.

The next morning Jem waited on Mr. Banks with Dr. Burney's compliments and a further plea for his company and Dr. Solander's; but 'they were Engaged at the Royal Society.' In the end they did call briefly at St. Martin's Street, bringing Omai at two o'clock after they had taken him to the House of Lords to hear the King make his speech from the throne. Except for Mr. Strange and another old friend, Mr. Hayes, who had come 'at their own Motion', it was a family party made up of Dr. and Mrs. Burney, the three unmarried sisters, Fanny, Susan, and Charlotte, with Jem and Dick, the last a child of six years. Fanny had been confined to her room with a cold for several days and delayed her appearance until the two escorts left when she came down 'very much wrapt up, & *quite a figure*'.[27]

On entering the room, she found the guest 'Seated on the Great Chair' next to her brother who was 'talking otaheite as fast as possible'; 'You cannot suppose how fluently & easily Jem speaks it', she wrote. Omai himself was in court dress and 'very fine': he wore 'a suit of Manchester velvet, lined with white satten, a *Bag*, lace Ruffles', and a sword which the King had given him. He was tall and very well made, much darker than Fanny had expected, '*by no means* handsome', but with a 'pleasing Countenance'. His hands were 'very much *tattowed*', but his face not at all. As Jem introduced them, Omai rose, made a 'very fine Bow', and then seated himself again. 'But', Fanny related,

when Jem went on, & told him that I was not well, he again directly rose, & muttering something of the *Fire*, in a very polite *manner*, without Speech insisted upon my taking his Seat, — & he *would* not be refused. He then drew his Chair next to mine, & looking at me with an expression of pity, Said, 'very well to-*morrow-morrow*?' — I imagine he meant *I hope* you will be very well in *two or 3 morrows* — & when I shook my Head, he said 'no? O very bad!'

'He makes *remarkably* good Bows', she added, '— not for *him*, but for *any body*, however long under a Dancing Master's care. Indeed he seems to Shame Education, for his manners are so extremely graceful, & he is

32 *Fanny Burney, after E. F. Burney*

so polite, attentive, & easy, that you would have thought he came from some foreign Court.'[28]

Omai continued to display the same courtly refinement in the course of the dinner. The moment he was served, he presented the plate to Fanny, who sat beside him, and on her declining it, had not, she explained, 'the *over shot* politeness to offer all around, as I have seen some people do, but took it quietly Again.' 'He Eat heartily', she went on, '& committed not the slightest blunder at Table, neither did he do any thing *awkwardly* or *ungainly*.' She particularly noted one instance of his courtesy which went beyond any mere question of formal manners: 'He found by the turn of the Conversation, & some wry faces, that a Joint of Beef was not roasted enough, & therefore when he was helped, he took great pains to assure mama that he liked it, & said two or three Times "*very dood* —, very *dood*."' 'It is very odd, but true,' she commented, 'that he can pronounce the *th*, as in *Thank you*, & the *w*, as in *well*, & yet cannot say *G*, which he used a *d* for. But I now recollect, that in the beginning of a word, as *George*, he *can* pronounce it.' Sometimes, she observed, he communicated silently: when being introduced to Mr. Strange and Mr. Hayes, for instance, he paid his compliments 'with great politeness' but 'without words'.[29]

As the meal progressed, Fanny was again struck by the guest's untaught command of manners, this time in dealing with a servant. He was given porter instead of the small beer he had asked for, but was too well bred to send it back and when the beer was brought also, he merely laughed, exclaiming 'Two!' During this contretemps one glass hit against the other which 'occasiond a little sprinkling' and prompted Fanny to further admiring comment: 'He was *shocked* extremely — indeed I was afraid for his fine Cloaths, & would have pin'd up the wet Table Cloth, to prevent its hurting them — but he would not permit me; &, by his *manner* seemed to *intreat* me not to trouble myself! — however, he had thought enough to spread his Napkin wider over his Knee.' When Mr. Hayes inquired, through Jem, how he liked the King and his speech, he 'had the politeness to try to answer in English, & *to* Mr Hayes — & said "*very well, King George!*"' Dinner ended with a toast to the King, proposed by Mrs. Burney, whereupon Omai 'made a Bow, & said "*Thank you, madam*," & then *tost off* "*King George!*"'[30]

They dined at four and after the meal Omai informed Jem that at six o'clock he was to go with Dr. Solander 'to see no less than 12 Ladies'. Jem in turn translated the speech to the rest of the company, watched by Omai who understood he was being talked about and, laughing heartily, 'began to Count, with his Fingers, in order to be understood — "1. 2. 3. 4. 5. 6. 7. 8. 9. 10. — *twelve* — *woman!*"' Before six o'clock he was informed of the arrival of his coach with the announcement, 'M^r omai's Servant.' He answered, '*Very well!*' but remained seated for about five minutes before rising to get his hat and sword. As Dr. Burney was speaking to Mr. Strange, Omai stood aside, 'neither chusing to interrupt him, nor to make his Compliments to any body else first.

When he was disengaged, Omai went up to him, & made an exceeding fine Bow, — the same to mama — then seperately to every one in the Company, & then went out with Jem to his Coach.'[31]

When summing up her impressions Fanny was abject in her praise. Omai was not merely 'a perfectly rational & intelligent man' but in understanding was, she claimed, 'far superior to the common race of *us cultivated gentry*'; otherwise he could not have 'borne so well the way of Life' into which he had been thrown. 'I assure you every body was delighted with him', she informed Mr. Crisp. Her regret was that she could not speak his language — unlike Lord Sandwich who had 'actually' studied it 'so as to make himself understood'. The bookish Burneys did, however, extract a timely moral from the recently published *Letters* of Lord Chesterfield to his son. Ever since the dinner, Fanny went on, their conversation had turned upon

Mr *Stanhope* & *omai* — the 1st with all the advantage of Lord Chesterfield's Instructions, brought up at a great School, Introduced at 15 to a Court, taught all possible accomplishments from an Infant, & having all the care, expence, labour & benefit of the best Education that any man can receive, — proved after it all a meer *pedantic Booby*: — the 2nd with no Tutor but Nature, changes after he is grown up, his Dress, his way of Life, his Diet, his Country & his friends; — & appears in a *new world* like a man [who] had all his life studied *the Graces*, & attended with un[re]mitting application & diligence to form his manners, & to render his appearance & behaviour *politely easy*, & *thoroughly well bred*! I think this shews how much *Nature* can do without *art*, than *art* with all her refinement, unassisted by *Nature*.

If she had been 'too *prolix*', Fanny told Mr. Crisp, she must be excused, for the fault was wholly owing to the 'great curiosity' she had heard him express for whatever concerned Omai. Her father, she promised, would arrange a meeting when the visitor from the South Seas returned to town after spending the holidays with Lord Sandwich.[32]

Before leaving for Hinchingbrooke Omai came under the calmer scrutiny of another observer, the Revd. Sir John Cullum, who met the 'Native of Ulaietea' on two occasions, once at a Royal Society dinner and again at Mr. Banks's house. The baronet (antiquarian, botanist, and country parson) laboured over the record of his impressions and finally asked his friend, the Revd. Michael Tyson, Fellow of Bene't College, Cambridge, whether he would care to read the result. Mr. Tyson, a man of similar interests, was glad to accept the offer, mentioning in his reply that he, too, had seen Omai when he visited the university and was 'much pleased with his appearance — there was an openess of countenance, and a native politeness that would do honour to any Englishman.' In his next letter Sir John accordingly included 'the Account of Omai' ('such as it is', he diffidently remarked), which he dated 3 December 1774.[33]

Cullum estimated the islander's age at 'about 30', described him as 'rather tall and slender', with an erect carriage, and thought his face 'on

the whole . . . not disagreeable'. In
more precise terms he listed the
salient features of this new specimen
of the human race — the 'somewhat flat' nose, the thick lips, the
ears 'bored with a large Hole at the
Tip', the swarthy complexion, the
hair 'of a considerable Length, and
perfectly black', the tattoo marks on
hands and posteriors, not in continuous lines, it was noted, but in
rows of 'distinct bluish Spots' — and
went on the pay the now customary
tributes to the 'tolerably genteel Bow,
and other Expressions of Civility' he
had acquired since arriving. The
man appeared to have 'good natural
Parts', had learned a little English,
and was 'in general desirous of Improvement'; in particular he wished
to learn to write which, he said,
'would on his Return enable him to

33 Silhouette of Omai

be of the greatest Benefit to his Country'; 'but ', commented Sir John, 'I do
not find, that any Steps have been taken towards giving him any useful
Knowledge, Mr Banks seeming to keep him, as an Object of Curiosity,
to observe the Workings of an untutored, unenlightened Mind.'[34]

As an amateur of science himself, Cullum followed with interest the
actions of this unschooled man of nature and recorded various 'Notices',
based on direct observation or inquiry. In a serious mood or while following what others were saying, Omai's 'Look' was 'sharp and sensible',
but his laugh was 'rather childish'. If he wanted you to understand
something he had seen, he used 'very lively and significant Gestures' —
he was in truth 'a most excellent Pantomime'. He was pleased with
trifling amusements ('as many of more improved Understandings often
are', added the fair-minded Cullum) and was unhappy when he had
nothing to entertain him. Here followed one of the scrupulous writer's
recent impressions:

when I dined with him, with the Royal Society, a small multiplying Glass had
been newly put into his Hands: he was perpetually pulling it out of his Pocket,
and looking at the Candles &c with excessive Delight and Admiration: we all
laughed at his Simplicity; and yet probably the wisest Person present would
have wondered as much, if that Knick-Knack had then for the first Time been
presented to him.

A further anecdote seems to refer back to Omai's Antarctic voyaging
and perhaps indicates the onset of his first English winter. He had, wrote

Cullum, seen hail before his arrival and was therefore not much surprised at a fall of snow which he called, naturally enough, 'white Rain'. But he was 'prodigiously struck' on seeing and handling a piece of ice; 'and when he was told, that it was sometimes thick and strong enough to bear Men, and other great Weights, he could scarcely be made to believe it.'[35]

Omai, on Cullum's authority, was entirely reconciled to European manners and customs, conformed to the English diet which he liked very well, denied ('against Self-Conviction') that his countrymen ate human flesh, and drank wine but was 'not at all greedy of it' — he had never been intoxicated since he arrived. In direct contradiction of Miss Banks's latest findings, he was said to like Englishwomen, 'particularly those of a ruddy Complexion, that are not fat.' He submitted 'most readily to the slightest Controul' without 'the least Appearance of a fierce and savage Temper'; Cullum had seen him, in the company of a gentleman who encouraged him, display 'all the cheerful and unsuspecting Good-Nature of Childhood'. The print recently engraved by Bartolozzi from Dance's drawing Sir John considered 'fine' in execution and 'extremely like' the subject.[36]

Tyson was grateful for his friend's impressions and hastened to add his own small quota. 'I thank you much', he wrote, 'for your admirable account of Omai, wch greatly entertained me'. He had seen the man at Cambridge, he repeated, and listened to a conversation between him and Banks. 'I have heard much of him', he went on, 'from people who have been long and frequently in his company — particularly the Bp of Lincoln — who said that he observ'd the two leading principles of his Mind were, a regard for Religion, and desire for revenge'. Tyson was evidently of the same opinion. He knew several academics, he said, to whom Omai paid special regard on finding out they were priests; and he was most offended when the Bishop of Lincoln sat at table between two ladies — 'a custom not allow'd the high-Priests in his country'. As for revenge, 'his desire to shoot his enemy the King of Bolabola is always uppermost, when his thoughts are not employ'd about novelties.' Tyson considered it would be impossible to teach him to form words and even more so to convey the art to his countrymen, though he might learn to make letters. And was Cullum not mistaken in suggesting that Omai's people ate human flesh? Surely the practice was confined to the New Zealanders.[37]

Meanwhile the subject of this solemn discourse was pursuing his heedless way in English society. After his glimpse of the London season, Omai set off to spend the holidays with Lord Sandwich. But in spite of what he had told James Burney, Banks did not join the Christmas gathering at Hinchingbrooke; nor did he attend the Handel festival held there to celebrate the New Year. At that time he seems to have been much occupied with his scientific pursuits. Late in November he had again been elected to the Council of the Royal Society — along with Solander and Constantine Phipps — and may have been engaged in discussions on the new voyage of discovery that was to leave for the Pacific after the *Resolution*'s return. More certainly he was fully employed in setting up at New Burlington Street a collection he had acquired from the estate of Philip Miller, for many years curator of the Apothecaries' Garden at Chelsea. 'Mr. Banks has bought Miller's *Herbarium*,' Solander informed John Ellis on 21 December, 'and we have been busy these two weeks in getting it home and into some order.'[38] His failure to pay the promised visit provoked somewhat excessive emotion among friends and admirers at Hinchingbrooke. 'We are all', wrote Sandwich on the 29th, 'extremely disappointed & unhappy at not having had the pleasure of seeing you according to the hopes you had

The North East View of Hitchinbroke Priory, *near* Huntingdon.

given us . . . .' Having decided he had no chance of winning, the sporting earl went on, he had 'with great concern' paid a bet of five shillings for Banks's failure to appear at breakfast that morning.[39]

Sandwich had other reasons for concern. In the same letter he explained:

Omai is the bearer of this — I own I am grown so used to him, and have so sincere a friendship for him, from his very good temper, sense, & general good behaviour, that I am quite distressed at his leaving me; &, knowing the dangers of a London life to an European of twenty one years old, am full of anxiety on account of the winter he is to pass in town in a Lodging, without the sort of society he has been used to, which has kept him out of dissipation.

He knew that Banks had the same feelings about their friend as he did, the conscientious First Lord continued, and hoped that when they met they would be able to discuss how they could manage Omai's situation to the best advantage. The visitor's safety, he summed it up, 'must depend upon you & me; & I should think we were highly blameable if we did not make use of all the sagacity & knowledge of the world which our experience has given us, to do every thing we can to prove ourselves his real friends'. Finally, he subscribed himself 'with great truth & regard' Banks's 'most obedient & most faithful servant *Sandwich*'.[40]

HIS LORDSHIP'S LETTER marked the climax of Omai's début in English society. Since his arrival in July this average Polynesian, casually enlisted and carried across the world by chance, had become a celebrity, the protégé of royal personages and aristocrats, the associate of scientists and savants, the focus of attention in public assemblies and polite drawing-rooms. How had this astonishing transformation come to pass in the space of a few short months? One answer to a complex question is at least clear: the way had been thoroughly prepared for the voyager before he disembarked. He had benefited from popular interest in the South Seas during recent years and from the work of numerous writers in periodicals, books, and newspapers. By the early seventeen-seventies Otaheite and the Society Islands had become familiar terms to most educated Englishmen. Hence it was not surprising that students of Bougainville should seek out the native from New Cythera or that readers of Hawkesworth should court the company of Oberea's supposed countryman. Their motives in so doing were inevitably mixed. To many Omai was merely the reigning lion; to some observers of scientific bent he was a specimen to be described and classified; to a few he was the embodiment of an idea, the personification of 'natural man'; to others — exemplified by Miss Burney and Sir John Cullum — he was a combination of all three.

Omai was also an individual and much of his success, it must be acknowledged, was due to qualities that were either peculiar to himself or derived from his antecedents and upbringing. With monotonous unanimity witnesses testified to his cheerfulness, his politeness, his obedience. He seems to have been amiable and tractable by nature, but in addition he was a representative of his class and his people. Society Islanders (with the possible exception of the Boraborans) were already noted for their friendliness and, unlike the Tahitians in this respect, European navigators had not found it necessary to batter them into civility. Moreover, as a member of the *raatira* (and incidentally as an exile), Omai had been deferring to his superiors since childhood. There was no novelty for him in a population ranging from the lowly and despised to the high-born and privileged; nor did he find it at all unusual to demonstrate his esteem by means of prescribed rites and formulas. After all, as some newspaper commentators perceived, he was not a naked 'savage' but the product of a settled and relatively sophisticated manner of life. He soon adapted himself to English society because in its hierarchical structure and its formality it resembled his own. Nor were all its customs and institutions wholly unfamiliar. It was obvious, for example, that a pantomime at Drury Lane was only an elaborate performance by the local *arioi*. As for the strange ritual of inoculation, was it not just a mild European equivalent to the ordeal of tattooing or the ceremony of supercision?

So this unexceptional denizen of the South Seas had taken his place in the new environment with comparative ease. It seems unlikely, however, that he would have scaled the heights, or even reached the foothills, had he not been aided by influential patrons. To the combined efforts of Banks and Sandwich he owed his introduction to Court and aristocracy, his tour of the provinces, his several meetings with members of the Royal Society, and his triumphs at Hinchingbrooke and during the London season. Now, towards the close of December, he was back in town and, as Banks again took over responsibility for the young man's well-being, he could reckon up the consequences of his own benevolent efforts in the past few months. While on the debit side his botanizing had suffered and the 'grand *Natural History Work*' still languished, the gains were considerable. Five years before, on the point of leaving Tahiti, he had announced his decision to carry off a substitute for his neighbours' captive lions and tigers. After the disappointment of Tupia's death, he had at length achieved his ambition. Probably, indeed, Omai filled the role of human curiosity far better than the 'proud and obstinate' Tupia would ever have done. Through the docile visitor's presence Banks had done much to assuage his nostalgia for the South Seas, he had consoled himself in some measure for the abandoned voyage, and he had restored or even enhanced his public reputation. Above all, he had mended the breach with his old friend Sandwich. From that reconciliation what inestimable benefits might not flow in the future? In accordance with His Majesty's wishes, Omai must be restored to his native sphere; a new expedition would be equipped and manned; doubtless, as in the past, naturalists would be included among the supernumeraries. Like Solander in his letter to Lind, Banks would hardly have dared to contemplate the exciting prospects before him.

For the present there were more urgent matters to consider — Omai's accommodation, his physical needs and desires, his moral welfare. And when the year 1774 at last came to an end, debts and credits in the most literal sense must be reckoned up. Among the Banks papers there survive a number of documents listing expenses incurred during the visitor's stay in England. As disclosed by the first of the series, his personal allowance in the previous six months had not been excessive. He had received two advances, both of five guineas, one a week after his arrival, the other on 27 August, the day he left London for the first house party at Hinchingbrooke. The episode at Hertford accounted for a couple of items: 15/6 for the servants of the inoculation house, twenty guineas for Baron Dimsdale, the fee already approved by Lord Sandwich. Banks's housekeeper, Mrs. Hawley, was paid £8-3-3 and one of his servants, Alex

Scott, £4-7-6, both for unspecified services. The remaining sums, ranging from 7/- to £8-12-6, probably represented transactions with tradesmen and firms, of whom only one can be identified: the hosiers Hunt and Cunningham supplied goods to the value of £11-5-0. Expenditure totalled £116-4-11, but one credit was scrupulously entered — £10-15-6, being 'Mr Omai's Wages for the Adventure Sloop'. Altogether he had cost his patrons or 'Government' (to follow Miss Banks) £105-9-5, a modest outlay in return for the vast entertainment he had provided.[41]

35 An early-nineteenth-century glimpse of Warwick Street

7. Omai and the Return
of the *Resolution*

WITH HIS ARRIVAL IN LONDON AT THE END OF 1774, THERE OPENED A NEW
and less eventful phase of Omai's stay in England. He was no longer the
guest of his two chief patrons, accommodated in their houses, exhibited
to their friends, and cosseted by their servants. Following the plan first
discussed in the middle of August, he entered lodgings kept by a Mr. De
Vignolles or de Vignoles or Vigniol (versions differ) and apparently
situated in Warwick Street which was no great distance from New
Burlington Street. His conduct could thus be readily supervised by Banks
and, as a further precaution against the dangers of metropolitan life, he
was placed in the care of Mr. Andrews, formerly surgeon on the
Adventure and his companion at Hertford.[1] Under this régime his public
activities seem to have been curtailed or perhaps he merely chose to
remain at Warwick Street without exposing himself to the full rigours of
his first northern winter. Whatever the reasons, in the opening weeks of
the new year his name was not mentioned in the popular press; nor did
it figure either in the correspondence of Banks and his friends or in his
sister's now infrequent jottings. Was it possible, then, that not only the
fickle London public but also his appointed guardians had lost interest
in the prodigy from the South Seas? The answer must be a qualified
negative, but Omai had clearly passed the peak of his current fame.

At the beginning of 1775, it is equally clear, both the newspapers and
members of the Banks circle were preoccupied with more serious matters
than the doings of a visibly fading celebrity. Grave news continued to
reach England from the American colonies, and late in January it was
reported that the aged Earl of Chatham had urged in a packed House of
Lords the withdrawal of all British troops stationed in Boston.[2] Of more
immediate concern to Banks and his friends (including Omai) were
recent discussions on a further voyage of exploration. Early in the previous year the Royal Society had proposed to the Admiralty the dispatch
of a ship or ships to sail up the north-western coast of America 'so as to
discover whether there is a passage into the European Seas.' After consultations between officials on both sides, the First Lord expressed his
interest in the expedition but, for financial and political reasons, decided
that it could not be sent until Captain Cook's return in 1775. As that

event grew nearer, plans for the new undertaking were actively can-
vassed by leading scientists, among them it is reasonable to assume,
Banks and his two friends on the Royal Society's Council. Another, with
greater certainty, was the Astronomer Royal, Dr. Maskelyne, who
approached James Lind of Edinburgh to see whether he would be willing
to go.[3]

For the second time Dr. Lind was delighted to accept an offer of
distant travel and scientific employment — but only on one condition.
'Nothing', he wrote on 30 January, 'will give me more pleasure than to
have the honour of going on the intended Voyage you mentioned, for
the making discoveries on the N.W. side of America beyond California,
provided my friend, Mr Banks, goes'. He wished to assure the Astronomer
Royal, however, that he would not go to oblige the Government after
their ungenerous treatment of him in return for the sums he had laid out
to equip himself for the last abortive venture to the Pacific. 'But', he
went on, 'to serve and attend on Mr Banks on whatever Expedition he
shall undertake, I shall esteem my Duty, as well as my greatest pleasure,
for the real regard I have for so noble and excellent a man.'[4]

A fortnight later, on 13 February, that paragon of human kind celebrated his thirty-second birthday, an occasion the devoted Sarah Sophia
marked by composing a prayer for his continued welfare and reviewing
his travels. These, she noted, covered a period of seven years, from the
time he left for Newfoundland in 1766 until he returned from Holland
in 1773.[5] Should his Scottish friend's hopes be fulfilled, a fresh cycle
would soon open. On 2 March Lind wrote to Banks, mentioning the
proposals outlined by Maskelyne and emphasizing his own continued
loyalty. 'If such a Voyage takes place, and you go,' he assured Banks,
'I shall think myself happy to be permitted to attend you: nor shall I
require any inducement from Government for doing what I shall ever
esteem my greatest pleasure.'[6] There matters were necessarily left to
rest until, with the *Resolution*'s return, arrangements for the latest
enterprise would be settled.

These affairs of the great outside world were also of moment to the
household in St. Martin's Street. Entering her diary early in the new
year, Fanny Burney remarked that her brother had left them some time
before; he had been posted to H.M.S. *Cerberus* which was ordered to
America. She was not at all pleased with the move, though she thanked
heaven there was no prospect of a naval engagement, the vessel's business
being only to convey army generals to Boston. In March, while the 'very
honest Tar' was still at Portsmouth, his name cropped up one afternoon
during a call Fanny paid at the Stranges' where she found Mr. Bruce
drinking tea with the ladies. 'His *Abyssinian Majesty*', as Mrs. Strange
called her fellow Scot and distant kinsman, first mentioned James, after
which, Fanny relates, the conversation turned to Omai and other
southern celebrities with whose names and reputations Mr. Bruce had
evidently made himself *au fait* since his arrival from Africa a year before:

When he found my brother was the person in question, and that he was going to America, he said he was sorry for it, as there was going to be another South-Sea Expedition, which would have been much more desirable for him. 'And,' said I, 'much more *agreeable* to him; for he wishes it of all things. He says he should now make a much better figure at Otaheite, than when there before, as he learnt the language of Omai in his passage home.'

'Ah, weel, honest lad,' said Mrs. Strange, 'I suppose he would get a wife or something pretty there.'

'Perhaps, Oberea,' added Mr. Bruce.

'Poor Oberea,' said I, 'he says is dethroned.'

'But,' said he archly, 'if *Mr. Banks* goes, he will reinstate her! But this poor fellow, Omai, has lost all his time; they have taught him nothing; he will only pass for a consummate liar when he returns; for how can he make them believe half the things he will tell them? He can give them no idea of our houses, carriages, or any thing that will appear probable.'

'Troth, then,' cried Mrs. Strange, 'they should give him a set of dolls' things and a baby's house, to show them; he should have every thing in miniature, by way of model; dressed babies, cradles, lying-in-women, and a' sort of pratty things.'

There was a humorous ingenuity about the suggestion, Fanny observed, and she really believed it would be well worth a trial.[7]

For some reason, perhaps connected with his son's posting to the *Cerberus*, Dr. Burney failed to arrange the promised meeting between Mr. Crisp and Omai, but both he and Jem were topics of discussion in the affectionate letters that passed between Newton House and Chessington Hall. She had no certain news of her brother's whereabouts, Fanny informed her old friend early in April, but she fancied he was still at Portsmouth. 'There is', she continued, 'much talk of [an in]tended South Sea Expedition: Now You must [know] there is nothing that Jem so earnestly desires as to be of the Party, & my Father has made great Interest at the Admiralty to procure him that pleasure: & as it is not to be undertaken till Capt. Cooke's return, it is just possible that Jem may be returned himself in Time from America.' She said nothing of the proposal to search for a passage through Arctic waters to Europe. This expedition, she explained, was to be the last: they were to carry Omai back and give him 'a *Month for liking*'; after which, if he did not again 'relish' his old home or found himself ill-treated, he was to have it in his power to leave again for England. Later in the month she was able to tell Mr. Crisp that the *Cerberus* had now sailed, bearing in addition to the ship's company three generals with their *aides* and entourage. 'Their stay is quite uncertain', she remarked. 'Jem prays for his return in Time to go to the South Seas.'[8]

Fanny and her friends might speak airily of Omai's future, but what of his present condition? And what if he should meet the sad fate of his solitary predecessor? Such were the questions raised at this time by two contributors to the *Gentleman's Magazine*. The first, who signed himself H.D., having read 'the entertaining narrative of the discoveries made by

Mr. Banks and Capt. Cook', expressed the pain he felt at learning his
countrymen had acted in a manner supposedly peculiar to the Spanish:
'I am shockt when I read, that these boasted discoveries, in three years
of the 18th century, made by men, by Britons, and by protestants, cost
the lives of many Indians.' With detailed citations, he gave instances of
unprovoked shooting and went on to remark:

> I might add to all the cruelties of discovery that of transporting a simple
> barbarian to a christian and civilized country, to debase him into a spectacle
> and a maccaroni, and to invigorate the seeds of corrupted nature by a course of
> improved debauchery, and then to send him back, if he survives the contagion
> of English vices, to revenge himself on his enemies, and die . . . .

The second writer, quoting from 'a late voyage' by an unnamed 'French
officer' (clearly Bernadin de Saint-Pierre), gave some particulars of
Aoutourou before and after his visit to France. While passing through
Mauritius with Bougainville, he was 'free, gay, and rather inclined to
libertinism'; when he returned to the island on his way home, he was
'reserved, polite, and well-bred'. He was 'enchanted' with the Parisian
opera and mimicked its songs and dances; he owned a watch from which
he could tell the hours for rising, eating, etc.; though 'very intelligent',
he knew little French and expressed his wishes by signs; he seemed
'much tired' at Mauritius and always walked out by himself. This poor
islander, commented the writer in his own person, never reached home,
for he died of smallpox just as he embarked for Ţahiti. 'May a better
fate attend Omiah, now in England!' he exclaimed. 'Hitherto our world
has been "a country from whose bourn/No *Taiti-man* returns."'[9]

WHILE HIS FUTURE WAS THUS DEBATED, Omai had appeared in public, not
noticeably debased or debauched but suffering from the rigours of the
northern climate. When speaking with him on 24 March, the young
German scientist and man of letters, Georg Christoph Lichtenberg,
asked how the winter in England suited him; to which he replied, '*cold,
cold*', and shook his head. 'Wishing to express that in his native land
only light shirts (if any at all) were worn,' his interlocutor went on, 'he
indicated this by taking hold of the frill of his shirt and pulling back his
vest.' The meeting took place during a function at the British Museum
when Lichtenberg was introduced to Dr. Solander and then to 'the man
from Ulietea' who offered his hand and shook the visitor's 'in the English
style'. Lichtenberg, who was not wholly free from racial preconceptions,
described Omai as 'large and well-proportioned', his skin 'yellowish-
brown', his face lacking 'the unpleasantness and protuberance of the
negro's'. Moreover, he 'had in his demeanour something very pleasant
and unassuming which becomes him well and which is beyond the range
of expression of any African countenance.'[10]
  Lichtenberg found Omai's English 'far from intelligible' and, had it
not been for the help of Mr. Planta, one of the Museum's librarians,

doubted whether he would have understood as much as he did. When asked if he liked England better than his native land, the islander assented; 'but he could not say *yes*, instead it sounded almost like *vis*.' Yet, oddly enough, he pronounced the English *th* quite well. His hands, the observer noted, were marked with blue stains which ran in rings round the fingers. Pointing to the right, Omai (lending some colour to Apyrexia's earlier assertion) 'said *wives*, then of the left hand he said *friends*.' 'That', remarked Lichtenberg, 'was all that I had the opportunity of saying to him that day; the company was very numerous, and we were both rather shy.' The young scientist ended his journal entry for 24 March on a reflective note: 'I found it not unpleasant to see my right hand in the grasp of another hand coming from precisely the opposite end of the earth.'[11]

For all his shyness, Lichtenberg was a persistent celebrity seeker (earlier in the month he had hunted out Boswell's hero, General Paoli), and again called on Solander and Omai the next day, this time apparently at New Burlington Street. Mr. Banks had gone hunting, but the visitor had luncheon with other guests, sitting next to Omai who was 'very lively'. No sooner had he greeted the company than 'he sat down before the tea-table and made the tea with all decorum.' He ate nothing baked or fried and, reverting to his own dietary customs, merely partook of a little salted and almost raw salmon. Lichtenberg bravely tried the dish, but it made him feel so ill that six hours later he had scarcely recovered from the effects. During and after the meal Solander entertained the gathering with familiar anecdotes. He repeated the story of their first meeting — in the coffee-house where Omai had stayed with Captain Furneaux on the night of their arrival — and confirmed the fact that, while the young native recognized Mr. Banks instantly and himself after some delay, they had no recollection of having seen him in Tahiti. He also spoke of Omai's visits to the theatre but apparently said nothing of the point made by Miss Banks — that he refused to return to Sadler's Wells because it was not patronized by the best people.[12]

Among miscellaneous observations, Lichtenberg noted that Omai's teeth were 'beautifully white, regular and well-formed'; that he had learned to play chess; that the name of his native island, as he spoke it, 'sounded almost like *Ulieta-ye*'; and that he could not pronounce *s*, at least at the beginning of a word, for he rendered Solander as 'Tolando'. Their conversation yielded novel particulars of Omai's family:

I asked him whether his father and mother were still alive; he turned his eyes upwards, then closed them, and inclined his head to one side, giving us thereby to understand that they were both dead. When I asked him about his brothers and sisters, he first held up two fingers saying *ladies*, then three fingers saying *men*, thereby indicating two sisters and three brothers.

As for his mental attributes, they were not impressive in this critic's opinion. He seemed to display little curiosity: he carried a watch but rarely troubled to wind it up and, while the rest of the company were looking at beautiful sketches of Pomona and other islands, Omai sat down by the fire and went to sleep. 'It is much to be doubted', Lichtenberg remarked, 'whether he will become the Czar Peter the Great of his nation, notwithstanding that he undertook this journey in order to increase his reputation.'[13]

After Lichtenberg's visit to New Burlington Street, nothing more was recorded of Omai for some weeks. Then, on 18 April, his presence was specially noticed by the *General Evening Post* at a gathering of high society to see the newly completed frigate *Acteon* launched at Woolwich. He was accompanied by the faithful Solander and for a time mingled with the Duke and Duchess of Gloucester, the Earl and Countess of Dartmouth, the Earl of Sandwich, and 'other persons of distinction' assembled for the event. Joseph Cradock, the First Lord's musical friend, was also there and entered in his memoirs a trifling incident that throws further light on the domestic habits Omai had acquired during his sojourn. He was 'very little entertained' by the launching ceremony, Cradock relates. So, to relieve his boredom, he stole away to the neighbouring tavern and, 'according to his custom, had very neatly cut the cucumbers and dressed the salad' by the time his friends in their turn arrived for the meal.[14]

Some days later he was again in the news to more surprising effect. A brief paragraph in the *London Chronicle* began: 'Omiah, the native of Otaheite, we are informed can read and write English well enough to hold a correspondence.' What followed was even more startling: 'It is still said he is going to be married to a young Lady of about 22 years of age, who will go with him to his own country.'[15] The identity of the young lady remains a tantalizing mystery. This is the first and last reference to her in the *Chronicle*, and she is not mentioned by any of its contemporaries. Was she perhaps one of the ladies of easy virtue whose favours, there is reason to believe, Omai sought and won at some stage of his stay in London? Had he escaped the vigilance of his guardians to frequent (in Cook's phrase) the purlieus of Covent Garden and Drury Lane? There is no certain answer. Up to this point he seems to have met only Miss Ray, Mrs. Burney and her step-daughters, the unnamed ladies of Leicester, and the womenfolk of his various hosts (but not certainly Miss Banks and her mother). Soon, however, he was to extend his acquaintance and enlarge his knowledge of sophisticated London society. If placed among the records of Omai's equestrian exploits, the undated account of his legendary ride up the Oxford Road seems to belong to the spring or early summer of 1775 and marks his association with the Chevalier D'Eon, duellist, diplomat, and transvestite.

The story is told by Henry, eldest son of the fashionable fencing and riding master Domenick Angelo, friend of Reynolds, Garrick, and the dramatist George Colman. One day Henry, then in his late teens, set out with D'Eon and Omai from his father's 'manège' in Carlisle Street, Soho, for the family's country house at Acton. The trio, 'mounted *en cavalier*, with cocked hats, long-tailed horses, and *demie-queue* saddles', pranced in good style along the Oxford Road until they reached the Pantheon, about half way up. There, much to the amusement of the crowd, Omai's horse came to a full stop, refusing to move, while D'Eon called out in French and the spectators shouted with laughter. Suddenly, 'preferring the stable, and finding out what sort of a rider he had', Angelo explains, the horse made for home. The Europeans rode on each side of their 'whitey-brown companion', using their whips, but in spite of their efforts his steed hurried back, with 'poor Omai trembling from head to foot'. At last they reached Carlisle Street where a more docile mount was found that took Omai safely to Acton. 'When I related the story', Angelo lamely concludes, 'it contributed very much to the amusement of my mother; not so of my father, who was angry with me for not telling him which rein to use.'[16]

Something might have been made of the limp anecdote by the creator of John Gilpin or perhaps by the satirists who indeed had again been active. Earlier in the year a contributor to the *London Magazine* wrote 'On the Advantages which Great-Britain may derive from the Discoveries of Travellers in the Reign of his present Majesty'. Hawkesworth's *Collection* and the *Travels* of Mr. Bruce need not, he held, serve merely to entertain the reading public; they could be of use to the nation at large. For example, Mr. Banks and Dr. Solander found that the people of Tahiti got on perfectly well without any kind of metal. What an advantage it would be to the British were they brought to the same situation. They would then be altogether independent of countries producing gold and silver; they would save the lives of many an unhappy wretch who falsified the coinage; and they would confer the blessings of health on their fellow citizens condemned to dig in mines or broil in forges. Again, since Tahitians managed perfectly well without horses, these animals could be slaughtered and the corn they ate distributed to the poor. True, this would eliminate cavalry, but surely English dragoons would be more suitably mounted on bulls trained for combat. The nation's foes would then feel with a vengeance the force of the epithet '*John Bull*', while no more effectual means could be devised for quelling the Bostonians. A further discovery of great utility had been brought from the same island: that it was perfectly natural to destroy children should they prove inconvenient. By adopting these excellent principles the British would, in a great measure, relieve themselves from the heavy burden of poor rates and make life easier and merrier for young people of both sexes. But New Zealand contributed a still more useful discovery, '*certain* intelligence of what was formerly considered by many to be *fabulous* — that mankind may feed even luxuriously upon the flesh of their own species.' 'Let us then', urged the writer, 'unite the child-murder of Otaheite with the eating of human flesh in New Zealand, and we shall realize the plan proposed by Dr. Swift for providing for the children of the poor in Ireland.'[17]

The next work was linked more closely to the Oberea cycle, though the monarch herself was nowhere mentioned by name. *An Historic Epistle, from Omiah, to the Queen of Otaheite* was published in the early summer of 1775 and dedicated by its professed 'Editor' to 'JOSEPH B—NKS, Esq.' 'To whom', he asked, 'can a curiosity be offered with such propriety as to you, who have traversed the globe in search of them? Particularly this, which may be termed *"A plant of your growth,"* from the unremitting attention you have bestowed on OMIAH's education; attention so wonderfully successful, that perhaps half the town will scarce believe this to have been *entirely* his own production.' Was that a slyly sarcastic allusion to Banks's failure, already voiced by Cullum, to improve his charge's mind and morals? Here and there the anonymous author-editor does, in fact, seem to possess first-hand knowledge of the islander's exploits. 'Sometimes I ride', Omiah proclaims — but his destination is Islington, not Acton. Perhaps he has the Chevalier D'Eon in mind when condemning 'Macaronies' 'Whose only care is in ambiguous dress / To veil their sex . . . .' He describes a contretemps at Court, not this time in greeting the King but when he attempts to seduce 'A nymph . . . just ripe for amorous sport' and is rejected, he supposes, through her fear of venereal disease ('BOUGAINVILLE's horrors' in the text or 'the *Neapolitan* fever' as a footnote has it). Elsewhere he speaks of his visits to 'the great Senate of the Realm' and among its orators refers to 'old CH-T-M' with his 'more than classic elegance of stile'.[18]

But the *Historic Epistle* is no mere versified chronicle of Omai in England; nor does it draw to any great extent on Hawkesworth. It is a satire, lengthier and more comprehensive than its predecessors, in which the 'wand'ring vagrant in the northern world' surveys the institutions of civilized society and finds them all wanting when measured by the 'natural' standards that prevail in the South Seas. He sums up his impressions in the opening pages:

> Where'er I turn, confusion meets my eyes,
> New scenes of pomp, new luxuries surprise . . . .

Then, using the artifices of European rhetoric, he emphasizes the contrast with his own unsophisticated island:

> Can *Europe* boast, with all her pilfer'd wealth,
> A larger share of happiness, or health?
> What then avail her thousand arts to gain
> The stores of every land, and every main:
> Whilst we, whom love's more grateful joys enthral,
> Profess one art — to live without them all.

Similarly, in condemning the involved processes of English law he compares them with the simple precepts that determine southern justice:

> Not rul'd like us on nature's simple plan,
> Here laws on laws perplex the dubious man.

> Who vainly thinks these volumes are more strong,
> Than our plain code of — thou shalt do no wrong.[19]

For the most part Omiah leaves his critical principles to be inferred. With only passing references to the virtues of his native sphere, he denounces the hypocrisies of established religion, the cruelties of European warfare, the pompous absurdities of the Law Courts, the corruption of art and letters (from which generalization he excepts the music of Handel and the painting of Reynolds). One of his main targets is science in all its eccentric manifestations. He attacks the impious probings of his hosts, the 'Virtuosi' of the Royal Society:

> This wond'rous race still pry, in nature's spite,
> Through all her secrets, and *Transactions* write . . . .

He interprets Constantine Phipps's northern expedition as a farcical and futile attempt to oil earth's 'axis at the pole'. He expends pages on the absurd theorizing of 'Philogræcos' with 'his scientific prejudice for tails' and in a footnote repeats a not implausible piece of gossip: When the famous Abyssinian traveller visited Edinburgh, he entered a court where the noble author was sitting in his judicial capacity; unable to restrain himself, the judge 'sent a message with lord M—'s compliments, begging to be *immediately* informed, if he had seen any of the *men with tails.*'[20]

His own protectors and patrons are not exempt from Omiah's satiric shafts. In a later section of the work he proclaims:

> Know, through the town my guide S—L—ND—R goes,
> To plays, museums, conjurers, and shows;
> He forms my taste, with skill minute, to class,
> Shells, fossils, maggots, butterflies, and grass . . . .

Banks is treated with similar indulgent derision in the prentice poet's somewhat limping couplets:

> O'er verdant plains my steps OPANE leads,
> To trace the organs of a sex in weeds;
> And bids like him the world for monsters roam,
> Yet finds none stranger than are here at home.

Nor is 'Religious S—NDW—CH' spared in a ponderous quip ridiculing both his oratory and his arithmetical skill. The First Lord's ungrateful protégé closes the epistle with a peroration that again contrasts degenerate Britain with his own uncorrupted island:

> Sick of these motley scenes, might I once more
> In peace return to *Otaheite's* shore,

Where nature only rules the lib'ral mind,
Unspoil'd by art, by falsehood unrefin'd;

There fondly straying o'er the sylvan scenes,
Taste unrestrain'd what Freedom really means:
And glow inspir'd with that enthusiast zeal,
Which *Britons* talk of, *Otaheiteans* feel.[21]

IN JUNE 1775, when the *Historic Epistle* was published, the supposed scourge of things British seems to have been quite happily reconciled to a further period of exile in the centre of all corruption. Since the beginning of the month he had again been enjoying naval hospitality, this time under the most distinguished auspices. He and Mr. Banks had been invited by Lord Sandwich to accompany him on the yacht *Augusta* during a 'visitation' or tour of inspection which took them to dockyards and depots as far distant as Plymouth. The impending departure of the yacht, its expected arrival at Portsmouth, and the First Lord's return were briefly noted by the newspapers, but only his visit to Chatham was given more extended treatment. Here, reported the local correspondent, when arriving late on 4 June his lordship was saluted with fifteen guns by H.M.S. *Ramillies*, a compliment the *Augusta* returned with seven guns. The next morning Lord Sandwich came ashore with his party, including 'Dr. Banks, and Omiah, the native of Otaheite'. Awaiting them were Commissioner Proby and the principal officers of the yard, while 'the grenadier company of marines were drawn up before the Commissioner's house, with drums beating, and fifes, and a band of music playing.' The visitors then 'took a view of the ships building and repairing, the storehouses, anchor wharf, &c.' 'Omiah', the writer continued, 'was conducted by Mr. Peake, builder's assistant, on board the Victory of 100 guns, now repairing in the dock-yard; his joy was amazing at seeing so large a ship.' The First Lord spent two more days inspecting vessels and men, after which he set out for Sheerness.[22]

The tour seems to have been a livelier, more informal affair than the newspaper report would suggest. Almost as if preparing himself for some lengthier expedition, Banks kept a minutely detailed 'Journal of a Voyage Made in the Augusta Yatch S\[r\] Richard Bickerton Commander', beginning on the morning of 2 June when after breakfast at the Admiralty they left from the Tower. He was in holiday mood from the outset and in describing their passage to Greenwich tells how the *Augusta* 'fell desparately in Love with a duch vessell' so that Sir Richard was forced to anchor her 'as a punishment for her Libidinous inclination'. There are many such pleasantries mingled with scientific jottings, nautical observations, and rather sparse allusions to the First Lord and the journalist's fellow guests — the Earl of Seaforth, Omai, and two of Lord Sandwich's staff, his secretary Mr. Bates, and an Admiralty official Mr. Palmer. Reaching Greenwich, they called at the hospital to eat heartily of 'the best pease' and drink as heartily of 'the best small beer imaginable' ('the food of the old Pensioners', Banks explained) and then passed on to the observatory. Here they found much that was curious but nothing more entertaining than the 'Camera obscura'. Banks remained outside the chamber, thinking the exclamations of those inside sufficient amusement: Lord Sandwich's recorded by a dash (too inaudible or possibly too improper to repeat); Lord Seaforth's 'a Cara'; and Omai's 'away te pereá' (perhaps *'aue! te piri e!'* or 'Oh! how strange!'). In the afternoon they were joined by Miss Ray, Sir William Gordon, and other friends who had travelled from London by coach. Sailing 'most merrily' down the river, they all partook of dinner until at nine o'clock the visitors disembarked and the yacht continued on its way to Chatham.[23]

Banks mentioned the compliments paid by the *Ramillies* when they anchored off Chatham on 4 June and conscientiously recorded the events of the following day: the progress through yards and storehouses; the inspection of a variety of vessels — warships, a hospital ship, a church ship (not a word, however, of the *Victory*); and their last official duty, a visit to the victualling office. He praised the neatness and order prevailing throughout the depot and the dryness and airiness of the ships; but by the evening he had evidently satisfied his curiosity about naval affairs. Lord Sandwich, he wrote on the 6th, had 'destin'd' that day for mustering the yard, 'a matter of infinite Consequence to him tho of no amusement to us'. So, borrowing a boat, he set out with his companions to explore the Medway. They admired successive sights — an old house 'in a romantick situation' commanding a view of Rochester castle and cathedral, the ruins of another house once, according to Camden, occupied by the Bishops of Rochester, a 'very beautifull' stretch of the river below the town. They also shot birds: gulls, herns, lapwings, and a turtle dove which they afterwards found juicy and good to eat. Sandwich continued his visitation on the 7th, but they had 'seen enough of the old ships', Banks again remarked, and preferred to spend the morning ashore watching artillery exercises. Later that day they rowed through the marshes, much amused by innumerable crabs 'amorously inclind', noting 'the vigorous attempt of the males & the prudery of the females'. On rejoining the yacht in the evening, they heard a skylark serenade 'as boldly as if it had been noon day'.[24]

A pattern had now been established for the tour. While the First Lord assiduously performed his official duties, Banks with equal assiduity followed his own interests, breaking off only on occasion to attend a formal reception or view a naval display. During his shore excursions he visited churchyards and castles and ruined abbeys and the homes of local gentlefolk. He was at particular pains to seek out and describe mechanical contrivances — at Sheerness a winch for drawing water from an enclosed well, at Hamble boat-shaped containers, fitted with wheels, to preserve lobsters and haul them ashore. He trawled for fish at sea, he angled in the rivers, he studied plants, he hunted wild life. Being 'botanicaly inclind', he wrote on 20 June, he left the yacht to find a rare species of grass mentioned in Ray's synopsis of British plants. Three days later, as Lord Sandwich was detained at the Isle of Wight preparing dispatches, Banks went 'a shooting' birds with Lord Seaforth and Omai, all three setting out 'a horseback'. Sometimes they picnicked — 'dining in the air' Banks called it — and more than once, at Omai's request, they ended the day at a nearby theatre: 'attended a play which Omai had bespoke', ran an entry for 21 June. Again, at the end of the month, after a fruitless attempt to reach Eddystone lighthouse, Banks noted: 'went to a play which Omai had bespoke'.[25] This was the last time he named his protégé in the *Augusta* journal, and there were only three previous references. Perhaps his interest in Omai had indeed evaporated; on the other hand, since the other guests were mentioned no more frequently, he may merely have taken the young man's presence for granted.

It was at this stage of the tour, while the *Augusta* was moored in Plymouth Sound, that the Admiralty received the first authentic intelligence of Cook since Furneaux's return. On 27 June the *General Evening Post*, bemused as ever, announced that an express had come from Portsmouth with 'news of the safe arrival of the Endeavour bark'. 'Yesterday', ran a note in the next issue, 'a Messenger was dispatched to the Earl of Sandwich at Plymouth.'[26] Actually, the *Resolution* was still in the Atlantic, a month's sail from England, and what the messenger conveyed to the First Lord was a letter from Cook written at the Cape of Good Hope in March to report his landfalls and discoveries after parting with the *Adventure*. He spoke of Easter Island, the Marquesas, the New Hebrides, New Caledonia, and went on to mention familiar places: Tahiti and the Society Islands, where for six weeks they again received 'hospitality altogether unknown among more civilized Nations'; Rotterdam in the Friendly Islands, a briefer anchorage; and Queen Charlotte Sound, once more a haven and depot for nearly a month. He described yet another sweep through southern waters 'strewed with Mountains of Ice' and a second unsuccessful attempt to find Cape Circumcision. He praised the 'constancy' of officers and crew, paid a special tribute to 'that indefaticable gentleman' Mr. Hodges, and referred with a certain reserve to 'other Gentlemen whom Government thought proper to send out' (meaning, it seems, Mr. Forster and his son). 'If I have failed in discovering a Continent', Cook concluded, 'it is because it does not exist in a Navigable Sea and not for want of looking . . . .'[27]

The letter was soon followed by one from Solander to Banks 'on road from Portsmouth to Plymouth'. 'As a Copy of Capt Cooks Letter was sent down to Lᵈ Sandwich,' he wrote, 'I take it for granted you know all concerning his Voyage.' His own special concern was with Odiddy, the Boraboran whom Cook had recruited at Raiatea and who, Solander's inquiries and calculations led him to believe, was still on the *Resolution*. 'If he should arrive before your return,' he asked Banks, 'shall it be mention'd to him, that Omai wishes he would live in the same house with him? It seems Mʳ Omai has desired Mʳ Vigniol to take him in, in case he should come.' Reverting to the voyage, he remarked: 'In all the Letters that are come from the Gentlemen on board the Resolution, they speak much in praise of our friends and all other Sth Sea Inhabitants that they have met with; and Nova Caledonia is described as a paradise without thorns or thistles.' There followed excited impressions culled from a report sent by Mr. Forster: '260 new Plants, 200 new animals — 71° 10′ farthest Sth — no continent — Many Islands, some 80 Leagues long — The Bola Bola savage an [in]corrigible Blockhead — Glorious Voyage — No man lost by sickness.' Solander sent greetings to his friends and a little personal news: Captain Phipps and he would represent Banks at a dinner on the *Bessborough*; he had seen Mrs. and Miss Banks that morning.[28]

In his *Augusta* journal Banks made no reference to these perhaps mortifying accounts of the Glorious Voyage he had forgone in a fit of pique. But he did full justice to the pleasures and minor triumphs that came his way during the last phase of the tour. The play which Omai bespoke at Plymouth on 30 June 'turnd out the worst acted we had seen for some years'. Resolutely cheerful, Banks merely added: 'as many of us were of opinion that plays should be either very well or very ill acted to be entertaining we went home not at all dissatisfied'. The next day, following two unsuccessful attempts, he landed on Eddystone, hardly a Nova Caledonia or even an island, yet full of interest, from its candle-powered lights to its pious keepers. After a spell of bad weather, they rowed up the Tamar on 4 July to enjoy the beauty of that 'romantick' river and dine with Lord Edgcumbe 'in the true style of our ancestors': 'a more agreable day I never wish to Spend', Banks remarked at its conclusion. Further diversions awaited them on their return to Plymouth: a dinner ashore and a final visit to the theatre on the 7th; and on the 8th an excursion to the Isle of Wight with local ladies and gentlemen — 'the best contrivd & Executed as well as the most successful Party of pleasure I remember', Banks commented. Rough seas, making everyone except Lord Sandwich 'excessively sick', marred the Channel passage, but by the 12th, as they approached Deptford, they were eating 'in a quantity which would have done credit to a troop of his majesties beef eaters'. On the 13th 'the Melancholy day of parting' arrived and Banks ended both entry and journal with the eloquent: 'I have been happy'.[29]

For the First Lord there was no immediate respite from his official labours. On 13 July 'and not before', as the *General Evening Post* expressed it, he returned to his house in the Admiralty after an absence of just six weeks spent in surveying the dockyards. He had found everything very satisfactory, the notice continued, 'except the shipwrights, who have declined working till their wages are raised.' In his account of their first stay at Portsmouth Banks referred in passing to 'some little dissatisfactions' in the yard. But the dispute was more serious than that suggests, for on the night of his arrival, the *Post* also noted, Lord Sandwich met other members of the Administration to consider how to set the men to work again, 'as their absence from the dock-yards at this time is much felt.' On the 14th, ran a further paragraph, he attended a levee at St. James's and presented to His Majesty a list of ships and stores 'by which it appears, that the royal navy is in very good condition.' Nothing more was said of the striking workmen, and the tour was not again mentioned until the following week when the newspaper printed another startling announcement: 'We hear that Omiah, since his return in the Augusta yacht, has been very bad from the sea sickness, so that there were but little hopes of his recovery.'[30]

The rumour was undoubtedly a libel on that seasoned navigator who had been sailing the seas since childhood and had recently traversed the oceans with no reported ill effects. Indeed, if published authorities are to be credited, he had already embarked on a further cruise in home waters. Banks's biographers, regrettably failing to supply their evidence, all state with varying degrees of certainty that soon after the return of the *Augusta* Sandwich left on a second yachting excursion, this time with Miss Ray, Banks, Omai, Constantine Phipps, and perhaps his brother Augustus.[31] Wherever they were (and, on the face of it, Hinchingbrooke would seem the most probable location), members of the little group were absent from London when the long heralded *Resolution* finally made its appearance.

WHILE HIS FRIENDS DIVERTED THEMSELVES, ashore or afloat, Solander stayed on in the capital, eagerly awaiting Cook's return. On Friday 21 July he explained to John Ellis that he would be unable to visit him on the coming Sunday: he was 'under an engagement' to see the captain who was now daily expected.[32] In the event he had to wait more than a week before sending Banks the dramatic and not quite accurate message: 'This moment Captain Cook is arrived.' He wrote at the beginning of August from some office or ante-room at the Admiralty where Cook, after his drive from Portsmouth, was closeted with his naval superiors. The explorer emerged in due course, looking 'better than when he left England', to pass on the warmest of greetings to Banks: nothing but his company, Cook said, could have added to the satisfaction he had in making the tour. He had some preserved birds for Banks's collection, Solander also reported, and would have written himself 'if he had not been kept too long at the Admiralty and at the same time wishing to see his wife.' Odiddy, it appeared, had not made the voyage after all (he had been left at Raiatea), and Solander had to content himself with examining likenesses of Omai's prospective fellow guest and potential rival — 'really a handsome man', he decided. The artist, Mr. Hodges, had produced a great many portraits, some very good; he seemed to be 'a very well-behaved young Man' and spoke with enthusiasm of the Tahitians and the Marquesans. Included in the letter were compliments to Miss Ray together with disjointed observations couched in a limited range of phrases: Solander had seen Cook's maps; he called the group near Amsterdam 'the *Friendly Islands*, because the people behaved very friendly'; those in the Hebrides were 'not so friendly' and he was 'obliged to kill some'; Nova Caledonia was 'a narrow strip of an Island', its 'People rather well behaved than otherwise.'[33]

Banks's response to this exhilarating news is not on record; perhaps it may be inferred from the fact that he apparently made no attempt to join Solander but continued his summer excursion with Omai and other companions. Sandwich, on the other hand, parted from his guests to travel to London where his presence was soon observed in official circles. The newspapers, inured to such events, had expended little space on the return of the *Resolution* which they still confused with the *Endeavour*. They merely noted the ship's safe arrival at Portsmouth and from its many landfalls and discoveries singled out for special mention 'an island in the South Seas, in lat. 22' (presumably New Caledonia) considered 'the most eligible place for establishing a settlement, of any yet discovered'. On 10 August, however, the *General Evening Post* reported: 'Yesterday Capt. Cook, who has lately been a voyage round the world, and made several discoveries in the South seas, was presented to his Majesty at St. James's by Lord Sandwich, and most graciously received.' The *London Chronicle* added that the captain made his own presentation of maps and charts and, further, that the *Resolution* was 'to be repaired for another voyage'.[34]

News of the forthcoming voyage was quickly confirmed in a letter from Dr. Burney to the anxious James Lind who had asked to be advised of any such proposal. 'When you last favoured me with a Letter', the doctor wrote on the 12th, 'I remember, & have constantly remembered that you wished to be apprised whether any new Expedition was in meditation for the South Seas.' For some time, he had already apologized, 'want of health & of Leisure' had delayed his answer, while in addition, he now explained, there had been no positive information to impart:

I c d get no intelligence worth communicating sooner as nothing was resolved on during the absence of Capt. Cook; but now he is come home & has made considerable discoveries another Expedition is not only talked of, but *determined* to take place between this Time & next X^mas — I yesterday Dined at the Admiralty & had (I speak it *inter nos*) the Information from L. Sandwich himself. Two Ships are to be sent out, in one of wch I believe my Son, who has already been a circumnavigator wth Capt. Fourneaux, will go out Lieutenant.

James had recently spent a fortnight in England with the *Cerberus* which had returned to take on reinforcements and supplies for the hard-pressed British forces in North America. He had left again for Boston, his father told Dr. Lind, but was expected back in November and that, said Lord Sandwich, would be time enough for him to leave for the South Seas.[35]

Dr. Burney failed to mention the purpose of the new expedition; nor did he discuss the question of its leadership. The opinion then prevailing was that Cook's first lieutenant would take charge. Mr. Clerke had been given the command, the *General Evening Post* announced a week later;

and the *Resolution*, after refitting, would 'prosecute' further discoveries, 'make a settlement on a large island in the South Sea, and carry back Omiah to Otaheite . . . .'[36] Whatever the First Lord may have been meditating at this stage, Cook certainly had no thought as yet of a third voyage to the Pacific. Writing to his friend John Walker of Whitby on 19 August, he remarked that the *Resolution* would 'soon be sent out again' but emphasized, 'I shall not command her'. For his part, he explained, he would be enjoying the 'fine retreat' and 'pretty income' ensured by the captaincy at Greenwich Hospital to which he had been appointed; whether he could bring himself 'to like ease and retirement', he added, time would show.[37]

Banks was kept abreast of these developments as he continued on holiday in the country. 'Mr Clerke was promised the command of the Resolution to carry Mr Omai home', wrote Solander on 14 August in describing a visit with Lord Sandwich to the ship, now moored in Galleon's Reach. Their excursion, he said, was 'quite a feast to all who were concerned': setting out from the Tower, they visited the Deptford yard, took on 'Miss Ray & Co' at Woolwich, and then made their way to the *Resolution*. There the First Lord made many of the ship's company 'quite happy' with his announcement of postings and promotions; not only Mr. Clerke but, among others, Captain Cook who was awarded a vacant place at Greenwich with 'a promise of Employ whenever he should ask for it'. Most of their time, Solander explained, 'was taken up in ceremonies', but he was able to see something of the expedition's trophies: '3 live Otaheite Dogs, the ugliest most stupid of all the Canine tribe'; 'a Springe Bock' with eagles and other birds, all brought from the Cape by Mr. Forster for presentation to the Queen; and, most diverting of spectacles, a severed head from New Zealand which 'made the Ladies sick'. All their friends looked as well 'as if they had been all the while in clover' and all, Solander assured Banks, inquired after him: 'In fact we had a glorious day and longd for nothing but You and Mr Omai.' Compliments went to that gentleman and also to Captain Phipps and his brother.[38]

Not all visitors to the *Resolution* were so amiable. The anonymous author of 'Harlequinade', a chatty, semi-satirical commentary in the *London Magazine*, claimed to have spent an hour on the ship at Woolwich and to have examined 'curiosities' never seen in Europe before. Furthermore, he spoke to the ship's officers about the last voyage and the coming one — with some surprising results. In their opinion the country best suited for settlement was New Zealand whose inhabitants were 'sober, civil, tractable and kind'. True, they had killed and eaten crewmen of the *Adventure*; but, as they explained to Captain Cook, they were driven to that cannibal act 'by the firing upon them unprovoked'; 'indeed', the writer commented, 'no people, if not properly restrained by their officers, are more wanton in their wickedness than the English sailors.' So it had been decided that 'Omiah, the senseless stupid native of Otaheite,' would be returned in the spring and the ship

would then 'proceed to settle New Zealand'. And who was to lead the
enterprise? None other than Captain Cook whose 'circumnavigable
pursuits' this voyage would terminate. Yet even the returned hero did
not meet with the critic's unqualified approval: his appointment as
'conditional captain pensioner at Greenwich Hospital' deprived 'some
veteran and infirm sailor of that situation.' 'But', moralized this
embryonic gossip columnist, now venting his spleen on Lord Sandwich,
'some men in power leap over all rules and institutions; and dispose of
places according to the pulse of interest, and the complexion of the
times.'[39]

Cook himself seems to have been unaware of the new appointment so
confidently predicted in the *London Magazine*. Writing again to John
Walker in mid-September, he referred to the coming venture with no
suggestion that he would take part. 'I did expect and was in hopes', he
remarked, 'that I had put an end to all Voyages of this kind to the
Pacific Ocean, as we are now sure that no Southern Continent exists
there, unless so near the Pole that the Coast cannot be Navigated for Ice
and therefore not worth the discovery; but the Sending home Omiah
will occasion another voyage which I expect will soon be undertaken.'
Nor was there the slightest hint of his own departure in a courteous
letter he sent earlier in the month to a would-be Pacific explorer,
Latouche-Tréville.[40] He was particularly well disposed towards his
French rivals as the result of an encounter during the homeward passage.
Soon after reaching the Cape of Good Hope, he was fortunate enough to
meet Captain Crozet, a man, as Cook described him, 'possessed of the
true spirit of a discoverer' with 'abilities equal to his good will'. This
disinterested navigator not only supplied a chart showing the southern
islands for which the *Resolution* and the *Adventure* had sought in vain
but gave details of de Surville's expedition and Marion du Fresne's. After
Aoutourou's death and a stay at the Cape, Cook learned, Marion had
made for New Zealand where he and many of his people were killed.
Crozet spoke with authority, for he had been Marion's second in command. And to some members of the ship's company he related an
historic sequel. In conversation with Rousseau, he had described the
'behaviour of the New Zealand savages'; whereupon the philosopher
exclaimed, "Is it possible that the good Children of Nature can really
be so wicked?"'[41]

However wicked in this instance, was the conduct of Pacific savages
really more culpable than that of their civilized betters? One more contribution to the unending debate was a 'Letter' from a nameless 'Officer
of the Resolution to his Friend', dated at Woolwich on 22 September
and published in the *London Magazine*. Purporting to give an account
of the voyage, he passed summarily over other anchorages to dwell on
Tahiti. There, he assured his friend,

we have established a disease which will ever prove fatal to these unhappy
innocents, who seem to have enjoyed a perfect state of simplicity and nature

till we, a more refined race of monsters, contaminated all their bliss by an
introduction of our vices. It is immaterial whether Bougainville or we communicated this disorder; but I am rather inclined to believe, by the account I
had from the natives, that it came from the first English who touched at this
spot.

While the islanders had medicinal roots which checked the disease, the
writer continued, so high was their 'venery' that it increased daily —
covered with sores, the victims died by inches. Worse still, it had now
spread through the whole group, so that Borabora, 'whilom the paradise
of women', was 'an island of Pandora's Ills'. The people, more particularly the Tahitians, had been very shy of the explorers and gave no
presents, he reported, but he could not explain whether this was through
a scarcity of supplies or a change of government; for 'the courteous
Oberea' had been dethroned and lived in retirement with a small retinue.
'The other circumstances of this island have been so often related before,'
the officer went on, 'that I shall conclude with saying, that I blush for
the honour of my country, which has suffered her people to destroy the
happiest race of mortals . . . .' His last word, however, concerned Omai:
the voyager's countrymen were looking out with impatience for his
return and, though not a priest or a man of any distinction among them,
'his exploring so far, will render him a prodigy . . . .'[42]

OMAI'S TRAVELS HAD EXTENDED EVEN FARTHER in the weeks since the
Resolution's return. On parting from Sandwich and Miss Ray early in
August, Banks journeyed north with his friends until they reached York
where they were joined by the playwright George Colman and his son,
another George, then in his thirteenth year. After attending the races,
they set off on an expedition which long remained in the memory of
Colman the Younger and found a place in the diffuse and elaborately
facetious reminiscences he aptly entitled *Random Records*. There were
six in the party — the Colmans, Constantine Phipps, his youngest
brother Augustus (a boy of George's age), Omai, and his 'bear-leader
and guardian', as Colman termed Banks. The *'Otaheitan'*, explained the
author for the benefit of his nineteenth-century readers, had shown
confidence in leaving 'his flock, (for he was a priest,)' to accompany
'European Savages, on board the Adventure' and, when he arrived, to
entrust himself to someone 'who had left a treacherous character behind
him, in the South Seas', a man who was reputedly 'the "gay deceiver" of
the Dido of Otaheite'.[43]
    They 'rumbled' from York in a coach, the 'ponderous property' of
Mr. Banks, 'as huge and heavy as a broad-wheeled waggon', yet not
too huge for its contents. Besides the half-dozen inside passengers, it
carried the luggage of Captain Phipps, 'laid in like stores for a long
voyage': 'boxes and cases cramm'd with nautical lore, — books, maps,
charts, quadrants, telescopes, &c. &c.' Even more formidable was
Mr. Banks's 'stowage': 'unwearied in botanical research, he travell'd

36 *A view of Scarborough in 1745*

with trunks containing voluminous specimens of his *hortus siccus* in whitey-brown paper; and large receptacles for further vegetable materials, which he might accumulate, in his locomotion.' Their progress, 'under all its cumbrous circumstances', was still further retarded by Mr. Banks's indefatigable botanizing. They 'never saw a tree with an unusual branch, or a strange weed, or anything singular in the vegetable world, but a halt was immediately order'd . . . .' Then out jumped the botanist, out jumped the two boys, and out jumped Omai. This was the excursion Banks had forgone in the previous summer, and their destination was the Phipps family estate at Mulgrave near Whitby; but instead of taking the direct inland route they travelled by way of Scarborough. It was from an eminence near the town that they saw 'the German Ocean' and George had his first glimpse of the sea. He was hugely disappointed, he confessed, and 'peremptorily pronounced' it 'nothing more than a very great puddle; — an opinion which must have somewhat astounded the high Naval Officer, who had not long return'd from his celebrated Voyage of Discovery towards the North Pole, and the Philosopher who had circumnavigated the globe.'[44]

On reaching Scarborough, George ran from the inn to the beach and early the next morning returned 'to take a dip, as the Cockneys call it'. He was on the point of plunging in from a bathing-machine, he relates,

when Omai appear'd wading before me. The coast of Scarborogh having an eastern aspect, the early sunbeams shot their lustre upon the tawny Priest, and

37 Mulgrave Castle, Yorkshire

heighten'd the cutaneous gloss which he had already received from the water: — he look'd like a specimen of pale moving mahogany, highly varnish'd; — not only varnish'd, indeed, but curiously veneer'd; — for, from his hips, and the small of his back, downwards, he was *tattow'd* with striped arches, broad and black, by means of a sharp shell, or a fish's tooth, imbued with an indelible die, according to the fashion of his country.

Omai hailed George as *'Tosh'* — he had, on Colman's doubtful authority, greeted His Majesty with *'"How do, King Tosh?"'* — and invited the boy to join him. George complied and, clinging to the islander's back, set out, 'as Arion upon his Dolphin'. But this Arion had no musical instrument to play, 'unless it were the comb which Omai carried in one hand, and which he used, while swimming, to adjust his harsh black locks, hanging in profusion over his shoulders.' His 'wild friend', Colman noted, 'appear'd as much at home upon the waves as a rope-dancer upon a cord' and safely delivered his passenger after spending three-quarters of an hour in the North Sea (the supreme test, surely, of Omai's adaptability and physical stamina). Awaiting them on the shore were the other members of the party — Augustus, 'vex'd' that he was not with them, Colman Senior, a little grave at his son's being so 'venturous', the captain and the philosopher, laughing heartily as they called George 'a tough little fellow'. Henceforth, he wrote, Omai and he were constant companions.[45]

The friendship thus begun continued to flourish when they reached Mulgrave. The commander of the North Pole expedition and the visitor to the South Seas, disdaining any game more common than a penguin or a bear, left the grouse on neighbouring moors to hired keepers. But Omai entered into the sport with abandon. Now quite familiar with European weapons, he 'prowl'd upon the precincts', gun in hand, popping at 'all the feather'd creation which came in his way; and which happen'd, for the most part, to be dunghill cocks, barn-door geese, and ducks in the pond.' Sometimes, as Colman tells, he reverted to his own more primitive methods of hunting:

One day, while he carried his gun, I was out with him in a stubble field, (at the beginning of September,) when he pointed to some object at a distance, which I could not distinguish; — his eye sparkled; he laid down his gun mighty mysteriously, and put his finger on my mouth, to enjoin silence; — he then stole onwards, crouching along the ground for several yards; till, on a sudden, he darted forward like a cat, and sprang upon a covey of partridges, — one of which he caught, and took home alive, in great triumph.

His treatment of other livestock could be quite as ungentlemanly. On another occasion, 'with the intent to take a ride', he seized a grazing horse by the tail, whereupon 'the astounded animal gallop'd off, wincing and plunging, and dragging his tenacious assailant after him, till he slipp'd from his grasp', leaving Omai in the mire but miraculously unhurt. 'He was not always so intrepid;' Colman continues, '— there was a huge bull in the grounds, which kept him at a respectful distance; and of which he always spoke reverentially, as the *man-cow*.'[46]

Encouraged by George, Omai continued his efforts to master English, while he in turn introduced the boy to his native tongue: 'reciprocally School-master and Scholar', they began by pointing to objects which each named in his own language. From words they advanced to phrases and short sentences until at the end of the first week they could hold something like a conversation, 'jabbering to each other between Otaheitan and English.' At the same time, under the tutelage of their elders, the two boys were extending their knowledge in other directions. Banks explained the rudiments of the Linnaean system in a series of nightly lectures, the first of which he illustrated by cutting up a cauliflower, and early every morning sent them to gather plants in the woods. Captain Phipps for his part organized expeditions to open 'the tumuli, or *Barrows*, as they are vulgarly call'd'. Since their archaeologizing took place at some distance from the house, they dined in a tent on dishes which they prepared themselves. Banks made very palatable stews in a tin machine, but 'the talents of Omai shone out most conspicuously; and, in the culinary preparations, he beat all his competitors.' As before at Hinchingbrooke, he built an earth oven to practise 'the Otaheitan *cuisine*', using English substitutes for native commodities: 'he cook'd fowls instead of *dogs* . . . . for plantain leaves, to wrap up the animal food, he was supplied with writing paper, smear'd with butter; — for yams, he had potatos; for the bread fruit, bread itself, — the best home-made in Yorkshire.' Nothing, Colman decided, could have been 'better dress'd, or more savoury' than Omai's dish; and he singled out for praise the special flavour, that *'soupçon* of smokiness', imparted to the fowls by 'the smouldering pebble-stones and embers of the Otaheitan oven'.[47]

One of Captain Phipps's guests lost no time in writing of their bucolic pleasures and exotic repasts to a friend who was equally prompt in his reply. 'My dear Colman,' David Garrick addressed the playwright on 29 August, 'I expect to see you as brown and as hearty as a Devonshire plough-boy, who faces the sun without shelter, and knows not the luxury of small beer and porter.' He sent compliments to 'those mighty adventurous knights', Banks and Phipps, if Colman was still risking his neck with them, and referred knowingly to their rustic feasts: 'I must lick my fingers with you, at the Otaheite fowl and potatoes; but don't you spoil the dish, and substitute a fowl for a young puppy?' He passed on obscure items of theatrical gossip — Foote had thrown the Duchess of Kingston 'upon her back' (in his *Trip to Calais*), Miss Pope the actress had sent her 'penitentials' — and spoke hopefully of his infirmities. He had been upon the rack since Colman left him, Garrick confessed, but at the Duke of Newcastle's an old Neapolitan friend commended a remedy which had worked wonders. Now his spirits were returned and he even meditated authorship on his own account. 'By the bye', he announced, 'I had some thoughts to make a farce upon the follies and fashions of the times, and your friend Omiah was to be my *Arlequin Sauvage*; a fine character to give our fine folks a genteel dressing.'[48]

THE GAY LITTLE COMPANY was dispersed by mid-September, just before Constantine Phipps succeeded his father as the second Baron Mulgrave and inherited the family estate.[49] By that time Omai was back in London, but until December there is a complete gap in the record of his doings save for one brief reference. In a letter written on 19 September to Edward Wortley Montagu at Venice, the physician and naturalist William Watson reported that he had dined twice with Captain Cook and was 'happy in hearing his relation.' Most of what the doctor heard covered familiar topics: the expedition had added greatly to knowledge of the globe; it had found no Terra Australis; it had brought back new plants and animals. Cook also dwelt on his two visits to Tahiti, making special mention of the native (Odiddy) he had picked up and returned; and he spoke with awed admiration of the great fleet gathered by the Tahitians, just before the *Resolution* sailed, to attack a neighbouring island — he thought it 'the finest Spectacle he ever Saw.' 'The whole account of this voyage', Watson continued, 'is, I am told, preparing for publication by Capt Cook, & Mr Forster, who, as Mr Banks & Dr Solander declined going, went in the capacity of a naturalist.' Winding up the bulletin, he sent the absent Montagu news of the next expedition:

Mr Clark, who came home Capt Cook's lieutenant, is, it is believed, to be appointed to a command, & Sent home with Omay, who is now So far acquainted with this country, that not long Since, & without any body attending him, he hired a horse, & rode to visit Baron Dimsdale, by whom he was inoculated, at Hartford.[50]

Omai's self-reliance was also mentioned by Fanny Burney when, on 14 December, she entered in her diary a lengthy account of his unexpected call at Newton House late one evening as the family entertained another guest, Miss Lidderdale of Lynn. He now walked everywhere quite alone, she wrote, and lived by himself in lodgings at Warwick Street, supported by a pension from the King. Since his first visit, twelve months before, he had, she noted, learned a great deal of English and, with the aid of signs and actions, could make himself tolerably well understood. He pronounced the language differently from other foreigners, sometimes unintelligibly, but he had really made great proficiency,

38 Newton House

considering the disadvantages he laboured under; for he knew nothing
of letters, while so very few persons were acquainted with his tongue
that it must have been extremely difficult to instruct him at all. Though
magazine scribblers might censure Omai for his stupidity, Fanny was
not of their opinion. On the contrary she spoke of him as 'lively and
intelligent', praising him further for the 'open and frank-hearted' manner
with which he looked everyone in the face as his friend and well-wisher.
'Indeed, *to me*', she remarked, 'he seems to have shewn no small share
of real greatness of mind, in having thus thrown himself into the power
of a nation of strangers, and placing such entire confidence in their
honour and benevolence.'[51]

In spite of goodwill on both sides, communication was not easy. 'As
we are totally unacquainted with his country, connections, and affairs,'
Fanny primly explained, 'our conversation was necessarily very much
confined; indeed, it wholly consisted in questions of what he had seen
here, which he answered, when he understood, very *entertainingly*.'
The first person discussed was Omai's friend James:

> He began immediately to talk of my brother.
> 'Lord Sandwich write one, two, three' (counting on his fingers) *'monts* ago,
> — Mr. Burney — come home.'
> 'He will be very happy,' cried I, 'to see *you*.'
> He bowed and said, 'Mr. Burney very *dood* man!'
> We asked if he had seen the King lately?
> 'Yes; King George *bid me*, — "Omy, you go home." Oh, very *dood* man,
> King George!'
> He then, with our assisting him, made us to understand that he was extremely
> rejoiced at the thoughts of seeing again his native land; but at the same time
> that he should much regret leaving his friends in England.
> 'Lord Sandwich,' he added, *'bid me,* "Mr. Omy, you two ships, — you go
> home." — I say (making a fine bow) "Very much *oblige*, my Lord."'[52]

Their later conversation, covering a variety of topics, threw some dim
light on Omai's occupations and diversions in the weeks since his return
from Yorkshire. When they asked how he liked the theatres, he failed to
understand, 'though, with a most astonishing politeness,' Fanny commented, 'he always endeavoured, by his bows and smiles, to save us the
trouble of knowing that he was not able to comprehend whatever we
said.' He made no mention of the excursion to Hertford or his other
equestrian feats, but amused the company (and apparently himself) by a
description of pillion riding which Fanny supposed he had seen on the
roads: '"First goes man, so!" (making a motion of whipping a horse)
"then *here*" (pointing behind him) "*here* goes woman! Ha! ha! ha!"'
Miss Lidderdale, who was dressed in a habit, told him *she* was prepared
to go on horseback, whereupon he made a very civil bow and, displaying
his knowledge of genteel usage, reassured her, '"Oh you, you *dood*
woman, you *no man*; dirty woman, beggar woman ride so; — not
you."'[53]

They went on to speak of Fanny's half-brother Dick. Omai remembered him from his previous visit and when told he now went to school at Harrow, 'cried, "O! to learn his book? so!" putting his two hands up to his eyes, in imitation of holding a book.' He then attempted to describe a school to which he had been taken and, prompted by Miss Lidderdale, discussed the friends he had made in aristocratic circles:

'Boys here, — boys there, — boys all over! One boy come up, — do so!' (again imitating reading) '*not well*; — *man* not like; man do so!' Then he showed us how the master had hit the boy a violent blow with the book on his shoulder.

Miss Lidderdale asked him, if he had seen Lady Townshend lately?

'Very pretty woman, Lady Townshend!' cried he; 'I drink tea with Lady Townshend in one, two, *tree* days; Lord Townshend my friend, Lady Townshend my friend. Very pretty woman, Lady Townshend! Very pretty woman, Mrs. Crewe! Very pretty woman, Mrs. Bouverie! Very pretty woman, Lady Craven!'

We all approved his taste; and he told us that, when any of his acquaintances wished to see him, 'they write, and *bid me*, Mr. Omy, you come, — dinner, tea, or supper, then I go.'[54]

Of all the subjects considered that evening the one nearest the Burneys' collective heart was music. When someone asked Omai whether he had been to the opera, 'He immediately began a *squeak*, by way of *imitation*, which was very ridiculous; however, he told us he thought the music was very *fine*, which, when he *first* heard it, he thought *detestable*.' Dr. Burney, who was absent when the visitor first arrived but returned later, asked him to repeat a song of his own country which he had sung at Hinchingbrooke. Omai complied but only with reluctance:

He seemed to be quite ashamed; but we all joined and made the request so earnestly, that he could not refuse us. But he was either so modest, that he blushed for his own performance, or his residence here had made him so conscious of the *barbarity* of the South Sea Islands' music, that he could hardly prevail with himself to comply with our request; and when he did, he began two or three times, before he could acquire voice or firmness to go on.

The song appeared to be 'a sort of trio' involving an old woman, a girl, and a youth. The two latter are entertaining each other with 'praises of their merits and protestations of their passions' when the woman enters and 'endeavours to *faire l'aimable* to the youth', displaying her dress and 'making him admire her taste and fancy'. He 'avows his passion for the nymph'; the old woman sends her away and, 'coming forward to offer *herself*, says, "Come! marry me!" The young man starts as if he had seen a viper, then makes her a bow, begs to be excused, and runs off.' Fanny was full of admiration for Omai's mimic talents. The 'grimaces, *minauderies*, and affectation' he assumed when impersonating the old woman, for example, afforded them 'very great entertainment of the *risible* kind'. On the other hand, the vocal side of his performance offended her sensitive ears. 'Nothing', she wrote, 'can be more *curious* or less *pleasing* than his singing voice; he seems to have none; and *tune* or *air* hardly seem to be aimed at; so queer, wild, strange a *rumbling of sounds* never did I before hear; and very contentedly can I go to the grave, if I never do again.' Her considered verdict on Omai was: 'His *song* is the only thing that is *savage* belonging to him.'[55]

Fanny may not have been the only member of her family to comment on their guest's singing. In the Royal Society's *Transactions* for 1775 there appeared a review of two papers by the learned Joshua Steele on musical instruments brought back by Captain Furneaux. While praising Mr. Steele for his 'minuteness of investigation' and the 'profusion of ancient musical erudition' he displayed, the anonymous writer considered the subject ill adapted to so laboured a treatment. The 'arbitrary, and indeterminate sounds, given by the reed pipes of the barbarous islanders of the South Seas' which, he affirmed, could be produced by blowing through a penny whistle, were 'here seriously, and scrupulously, compared with the *diatonic* and *chromatic* genera of the polished Greeks.' Indeed, were the author not perfectly serious throughout, the two papers might seem intended as a 'solemn mockery of ancient wisdom'. Yet, the reviewer conceded, the Tahitians did 'practise the intervals of the diesis, and still minuter divisions of the tone'; and in support of his assertion he cited 'the testimony of a sober and discreet person, who has a tolerable good ear, and has heard Omiah sing one of his country songs.' According to this witness, 'The melody . . . seemed to be wholly *enharmonic* — slubbering and sliding from sound to sound by such minute intervals, as are not to be found in any known scale, and which made it appear to him as music, — if it could be called music, of another world.' Evidence for the authorship of these remarks all points in one direction. The style, with its mingling of the technical and the colloquial, is close to Dr. Burney's; moreover, he had been elected to a fellowship of the Royal Society the previous year and early in 1776 would publish the first volume of his *History of Music*, much of it concerned with the Greeks. Thus it is more than likely that both reviewer and discreet person were none other than Dr. Burney himself and that the article conveys the impressions he had formed at Hinchingbrooke and St. Martin's Street.[56]

Omai sang no more for the Burneys. When he next appeared at Newton House late in December he was accompanied by Mr. Andrews, a gentleman who was hitherto unknown to Fanny and who, she said, spoke Tahitian very well. This, she complained, they had reason to regret, as it rendered their guest far less entertaining than during his previous call when he was obliged, in spite of the difficulties, to explain himself as well as he could. Now, with Mr. Andrews ready as interpreter, he gave himself very little trouble to speak English. Omai was, of course, no longer a novelty and in any case this latest visit was overshadowed by a more momentous event recorded in the same entry of Fanny's diary. 'My brother James,' she wrote, 'to our great joy and satisfaction, is returned from America, which he has left in most terrible disorder.' He was extremely well in health and spirits, she reported, and though suffering great hardships, had nevertheless honourably increased his friends and gained in reputation. He was, she concluded, in good time for 'his favourite voyage to the South Seas' which was to 'convoy' his friend Omai home and would, they believed, take place in February.[57]

Time was indeed running out. When the year ended, Mr. Banks or his book-keeper drew up a second financial statement, 'Expences incurrd on account of Omai in the Course of the Year — 1775'. The largest single item was £160-0-0, being 'One Years Board & Lodging for Himself and Mr Andrews' paid to 'Mr D^e Vignolles' and already authorized by Lord Sandwich in August 1774. (Mr. Andrews's emolument seems to have been more than adequate since his only recorded appearance as escort was at St. Martin's Street.) Omai's landlord also received £6-14-0 for 'Necessaries laid in, when he came into his Lodgings' and a further £18-4-1 for 'Necessaries' bought later in the year. One composite item, 'Money advanced by me', covered Banks's allowance to his charge, varying from quarter to quarter: ten guineas for the first, sixteen for the second, five for the third (mainly taken up by the *Augusta* cruise and the northern tour), and fifteen for the last. 'Cash Advanced by Lord Sandwich' was a modest two guineas, while 'Roberts' (presumably Banks's servant) received £2-19-6½ for undisclosed services. This account was more explicit than the first regarding Omai's transactions with various tradesmen: his 'Taylors 2 Bills' amounted to £52-0-4, and he spent £16-10-0 on wine; among lesser items, £3-13-0 went to his hair-dresser, £4-0-0 to his shoemaker, and three guineas to his apothecary. The total amounted to the not inconsiderable sum of £317-11-11½, and on this occasion there was no credit entry. Perhaps his patrons had reason for urging, 'Omy, you go home.'[58]

8. Omai's Farewell

THE YEAR 1776 OPENED WITH A SPELL OF SEVERE WEATHER UNPARALLELED IN England for decades. On 7 January much of the country was covered by the 'greatest fall of snow . . . in the memory of man', accompanied by a strong easterly wind that piled up drifts to 'an incredible depth'. Flocks of sheep were buried, carriages overturned or immobilized, roads made impassable. Deaths from accident or exposure were of daily occurrence, while the miseries of the poor were such that charitable public men took the lead in raising funds for their relief.[1] Among these benefactors the newspapers specially singled out Henry Thrale Esq., wealthy brewer and member of parliament, who gave a hundred guineas for distribution in his constituency of Southwark. As one bleak day succeeded another, there was no sign of improvement; conditions, in fact, seemed to worsen. By the middle of the month many ships loaded and ready for sailing were frozen up in the Thames and soon their crews were walking over the ice to exchange visits. On the 20th, stated the *General Evening Post*, the degrees of cold on a thermoscope owned by Robert Chequeleigh Esq. of Marybone 'exceeded any felt in England for these twenty years past.' A black servant who was employed by the same gentleman and had been in the country about half a year, the report continued, on being asked to go an errand, absolutely refused, 'as he had never seen any snow in his life before'. Then, by accident or design, followed another paragraph: 'Omiah, the native of Otaheite, has, for some days past, been endeavouring to skait on the Serpentine river in Hyde-park, and considering the short time he has practised, is wonderfully proficient.'[2]

Lichtenberg, the witness to Omai's discomfort in the previous winter, might have found in these contrasting items further proof of the Polynesian's superiority to the Negro. He certainly seems to have adapted himself with remarkable ease to the inclemencies of the English climate and now pursued the art of ice-skating with the zeal he had already displayed for shooting and horse-riding. His latest exploit had indeed brought him belatedly to the notice of the supreme connoisseur of celebrities. Writing on 28 January to Sir Horace Mann in Florence, Horace Walpole, stricken with gout after a drive through 'mountains of snow and quarries of ice', complained of the bitter weather: it was made for the North Pole, had lasted three weeks, grew worse every day. Parliament, he informed his correspondent, had met but two-thirds of the members were 'frozen in the country'. 'Omiah, the native of Otaheite,' he went on, 'breakfasted with Mr. Conway to-day, and learns to skate. He had no notion of ice, and calls it *stone-water*; a very good expression. If he was in Ireland they would advise him to carry some over in spirits.' The brief anecdote with its last obscure quip relieved the gloom of a letter deploring not only the weather but the course of American affairs: the government was raising a great army of Hessians and Brunswickers that would cost millions; Boston was famishing; the fate of Quebec was not yet known.[3]

There is no evidence — and small probability — that Horace Walpole sought out the denizen of a region he held in so much contempt. But in his cousin Mr. Conway Omai had made a notable and sympathetic addition to the circle of his aristocratic acquaintance. General the Hon. Henry Seymour Conway, M.P. for Bury St. Edmunds, was not only distinguished as a soldier and politician but known for his liberal and independent views. He supported the cause of the American colonists and ten years earlier had arranged for the award of a royal pension to Rousseau while he sheltered in England from his enemies. In the long succession of Omai's hosts Conway was as likely as any to have examined him in the light of that philosopher's theories. Did he then attempt to discern beneath European costume and European manners the lineaments of natural man? Did he probe through the visitor's cara-pace of politeness to discover his real views on the world about him? Possibly the veteran of Fontenoy and future field-marshal preferred to discuss military tactics with the warrior from the South Seas.[4] Or in the absence of an interpreter (for by this time Mr. Andrews seems to have relinquished his sinecure), their conversation might well have foundered on the rock of Omai's incomprehensibility.

Breakfast at Mr. Conway's did not mark the close of Omai's career in English society, but an end was now in sight. The day before that regrettably unrecorded function a paragraph appeared in the news-papers:

Captain Cook in the new voyage which he is going to make (Captain Clarke the commander of the second ship) is to take Omiah to Otaheite, and from thence to proceed upon the discovery of the North-West Passage to the north-ward of California. Parliament has just offered 25,000 l. reward, 20,000 l. to those who approach within one degree of the Pole; but there are to be no Botanists, Designers, &c. to accompany them.[5]

The announcement was not wholly accurate and seems to have been a trifle premature. In the previous December, after further discussions between the First Lord and members of the Royal Society, a bill had been passed offering £20,000 for the discovery of a northern route between the Pacific and the Atlantic, with an additional prize of £5000 for the first ship to sail within a degree of the North Pole. The prospect of sharing in this reward doubtless had some part — if only a minor part — in Cook's actions. He had already been drawn into negotiations for the purchase of a ship to accompany the *Resolution*, but it was not until 10 February that he offered his services as leader, prudently requesting that on his return he should be restored to his post in Greenwich Hospital or receive some 'other mark of the Royal Favour'. The same day he wrote to his French correspondent Latouche-Tréville to tell him the news. Arrangements, he said, had just been completed for the dispatch of two ships to the Pacific towards the end of April with himself in command. He passed over the expedition's larger aims, merely stating that its first object would be 'de reconduire Omaï dans son isle'.[6]

THE PROSPECT OF OMAI'S EARLY DEPARTURE brought to the surface issues which had long been impending. From time to time in the past eighteen months critical observers had complained of the manner in which the visitor from the South Seas had been decked out like a 'macaroni', paraded as a 'shew' by his worldly patrons, and denied the tuition he himself craved for. Only recently Sir John Cullum, who had already censured Banks on this score, gave a further hint of his disapproval while discussing with Michael Tyson his latest excursion to London. He had spent an evening at Enfield, he told his friend, and at the house of Captain Blake seen a unique volume of Chinese botanical drawings 'executed by Artists of the Country, under the Inspection of the Captain's Son'. In addition he had met Blake's Chinese pupil who was then on the eve of leaving England. Unfortunately he failed to give the exotic visitor's name but did remark that the captain's daughters had 'taken great Pains with him in teaching him to read, and to behave himself properly.' He had, Cullum commented, 'infinitely the Advantage of Omai, by having been in better Hands . . . .'[7]

Other high-minded persons held similar opinions and marshalled their forces to remedy the shortcomings of Lord Sandwich and Mr. Banks. On 14 January (a Sunday) the pious Sir Harry Trelawny expressed his feelings in a letter to the Revd. Mr. Broughton of the Society for Promoting Christian Knowledge:

My present business justifies me I trust in writing on this sacred day, — it is to hint to you what has I doubt not, appeared to you as it does to me a strange and diabolical neglect — the non baptism & non instruction of the Indian omiah — he is brought here where the full light of the glorious Gospel shines unclouded; — and what has he learned. why, to make refinements on sin in his own country — . . . . Does it fall within the province of our Society to take some step in this basely neglected business? Zeal of souls with God's blessing might I should think suggest to us some method whereby to get him instructed, & ordained if found right.

Perhaps, Trelawny suggested, they should approach Lord Dartmouth;

he was now in power and a man 'rooted & grounded in the love of Christ'. Or might it not be worth while, he asked, to lay these considerations before a meeting of the Society?[8]

Either as a result of this move or independently, Omai's plight soon afterwards became the concern of a group of London philanthropists whose most active member was Granville Sharp. This dedicated man had already taken up the cause of African slaves and now through his brother William, a surgeon practising in the City, sought the help of Lord Sandwich's secretary, Mr. Joah Bates, in meeting the benighted voyager from the South Seas. 'Pray tell your brother Granville', wrote Bates, 'that I will not forget his commission about Omai. If it should be practicable to bring about an interview between them it will give me great pleasure, as well as himself.' In a diffident reply Granville sent thanks to Mr. Bates but didn't think he was capable of expressing himself properly in discourse with the islander, for he had 'no talent at talking'. He meant to consult the Bishop of Llandaff, he said, about some proper person to instruct the young man in the first principles of the Christian religion. Writing on 17 February, Dr. Jekyll, another member of the circle, praised Granville for the benevolent interest he was taking in Omai. 'But', he hinted darkly, 'if the representations made of him to me are just, I fear that you will have more difficulties than that of language to encounter.' At the same time he thought the present peace and welfare of a fellow creature (and perhaps of hundreds through him) was an object of sufficient importance to support a Christian in the most arduous undertaking. 'I shall be happy in attending you on Monday morning,' he concluded, 'and wish it may be in my power to contribute to the charitable work.'[9]

From his own notes it is clear that, with or without the Bishop of Llandaff's advice and largely on his own account, Sharp had already committed himself to the undertaking so inauspiciously begun two years before in Queen Charlotte Sound. On 12 February he called on Mr. Bates at the Admiralty and received the First Lord's permission to proceed with the scheme. The following day he visited Mr. Banks and Omai 'by appointment' and on the 14th seems to have begun serious teaching at his brother's house in the Old Jewry. From then on for about a month he gave regular instruction, sometimes with Dr. Jekyll's assistance. A typical entry in his March notes reads: '8th. Omai came for three hours; and 9th, for two hours with Dr. Jekyll.' On the 11th and the 13th he again came for two hours, but there is no further entry until the 26th when 'Omai called, but had no time for a lesson.' On both 28 March and 4 April he was with Sharp 'for a very short time' and on the 6th, the final entry: 'Omai was so taken up with engagements that I could have no more opportunity of giving him lessons, which were but fifteen in all.' However, Sharp consoled himself, he had taught his pupil the use of English letters and made him sound 'every combination of vowels and consonants that letters are capable of: and he afterwards wrote a letter to Dr. Solander . . . .'[10]

39 *Miss Martha Ray, after Nathaniel Dance*

Apart from Sharp's own modest claim, there is no evidence of the success or failure of his didactic efforts. Neither the letter to Solander nor any other example of Omai's penmanship seems to have survived. That his mentor possessed even less talent for teaching than he did for talking is strongly suggested by *An English Alphabet, for the use of Foreigners: wherein the Pronunciation of the Vowels, or Voice-Letters, is explained in Twelve short general Rules, With their several Exceptions, As Abridged (For the Instruction of Omai) From a larger Work*. This pamphlet by Sharp, published a decade later, is hardly a model of lucid exposition. What, for example, did Omai make of Rule 2 ? It ran:

> *The* vowels *are pronounced short in all syllables ending with a consonant, (except in the particular cases hereafter noted,) and the three first vowels have the foreign articulation, without any other material difference except that of being pronounced short.*

Appended texts — the Lord's Prayer, the Creed, the Ten Commandments — would also have created formidable problems for the Polynesian eye and mind, even though they were 'divided into syllables, (according to the *rule for spelling* recommended by the learned Bishop Lowth,) with references placed to those syllables which are *exceptions* to the several *rules* laid down in this book respecting the pronunciation of vowels and diphthongs.'[11]

Sharp's concern, as his biographer emphasizes, was not merely with language nor with one solitary proselyte. Through Omai he hoped to diffuse 'Christian light over a new race of men'; and in attaining that object the teaching of English was only a preliminary step. How far he succeeded in these larger aims is also uncertain. There is nothing to suggest that his pupil was ever baptized, let alone ordained. To judge from Sharp's own testimony, however, he did contrive to impart to the young pagan (or more accurately to elicit from him) some understanding of moral principles. One day, he relates, when they were sitting at table after dinner, he thought it a good opportunity to explain the Ten Commandments. He proceeded with tolerable success through the first six, pausing occasionally to define a term, but when they reached the seventh Omai asked: '"Adultery! what that? what that?"' Sharp described the ensuing debate in an address he prepared long afterwards for the Maroons of Sierra Leone (a people regrettably addicted to the practice of polygamy):

> 'Not to commit adultery,' I said, 'is that, if a man has got one wife, he must not take another wife, or any other woman.' — 'Oh!' says he, 'two wives — very good; three wives — very, very good.' — 'No, Mr. Omai,' I said, 'not so; that would be contrary to the first principle of the law of nature.' — 'First principle of the law of nature,' said he; 'what that? what that?' — '*The first principle of the law of nature,*' I said, 'is, that *no man must do to another person any thing that he would not like to be done to himself*. And, for example, Mr. Omai,' said I, 'suppose you have got a wife that you love very

much; you would not like that another man should come to love your wife.'
This raised his indignation: he put on a furious countenance, and a threatening
posture, signifying that he would kill any man that should meddle with his
wife. 'Well, Mr. Omai,' said I, 'suppose, then, that your wife loves you very
much; she would not like that you should love another woman: for the women
have the same passions, and feelings, and love towards the men, that we have
towards the women . . . .'[12]

At the end of this speech Omai lapsed into reflective silence, but he
soon gave ample proof that he understood Sharp's meaning and, more
than that, the nature of the relations between the First Lord and Miss
Ray (or Miss Wray, as she was known to many of her contemporaries).
Taking one pen from an ink-stand, he laid it on the table with the
explanation:

'There lies Lord S———' (a Nobleman with whom he was well acquainted,
and in whose family he had spent some time); and then he took another pen,
and laid it close by the side of the former pen, saying, 'and there lies Miss
W———' (who was an accomplished young woman in many respects, but,
unhappily for herself, she lived in a state of adultery with that nobleman); and
he then took a third pen, and placing it on the table at a considerable distance
from the other two pens, as far as his right arm could extend, and at the same
time leaning his head upon his left hand, supported by his elbow on the table,
in a pensive posture, he said, 'and there lie Lady S———, and cry!'

Sharp was convinced that his pupil thoroughly understood 'the gross
injury done to the married lady by her husband in taking another woman
to his bed.' 'There was no need', he ended, 'to explain the rights of
women any farther to Mr. Omai on that occasion.'[13]

IT IS AGAIN DOUBTFUL whether Omai profited from Granville Sharp's
moral teaching; the meagre records that survive of his final weeks in
England tend to suggest otherwise. If Fanny Burney's testimony is
accepted, he seems to have continued his wayward course through the
world of fashion. Indeed, the last glimpse she provides of Jem's shipboard friend depicts him — and also herself — in a most unflattering
light. Writing to Mr. Crisp early in April (when Omai was forced to
give up his lessons through the press of 'engagements'), she described a
visit to the Park one Sunday morning and her surprise at the 'undressed
& slaternly' appearance of the 'Young & handsome' Duchess of Devonshire. Two of her curls came quite unpinned, falling lank on her shoulder,
one shoe was down at heel, the trimming of her jacket and coat was in
some places unsewn, her cap was awry, and her cloak, which was rusty
and powdered, was flung half on and half off. 'Had she not had a servant
in a Superb Livery behind her,' Fanny commented, 'she would certainly
have been affronted.' The duchess certainly was affronted, as Fanny
herself disclosed; she concluded her account: 'Omai, who was in the
Park, called here this Morning, & says that he went to her Grace, &

asked her why she let her Hair go in that manner? Ha, Ha, Ha, — don't you Laugh at her having a Lesson of Attention from *an* Otaheitan?'[14]

Perhaps in response to a recent change in fashionable opinion, Fanny had evidently revised her former estimate of Omai. But even as she wrote he was enhancing his reputation for social poise and good manners in one of London's most exalted literary circles. It was about this time, in late March or early April, that he seems to have been taken up by the blue-stocking and ardent lion-hunter, Mrs. Thrale, who introduced him to the other celebrities she had gathered round her indulgent husband and herself at Streatham Park in Surrey. The principal and most formidable of her lions, Dr. Johnson, was, according to Boswell, struck by the elegance of Omai's behaviour and accounted for it thus: 'Sir, he had passed his time, while in England, only in the best company; so that all that he had acquired of our manners was genteel.' As proof of his statement, Johnson cited his experience with another member of Mrs. Thrale's entourage, the former Captain Phipps, to whom Omai required no introduction: '. . . Sir, Lord Mulgrave and he dined one day at Streatham; they sat with their backs to the light fronting me, so that I could not see distinctly; and there was so little of the savage in Omai, that I was afraid to speak to either, lest I should mistake one for the other.'[15]

The point of the comparison is somewhat blunted not only by the notorious fact of Johnson's short-sightedness but by Mrs. Thrale's recorded opinion that Mulgrave was 'Rough as a boatswain, and fond of coarse merriment approaching to ill manners'. There are, in addition, some grounds for supposing that in the Streatham circle the South Sea Islander's social graces, real or imagined, formed a convenient stick with which to beat one's adversaries. Of Johnson's old friend, who held the post of Italian master to her eldest daughter, Mrs. Thrale remarked, 'When Omai played at chess and at backgammon with Baretti, everybody admired at the savage's good breeding and at the European's impatient spirit.' Or, as another version has it, 'You would [have] thought Omai the Christian, and Baretti the Savage.'[16]

Boswell, one of Rousseau's most fervent British disciples, apparently made no attempt to inspect this specimen of natural man (another fact suggesting a recent slump in Omai's reputation). But the assiduous hero-worshipper sought out Captain Cook several times in the spring of 1776. They first met on 3 April, soon after Cook's election to a fellowship of the Royal Society, when the 'celebrated circumnavigator' and his wife were among the guests at a dinner given by Sir John Pringle. The host had already described the captain as 'a plain, sensible man with an uncommon attention to veracity' and to illustrate the last quality mentioned an incident concerning Lord Monboddo. The judge had been very pleased to hear that Cook claimed to have seen a nation of men like monkeys, but when Sir John mentioned this to Cook himself he denied having spoken in such terms: '"No," said he, "I did not say they were like monkeys. I said their faces put me in mind of monkeys."' Boswell thought the distinction 'very fine but sufficiently perceptible' and at this function found the captain not only 'very obliging and communicative' but modest — he 'seemed to have no desire to make people stare'. In their conversation (apparently confined to the South Seas) Cook, 'being a man of good steady moral principles . . . did not try to make theories out of what he had seen to confound virtue and vice.' Hawkesworth, he complained, had drawn 'a general conclusion from a particular fact, and would take as a fact what they had only heard.' A 'disregard of chastity in unmarried women', he instanced, 'was by no means general at Otaheite'. As for the assertion that he and Mr. Banks had revised all the book, it was quite untrue — Hawkesworth, asserted Cook, would make no alteration (or such was Boswell's impression).[17]

At one point the discussion turned to Omai who, according to Cook, begged to have two things to carry back, 'port wine, which he loved the best of any liquor, and gunpowder'. He would not let him have 'the power of fire-arms', Cook declared, because he supposed the young islander wished to have them 'from some ambitious design'. 'He said', Boswell continued, 'that for some time after Omai's return home he would be a man of great consequence, as having so many wonders to tell.' Yet Omai 'would not foresee that when he had told all he had to tell, he would sink into his former state, and then, the Captain supposed, he would wish to go to England again'; however, Boswell reported, 'the Captain would take care to leave the coast before Omai had time to be dissatisfied at home.' 'It was curious', the diarist finally reflected, 'to see Cook, a grave steady man, and his wife, a decent plump Englishwoman, and think that he was preparing to sail round the world.'[18]

Inspired by this meeting, Boswell now pictured himself in the role of circumnavigator and hastened to discuss the idea with Dr. Johnson. Arriving at Bolt Court the next morning, he found the sage, gloved and dusty, putting his books in order, 'quite in the character which Dr. Boswell drew of him: "A robust genius! born to grapple with whole libraries!"' The ensuing interchange, as recorded in Boswell's journal, went thus:

I gave him an account of Captain Cook, and told him I felt, while I was with the Captain, an inclination to make the voyage. 'Why, so one does,' said the Doctor, 'till one considers how very little one learns.' I said I was certain a great part of what we are told by the travellers to the South Sea Islands must be conjecture, because they cannot know language enough to understand so much as they tell. The Doctor was of that opinion. 'But,' said I, 'one is carried away with the thing in general, a voyage round the world.' 'Yes,' said he, 'but one is to guard against taking a thing in general.'[19]

Boswell's ardour was not entirely quenched by this mild rebuke, and a fortnight later he returned to the exciting topic of global travel. On that day, 18 April, while dining at the Mitre with Sir John Pringle, Dr. Solander, Mr. Banks, and other notables of the Royal Society, he contrived to place himself next to its latest luminary. Cook discussed the problems of interpreting an unknown tongue and, confirming Boswell's own belief,

III Head of Omai by Sir Joshua Reynolds, c. 1775

candidly confessed . . . that he and his companions who visited the South Sea Islands could not be certain of any information they got, or supposed they got, except as to objects falling under the observation of the senses; their knowledge of the language was so imperfect they required the aid of their senses, and anything which they learnt about religion, government, or traditions might be quite erroneous.

As an example of direct sensory experience, he gave Boswell 'a distinct account of a New Zealander eating human flesh in his presence and in that of many more aboard' so that 'the fact of cannibals' was 'now certainly known.' They next discussed 'having some men of inquiry left for three years at each of the islands of Otaheite, New Zealand, and Nova Caledonia, so as to learn the language and . . . bring home a full account of all that can be known of people in a state so different from ours.' The scheme made a strong personal appeal to the mercurial but not wholly disinterested Boswell. 'I felt', he wrote, 'a stirring in my mind to go upon such an undertaking, if encouraged by Government by having a handsome pension for life.'[20]

The last meeting took place at Cook's home in the Mile End Road where they had tea in the garden and a blackbird sang — a 'quite pleasant' experience that apparently did nothing to quell Boswell's enthusiasm for his latest project. He was given no encouragement, however, when towards the end of April he followed Johnson and the Thrales to Bath and again aired his aspirations. As he relates the incident in the *Life*, 'a gentleman' (obviously Boswell himself)

expressed a wish to go and live three years at Otaheité, or New-Zealand, in order to obtain a full acquaintance with people, so totally different from all that we have ever known, and be satisfied what pure nature can do for man. JOHNSON. 'What could you learn, Sir? What can savages tell, but what they themselves have seen? Of the past, or the invisible, they can tell nothing. The inhabitants of Otaheité and New-Zealand are not in a state of pure nature; for it is plain they broke off from some other people. Had they grown out of the ground, you might have judged of a state of pure nature . . . .'[21]

Nothing more was heard of Boswell's plan for self-exile in Tahiti or New Zealand (preferably the former, one would imagine). Soon, however, another member of the Streatham circle, scarcely less illustrious than Dr. Johnson, was to present to the public his own eloquent comment on the theme of savage man. Since he last exhibited at the Royal Academy in the spring of 1775, Sir Joshua Reynolds had been pursuing his industrious, prolific career. He had painted numerous portraits of aristocrats and other personages of the fashionable world — among them 'Richard, Earl Temple', 'Georgiana, Duchess of Devonshire', 'David Garrick', and perhaps 'Henry Thrale'; he had painted more of those renderings of childhood in which he sometimes anticipated the mood of his romantic successors — the 'Infant Samuel', 'Master Crewe'; and he had painted contrasting studies of two migrants from distant parts of the earth. To this period probably belongs the modest and

charming likeness of an oriental youth known as 'Wang-y-tong' (whose
model, it seems, was none other than Captain Blake's nameless pupil
mentioned in Cullum's letter to his friend Tyson). And to the years 1775
or 1776 can be assigned with greater certainty the elaborate full-length
'Omai'.[22]

Owing to the loss of Reynolds's engagement books for the years 1774
to 1776, 'Omai' cannot be dated with absolute precision. All things
considered, the sittings were most likely arranged during the obscure
weeks late in 1775 after the excursion to Yorkshire. Probably uncom-
missioned (for it was still in the studio four years later), the work was
carried out with exceptional care. Contrary to his usual practice,
Reynolds did not paint directly on the canvas but first made two preliminary studies of the subject's head. One, a pencil drawing, is a
masterly rendering of the young man's features — the long, straight,
black hair, the broad forehead, the alert dark eyes, the flat, fleshy nose,
the full lips, the slightly receding jaw. This is not the Europeanized
native of a Cipriani or a Bartolozzi but recognizably the representative
of a new race, a Polynesian. Equally striking in its own way is a sketch
in oils which long afterwards Hoppner thought 'as fine as Titian'.[23] It is
certainly a fine work of art but as a likeness it falls far short of the
drawing. Though pose and features are similar, the sharp clarity of the
pencil study has gone and Omai is shown as a brooding, enigmatic
presence, handsome half-brother to Caliban.

Poetic transformation went a stage farther in the finished painting
which Reynolds showed at the Royal Academy's exhibition in Pall Mall
early in May. Oddly enough in the light of Fanny Burney's remarks,
'Omai' hung with another work of the same large dimensions, 'Georgiana,
Duchess of Devonshire'.[24] No longer in slatternly disarray, her grace is
seen in park-like surroundings, her abundant draperies and lofty coiffure
combining with the sylvan properties of the picture to reduce her glazed,
doll-like face to insignificance. The painting is not so much an example
of portraiture as a tribute from the high priest of eighteenth-century art
to one of the avatars of rank and fashion. 'Omai' is equally remote from
the literal truth of the model's appearance as it was rendered by
Nathaniel Dance or Reynolds himself in his preliminary drawing. Robed
and turbanned, he is flanked on his right by a tropical palm while to
the left a romantic landscape recedes into the distance. In this exotic
setting he stands like an African princeling, one tattooed hand out-
stretched as if in declamation, his handsome, now somewhat negroid
features composed in an expression of benign authority. The painting
depicts not only an idealized Omai but one of the several conceptions
he embodied in the eyes of European observers — the nobility and
dignity of natural man. At some time the portrait was copied by one of
Reynolds's assistants, James Northcote, and in 1777 engraved by a visiting
German, Johann Jacobé (or John Jacobi). It was through the latter
version that the most exalted image of Britain's first Polynesian visitor
became familiar to the eighteenth-century public.[25]

40 *Head of Omai by Sir Joshua Reynolds, c. 1775*

41
*Georgiana
Duchess of
Devonshire
by Reynolds*

APRIL HAD COME AND GONE, the month of May was slipping by, but there was still no sign of the expedition's early departure. Apparently Cook had underestimated the time needed to organize the new venture and, furthermore, had failed to anticipate the problems that would arise when he became chronicler — or co-chronicler — of the previous voyage. On this occasion Sandwich and his advisers, firmly ruling out the possibility of another Hawkesworth, decided in favour of two authors with first-hand experience of the events recorded, John Reinhold Forster and Cook himself. Their association on the *Resolution* had not been happy, but no open breach had occurred and soon after their return they agreed on a loosely defined scheme of collaboration. By September, as the letter from William Watson to Edward Wortley Montagu indicates, the fact was common knowledge. For some months, under the First Lord's general direction, both men worked independently on their manuscripts, Cook with editorial assistance from the Revd. John Douglas, Canon of Windsor. By April it was apparent that the narratives overlapped, and on the 13th Sandwich arranged a conference with the authors to determine their respective limits. An understanding was then reached that the account of the voyage would be issued in two volumes — the first Cook's revised journal, the second a treatise, part scientific, part philosophical, on Forster's discoveries in natural history and his observations of native peoples. The authors would share both the costs and the profits of publication and the Admiralty would pay for the engraving of plates.[26]

Since February Cook's literary labours had been combined with his exacting duties as leader of the expedition. Even before finally committing himself, he had been called on to advise on the purchase of an escort vessel, the *Diligence*, which was renamed the *Discovery*. A month later, on taking command of the *Resolution*, he opened a vast correspondence with Admiralty officials on the equipment and provisioning of the two ships. With a strict regard for the courtesies and the formalities, he asked whether it might not please the Lords Commissioners to order the Commissioners of the Sick and Hurt to supply His Majesty's sloops with portable soup. It was well known, he observed in his next communication, that the crews of His Majesty's sloops during the late voyage received great benefit from 'Sour Krout and Malt'. Might it now please the Lords Commissioners to order the Victualling Board to supply those items to the *Resolution* and the *Discovery*? Early in March he took the liberty of enumerating articles which might be ordered if they met with their Lordships' approbation; they would be exchanged with the natives for refreshments or 'distributed to them in presents towards obtaining their friendship'. There followed a lengthy list of axes, hatchets, chisels, beads, fish-hooks, etc. with such additional commodities as 'Old Shirts, not patched', 'Red Baize', 'Old Cloathes', and 'Fine old Sheets'. Polite requests were sent for 'Inspissated Juice of Wort' and 'Corn'd Powder', requisitions went out for worsted caps and kersey jackets and linsey drawers, for an azimuth compass and a tent observatory, for port wine, muscovado sugar, and a thousand things more.[27]

The manning of the two ships was not entirely Cook's responsibility, but there is little doubt that his views on the choice of officers and men were decisive. Tried veterans, it is noticeable, filled the senior posts. Charles Clerke, who according to Solander and the newspapers was first chosen to carry Omai home, had sailed with the two previous expeditions and was now in charge of the *Discovery* and second in command. His first lieutenant was James Burney, while Cook's was Banks's companion in Iceland, the widely travelled John Gore, setting out on his fourth voyage of circumnavigation. Other veterans held various appointments on both ships: the *Resolution*'s surgeon was the talented William Anderson, the quartermaster Patrick Whelan, the master's mate William Harvey; George Vancouver, still classed as midshipman, travelled on the *Discovery* with such old Pacific hands as William Peckover, gunner, and Peter Reynolds, carpenter's mate. All had already served on the *Resolution* or the *Endeavour* or both. Among newcomers notable for one reason or another were Second Lieutenant King of the *Resolution*, its master William Bligh, one of its midshipmen, John Watts, Anderson's mate David Samwell, and Second Lieutenant John Rickman of the *Discovery*.[28]

In the matter of supernumeraries Cook's opinion again seems to have been decisive. Perhaps it was he who inspired the emphatic conclusion to the newspaper report announcing his appointment: that on the coming voyage there were to be 'no Botanists, Designers, &c.'. Some support is given to this conjecture in a conversation recorded by the elder Forster. On being posted to the *Resolution*, he wrote, Mr. King

'visited the Captain, and told him he considered himself fortunate to be making this important voyage with so great a navigator, but at the same time he expressed his regret that there were no scientists accompanying the expedition, as had been the case with the former expeditions. Cook, whose head had been turned by Lord Sandwich, said, "Curse the scientists, and all science into the bargain." This discourteous reply so shocked Mr. King that he repeated it to me the next day, and his respect for the man under whose command he was to sail was considerably diminished until I took the opportunity of setting things right by describing Cook's character and pointing out that it was in reality not so bad as it appeared, but that he was a cross-grained fellow who sometimes showed a mean disposition and was carried away by a hasty temper . . . .'[29]

Forster's assertions, coloured as they were by his manifold grievances, must be treated with reserve. But Cook's words at least have the ring of truth, and the fact remains that on this voyage, apart from the veteran Mr. Bayly who was astronomer on the *Discovery*, there were no professional men of science. Rather than risk another quarrelsome Forster or temperamental Banks, the commander evidently decided to draw on Anderson's talents in natural history and, for astronomical expertise on the *Resolution*, to rely on the scholarly King and himself.

As for 'Designers', nothing was done until the last possible moment when, fortunately for posterity, enlightened Admiralty officials engaged 'Mr John Webber Draughtsman and Landskip Painter' and dispatched him to the *Resolution*.[30]

The two ingenious gentlemen, it is reasonable to assume, had long since realized they would not be asked to accompany Cook and witness Omai's restoration to his native sphere. Dr. Lind must also have learned for a second time not to put his trust in the impetuous proposals of his English colleagues. If the little group of friends exchanged condolences or recriminations, the letters have not survived; but there is clear testimony that Solander, for one, continued to reflect on Tahiti and its bounteous resources. Writing to John Ellis on 4 May, he asserted: 'The Bread Fruit of the South Sea islands within the tropics, which was by us during several months daily eaten as a substitute for bread, was universally esteemed as palatable and as nourishing as bread itself.' It was undoubtedly of the greatest consequence, he urged, to bring so valuable a fruit to other countries where the climate favoured its cultivation.[31] Banks, too, while resigning himself to the bleak conclusion that he would not again botanize through the Pacific in person, contrived to salvage something from the wreck of half-formulated plans and hopes. He arranged for one of the Kew gardeners, David Nelson, to sail on the *Discovery*. Listed in the muster-roll as Mr. Bayly's servant, he was actually sent out to gather plants for his royal master and Mr. Banks.[32]

If less lavishly provided with men of learning than its predecessors, this expedition was better equipped to civilize the Pacific and demonstrate British power and goodwill. There was no question, as earlier rumoured, of establishing a settlement in New Zealand or New Caledonia, but everything possible was done to equip Cook and his men for their patriotic mission. The King himself supplied animals for the cause — a bull, two cows with their calves, a number of sheep — and one noble benefactor, Lord Bessborough, contributed a peacock and hen.[33] Sundry drafts and jottings among his papers also indicate that Banks was called in to advise on the choice of gifts: 'if his majesty should be graciously pleased to send any in his own name they must', he recommended, 'be of the finest materials such as cannot be Equald by those of the officers or seamen'; they should, moreover, be distributed 'among those Cheifs only who have shewn themselves best deserving of such honours'. A list of articles for worthy recipients is more varied and imaginative than Cook's. It includes such staple items as adzes and iron tools but also *'Lacd Hats & Feathers'*, *'Loose Gowns of Fine materials'*, *'Trousers of fine Linnen'*, *'Broad swords'*, *'Bowls of cut glass'*, *'Cases of Knives & Forks'*, *'Multiplying glasses'*, *'chess boards'*, *'spy glasses large'*. A corresponding list 'For the Ladies' similarly emphasized the ornamental rather than the useful: *'Paste pinns'*, *'Earings of cut paste'*, *'Coloured gauses'*, *'perfum'd waters & oils'*, *'Fanns'*, *'Hand skreens'*, *'Broad ribbons* of various colours', *'Handkercheifs with Great Britain* printed on them', then, more prosaically, *'Needles & thread Housewifes Pins bodkins'* and *'Soap'*.

A scribbled note mentioned *'the Kings picture'*, 'the Queens dº', 'Silver watches', and finally came an eloquent addendum, 'Medecines for the Venereal disease'.[34]

Banks singled out two inhabitants of the South Seas for special consideration. A brief memorandum headed 'Things intended to be sent to Odidde, an Indian who embarked on board the Resolution in order to have come home with Captain Cook, but left him on his second visit to the Island Otaheite' specified only '2 suits of cloaths with suitables' and 'a sword'. Articles to the value of nearly £50 were ultimately assigned to Cook's favourite, but in number and cost they were insignificant compared with the gifts lavished on Omai. At the behest of Sandwich a suit of armour had already been fashioned for him by artificers in the Tower. Now Banks ensured that on his return the young man would not entirely lack the luxuries and the conveniences of the life to which he had been introduced two years before. He was to be supplied with '4 Suits of cloaths of light materials, with a proper assortment of suitables', 'A few shoes & stockings extra', 'An assortment of linens', '2 suits of Women's cloaths compleat' (the last perhaps for presentation to his sisters). As a means of introducing European crafts and domestic habits to his fellow islanders he would be equipped with 'Assortment of Iron', '2 Whip saws', 'Planes', 'Files', 'A case of knives & forks', '12 pewter plates', 'Sauce pans & kettles for boiling', 'Mugs, glasses, & spoons', 'Flints & steels for striking fire', 'a table to be made on board', 'a Chair Ditto', 'a Field bed', 'a Chest of drawers', 'a Wheelbarrow to be made on board'. With '2 Drums' he would, in a modest way, be able to extend the range of Polynesian music; an 'Assortment of beads' would supply both personal ornaments and local currency; and with the aid of 'Toy models of horses, coaches, waggons, sedan chairs &c' he would, as Fanny Burney's friend Mrs. Strange had suggested, be more likely to convince sceptical islanders that these wonders really did exist. An afterthought, inserted beside the main list, recommended the highest honours: though not of chiefly rank, Omai would, like his betters, receive 'Kings picture', 'Queens dº-', 'Multiplying glasses', 'glass bowls', 'Hand skreens'.[35]

Thus Banks laboured to ensure Omai's future welfare and before the final parting did something to ensure that their association would be suitably commemorated. It was probably he who commissioned William Parry, a former pupil of Reynolds lately returned from Italy, to paint a large conversation piece set in the study of his country home — or such is the suggestion of a wooded vista seen through an open window at the right of the picture. Beneath it is the plump, benign Solander seated, pen in hand, at a writing-table. In the centre, dominating the composition, stands the masterful Banks who points with didactic or proprietary gesture towards the full-length figure of Omai on his right. This is the Omai of Dance rather than Reynolds, a native clad in stiff white robes, his plain Polynesian features marked by an expression of resolution mingled with sadness. Whether the painting represents the young man's mood towards the end of his stay cannot be ascertained, for its exact date is uncertain and neither Banks nor Solander left any record of their protégé at this period.[36] Indeed, of the whole Sandwich coterie only Joseph Cradock, writing half a century later, provides a glimpse of Omai on the eve of embarkation. At his home in Leicestershire, Cradock relates, he heard that the visitor was 'not at all concerned at the thoughts of leaving any of us' and consequently he himself felt 'rather vexed that we should have wasted so much anxiety about him'. But on returning to London, he 'met Omai on the raised pavement in Parliament-street, leading to the Admiralty,' and was strongly convinced to the contrary. 'He was miserable,' wrote the tender-hearted impresario, 'and I was never much more affected.'[37]

Whatever his feelings, Omai must again follow his destiny as preparations for departure went inexorably forward. His Majesty's ships *Resolution* and *Discovery* were completely fitted out for sea at Deptford, announced the newspapers on 28 May, and waited for nothing but sailing orders before they proceeded on their voyage to the South Seas for further discoveries. 'Yesterday', ran a brief paragraph on 11 June, 'Omiah, the Otaheitean, took his leave of his Majesty, and this day set out for Portsmouth, where he is to embark on board Capt. Cook's ship, in order to return home.' On the 13th, it was further reported, the captain had been similarly honoured by the King and in a few days would sail in company with the *Discovery*, Captain Clerke, now at Gravesend.[38] Finally, on the 18th, members of the public — in particular Granville Sharp and his friends — were doubtless gratified to read:

Omiah, who is now on board the Resolution, in order to return to Otaheite, has made such good use of his time while in England, that he was able to write his sentiments in our language: the following is a copy of the card he sent to several of his friends, which we give upon the best authority.

'Omiah to take leave of good friend. He never forget England. He go on 'Sunday. God bless King George. He tell his people how kind English to him.'[39]

Some of these statements (though not certainly the last) conveyed speculation and intention rather than accomplished fact. Omai did not board the *Resolution* until later in the month and then he was in Cook's company, bound not for Portsmouth but Plymouth. Various complications had held up both captains and delayed their departure. The quixotic Clerke, who had made himself responsible for his brother's debts, was detained in the King's Bench prison. So, when the *Discovery* sailed from Long Reach on 16 June, Lieutenant Burney was temporarily in command.[40] Cook for his part was still putting the finishing touches to his account of the previous voyage and received permission to stay on till arrangements for its publication were settled. Not surprisingly, the scheme of joint authorship had broken down, mainly through Forster's refusal to permit alterations to his work. Troubled by no such scruples, Cook continued in amicable consultation with Canon Douglas. Writing on the 14th, he told his editor that the night before he had used all arguments to persuade Dr. Forster to submit, 'but to no manner of purpose'. He went on to discuss the plates for his book and enclosed further copy, 'a paper concerning Omai' prepared by 'My Lord Sandwich' and 'tack'd in its proper place' in the manuscript. The introduction, he promised, would go 'by the Stage' tomorrow. On the 23rd he sent Douglas his last message: it was now settled that he was to publish without Mr. Forster; the next morning he would set out to join his ship at the Nore whence it would make for Plymouth.[41]

THE 'PAPER CONCERNING OMAI' was the basis for one of several valedictory compositions that appeared after the visitor's departure. When published a year later in *A Voyage towards the South Pole*, it combined the views of both Cook and Sandwich whose drafts had doubtless been reconciled and edited by Douglas. For these reasons it is not easy to identify the separate contributions. Cook, the nominal author, was probably responsible for introductory remarks where he made handsome amends for his earlier uncomplimentary description of Omai as 'dark, ugly and a downright blackguard'. Heavily deleting those words, he wrote more mildly in his account of the *Resolution* and the *Adventure* at Huahine:

> Before we quitted this island, Captain Furneaux agreed to receive on board his ship a young man named Omai, a native of Ulietea, where he had some property, of which he had been dispossessed by the people of Bolabola. I at first rather wondered that Captain Furneaux would encumber himself with this man, who, in my opinion, was not a proper sample of the inhabitants of these happy islands, not having any advantage of birth, or acquired rank; nor being eminent in shape, figure, or complexion. For their people of the first rank are much fairer, and usually better behaved, and more intelligent than the middling class of people, among whom Omai is to be ranked.

Since his own arrival in England, Cook generously acknowledged, he had become convinced of his error; for, except in the matter of complexion (and Omai's was undoubtedly of a deeper hue than that of 'the *Earees* or gentry' who lived a more luxurious life and were less exposed to the sun), he much doubted whether any other native would have given more general satisfaction by his behaviour.[42]

There followed a catalogue of the exemplary native's virtues: his 'very good understanding'; his 'quick parts'; his 'honest principles'; the 'natural good behaviour, which rendered him acceptable to the best company'; and 'a proper degree of pride, which taught him to avoid the society of persons of inferior rank'. With his limited knowledge of Omai at this period, Cook could hardly have committed himself to such specific and undiluted praise. But, after observing his guest at close quarters on the *Augusta* and at Hinchingbrooke, Sandwich was well qualified to do so; and in a further tribute there seem to be faint echoes of the solicitous letter he wrote to Banks in December 1774:

He has passions of the same kind as other young men, but has judgment enough not to indulge them in an improper excess. I do not imagine that he has any dislike to liquor . . . but fortunately for him, he perceived that drinking was very little in use but among inferior people, and as he was very watchful into the manners and conduct of the persons of rank who honoured him with their protection, he was sober and modest, and I never heard that, during the whole time of his stay in England, which was two years, he ever once was disguised with wine, or ever showed an inclination to go beyond the strictest rules of moderation.[43]

In a final paragraph, where it is even more difficult to disentangle the views and compliments of His Majesty's loyal subjects, the events of Omai's stay were summarized. Soon after his arrival, in this version, the Earl of Sandwich introduced him to the King at Kew 'when he met with a most gracious reception, and imbibed the strongest impression of duty and gratitude to that great and amiable prince' — an impression, it was confidently predicted, he would 'preserve to the latest moment of his life'. During his stay, the account continued, 'he was caressed by many of the principal nobility, and did nothing to forfeit the esteem of any one of them; but his principal patrons were the Earl of Sandwich, Mr. Banks, and Dr. Solander'. While Omai lived in the midst of amusements in England, it was noted, his return was always in his thoughts and, though not impatient to go, he expressed satisfaction as the time approached. 'He embarked with me in the Resolution,' anticipated the author, '. . . loaded with presents from his several friends, and full of gratitude for the kind reception and treatment he had experienced among us.'[44]

These proceedings were viewed in a rather different light by two satirists who, a little belatedly, had been sharpening their quills. Some weeks after the *Resolution* sailed, G. Kearsly of Fleet Street published the anonymous *Omiah's Farewell; inscribed to the Ladies of London*. A further but not final addition to the Oberea sequence, it marked another stage in the reaction against earlier journalistic excesses and fashionable adulation. A long, rambling, often incoherent preface opened: 'When we consider the great civilities which have been shown to OMIAH, the native of *Otaheitée*, it is no longer a surprize that he should leave such a situation with regret, as the great personages of this kingdom were assiduous to do him favours.' Like the Duenna, this 'exotic' had become 'a very favourite' and people contended who could see him most, not for his intrinsic merits but 'to surpass each other in an extravagant absurdity'. Besides correcting popular misconceptions, the writer supplied details of Omiah's origins, appearance, and attainments. He was 'an Indian of a low descent, and not of the order of priesthood, as hath been erroneously represented.' His visit to Europe was not at first approved by 'OBEREA, his Queen', but her favourite voyagers overruled her objections and he followed the ill-fated Tupia. His age was twenty-three, his complexion a dark copper colour, and though well made, his

legs were 'of that particular bowed make peculiar to all the natives of
Guinea'. His 'address' was 'uncommonly courteous' and even carried
with it 'the air of some breeding'. On the other hand, his 'parts' were
but dull, for, despite his long stay in England, he could scarce speak
the language, 'only uttering incoherent words'. He could give but little
account of his own country, and it was to be feared he would be unable
to describe what he had seen in this one. Not for the first time he was
unfavourably compared with another voyager from distant parts: 'The
Chinese man brought over by Captain BLAKE, was in ability a *Confucius*
to him, and in very good English he would relate the customs and
produce of *China* in an informing and most pleasing manner.'[45]

The same process of critical deflation was applied to Omiah's guardians
who were censured for 'dressing him out in a bag and sword, and leading
him forth to all public spectacles'. At this point the writer introduced a
novel variation on the views of previous commentators. In his opinion
Omiah should have been instructed not in spiritual matters or the art of
writing but in medical knowledge which, on returning home, he could
have applied to his 'uninformed fellow creatures' — those once 'innocent
mortals in a simple state of nature' now afflicted with 'dreadful diseases'.
Possibly through some association of ideas, there followed references to
Omiah's intimacy with 'women of quality' coupled with sly allusions to
'the depravity of female inclinations'. No mention was made of Banks
and Solander, but the First Lord was singled out for special consideration:

OMIAH's introduction to Court was by Lord S*******, who has always honoured
him with a peculiar attention, and carried him over the most pleasing parts of
the kingdom: OMIAH in return, has not been ungrateful in his particular
attentions to his Lordship's family. There are various little anecdotes related
of him at H*************, but as trivial as possible, and unworthy a repetition; his animal powers were his best, and those he used with freedom and
success . . . .[46]

From Lord Sandwich and Omiah's unnamed — or perhaps unspeak-
able — liberties at Hinchingbrooke the censorious spotlight was turned
on His Majesty who, without benefit of asterisks, was castigated for
speaking of navigators as 'the first ornaments of his reign' and for the
attention he paid at St. James's to this 'human exotic in his native dress'.
Finally a picture is conjured up of Omiah returning home, 'fraught by
royal order with squibs, crackers, and a various assortment of fireworks,
to show to the wild untutored Indian the great superiority of an enlightened Christian prince.' He leaves England dejected, and the contrast is
striking: 'here he is honoured with the smiles and favours of red and
white goddesses, and from their arms dashed at once to be a naked
fisherman.'[47]

As the last theme is elaborated in the verses that follow, asterisk,
innuendo, and explanatory footnote fall thick upon the page. Now
presented in the guise of a promiscuous Othello and speaking in his own
person, Omiah deplores his 'dark Numidian' hue while he farewells a

pantheon of white goddesses. His opening tribute is paid to 'Lady ******
fair', 'beauteous Christian, and the Indian's friend'. He praises her 'art
of painting white and red', comparing it with the practice of his own
'savage race, / To daub ignoble parts — nor mend the face', and wonders
whether he might not introduce the cosmetic art to Oberea, so that

> On her brown cheek the blushing Rose should blow,
> And her tann'd neck appear more white than snow.

Why, he asks, should the women of his country 'give the tail, what they
deny the face?' And, perhaps in passing allusion to Monboddo, he
reflects:

> How customs vary, yet how like each kind,
> The Man, the Monkey, differ but in mind.[48]

Mighty Christians may leave their 'Beauties to explore the Poles', he
concedes, but such exploits are not for him:

> Untutor'd, wild, unletter'd, I proclaim
> Myself an Indian — not the slave of Fame;
> The slave of Love — no other God I own,
> No other God is to OMIAH known.

Momentarily his courage fails him and he asks to be left in Britain with
his goddesses, safe from the perils of his native islands:

> Here let me run the golden sand of life,
> Free from all hostile broils and civil strife,
> Free from the rage of BOLABOLA's slaves,
> Of wounds unpitied — and untimely graves.

Or, if he must sail away, let Lady ******* accompany him, like Europa
on the back of Jupiter, 'to leave this clouded sky, / And with OMIAH
share Eternity.' From her he turns to drink a toast to other charmers:
first to Lady C*****, then in succession to 'beauteous B******' and
'courteous C***' and 'lovely T*******'. But in gratitude for past favours
he reserves the final tribute for his noble benefactor S*******, referring
to his musical accomplishments and those of Miss Ray:

> Hail gallant Peer, the Neptune of this day,
> Illumin'd too by a cœlestial *Ray*:
> May'st thou be ravish'd while she sweetly sings,
> And VIRTUE shade thee with her silver wings:
> May'st thou with HONOUR long direct the fleet,
> And CUPID's kettle drums with rapture beat![49]

Sandwich, under his popular nickname of Jemmy Twitcher, also

figures in a second set of valedictory verses, 'Omiah: an Ode', which
perhaps on account of its mildly scurrilous nature remained in manuscript until published some years later in *The New Foundling Hospital
for Wit.* The ode, reputedly by John Townshend, is addressed to
Charlotte Hayes, a notorious bawd, who is urged to collect her 'vestals',
descend on Jemmy Twitcher, and with their 'sugar'd kisses' persuade
him 'To waft OMIAH home, in charge of 'patriot P--PPS'. 'But first',
she is advised, 'bribe madam Ray.' In an abrupt transition, Omiah is
shown restored to his country where, surrounded by queen, wives, and
virgins, he 'displays / His splendid arms and dress', while he 'flourishes
his fork and knife', and, now quite explicitly presented as a South Seas
Othello, relates his experiences:

> Of wondrous sights, OMIAH tells
> Of asses — apes — and Sadlers Wells!
>   And of our smooth cestinos!
> — How he admir'd a masquerade,
> Was sometimes 'prentice to the trade
>   Of op'ras — and festinos!

Whereupon:

> Capricious beauties — fond to change,
> Will cry, ''tis strange, 'tis wondrous strange,'
>   And hug their dear OMIAH![50]

   The erotic note introduced by Charlotte Hayes and her maidens (with
its suggestion that Omiah's associates were not always drawn from the
world of fashion) is combined with social and political satire. The brief
ode is studded with allusions to topical events and personages of the time
while others are supplied in the footnotes that crowd each page. There
are such generalized targets as 'MACARONIES' and 'fops' but most are
named or lightly disguised. The 'patriot P—PPS' appears not only as a
possible escort for Omiah but as the 'present L—rd M—LGR—VE',
rejected parliamentary candidate for Newcastle and now 'in the service
of Lord S—NDW—CH'. The two ingenious gentlemen make brief appear-
ances in minor roles: B——KS is given credit for teaching Omiah 'to play
at chess'; Dr. S—L—D—R is shown complaining because he, a Swede,
was not allowed to instruct the visitor in the northern art of skating.
Less trivial in their significance are the references to American affairs.
'Omiah', runs one note, 'has been presented with a rich suit of armour,
to enable him to conquer Otaheite. He is to hold it by charter from the
Crown, and has promised to acknowledge the right of taxation, and
the supremacy of the British parliament.' The writer elaborates the
idea in his closing stanzas where he pillories 'bold G—RM—NE' (Lord
George Germain, secretary of state for the colonies), attributes to him
recent American losses, and predicts the establishment of British power
in the Pacific:

My Lord applauds OMIAH's skill,
.   .   .   .

— Resigns an Isle, and Boston town,
Joins Otaheite to the Crown,
    And makes OMI' —— VICEROY![51]

Satirical criticism of Omai's frivolous tastes and manner of life is borne out to some extent by a further source. Late in June Banks and his clerks drew up their last reckoning, 'Expences incurrd on account of Omai in the Year 1776'. Certain basic items showed no great change when compared with the previous record. 'Mr de Vignoles', as he was now termed, was paid £80-0-0 for 'Board and Lodging' with £9-15-6 for 'Necessaries' — perhaps a larger sum than he was entitled to since no reference was made to similar services for Mr. Andrews. Omai himself was treated rather more liberally in the matter of pocket money, receiving five guineas a month or thirty in all. In other respects, however, there were marked increases, and the grand total was £395-8-9, exceeding the £317 odd spent during 1775. The difference was partly due to the fact that payment for some of the gifts recommended by Banks was included in this account. Among such entries was £4-0-0 for 'Drums', £10-2-4 for 'Beads', £4-14-6 for '2 Women's Dresses', with £20-7-7 paid to 'Iron-mongers', £2-12-6 to 'printsellers' (for royal likenesses?), £3-17-6 for 'Toyman's Bill', and £5-19-0 'payd for a Sword'. Current expenses were not always listed separately: one large item of £135-2-0 was described as 'Account of presents for Messrs Omai and Odidde in which Mr Omais Cloathing for the last half year and the Voyage are included'. But Omai acquired many other articles of apparel, as successive entries show: a tailor's bill for £86-1-6, two from linen drapers for £33-9-6, two from a shoemaker for £10-5-6, one from a hosier for £12-4-0, and another from a hatter for £3-5-6. Nor was this all, for there was a supplementary list of his purchases, mostly for clothes and footwear, amounting to the sum of £20-19-9. He spent a relatively modest £3-2-6 with his apothecary and only £12-4-0 with his wine merchant, but the bill from his hair-dresser showed a spectacular rise — from £3-13-0 for the previous year to £10-14-0 for the last six months of his stay.[52] Altogether, the accounts suggest Omai's vanity and extravagance but there was little evidence of dissipation. Proof of that was still to come.

9. Omai on the *Resolution*

MEANWHILE OMAI HAD SET OUT ON HIS SECOND OCEAN VOYAGE, NOT consigned this time to the crew's quarters of the escorting vessel but accommodated in the *Resolution* as an honoured charge of the commander. On the road from London to Chatham, Cook related, the young man was moved by 'a Mixture of regret and joy'. When they spoke of England and of those who had honoured him with their protection and friendship, he became very low-spirited and with difficulty refrained from tears; 'but turn the conversation to his Native Country and his eyes would sparkle with joy.' He was, in the captain's opinion, 'fully sencible of the good treatment he had met with in England and entertained the highest ideas of the Country and people.' On the other hand, 'the prospect he now had of returning home to his native isle loaded with what they esteem riches, got the better of every other consideration and he seemed quite happy . . . .' They had left London at six o'clock on the morning of 24 June and some five hours later arrived at Chatham where Omai's acquaintance Commander Proby entertained them at dinner and very obligingly arranged for his yacht to take them to Sheerness. There they boarded the *Resolution* and about noon the next day set sail. On the 26th they anchored off Deal to pick up two boats, but Omai did not go ashore, 'to the great disapointment', Cook recorded, 'of many people who I was told had assembled there to see him.' Soon he was on the best of terms with his new shipmates. 'Omiah is a droll Animal & causes a good deal of Merriment on Board', wrote David Samwell, the surgeon's mate, on the 29th. At the end of the month they reached Plymouth, only three days behind the *Discovery*.[1]

During his brief stay in port Cook busied himself with last-minute preparations and took on board supplies to replace those already expended. On 8 July he received 'by express' his 'Secret Instructions' which contained little that was novel since they had obviously been drawn up with his knowledge and embodied his own views and plans. He was first to make for the Cape of Good Hope, calling if necessary at Madeira, the Cape Verde, or the Canary Islands to purchase wine. Having refreshed his men and provisioned his ships at the Cape, he was to seek out the southern islands recently discovered by the French and examine them for harbours and other facilities that might aid shipping.

*enough to admit of your giving the
Sloops Companies the Refreshment they
may stand in need of, before you prosecute the farther Object of these Instructions.*

*Upon your arrival at -
Otaheite, or the Society Isles, you
are to land Omiah at such of them
as he may chuse, and to leave him
there.*

*You are to distribute -
among the Chiefs of those Islands
such part of the Presents with which
you have been supplied as you shall
judge proper, reserving the remain*

42 *From Cook's secret instructions*

Next, after touching if convenient at New Zealand, he was to carry out his first mission. 'Upon your arrival at Otaheite, or the Society Isles,' he was enjoined, 'you are to land Omiah at such of them as he may chuse and to leave him there.' He was then to commit himself to his second objective, the attempt to find a passage, either to the north-west or the north-east, from the Pacific to the Atlantic or the North Sea. The minutely detailed document included a wildly optimistic timetable, warned Cook against offending the Spaniards, and anticipated every contingency save the one that ultimately overtook the expedition and himself.[2]

In his punctilious fashion Cook reported receipt of the instructions and, as the fleeting interlude drew to a close, discharged his obligations to subordinates, friends, and patrons. Clerke, still detained by minions of the law in London, was informed of the *Resolution*'s imminent departure and directed on his release to follow 'without a moments loss of time'. Sandwich received effusive acknowledgements for his many favours, in particular for the very liberal allowance made to Mrs. Cook. 'This,' wrote her husband, 'by enabling my family to live at ease and removing from them every fear of indigency, has set my heart at rest and filled it with gratitude to my Noble benefactor.' The Revd. Dr. Kaye

Gio. Chicêr Ad vivum pinx.　　　　　　　　　　　　Apud Theodorum Viero Venetiis.

Il Cap.^{io} Giacomo Cook　　　　　　*Le Cap.ⁱⁿ Jacques Cook*
Membro della Reale Società di Londra , e　　*Membre de la Societé Royale de Londres, et*
rinomat.^{mo} per li suoi Viaggi e scoperte .　　*trés rennommé pour les Voyages, et les decouvertes*

of St. James's Palace was likewise thanked for his kind tender of service
to Mrs. Cook and assured that his name would be commemorated should
it please God to spare Dr. Kaye's humble servant. Banks in turn was
favoured with a letter largely taken up with his part in preparing the
new publication for the press. Cook was obliged for these services and in
addition, he said, for the 'unmerited Honor' conferred on him by the
award of the Royal Society's medal. Of his charge he wrote amiably:
'On my arrival here I gave Omai three guineas which sent him on shore
in high spirits, indeed he could hardly be otherwise for he is very much
carressed here by every person of note, and upon the whole, I think, he
rejoices at the prospect of going home.' He only waited for a wind to put
to sea, Cook added, and in conclusion sent Dr. Solander and Mr. Banks
his best respects in which he was joined by Omai.[3]

By the evening of 12 July 1776 the wind was favourable and, delivering
Clerke's sailing orders to Lieutenant Burney, Cook set out. So it was that
Omai left England almost exactly two years after his arrival with
Captain Furneaux. Having acted as the agent of providence, that
veteran of the South Seas had again taken up regular service and was
now winning modest renown in American waters. His ship the *Syren*,
ran a recent announcement from the Admiralty, had captured a brigan-
tine carrying rebel troops from Philadelphia to Charleston. The news
afforded some slight encouragement to counter the gloomy bulletins
that continued to cross the Atlantic. As Townshend had mentioned in
his ode, the British forces had been compelled to abandon the town of
Boston, while the fate of Quebec still hung in the balance. But the
government was marshalling its forces to quell disaffection. While he lay
at Plymouth, Cook noted the arrival of a flotilla, driven into the Sound
by adverse winds. Made up of His Majesty's ships, *Diamond, Ambuscade*,
and *Unicorn* with sixty-two transports, it was bearing to America a
division of Hessian troops and their mounts.[4]

Committed to a more peaceful mission on his country's behalf, Cook
followed an uneventful course for the next four weeks. At this early
stage of the voyage the live cargo for the Pacific was already influencing
his actions. Finding that the hay and corn on board would be insufficient
until they reached the Cape, he decided to call at Tenerife where he
thought the fodder would be more plentiful than at Madeira. He
anchored in the roadstead of Santa Cruz on 1 August and until the 4th
busied himself attending to the needs of his voracious animals and his
crew. Supplies were plentiful and, though the local wine was to his taste
far inferior to the best Madeira, he found it much cheaper. While he
and some of his officers dealt with purveyors or paid official calls, others
were at leisure to inspect the sights. One afternoon Mr. Anderson with
three companions hired mules to take them to the city of Laguna, a
disappointing excursion enlivened by the cheerful songs of their guides.
The surgeon was impressed by the island's remarkably healthy climate
and wondered why consumptive patients were not sent here rather than
to Lisbon. He admired the dark-clad, dark-eyed women and noted that,

while the British saw no marked similarity between their own ways and those of the Spaniards, Omai did not think the difference great: 'He only said they seem'd not so friendly & in person they approach'd those of his own country.'[5]

They continued on their way, narrowly escaping disaster on a submerged reef in the Cape Verde Group where Cook decided to call in case their consort awaited them at St. Jago. A brief inspection of the shipping anchored off the island showed that the *Discovery* was not there, so on 16 August they turned again to the south. Within a week they were well inside tropical waters and Omai had the first chance to display his native talents. Not only had he shown his shipmates how to catch dolphins with a white fly and rod, Cook observed on the 23rd, but he hooked twice as many of the fish as anyone else. Anderson also called on the versatile supernumerary to identify a novel species of shark. He was able to supply its Tahitian name, adding that it was considered the best to eat, far superior to the shore variety. When the ship crossed the line at the beginning of September, as one of the veterans Omai was presumably exempt from what the enlightened Anderson called 'the old ridiculous ceremony of ducking'. Because of scamped workmanship in the royal dockyards the final weeks passed in damp discomfort. Rain poured through the badly caulked decks and sea water invaded the cabins. It was with relief that they sighted the Cape on 17 October and early the next afternoon anchored in Table Bay.[6]

David Samwell for one had no complaints. It had been a pleasant passage, he informed his friend Matthew Gregson on the 22nd, and as this was 'a very plentiful Country' they would live on 'the Fat of the Land' for the next month. Then they would set off for Tahiti where he supposed they would not stay long since they must use the summer season to try for the North-West Passage. And if that was found, they would be back in England by the following winter. He went on to give impressions of his fellow passenger based on more than three months' observation:

Omiah is very hearty and I do not doubt but he will live to see his own Country again, he is not such a stupid fellow as he is generally look'd upon in England, 'tis true he learn'd nothing there but how to play at cards, at which he is very expert but I take it to be owing more to his want of Instruction than his want of Capacity to take it. he talks English so bad that a person who does not understand something of his language can hardly understand him or make himself understood by him they have made him more of the fine Gentleman than anything else. he is a good natur'd fellow enough, and like all ignorant People very superstitious, Seeing on our Passage here a very bright Meteor pointing to the Northward, he said it was God going to England & was very Angry that anyone should offer to contradict him, looking upon it as no less than Blasphemy.

He himself was now on shore, Samwell explained, living in a tent near the town which was without exception the most beautiful he had ever seen. 'Today', he proudly announced, 'Capt. Cook din'd with the Governor at the Garrison — 3 royal Salutes of 21 Guns each were given with the Toasts at Dinner.' The governor and everyone else, Samwell added, paid the captain extraordinary respect; he was as famous here as in England and perhaps even more noted.[7]

While he discharged official and social obligations, Cook also attended to his pressing duties as leader of the expedition. At first the site chosen for an encampment was occupied by local militiamen, but he set the caulkers to work on the leaky *Resolution* and with the aid of his old friend Mr. Brand ordered supplies from various purveyors. By the 23rd he had set up tents for sailmakers and coopers, brought the animals ashore to graze, and begun taking astronomical measurements in his observatory. That day he addressed to Sandwich a short letter which he sent off by a French Indiaman leaving for Europe. 'My Lord', he began, 'Before I sailed from England your Lordship was pleased to allow me the Honour of Writing at all oppertunities.' He now embraced this one, he wrote, to inform his lordship of his safe arrival with Omai and the animals, all 'in a fair way of living to arrive at their destined spot'. The *Discovery* had not yet joined them, he reported, but that very moment a ship had been signalled and was probably their consort. 'Omai', he concluded, 'desires his most dutifull respects to your Lordship, and I am well assured it is from the sincerity of his heart, for no man can have a more juster sence of your Lordships favours except Your Lordships most Obedient & faithfull Humble Servant Jam^s Cook'. A postscript followed: 'I am just told that the ship in the offing is too large for the Discovery.'[8]

Clerke did not in fact reach Cape Town until 10 November. He had made a swift passage and would have arrived at least a week earlier but for a storm which also caused havoc in the *Resolution*'s shore station and nearly ruined the astronomical quadrant. Nor was this the last of their misfortunes. On the night of the 13th 'some person or persons', as Cook judicially expressed it, put dogs among the sheep penned near the encampment, killing four and dispersing the rest. In the governor's absence, the incident was reported to his deputy Mr. Henny (or Hemmy in Cook's version) and the public prosecutor. Both 'gentlemen' promised to 'use their best endeavours' to have the animals found; 'and', Cook darkly commented, 'I shall beleive they did when I am convinced that neither they nor any of the first people in the place had any hand in this affair.' In the end by bribing 'the meanest and lowest scoundrels' he succeeded in recovering most of the sheep and bought a few more of the Cape variety. Mr. Henny, evidently a farmer or breeder on his own account, 'very obligingly' offered to replace an injured ram by one he had imported from Lisbon, but the offer was declined. From his lavish use of sarcasm and innuendo it becomes obvious that Cook suspected the deputy governor of coveting the royal flock and using these despicable measures to make it his own.[9] Mr. Henny again figures in the annals of the voyage through his association with a relic of slightly more than antiquarian interest. While visiting the house he owned or occupied at the time, Omai and Clerke scratched their autographs on one of the windows. The inscriptions survived for many years and in the late eighteen-fifties, when the building had become the property of the South African Bank, efforts were made to transfer the pane to the local museum. It has since vanished and with it perhaps the only authentic evidence that Granville Sharp had not laboured in vain.[10]

In spite of the fame or notoriety Omai now enjoyed, the early weeks of his second visit to the Cape are but sparsely recorded. Was the incision on Mr. Henny's window the climax of some riotous evening or was it perhaps a ceremony carried out on a more formal occasion? And did the young dandy array himself in velvet suit and dress sword to call on the Dutch lady who had won his regard (but not his love) in 1774? One can merely speculate. There is some slight evidence, however, that he made a lasting impression on the daughters of Mr. Brand, and towards the end of his stay explicit references to his actions become more frequent. From 16 November until the 20th he was one of a small party that went to the district north-east of Cape Town to collect specimens for Mr. Banks. His companions included David Nelson, the *Discovery*'s supernumerary, Lieutenant Gore, and Mr. Anderson who wrote to the botanist on the 24th to tell him of the excursion. The results, he had to confess, were disappointing. Their two 'shooters', Mr. Gore and Omai, had with the utmost diligence only killed a few small birds. Nor had Nelson had much success in gathering botanical samples, for at this time of the year not many plants were in flower. 'Omai has just desired me to present his respects to you', he informed Banks, concluding with the abrupt disclosure: 'He brought a pox with him but is now well.' Evidently Omai was not alone in his affliction. On leaving Plymouth they had 'a little of the Small and abundance of the French Pox' but all hands were again 'perfectly healthy', wrote Clerke when reporting to Banks his arrival at the Cape and imminent departure.[11]

More discreet than Anderson and Clerke, Cook ignored medical details in the letters he sent on the eve of sailing. At length they were ready to put to sea, he informed Lord Sandwich on the 26th. Nothing was wanting, he jested, 'but a few females of our own species to make the *Resolution* a Compleat ark'; for he had taken the liberty of adding considerably to the number of animals transported from England; but, as he had done so for the good of posterity, he had no doubt the measure would meet with his lordship's approbation. 'The takeing on board some horses has made Omai compleatly happy', he added; the obliging passenger had 'consented with raptures' to give up his cabin in order to make room for the new arrivals, his only concern being that there would not be enough food for all the stock they carried. 'He continues to injoy a good state of health and great flow of Spirits', Cook reported, 'and on every occasion expresses a thankfull rememberence of your Lordships great kindness to him.' The captain went on to assure Sandwich that his lordship's efforts had not been lost on Omai who, during his stay in England, had obtained 'a far greater knowlidge of things than any one could expect or will perhaps believe.' 'Sence he has been with me', the tribute ended, 'I have not had the least reason to find fault with any part of his conduct and the people here are surprised at his genteel behaviour and deportment.' The same day similar pleasantries and sentiments went to Mr. Banks who was desired to receive Omai's best respects for himself and convey them to Dr. Solander, Lord Seaforth, and 'a great many more, Ladies as well as Gentlemen'. Their names he could not insert, Cook explained, because they would fill up the whole sheet of paper.[12]

At the end of November the two ships at last weighed anchor and sailed from Table Bay. They carried provisions for more than two years and a live cargo of which Anderson took a census on the day they left. Besides the bull, the two cows, and their calves presented by His Majesty, there were two stallions, two mares, three young bulls, three heifers, twenty goats, with an unspecified number of sheep and an assortment of pigs and poultry. Samwell and other uninformed members of the expedition may have been both surprised and aggrieved when they made off not in the direction of Tahiti but towards the south. Following his encounter with Captain Crozet on his previous visit to the Cape, Cook had resolved to examine the islands which had eluded him in his earlier exploration of the Antarctic. In case they became separated in those hazardous waters, he thought it prudent to give Clerke a copy of his instructions and appoint Queen Charlotte Sound their first rendezvous.[13]

EXPERIENCES IN THE NEXT PHASE OF THE VOYAGE, while they sought out the French discoveries to the south-east of the Cape, were by no means novel to veterans of the second expedition. Thanks, however, to the chart Crozet had supplied, the search was brief and rewarded by occasional glimpses of land. Within a few days of leaving port they met with violent gales which damaged the *Resolution* and proved fatal to some of its animals. Notwithstanding all their care, Cook lamented, the rolling of the ship, combined with increasing cold, killed several goats, especially the males, and a number of sheep. On 12 December, heralded by sportive porpoises and a seal, two islands appeared where they could discern neither trees nor shrubs and not many birds. Cook called the smaller Prince Edward Island, after the King's fourth son, and the larger one, whose peaks were covered with snow, Marion Island after Aoutourou's unfortunate benefactor; a larger group to the east he gratefully honoured with the name of Captain Crozet. Pushing farther on their south-easterly course towards the island found by Kerguelen, the two ships were for days at a time shrouded in fog and kept in touch only by the constant firing of guns. The bitter weather resulted in further casualties among the goats and, again through faulty caulking, the men of the *Resolution* suffered in leaky discomfort. On Christmas Eve they sighted what appeared to be lofty peaks enveloped in mist. Old Antarctic

THE
TRAVELS OF OMAI
TO ENGLAND ----   FROM ENGLAND ——

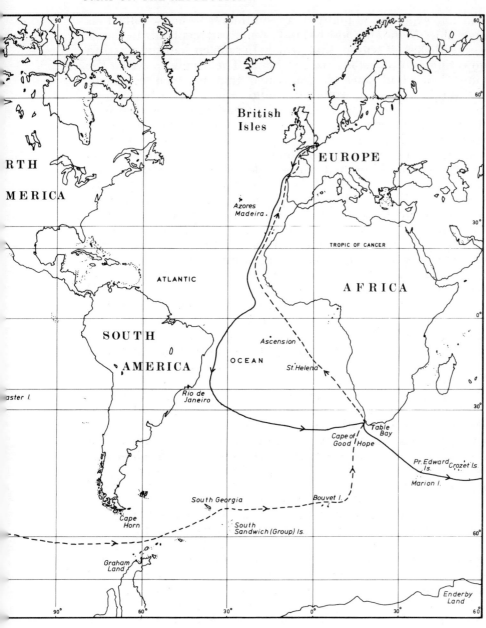

hands, who 'had experienced many disappointments from the fallacious resemblance of ice islands to those of land', remained sceptical.[14]

Land, nevertheless, it was — that which Kerguelen had supposed to be the projecting part of a southern continent. The 'English', wrote the self-effacing Cook, had since demonstrated that no such continent existed; as for the projection, it was an island of no great extent which because of its 'stirility' he called 'the *Island of Desolation*'. The men who landed at points on the deeply serrated northern coast found no signs of trees or shrubs and only small patches of coarse grass which they gathered for the famished cattle. Streams ran down the bare hills in torrents, so they had no trouble in filling their water casks, while seals and sea lions provided oil for the ships and a change of diet for the less fastidious. Among the multitude of sea birds the penguins excited most interest. They lined the shore to watch the newcomers, standing upright in regular rows and looking, as Samwell observed, not unlike a regiment of soldiers. The poor creatures, he added, did not at first move out of the sailors' way but grew more shy when great numbers were knocked on the head in wanton sport. One forager lighted on a memento left by the French discoverers, a bottle containing a document. This was inscribed with details of the present visit and replaced in the bottle which was then buried under a cairn of stones. Here Cook formally named his anchorage Christmas Harbour and raised the British flag — a ceremony the unpatriotic Anderson thought 'perhaps fitter to excite laughter than indignation'. After a little further exploration by land and sea, Cook set off for New Zealand on 30 December. There had been more deaths among the animals (variously ascribed to cold, neglect, the sudden change of diet, or the penguin dung on the island grass), and it was imperative to seek milder weather and fresh fodder.[15]

Following an uncomfortable passage from Kerguelen Island, it was again the pressing needs of his 'cattle' that persuaded Cook to call at Van Diemen's Land for a few days late in January 1777. The appointed rendezvous was Captain Furneaux's Adventure Bay where they arrived on the 26th. Boats immediately put ashore from both ships and reported wood and water in plenty, though grass, which they needed above all else, seemed scarce. The next morning parties dispersed to collect supplies while some men went fishing in a brackish lake not far from the anchorage. In accounts of that enterprise Omai at length emerged from the obscurity which had enveloped him since he left the Cape of Good Hope. Lieutenant Gore mentioned him hooking or netting 'several Goose Dishes'; rather more comprehensibly Samwell spoke of him as 'by far the best fisherman' — 'he catched a great many more than any single person beside.'[16]

For the second time Omai had survived the rigours of sub-antarctic latitudes and would henceforth be the subject of comment not only among his companions on the *Resolution* but from voyagers less conveniently placed on the *Discovery*. Those assiduous journalizers, Burney and Bayly, again travelling together on the escort vessel, both made occasional mention of their old shipmate when he fell under their notice. Unfortunately Burney kept nothing like the informal narrative of his previous voyage, but his fellow officer John Rickman was the author of an unbuttoned record in which Omai was a conspicuous figure. Much of what Rickman wrote — and surreptitiously published — must be discounted if only because he could not have witnessed many of the incidents he related in circumstantial detail. However, when allowance is made for his tendency to invent and exaggerate, he adds, not always implausibly, to the evidence of more pedestrian writers.

At Van Diemen's Land observers on both ships dwelt at length on the indigenous inhabitants who had eluded Furneaux and his crew in 1773. This time their distant fires had been seen from the outset, and on the 28th eight men and a boy, showing no signs of surprise or fear, emerged from the woods to greet a working party. They were dark in colour, carried no weapons except pointed sticks, and went completely naked. The next day a larger crowd assembled, including females of all ages who were as naked as the men unless for an animal's skin which some wore to support their children. These primitive beings dwelt in rude shelters or hollow trees, subsisted mainly on shell-fish, and showed little interest in European tools and ornaments. As the more literate navigators seem to have recognized, they were face to face with living representatives of that philosophical abstraction, 'natural' man — a spectacle that was scarcely inspiring. Few people, Burney considered, might 'more truly be said to be in a state of Nature'; and he went on to castigate the men who had so little sense of decency that, whether sitting, walking, or talking, they would pour forth their 'Streams' without any preparatory action or guidance. 'The Inhabitants', wrote the less censorious Clerke, 'seem to have made the least progress towards any kind of Improvement since Dame Nature put them out of hand, of any People I have ever met with . . . .' They lived in 'the rudest State of Nature', remarked Samwell, noting the men's habit of idly 'pulling or playing with the Prepuce' as they stood before the outraged visitors. The erudite Anderson made similar observations which he used for the text of a discourse on the origins of modesty — whether implanted in mankind by nature or acquired from some person of uncommon delicacy. He ascribed the peacefulness of these 'indians' to their lack of possessions and thought their use of hollow trees for shelter authenticated the ancient legends of fauns and satyrs.[17]

One thing at least was certain: Omai belonged to an entirely distinct order of human kind. According to Samwell, he did not understand a word of the local tongue which was 'quite different from that of the South Sea Islands.' The same informant described how in fun — or possibly to deride the man's nakedness — he threw a piece of white cloth, 'cut in the Otaheite Fashion', over the shoulders of 'a little deform'd hump-backed fellow' who 'expressed great Joy by laughing shouting & jumping'. His conduct towards these unsophisticated aborigines was not always so graciously condescending. Most accounts of his first meeting

with them say that, to their consternation, he fired his musket to show
the superiority of European weapons to their pointed sticks. In another
more doubtful version of the incident Rickman asserts that Omai,
'though led by natural impulse to an inordinate desire for women', was
so disgusted by the females of Van Diemen's Land that he fired into the
air to frighten them away. Cook wrote little on such carnal topics,
merely reporting from hearsay that the women rejected with great
disdain addresses and large offers made by gentlemen on the *Discovery*
(less fastidious, apparently, than Omai). His time was taken up in super-
vising shore duties and initiating his campaign to diversify southern
resources. He considered freeing an assortment of his animals but, fearing
the natives would destroy them, left only a boar and a sow which he
took a mile or so into the woods in the hope they would be left there to
breed and multiply. In addition, some unnamed benefactor — probably
David Nelson — planted beans, potatoes, the stones of apricots and
peaches. Cook made other short excursions into the interior but, less
inquiring than usual or perhaps only pressed for time, he failed to test
Furneaux's theory that this country formed part of the northern main-
land. The ships pulled out again on 30 January and after a fairly smooth
passage in fine weather reached Queen Charlotte Sound on 12 February.[18]

Their stay of less than a fortnight in that familiar spot was overshadowed by memories of the affair in Grass Cove three years earlier.
Omai was well to the fore when the *Resolution* came to anchor, waving
a handkerchief to greet three or four canoes as he announced that 'Toote'
had returned. At first the crews were shy about approaching at close
quarters and few ventured on board. They were apprehensive, Cook
supposed, that he had come to exact vengeance, and their fears were the
more acute because Omai, whom they remembered on the *Adventure*,
spoke openly of the massacre. Intent on reconciliation, Cook did everything in his power to reassure the anxious natives, with the result that
they soon flocked to Ship Cove from all parts of the countryside. Among
the early arrivals was a youth about seventeen years of age called Te
Weherua (rendered as '*Tiarooa*' by Cook), remembered for his friendliness and honesty during previous calls at the Sound. A more sinister
visitor was a chief known as Kahourah, 'very strong, & of a fierce
Countenance tattowed after the Manner of the Country', who was
pointed out as a leader of the murdering band and the killer of Jack
Rowe. Some of his countrymen urged the commander to slay this villain
and were surprised when he refused, 'for', he acknowledged, 'accord[ing]
to their ideas of equity this ought to have been done.' Had he followed
the advice of these and other pretended friends, Cook remarked, he
'might have extirpated the whole race'. The same note of mildly grim
humour was repeated elsewhere in his account of the stay. The New
Zealanders brought them three articles of commerce, he wrote, 'Curiosities, Fish and Women'; 'the two first', he went on, 'always came to a
good market, which the latter did not: the Seamen had taken a kind of
dislike to these people and were either unwilling or affraid to associate

with them; it had a good effect as I never knew a man quit his station to go to their habitations.'[19]

Cook was forgiving but more vigilant than ever before. Mindful not only of the loss of his own compatriots but of the more appalling slaughter of Marion du Fresne and his men in 1772, he redoubled the usual precautions. A guard of ten marines was appointed to protect the encampment where, on the 13th, Mr. Bayly set up his observatory and sailors from both ships began their varied tasks — filling water casks, mending sails, brewing spruce beer, rendering down the blubber brought from Kerguelen Island. The same day, 'to the great Astonishment of the New Zealanders', as Samwell wrote, 'Horses, Cattle, Sheep, Goats &c. with peacocks, Turkeys, Geese & Ducks' poured out from the 'second Noahs Ark' to graze or disport themselves ashore. Surrounded by these domestic creatures, observed the same imaginative scribe, the visitors almost forgot they were 'near the antipodes of old England among a rude & barbarous people.' And even the natives seemed to shed some of their savage propensities when viewed at close quarters through Cook's indulgent eyes. He praised the speed and skill shown by the men in building temporary huts in all parts of Ship Cove while the women busied themselves gathering provisions or dry sticks for fires to cook their victuals. As he watched their combined labours, he emptied his pockets of beads for which the old people and children scrambled in competition. This and similar acts of munificence were amply rewarded. He and his men received no little advantage from their neighbours, he remarked, and went on to acknowledge in particular almost daily tributes of fresh fish.[20]

In his earlier expectations that Europeans might one day profit from their own benevolent efforts, Cook was bitterly disappointed. Not a vestige remained of the gardens Mr. Bayly and his companions had established near the observatory, and there were no signs of animals or poultry. A search elsewhere in Ship Cove was, however, slightly more encouraging. Cook found cabbages, onions, leeks, etc., with a few potatoes, all overrun with weeds. The potatoes, originally brought from the Cape, had improved with the change of soil, he noted, and were highly esteemed by the natives. Yet they had not troubled to plant out a single one, much less any of the other vegetables. Nevertheless, on Samwell's authority, the altruistic navigators cultivated the plots and sowed more seeds in the belief that they would be 'of Service to the Country'. As for the livestock left during previous visits, unconfirmed rumours reached Cook that a hog and some poultry still survived in distant parts of the Sound. He had intended leaving sheep and cattle but now limited his gifts to a pair of goats, male and female, with a boar and sow which he bestowed, not very hopefully, on two importunate chiefs. A variation on the normal flow of commerce was the purchase, towards the end of the visit, of several New Zealand dogs, priced at a hatchet apiece. Finally, Cook bestowed on this barren land two animals which had not previously figured in records of the voyage:

in the interests of posterity he released on Motuara Island a pair of rabbits.[21]

On many of his excursions Cook was joined by Omai not only as companion but, somewhat surprisingly, in the role of interpreter. For, though showing no linguistic aptitude on the previous voyage, he had with enhanced social status acquired the gift of tongues. The commander described him speaking to a ring of attentive New Zealanders and elsewhere asserted quite explicitly that he understood them 'perfectly well'. Anderson did not go quite so far, merely stating that he followed their language 'pretty well' since it was 'radically' the same as his own, 'though a different dialect'. The only dissentient voice was Rickman's. In his view Omai knew less of what these natives said than many common sailors and was preferred to them only because he was Cook's favourite. Proficient or not, he was the go-between when a large party, including both captains, visited Grass Cove to collect fodder and make inquiries at the scene of the affray. The inhabitants showed manifest signs of alarm when Cook arrived with his entourage, but he allayed their fears with a few presents and induced them to give an account of the fatal clash. It had occurred in the late afternoon while the men of the *Adventure* were eating their meal at a distance from the cutter, surrounded by natives. When some of the latter snatched bread and fish, a quarrel broke out which led to the shooting of two New Zealanders; but before the sailors could reload they were overwhelmed and killed. Another informant put the blame on Captain Furneaux's black servant who had been left in charge of the boat and — so this story went — struck a man he caught stealing from it. On hearing the victim's cries, those gathered round the other sailors had taken fright and begun the attack. What happened to the cutter could not be established: some said it had been burnt, others that it had been carried away by strangers. Whatever the precise facts of the whole affair, Cook was satisfied that 'the thing was not premeditated' and, further, that the clash had arisen from thefts committed by the natives and 'too hastily resented' by Rowe and his companions.[22]

These conclusions were of no comfort to anyone and did nothing to endear the New Zealanders to their visitors. The forthright Samwell roundly condemned them as 'the most barbarous & vindictive race of Men on the face of the Globe'. Anderson expressed himself more temperately; indeed, in a lengthy survey of their customs he did justice not only to their artistic skill but to the humane feelings that coexisted with their cruelty. To remedy their horrid practice of destroying one another it would, he thought, be necessary to bring in plenty of animal food, but on a more extensive and certain plan than Captain Cook's. Their present condition, he felt, was 'little superior to that of the Brute creation'. 'No Beast can be more ravenous or greedy than a New Zealander', echoed Burney who attributed the natives' troublesome conduct on this visit to the commander's misguided clemency. In that opinion he was supported by Omai. Towards the end of their stay, Cook himself records, just as he and Omai were re-embarking after a visit ashore, the notorious Kahourah left the ship. More vengeful than his master, the officious young man urged Cook to shoot Rowe's murderer and then proclaimed that he himself would be the executioner if the chief ever came back. Ignoring these threats, Kahourah appeared the next morning with his family and was taken to the captain's cabin by Omai who ordered that the villain should meet his desserts. On his return soon afterwards, he saw that Kahourah was untouched and, as Cook relates, reproached him bitterly: '"why do not you kill him, you tell me if a man kills an other in England he is hanged for it, this Man has killed ten and yet you will not kill him, tho a great many of his country-men desire it . . . ."'[23]

Following an independent line, as he did so often, Rickman took a favourable view of the place and gave qualified praise to its people. Of the expedition's arrival he wrote, 'Not a man on board who did not now think himself at home, so much like Great-Britain is the Island of New Zealand.' And he included in his narrative the story of a youth on the *Discovery* who, 'desperately in love' with a local maiden and 'charmed with the beauty of the country', deserted with the intention of settling ashore and founding a dynasty. Such love was only found 'in the region of romance' he remarked of the touching affair which ended with the hero's recapture and the relatively mild sentence of twelve lashes (incidents mentioned by no other annalist). But even this man of sensibility was compelled to acknowledge that love between visitors and denizens generally assumed less idyllic forms. Among the seamen, he wrote, the traffic with women was 'carried to a shameless height' and though the first price might be trifling — 'nails, broken glass, beads, or other European trumpery' — it 'cost them dear in the end.' Another offender he singled out was Omai 'who, from natural inclination and the licentious habits of his country, felt no restraint', indulging 'his almost insatiable appetite with more than savage indecorum.' If the same observer can be credited, whenever he could escape Cook's watchful eye, Omai was hardly the paragon of discreet moderation Sandwich had conjured up: 'he set no bounds to his excess, and would drink till he wallowed like a swine in his own filth.' On such occasions he was surrounded by the common sailors who taunted him as he did 'the poor Zealanders'. Yet, Rickman added with a touch of compassion:

He was indeed far from being ill-natured, vindictive, or morose, but he was sometimes sulky. He was naturally humble, but had grown proud by habit; and it so ill became him, that he was always glad when he could put it off, and would appear among the petty officers with his natural ease. This was the true character of Omai, who might be said, perhaps, by accident, to have been raised to the highest pitch of human happiness, only to suffer the opposite extreme by being again reduced to the lowest order of rational beings.[24]

Rickman is the most critical of several witnesses to one of the strangest episodes in this unhappy voyage. His newly acquired pride, combined

with notions he had picked up from high-born English friends, persuaded Omai that he must now have retainers of his own. Even before
reaching New Zealand, Cook explains, his charge had expressed the
wish to carry one of its natives away with him. Now in the amiable
Tiarooa he found a willing recruit. Once he elected to go, the youth
took up his quarters on the *Resolution* and, thinking he would disappear
once he had got all he could from Omai, Cook at first paid little attention. But when he stayed on it looked as if Omai had deceived the young
New Zealander and his family by assuring them he would come back.
'I therefore caused it to be made known to all of them', Cook emphasized,
'that if he went away with us he would never return'. The announcement
made 'no sort of impression' and Tiarooa persisted in his determination.
Since he was of chiefly rank (the son, it was said, of a tribal leader killed
in a recent raid), another youth was chosen to go as his servant but was
later removed from the ship. At the last moment a replacement was
found in a boy of about nine or ten named Coaa (more properly Koa)
who was enlisted in a manner Cook described: 'he was presented to me
by his own Father with far less indifference than he would have parted
with his dog; the very little cloathing the boy had he took from him and
left him as naked as he was born.' The captain again tried to make the
natives realize the improbability, or rather impossibility, of the boys'
return, but with no effect: 'Not one, even their nearest relations seemed
to trouble themselves about what became of them.' He therefore consented to their going, the more willingly, he wrote, because he 'was
well satisfied the boys would not be losers by exchange of place'; and he
went on to describe how the New Zealanders lived 'under perpetual
apprehinsions of being distroyed' through unending tribal wars and
their insistence on revenge.[25]

The incident obviously troubled Cook who, in Rickman's view, was
party to a transaction, the possibility of which he had formerly denied
— the selling of their children by New Zealand parents. Omai paid two
hatchets and a few nails for his two retainers, alleges Rickman, and
Cook himself mentions Tiarooa's mother coming on board the afternoon
before they sailed to 'receive her last present from Omai'. In whatever
light the affair might have appeared to the New Zealanders, whether
as the bartering of their own flesh and blood or the ceremonial exchange
of courtesies between equals, all observers agreed that they displayed
natural human feelings when finally parting with the boys. Their
friends, noted Rickman, expressed their grief 'very affectingly', while
Cook spoke of Tiarooa and his mother exhibiting 'all the Marks of tender
affection that might be expected between a Mother and her Son who
were never to meet again.' Not only did she weep aloud, wrote Samwell,
but 'cut her head with a Shark's Tooth till the blood streamed down her
Face.'[26]

In the initial phase of their new life the boys were closely watched by
sympathetic witnesses of whom Samwell was the most eloquent. As the
expedition left the Sound and the last canoes put back to shore, Tiarooa

and Coaa wept but made no attempt to leave the ship. They remained in fairly good spirits until land began to disappear when, with the onset of seasickness, 'they gave way to that grief which in spite of all their Resolution lay heavy at their Hearts'. They 'cryed most piteously' and 'in a melancholy Cadence' chanted a song in praise of their native land and its people — or so their audience interpreted it. The first night they lay on the bare deck, covered with their cloaks, and with the dawn of another day resumed their weeping and their mournful singing. Omai vainly tried to comfort his forlorn charges, while Cook, in an attempt to win them over, ordered them to be fitted out with jackets of the red cloth so prized by New Zealanders; but the boys took little notice of this finery. With Omai's encouragement, Tiarooa might have become reconciled to his situation had it not been for Coaa who sat each day for hours weeping and repeating his plaintive song. On hearing it, the young chieftain would go and sit beside his servant to chant with him and 'partake of his Grief'. They had not been at sea a week when an incident occurred recalling Omai's similar experience on the *Adventure*. One day early in March the weather was calm enough for Captain Clerke and Lieutenant Burney to pay Captain Cook a visit. On their arrival, the panic-stricken boys fled from the deck to hide, fearing 'some design on their lives, as in their country', Rickman explained, 'a consultation among the chiefs always precedes a determined murder.' They continued in the same unhappy state for many days until, reported Cook:

their Sea sickness wore of[f], and the tumult of their minds began to subside, these fits of lamentation became less and less frequent and at length quite went of[f], so that their friends nor their Native country were no more thought of and [they] were as firmly attached to us as if they had been born amongst us.

Gradually they picked up English words and adopted English habits. At first they preferred fish to all other food, but later grew accustomed to shipboard diet and acquired a taste for wine, though, Samwell noted with approval, they never became 'in the least intoxicated'.[27]

On recovering appetites and spirits, the New Zealanders were able to answer Cook's numerous questions about their homeland. From Tiarooa he learned of the perpetual feuds among his people and of the existence (confirmed by the informant's life-like drawings) of enormous snakes and lizards, the latter 'Eight feet in length and as big round as a mans body'. These creatures sometimes seized and devoured men, tunnelled into the ground, and were killed by means of fires lit at the mouths of their burrows. Both boys spoke of a ship which had reached their country before the *Endeavour* (known to them as 'Tupias Ship'). The captain had fathered a son, still living, by a New Zealand woman, and the crew, stated Tiarooa, had first introduced venereal disease. Cook derived whatever comfort he could from the last revelation and went on to say that the disorder was now 'but too common', though the natives did not find its effects 'near so bad' as on its first appearance; their remedy was 'a kind of hot bath arrising from the Steam of green plants laid over hot stones'.[28]

The two boys did something to restore the reputation of their compatriots among members of the expedition. They were both 'universally liked' wrote David Samwell. When he overcame his homesickness, Coaa (or Cocoa, as the surgeon's mate engagingly called him) proved to be of a 'very humoursome & lively' disposition and used to afford his shipmates 'much Mirth with his drolleries'. Tiarooa was described more summarily as 'a sedate sensible young Fellow'.[29] Except for the ill-fated Ranginui, kidnapped by de Surville, they were the first New Zealanders in recorded history to leave their country. And all unknowingly they now followed the path of their forbears towards the ancestral Hawaiki.

COOK HAD LEFT QUEEN CHARLOTTE SOUND on 25 February and, with the aim of reaching the Arctic in the northern summer, pressed forward with an urgency that provoked muttered criticism from the lower decks. Contrary winds, however, impeded the north-easterly passage, added to which he again found himself in trouble with the live cargo. He had thought the hay and grass taken on at New Zealand would last until they reached Tahiti, but by the middle of March fodder was running out and he was forced to sacrifice some of the sheep in order to save more precious livestock. Visiting the *Resolution* on the 24th, Clerke and Burney found an 'alarming' situation on that vessel through the shortage of fresh supplies. Many animals had been killed and served to the ship's company, others were reduced to 'mere skeletons', while the crew had been placed on a daily allowance of two quarts of water. The officers said nothing of Omai, but it seems not unlikely that his spirits were rising with increasing temperatures and remembered signs of his old environment. For Anderson's benefit he had already identified a red-tailed bird 'call'd Ta'wy by the natives of the Society isles'. On 27 March they entered the tropics and two days later sighted land, an island of no great size protected by a reef against which the surf broke 'with great fury'.[30]

It was Mangaia, hitherto unknown to Europeans, the southernmost of the group which now bears Cook's name. On the morning of the 30th warriors were seen gathered on the reef brandishing their weapons and uttering cries of defiance much in the manner of the New Zealanders. Viewing them through his spyglass, Anderson found them a tawny colour, most of them naked except for a sort of loin-cloth, though some wore a cloak thrown over the shoulders. Two men soon approached the *Resolution* in a small canoe, showing extreme signs of fear until Omai, who addressed them in his own language, reassured them to some extent. He was tactless enough to ask whether they ate human flesh — a charge that was indignantly denied — and they left after accepting a few presents. Later in the day the more commanding of the two was persuaded to come aboard and shown over the ship, Omai again acting as interpreter. Cook expressed disappointment that the man was not more surprised by the 'Cattle' and mentioned that on leaving the cabin he stumbled over a goat 'and asked Omai what bird it was'. Barred from landing by the reef and heavy surf, the captain reluctantly left 'this fine island' which appeared capable of supplying all his wants. Its inhabitants seemed 'both numerous and well fed', the men 'stout, active and well made', in actions and language 'nearer to the new Zealanders than the Otaheiteans', in colour 'between both'.[31]

They continued their northward course and in a couple of days reached the island of Atiu whose people closely resembled the Mangaians but seemed more friendly. Led by a chief carrying the symbol of peace, a coconut branch, men came aboard and were greeted by Omai who understood them 'perfectly', making the appropriate responses to the chief's incantations. When taken over the ship, the visitors displayed gratifying wonder at the animals and returned with pigs, coconuts, and plantains, in return for which Omai generously gave them the prize they most coveted, a favourite dog he had brought from England. Since there was again no passage through the encircling reef and no safe anchorage, Cook decided to make an attempt to take on urgently needed fodder by boat. On 3 April a party set out and succeeded in reaching the island by transferring from their boats to native canoes which carried them over the reef. Lieutenant Gore was in charge, accompanied by Mr. Anderson, Lieutenant Burney, and Omai who went as interpreter and who, by all accounts, proved himself the hero of the occasion.[32]

Greeted by emissaries bearing green boughs, they were escorted through a great throng of people and presented to a succession of dignitaries, culminating in the principal chief or 'Aree' who entertained them, 'much in the Stile of the Friendly Isles', with ceremonial displays performed by young women and armed warriors. In return Omai delivered a speech and gave the Aree a bunch of red feathers. Then, 'perhaps to shew his Gallantry, [he] took a Cocoa nut & drawing a very handsome Dirk which had been given him in England, broke it open and presented it to one of the Ladies.' Both he and Gore explained their purpose in coming, but neither the chief nor his subjects paid much heed, intent as they were on satisfying their curiosity. As they pressed round the four men, the dense crowd (at least two thousand, Anderson estimated) examined their clothing and persons while displaying the same dexterous skill in theft as their Tahitian cousins. They continued to pester and pilfer the visitors for the rest of the day and firmly resisted any attempts at escape. Omai was greatly alarmed when he saw an earth oven being heated and, to his companions' annoyance, asked the natives whether they were cannibals. He also wondered if they were preparing to kill the strangers and burn their bodies, as the Boraborans did, to conceal the crime. His fears were allayed when a pig was brought to the oven, and he eased the tension by taking a club and demonstrating how it was used in his own country — a performance that vastly entertained the audience. Cook's report of the affair also made it clear that his favourite, with a lavish use of hyperbole, had taken every opportunity to emphasize British prestige and martial power:

Omai was asked a great many questions concerning us, our Ships, Country, &c^a and according to his account the answers he gave were many of them not a little upon the marvellous as for instance he told them we had Ships as large as their island, that carried guns so large that several people might sit within them and that one of these guns was sufficient to distroy the whole island at one shot. This led them to ask what sort of guns we had, he said they were but small, yet with them we could with great ease distroy the island and every soul in it; they then desired to know by what means this was done, accordingly fire was put to a little powder, the sudden blast and report produced by so small a quantity astonished them and gave them terrible ideas of the effects of a large quantity, so that Omai was at once credited for every thing he told them.

Anderson gave Omai deserved praise for his resourcefulness, while Burney attributed their final release to his spectacular display. After feasting the guests with roast hog and plantains, towards nightfall the islanders informed them they could now leave. Stripped of their loose possessions, including Omai's precious dirk, they were carried in canoes to their boats and made their way back to the ships.[33]

As he reflected on his experiences ashore, Anderson regretted that the brevity of the visit and the behaviour of the natives had frustrated an opportunity he had long wished for — 'to see a people following the dictates of nature without being bias'd by education or corrupted by an intercourse with more polish'd nations, and to observe them at leisure . . . .' He was inclined to think that in detaining his companions and himself they were impelled only by curiosity or the desire to steal what they coveted or perhaps by a combination of both motives. One event he recorded with special interest was Omai's meeting with three of his countrymen living on Atiu. They were survivors from a canoe which had been driven from its course and eventually, after a harrowing voyage, carried to this island. When the incident happened was uncertain but it must have been at least twelve years earlier, for the men had not heard of Captain Wallis and knew nothing of the conquest of Raiatea by Opoony and the Boraborans. It was a 'circumstance', commented Anderson, 'which may easily explain the method by which many of these places are peopled.' In his account of that memorable day, Cook remarked that the castaways were now so satisfied with their situation that they refused Omai's offer of a passage back to their native island. Slightly enlarging on Anderson, he too theorized on the implications of the affair. 'This circumstance', he wrote, 'very well accounts for the manner the inhabited islands in this Sea have been at first peopled; especially those which lay remote from any Continent and from each other.'[34]

The episode at Atiu had yielded no supplies worth mentioning, so, rather than run further risks among these difficult people, Cook decided to continue the search elsewhere. He first made for the neighbouring islet of Takutea which was found to be without inhabitants, though there were signs of occasional visitors. Here two boat crews under Mr. Gore managed to negotiate the reef at great risk to themselves and collected coconuts and fodder, in return for which the scrupulous lieutenant deposited nails and a hatchet in one of the deserted huts. Omai, reported Anderson, 'dress'd' some of the spoils for dinner, the fruit of a plant 'eaten by the natives of Otaheite in times of scarcity'; but the dish proved 'very indifferent'. With the appetites of animals and men whetted rather than appeased by this perilous interlude, they next headed for the Hervey Islands, first charted during the previous voyage.[35]

When land came in sight on 6 April, to Cook's surprise (for he had supposed the place uninhabited), canoes put out from the shore. The occupants, though they seemed darker than the people of Atiu, were clearly related and Omai again understood their speech. He persuaded them to come alongside and answered their numerous questions about the ship, its name, its captain, the size of its crew — 'a bad thing' he told Anderson, for in his country that meant they intended an attack. The surgeon himself spoke of their 'disorderly and clamorous behaviour' and mentioned their 'fierce rugged aspect resembling almost in every respect the natives of New Zeeland'. Their conduct did indeed recall early European encounters with that barbarous nation. They refused to board the ships, attempted to kidnap Mr. Bayly's servant, and stole anything they could lay their hands on. One particularly audacious theft was their seizure of a piece of beef which someone on the *Discovery* had enclosed in a net and placed in the water to 'freshen'. They then took their prize to the *Resolution* and sold it or, according to another witness, restored it as a result of Omai's threats. In their 'Manners', commented Midshipman John Watts, using the stock comparison, they were like 'the New Zealanders, great Thieves & horrid Cheats'. It was in these circumstances that Omai's boys reappeared after a prolonged eclipse. 'Here', wrote Samwell, 'we found our New Zealand Ship mates as expert as any of us at trafficking, the younger boy Cocoa bought a fine Fish for a piece of brown paper he picked off the Deck & was highly delighted at having overreached the poor Indian.' Their native propensities were again in evidence when two boats, after vainly searching for an anchorage, reported that the islanders, armed with pikes and clubs, had lined the reef as if to oppose a landing. 'The two new Zealanders', Samwell further commented, 'express their Astonishment, that of the great number of people we have had in our power we have not yet killed any.'[36]

Less bloody-minded than Omai's retainers, Cook was not prepared to risk men and ships in this inhospitable spot. Frustrated in the fourth successive attempt to obtain provisions and water (for the supplies taken on at Takutea were quite insufficient), he was compelled to take stock of the situation. He had been disappointed at every landfall since leaving New Zealand, he had been held back by unfavourable winds, and he now concluded it would be impossible to reach the Northern Hemisphere in time to carry out the intended exploration in the coming summer. Everything possible had thus to be done not only to preserve the animals but also to save stores so that the search for a northern passage could be made a year later than originally intended. Instead of continuing towards Tahiti, therefore, he redirected his course towards the Tongan Group whose lavish hospitality, twice enjoyed in the previous voyage, had earned them the name of the Friendly Isles.[37]

Such was the plight of the expedition that Cook decided to sail by night as well as by day, with the *Discovery*, the more navigable of the two ships, acting as pilot. When they approached land on 14 April, boats were immediately ordered ashore; 'for now', explained Cook, 'we were under an absolute necessity of procuring from this island some food for the Cattle otherwise we must lose them.' It was an uninhabited islet of the Palmerston atoll, already sighted in 1774, and although difficult of access, it supplied 'a feast for the cattle' in an abundance of scurvy grass and young coconut trees. The men also found ample provisions for themselves in the varied fish of the lagoon and the tropical birds, so tame they allowed themselves to be lifted from the trees. Now restored to his native element, Omai came into his own, winning praise on all sides. He settled ashore with his two young followers and in a very short time, acknowledged the grateful commander, caught with his scoop net enough fish to serve the whole party and in addition to supply the crews left on both ships. He showed his companions how to procure fresh water by digging in the sand and introduced them to a large eel which they found delicious eating, though so repulsive in appearance that without his guidance they would have shunned it. The well-read Anderson likened him to the Mosquito Indians used for a similar purpose by the buccaneers. His talents, however, went beyond those of a mere forager: assisted by the New Zealanders, he 'dressed' fish and birds 'in an oven with heated stones after the fashion of his country with a dexterity and good will which did him great Credit.' In short, as his old friend Burney testified, he was 'a keen Sportsman an excellent Cook and never idle — without him we might have made a tolerable Shift, but with him we fared Sumptuously'. Omai himself was so delighted with the place that he often declared his intention of returning to live there and become 'King'. Yet he could never, by sun or compass, point out in which direction it lay, observed Samwell, who was pretty sure he would not be so foolish as to make the attempt.[38]

Refreshed by three days spent on this and neighbouring islets, the navigators resumed their westward passage. They sailed past Niue, called Savage Island on the previous voyage because of the implacable hostility of its people, and after experiencing wet and sultry weather for the final week caught the first glimpse of the Tongan Group on 28 April. They touched at the small island of Mango and at the beginning of May came to rest in the *Resolution*'s former anchorage at Nomuka, relieved to find themselves, as Rickman expressed it, 'in safety on a friendly coast'. 'We forgot the dangers we had escaped,' he went on, 'and thought only of enjoying with double pleasure the sweets of these happy islands . . . .'³⁹

THE TROPICAL SOUTH continued to inspire impressionable minds and imaginations. Viewing a Pacific island at close quarters for the first time, Samwell thought Nomuka realized 'the poetical Descriptions of the Elysian Fields in ancient Writers'. In a more extended account Rickman, another newcomer, responded with all the enthusiasm of a Bougainville or a Banks. While still at sea he found its fragrance 'inconceivably reviving' and, on approaching the shore, was delighted by the prospect before him: the plantations with their intermixture of various blossoms, the trees of vivid green, the little rising hills, the verdant lawns, the rich low valleys. As the ships moored in the harbour, he admired the innumerable canoes, curiously constructed and filled with fruits from the plantations or articles of local manufacture — cloth of different fabrics, calabashes, bracelets and breastplates ornamented with vivid feathers, mantelets artfully and beautifully arranged. With growing intimacy, he found the people friendly, generous, hospitable, ready to oblige (though some, alas, were 'villainously given to thieving'), while the chiefs did everything in their power to serve and honour the visitors. Under their direction, he noted, such was the quantity of hogs and fruit supplied that it exceeded the daily consumption on both ships. Nor did their attentions cease there. They conferred on Captains Cook and Clerke the richest offerings they could make, breastplates decorated with red feathers; they feasted them 'like tropical kings' on barbecued pigs and poultry and most delicious fruit; and they entertained the entire expedition with music, dancing, pantomime. The captains in their turn were not wanting in generosity, Rickman emphasized, for they loaded the chiefs with hatchets, knives, linen cloth, glass, and beads. 'Who knows', speculated the eager young officer, 'but that the seeds of the liberal arts, that have now been sown by European navigators in these happy climes, may, a thousand years hence, be ripened into maturity . . . .'⁴⁰

Accustomed to such experiences, Cook passed summarily over the welcoming functions but made special mention of a grass 'plat' in front of the principal chief's doorway, used for wiping the feet — a mark of cleanliness he had not encountered in these seas before. Once the civilities were ended, working parties were sent to gather wood and water, the observatories were set up, and the ailing animals transported from the *Resolution*. Omai's linguistic gifts, so conspicuously lacking on his previous visit to the group, were again employed for the benefit of his companions. He was of great use not only as an interpreter, reported Second Lieutenant King, but in fostering good relations with the natives, 'for they pay him great attention & listen to the stories he tells them about Britannee, which doubtless tends to keep up our consequence, too apt to be lessen'd by the familiarity of our intercourse . . . .' He accompanied the captains on their daily excursions and acted as go-between in the brisk trade that soon sprang up in local produce and curiosities. In

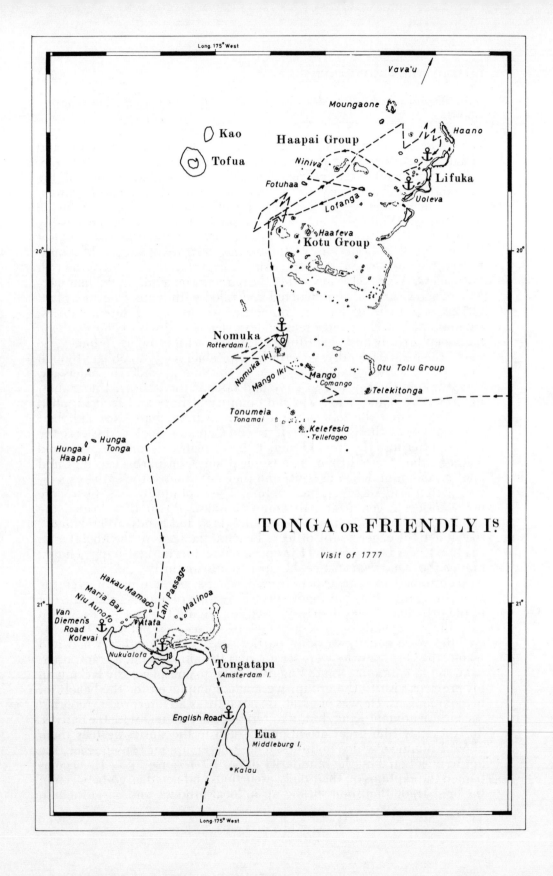

Long. 175° West

Vava'u

Moungaone

Kao

Tofua

Haapai Group

Haano

Niniva

Lifuka

Fotuhaa

Uoleva

Lofanga

20°   20°

Haafeva

Kotu Group

Nomuka
Rotterdam I.

Otu Tolu Group

Nomuka Iki

Mango Iki

Mango

Comango

Telekitonga

Tonumeia
Tonamai

Kelefesia

Tellefageo

Hunga
Tonga

Hunga
Haapai

TONGA or **FRIENDLY I**s

Visit of 1777

Hakau Mamao

Maria Bay

Niu Aunofo

Lahi Passage

Malinoa

Van
Diemen's
Road
Kolevai

Atata

Nuku'alofa

Tongatapu
Amsterdam I.

English Road

Eua
Middleburg I.

Kalau

return for some of the articles brought from England, he himself laid in a stock of the red feathers so abundant here, so rare and precious in his own islands. And, reverting to Polynesian custom, he began the practice of spending the nights ashore with the 'Wife' provided by his considerate hosts.[41]

Omai had scarcely settled in with his new friends when he acquired another influential patron in a man of commanding presence who came from Tongatapu with a retinue of followers. His name was Finau — Feenough in Cook's rendering — and he was introduced as 'King of all the friendly isles'. Though he had some doubts about the propriety of the title, Cook entertained the supposed monarch in his cabin and conferred on the royal person a gown of printed linen with lesser gifts. Feenough secured the return of a large axe stolen before his arrival but seemed powerless to curb his subjects' continual pilfering. One of them, a minor chief, was detected carrying off an iron bolt hidden beneath his clothes. For this crime he received twelve lashes and was confined on the *Resolution* until ransomed with a hog — penalties that deterred his fellow chiefs but not their servants until Clerke hit upon the device of shaving the heads of all culprits. Otherwise things went amicably enough and, while Omai cultivated his latest protector, Cook supervised shore activities and, with invincible optimism, the planting of English fruits and vegetables. At the end of ten days, since he found they 'had quite exhausted the island of all most every thing it produced', he thought it time to move elsewhere. He first intended making for Tongatapu but Feenough persuaded him to visit instead the islands in the north-east. Since his arrival the live cargo had 'amazingly recovered'—'from perfect skeletons, the horses and cows were grown plump, and as playful as young colts.' Not every member of the expedition, however, had benefited from the visit to Nomuka. Before the ships weighed anchor on 14 May the sharp-eyed Lieutenant Burney noticed that the older of the two New Zealanders had 'contracted the Venereal Distemper'; 'so it is,' wrote Mr. King, 'that wherever we go, we spread an incurable distemper which nothing we can do can ever recompence.'[42]

After a tedious and sometimes hazardous passage from Nomuka, on the 17th the ships reached the island of Lifuka for a stay which marked the idyllic climax of this visit, perhaps of the entire voyage. Escorted by Feenough and Omai, Cook went ashore the next morning to receive a ceremonial welcome more elaborate and more protracted than any he had experienced before. First of all two long lines of natives appeared bearing gifts — yams, breadfruit, plantains, coconuts, sugar-canes, pigs, fowls, turtles — which they placed in separate piles, one for Omai and the other, twice as large, for Cook. It far exceeded any present he had ever received from an 'Indian Prince', wrote the grateful commander. The guests, surrounded by thousands of spectators, were then diverted by athletic competitions: wrestling bouts in a style resembling that of 'our Cornish men'; boxing matches between Amazonian women; duels among pairs of young men armed with clubs. In return for this

44 *Night dance by Tongan women, after John Webber*

45 Night dance by Tongan men, after Webber

virile entertainment, at Feenough's special request, the marines from both ships carried out military exercises and fired volleys from their muskets. The islanders again responded with a dance performed by a troupe moving 'as one man' to the beat of drums. At nightfall the Europeans let off sky and water rockets with gratifying effects on the vast concourse. As Mr. King observed, Omai used the occasion to emphasize British power, pointing out how easy it was for his shipmates to destroy not only the earth but the water and the sky. Cook for his part noted with satisfaction that the fireworks pleased the natives beyond measure 'and intirely turned the scale in our favour.' The Tongans, nevertheless, had the last word in this contest of spectacles. By the light of burning torches they staged a succession of formal dances, including one by young women who carried out their movements with the precision of a European ballet. These performances, like other events in a memorable interlude, were beautifully commemorated by the artist John Webber and moved David Samwell to poetic speculation. Had the navigators 'at last found the fortunate Isles where all those Blessings are contained that "fancy fabled in her Age of Gold"'? He was inclined to think so but felt compelled to condemn two evils that marred this earthly paradise, the 'exorbitant Power of the Chiefs' and their 'barbarous Treatment of the common People'.[43]

The festival, spread over several days, made an auspicious beginning to an interlude marred rather less here than elsewhere by pilfering. Cook merely reported the loss of 'a Tarpauling and some other things' which were spirited away before the thieves could be apprehended. The *Discovery* suffered more severely with the disappearance of various iron objects and, even more annoying, the ship's cats. On the 20th a man was caught purloining one of the animals and, to the consternation of Europeans and Tongans alike, he turned out to be an important chief. Consulted about what should be done, Omai recommended a sentence of a hundred lashes, sternly pointing out that the higher the rank the more reprehensible the crime. The less doctrinaire Clerke awarded a token punishment of one lash and freed the malefactor, an act of clemency which won the abject gratitude of his subjects and fellow chiefs. In this incident Rickman found further proof of their friendly and pacific disposition. 'They seem to be', he claimed, 'the only people upon earth who, in principle and practice, are true christians.' Irritated by petty thefts, the visitors remained blissfully unaware that their hosts were meditating plunder on a truly prodigious scale. In the midst of feasts and entertainments these kindly islanders were, according to their own traditions, plotting the slaughter of their guests and the seizure of the ships. Happily for European illusions and lives, the plans miscarried, and on 23 May Feenough, one of the leading conspirators, left for an island in the north to get red feathered caps for Cook and Omai to carry to Tahiti. He promised to be back in a few days and asked the commander to wait at Lifuka until he returned.[44]

Cook had already discharged his debt to posterity by sowing Indian corn, melons, pumpkins, etc. in the well-kept plantations and spent the next few days adding to his knowledge of Tongan customs. He watched as a mother operated with wooden probes on the eyes of a blind infant while another woman in the same house used a shark's tooth to shave her child's head. Since there was no sign of Feenough by the 26th and provisions were becoming scarce, he decided to seek fresh supplies elsewhere. The ships had not yet cleared the island when, at noon on the 27th, a large sailing canoe reached the anchorage with an imposing passenger, Polaho (Paulaho), who was introduced as 'King of all the Isles'. This was the second of Feenough's rivals to appear within a week, for at the close of the festivities there arrived a personage of 'sullen and stupid gravity' claiming to be 'King'. But he refused to visit the *Resolution* and, following Feenough's example, the commander ignored him. Polaho was a more formidable pretender. He did not hesitate to come aboard, bearing a present of two fat hogs, 'though not so fat as himself,' Cook jested, 'for he was the most corperate plump fellow we had met with.' The commander found him sedate and sensible and, for the present, was not disposed to inquire into the legality of the titles assumed by 'all these great men'. It was otherwise with Omai 'who', again to cite Cook, 'was a good deal chagrined at finding there was a greater man than his friend Feenough, or Omai as he was now called for they had from the first chang'd names.' The jealous young man closely questioned the monarch in an attempt to dispose of his pretensions and refused to accompany him and Cook when they went ashore.[45]

Followed by Polaho in the royal canoe, the two ships finally got away at daybreak on the 29th, heading south to continue their locust-like progress through the islands. By this time, reported Mr. Bayly of the *Discovery*, the people of Lifuka had very few things to dispose of except their women. The commerce, he added, was highly advantageous to the local men who received payment at the rate of a hatchet or a shirt per night. That, however, was only 'the Common run of trade' — in some instances he had seen 'two hatchets & a shirt or sheet given for a Nights lodging with a fine young Girl.'[46]

Though his ultimate objective was Tongatapu, Cook had arranged to meet Polaho at Nomuka whither he sailed by the route he had previously taken on his passage north. The weather was squally and the ships often in danger from submerged reefs and sand-banks; but such hazards, the commander acknowledged with resignation, were 'the unavoidable Companions of the Man who goes on Discoveries.' They again landed at Nomuka on 5 June to find the islanders harvesting their yams which were 'in the greatest perfection' and, acquired for pieces of iron, did something to replenish supplies. On inspecting his own gardens, Cook saw to his 'Mortification' that only the pineapples were flourishing; most of the other plants had been destroyed by ants. He suffered a further disappointment when Feenough at last turned up on the 6th with news that the spoils of his northern expedition had been lost at sea. Cook disbelieved the supposed monarch's story and was fully convinced of his duplicity on Polaho's arrival the next morning. When they met ashore, the two royal pretenders spoke to each other but to what effect no one could tell, for out of loyalty to his new patron, King alleged, Omai misinterpreted the conversation. Polaho certainly seemed the greater and when they went aboard to dine there could be no more doubt. In accordance with Tongan protocol, Feenough was not permitted to eat in the presence of a superior and withdrew from the cabin when the meal was served. His larger claims were thus unfounded, but he still exerted some authority and appointed two of his underlings to guide the ships to Tongatapu where they arrived on 10 June. Among the first callers was Otago, Cook's major-domo during his first visit. Testimonies of friendship were exchanged, he reported, but the man's name was not again mentioned.[47] Otago had served his purpose and now gave way to more influential figures.

As this was meant to be their last anchorage before they left for Tahiti, a camp, trading-post, and observatory were set up under the protection of marines and the animals unloaded (to the astonishment, as usual, of the native audience). Omai now spent most of his time ashore and built a small house for his 'Girl' and himself near the encampment. Because he was always in the company of Captain Cook and other officers, Samwell noted, he was considered a chief of great consequence by the Tongans and, as such, highly respected. The New Zealanders were 'pretty well understood', wrote the same informant, and spent most of their time with the local people who were very fond of them and paid them much attention. After once dancing their war 'Heivah', the two boys were often called on to repeat the performance — 'which they did & were much caressed & admired for it.'[48]

Several times during the visit the islanders entertained their guests with feasts, concerts, athletic contests, and ballets which, if less spectacular than those seen at Lifuka, continued to draw admiring comment from some members of the expedition. Cook was evidently becoming sated with such junketing and ventured to criticize 'a sort of sameness' in the 'Circular dance', though he admitted that uninformed outsiders would view English country dancing with similar prejudice. His own interests attracted him more strongly to other aspects of Tongan life, in particular its highly developed ritual and its baffling social structure. At the request of his hosts, he attended one of their ceremonies of mourning and, much against their will, took part in an elaborate festival of initiation — the *inasi* — where following the example of other celebrants (and of Mr. Banks on a famous occasion), he stripped to the waist. Omai was his companion at both functions and assisted him in his determined efforts to unravel the intricate relationships of Tongan royalty. Polaho, there seemed little doubt, was 'King', yet one of his venerable relatives, *'Mariwaggy'* (Maealiuaki), was described as 'the first man on the island', while Polaho himself was seen to do obeisance to an unnamed woman of prodigious sacredness. Feenough was clearly of lower status but was found to be 'a man of consequence and property' — certainly endowed with sufficient authority to offer Omai the chieftainship of the island of Eua.[49]

Under the strain of his combined roles as interpreter, diplomat, go-between, and chief-presumptive, Omai apparently suffered a temporary lapse from decorum. In the course of a dispute, relates Samwell, 'in a drunken fit', alleges Burney, he struck the Corporal of Marines who returned the blow. Highly offended by this insult, he complained to Captain Cook, but when his protector refused him any redress, Omai announced his intention of staying behind in these islands. He then left the encampment, taking with him his New Zealand retainers. Happily the quarrel was soon settled. A messenger was sent after him and, on his return the next day, Samwell concludes, 'matters were made up to his satisfaction, tho' Capt[n] Cook would not punish the Corporal as Omai had struck him while upon duty.'[50]

During their month-long stay on the island Cook, too, seems to have suffered under the strain of his manifold duties, more especially the self-imposed duty of imparting to his hosts civilized notions concerning the sacredness of private property. The pilfering experienced elsewhere in the group here reached wholesale proportions. In spite of their vigilance, and in the very midst of ceremonies held in their honour, the commander lamented, they were plundered 'in every quarter and that in the most daring and insolent manner'. The penalties previously imposed having proved quite ineffective, he increased their severity; and in his efforts to stem the tide of theft he showed no respect either for high-born persons or the laws of hospitality. To secure the return of some stolen articles, he detained Polaho and Feenough, whom he had invited to dine with him on board, and released them only when they promised that everything would be restored. The common people suffered far more severely: one man received six dozen lashes for stealing a knife; another three dozen for removing a few glasses; a third, for stoning a sentry, had his arm cut to the bone — a punishment he bore without complaint, though the sight moved Feenough to tears. 'It is not to be wondered,' remarked the humane Rickman, 'that after such wanton acts of cruelty, the inhabitants should grow outrageous; and, though they did not break out into open acts of hostility, yet they watched every opportunity to be vexatious.' Other writers spoke of growing coldness among the Tongans, of the closed doors that now confronted the visitors, of the insults and violence to which they were sometimes subjected. While they were out on a shooting expedition, Mr. Bligh, master of the *Resolution*, and a companion were set upon and robbed of their muskets and other possessions. On returning to the encampment, they got Omai to complain to his royal friends, but the only result was that Polaho and Feenough, fearing the commander's wrath, withdrew from the neighbourhood of the ships and returned only when assured that he did not hold them responsible. He was 'very much displeased' by the incident, Cook wrote, and 'gave Omai a reprimand for meddling in it'.[51]

Suspecting that his precious livestock might be the next target for native 'Thievery', Cook thought it prudent to distribute the selection he intended to leave. So on 19 June he assembled the chiefs and made a formal presentation. To Polaho he gave an English bull and cow, to Mariwaggy a Cape ram and two ewes, to Feenough a horse and mare. Omai was not at all pleased by this move, claiming that the 'Cattle' were intended for him. Nevertheless, at Cook's prompting, he told the recipients

that there were no such animals within many Months sail of them, that they had been brought them at a vast trouble and expence, and therefore they were not to kill any till they became very numerous, and lastly, they and their Children were to remember that they had them from the men of Britane . . . .

He also passed on what practical instruction he could which, as Cook remarked, was little enough. The cows and horses were well cared for by their new owners, but, finding the sheep neglected and fearing that dogs might destroy them, Cook revoked the gift and took them back on board. Towards the end of the visit, with the object of improving the local breed, he gave his friends an English boar with three young sows and, one last tribute, a buck rabbit and doe. On 9 July he ended his journal entry on a note of self-congratulation: 'If the Cattle succeed, of which I have no doubt, it will be a vast acqu[i]sition to these islands, and as Tongatabu is a fine level country the horses will prove a usefull animal.' Final preparations having already been made, the ships left the next morning for Eua where they anchored on the 12th.[52]

The return to Eua marked one of the peaks in Omai's erratic career. Less than four years earlier he had touched at this self-same place, an inconspicuous follower of his European masters, an anonymous native rather overshadowed by the more attractive Odiddy. Now he was the commander's trusted interpreter and companion, a great favourite, as Cook himself said, of the influential Feenough who had offered to make him chief of the island. His sponsor, detained at Tongatapu by a funeral ceremony, was not present to urge the aspirant's claims, and the scheme fell through. Cook considered it not unlikely that Omai would have chosen to stay, but he withheld his own approval, 'not', he added darkly, 'because I thought he would do better in his own Native isle.' Had he been allowed to accept the office, Burney foretold, 'his continuance in it, after the departure of the Ships, would have been very precarious.' No one else in the expedition seems to have referred to the affair, and neither Cook nor Burney mentioned whether the New Zealand retainers were included in the proposals for their master's ennoblement.[53]

Cook may not have taken Feenough's offer very seriously, for he gave it far less space in his journal than he did more prosaic and practical matters. He had come in the first instance for fresh water, but accessible springs were as brackish here as at Tongatapu and he was forced to make do with what he already had. To his satisfaction, he was able to partake of a dish of the turnips sown on his previous voyage and, thus

encouraged, planted more seeds in the local chief's garden. That func-
tionary (whose attitude to the potential usurper is also ignored) supplied
what provisions he could and in return received a splendid gift, the three
sheep reclaimed from Mariwaggy. As the dogs he himself had introduced
to Tongatapu had not yet reached Eua, Cook thought it the 'properest
place' to leave the small flock. On climbing a hill whence he could view
'a very beautiful Landskip', he indulged in a vision of some future
navigator standing on the same spot to 'behould these Medows stocked
with Cattle, the English have planted at these islands.' Only one incident
marred the felicity of the brief visit. While he wandered alone, the
captain's servant was surrounded by a crowd who knocked him down
and stripped him of everything but his shoes. Cook immediately seized
two canoes and a hog by way of reprisal and in addition demanded the
surrender of the thieves and the return of all they had stolen. His resolute
methods were fully vindicated and the principles of British justice
upheld. By the time the ships sailed on 17 July, one offender had been
handed over and the last of the victim's garments given up — reduced
to fragments. The final gesture from the Friendly Isles was, however,
wholly in harmony with Cook's designation of the group. Canoes put
out from Tongatapu, laden with coconuts and shaddocks and bearing
farewell messages from the chiefs.[54]

In the next stage of the voyage when the annalists of the expedition
attempted to sum up their impressions, they were able to appreciate the
virtues of their hosts and view their shortcomings in calmer perspective.
The high-minded Anderson thought their countenances remarkably
expressive of their mild good nature and 'entirely free from that savage
keenness which marks nations in a barbarous state.' Their peaceable
disposition was sufficiently shown by the reception they had given to all
European voyagers; they had 'never appear'd in the smallest degree
hostile'. On the whole, they possessed many of the most excellent
qualities that adorned the human mind — 'Industry, Ingenuity, Perseverance, affability'. One thing alone, in Anderson's opinion, sullied
the Tongans' reputation, their habit of pilfering, a defect found to an
uncommon degree in people of both sexes and all ages. Yet the vice
appeared mainly in their dealings with Europeans, for among the natives
themselves dishonesty was, if anything, less common than in other
countries. Their thefts, indeed, seemed to arise solely from 'an intense
curiosity or desire to posess something which they see belongs to a sort
of people so different from themselves . . . .'[55]

If Cook did not go quite as far as the charitable surgeon, in the seclusion of his cabin he acknowledged the state of 'most cordial friendship'
which had prevailed during a stay of between two and three months.
True, 'some accidental differences' had now and then occurred owing
to the natives' 'great propensity to thieving'. On the other hand, such
differences had been 'but too often incouraged by the negligence of our
own people' and, furthermore, had never been 'attended with any fatal
consequences'. Some degree of remorse seems to be implied in such

remarks, and the sentiment became even more explicit when the commander reflected on a further consequence of his voyaging. There was inescapable evidence that venereal disease was now prevalent in these islands, for some of his men had become infected soon after they arrived. He thus had the 'Mortification' of learning that all the care he had previously taken to prevent 'this dreadfull desease' reaching the inhabitants had proved quite ineffectual.[56]

Possibly it was through his fear of spreading the dread contagion that, to the surprise of later commentators and some of his own men, Cook failed to visit either the Fiji or the Samoan Islands of which he had heard much from the Tongans. In any case, he was now anxious to complete his first mission, the restoration of Omai, and then push on with his voyage towards the Arctic. The month-long passage to Tahiti was marred by only one mishap. During a heavy squall on the night of 29 July the men of the *Resolution* observed lights moving on their consort and the next morning saw that its maintopmast was gone. With temporary repairs effected, the ships pursued their course until on 8 August land was unexpectedly sighted, the island of Tubuai, hitherto unknown to Europeans. Canoes resembling those of New Zealand came out to greet the voyagers and, though Omai could not persuade the crews to approach closely, he found they spoke his own tongue. Mr. Bayly was convinced these people had originally come from Tahiti and, subscribing to the now familiar theory, considered it probable they had been 'driven out to sea by some Accidental Winds & not able to get back again.' One man, Cook noted, continuously blew a conch which he had never found 'the messinger of Peace'. He thought it a place of little consequence, not worth the risk of losing a favourable wind to examine more thoroughly, and continued on his way. By the 12th the expedition was within sight of its next objective, Vaitepiha Bay in Tahiti Iti. 'Our two New Zealand Friends', wrote David Samwell, 'were not backward in testifying their Joy at seeing the Promised Land of which they had heard so much from Omai & others in the Ship.' As for their master, according to the same tender-hearted witness, he 'sat all day on the forecastle viewing his Native Shores with Tears in his Eyes.'[57]

10. Omai's Homecoming

RESTORED AT LAST TO HIS NATIVE SPHERE, OMAI NOW BECAME THE CENTRAL figure in an extended performance, part social comedy, part social drama, of which his shipboard companions were the absorbed and sometimes self-conscious spectators. 'Many in England envy'd us the sight of Omai's return to his Countrymen', wrote Second Lieutenant King who, supremely aware of his privileged role, supplied a circumstantial account of the episode. As they approached Tahiti, he observed, their charge became more and more the object of their attention, while with anxiety equal to their own he grew increasingly thoughtful. Even before reaching Vaitepiha Bay on the evening of 12 August, they waited impatiently for canoes to arrive and when at last one man boarded the *Resolution*, Omai clasped him by the hand with emotion to ply him with questions. The visitor showed no sympathy in return and hardly the least surprise at being spoken to in his own language by a stranger dressed differently from himself. Nor was there any 'wild Demonstration of joy' from another canoe bearing a chief and Omai's brother-in-law. The voyager embraced his relative with 'marks of strong feeling & great tenderness' but was received 'rather Coldly than cordially' until he took the men below to confer on them gifts of the red feathers he had brought from the Friendly Isles. King was a disgusted witness of 'the farce of flattery & vanity' that followed. The chief, who had scarcely noticed him before, now began to caress Omai, asked him to exchange names in token of friendship, and sent ashore for a hog in return for the precious feathers. As for the brother-in-law, a person of 'most forbidding countenance' in King's view, he shed his distant manner and stayed on the ship till morning.[1]

In conversation with his compatriots, Omai managed to pick up some news of local affairs. The first man aboard had spoken of a ship which reached the bay after Captain Cook's previous visit, but he added such unlikely details that Omai doubted his word. The others, however, were able to verify and amplify the report. There were, they said, two ships which had come twice from a place called Rema. The first time the strangers had built a house and left behind four men — two priests, their servant, and another man. At the end of ten months the same ships had returned to take the settlers away, leaving the house and near it a cross to mark the grave of their commander who had died ashore. Furthermore, they concluded, the strangers had left behind animals much finer than those on the *Resolution*. When his shipmates heard the last particulars, King related, disappointment and vexation were visible on every countenance: 'We saw that our Act of benevolence from its being too long deferrd, had lost its hour & its reward; We saw the loss of a season & an immence deal of trouble all thrown away to no purpose . . . .' There this tantalizing intelligence had necessarily to rest for the present. Since there was no wind and the moon was up, they attempted to tow the two vessels in with the aid of their boats; but they had no success and were compelled to lie off the coast for the rest of the night.[2]

By morning, news of the rarities acquired in Tonga had spread ashore and, as they moved into the bay, the ships were surrounded by a multitude of canoes filled with hogs and fruit for barter. Above all else the Tahitians demanded red feathers in return for their produce, so that, as Cook jested, 'not more . . . than might be got from a Tom tit would purch[ase] a hog of 40 or 50 pound weight'. They still set a high price on hatchets and knives, 'but', he noted, 'Nails and beads, which formerly had so great a run at this island, they would not now so much as look at.' Some favoured visitors were taken below and one chief, who was allowed to deck himself out in feathered finery, spent the rest of the day at the cabin windows displaying himself to his fellow islanders, 'like some eastern Monarch adored by his Subjects'. Soon after they anchored, about nine o'clock, Omai was joined by his sister in a meeting that satisfied all the expectations of sentimental observers. Cook passed the scene over as 'extreamly moving and better concieved than discribed', but the less delicately reticent Samwell gave some details. He mentioned the young woman's cries of distress when she arrived in a canoe laden with hogs, breadfruit, and other refreshments for her brother. She was so deeply affected, he said, that she seemed hardly able to bear an interview with one 'whom she had been so long without seeing'. As she came on board weeping, Omai embraced her but, to hide his own tears, took her below whence she returned to thank Captain Cook and his officers for bringing her brother back in safety. She, too, received a quota of red feathers and so did 'all who had art to profess friendship', added the disapproving Mr. King.[3]

After initiating routine activities, Cook went ashore later in the morning with Omai and some of his officers to wander, observe, and question in his usual manner. Otoo and other friends were flourishing, he learned, but there had been two recent fatalities. The elusive Vehiatua of his last voyage, Mr. Banks's 'little olive liped boy', was no more. He had succumbed to an illness (some said to intemperance) and been succeeded by a brother who was now visiting another part of his domain. Of far greater moment to the outside world, the 'celebrated Oberea' had died since the *Resolution* last touched at Tahiti in May 1774. Cook recorded

the fact without comment, but the gentle Clerke wrote in elegiac strain:
'I felt severely for the loss of this good old Lady, for she was a most
benevolent Being, and a firm Friend to our cause.' In the absence of
the new Vehiatua, they paid their respects to a venerable man from
Borabora known as Oro, after the supreme god of the islands, though
Cook declared his real name was Etary (more accurately Etari). Despite
his sinister origins, Omai treated the sage with reverence, gave him a
tuft of red feathers, and was conversing with him 'on indifferent matters'
when his attention was drawn to an old woman. She was his mother's
sister and behaved with becoming emotion — she fell at her nephew's
feet and 'bedewed them plentifully with tears of joy'. Leaving Omai
with his aunt and the crowd which had gathered round them, the commander walked on to inspect the house said to have been left by the
mysterious strangers.[4]

The place was closely examined by Cook and his companions. It was
built of timber specially brought for the purpose, since each plank was
separately numbered. The walls were pierced by shuttered apertures
that ventilated the house and would, if necessary, have served for the
firing of muskets from within. There were two rooms, each about five
or six yards square, the inner one still containing a bedstead, a table,
stools, and some articles of European clothing which the Tahitians
carefully preserved. They had also protected the house by erecting a
large shed over it so that it had suffered no damage from sun or weather.
At a little distance stood a cross bearing the inscription, 'Christus Vincit
Car[o]lus III imperat 1774'. A few neglected cabbages grew near the
house and a vine 'in a bad state', the only remnant of a plantation which
the islanders had trampled underfoot when they tasted the unripe grapes
and decided they were poisonous. In addition, the strangers had left
several animals, though, to Mr. King's relief, they hardly compared in
number or variety with those on the Resolution. There were neither
sheep nor horses but only goats, some hogs much larger than the local
breed, cats which had gone wild, dogs of various kinds, and a solitary
bull, now living elsewhere on the island.[5]

Cook had difficulty in piecing together an account of the visitors, for
most islanders, he complained, were quite unable 'to remember, or note
the time when past events happened; especially if the time exceeds ten,
or twenty months.' Indeed, the voluminous European records of the
episode are themselves sometimes obscure or contradictory. As the
Englishmen had already divined, the strangers were Spaniards from
Peru. On three separate occasions (not two, as Omai's informants told
him), they had come to assert His Catholic Majesty's rights in the Pacific
and in consequence had increased the score of Polynesian voyagers and
Polynesian victims. They first called at Tahiti late in 1772, so giving rise
to the rumours Cook had picked up on his previous visit to Vaitepiha
Bay. After staying a month, they had left with four native volunteers;
of these one died when they reached Valparaiso and another at Lima.
The remaining two, having lived about eighteen months in the Viceroy's

palace and received Christian baptism, returned with the second
expedition. They reached home in November 1774, accompanied by
two Franciscan friars, their servant, and a translator, supplied with a
portable house to accommodate them. This time the Spaniards spent
two months in Tahitian waters, leaving behind the tiny mission and the
body of their dead commander who had been buried near the house.
Once more native volunteers travelled to South America with the
Spaniards, but reports differ as to their number. According to one
version, there were again four, of whom two died, while a third
remained in Peru and the fourth returned to Tahiti. Another source
mentions two men but says nothing of their subsequent fate. The
survivor or survivors went back with the final expedition which called
briefly at Vaitepiha Bay in November 1775 and then sailed off with the
four Spaniards, Tahiti's first European settlers.[6]

Whatever the precise facts, it was certain that the whole protracted
enterprise had done virtually nothing to change the Tahitians' manner
of life or wean them from their ancient beliefs. In the period they spent
on the island — little short of a year — the Franciscans had not made
a single convert. Even more discouraging, the two survivors of the first
expedition had deserted the mission they were intended to serve, rejected
Christianity, and returned to the faith and practices of their ancestors.[7]
The prospect that Omai, still in his pagan state, might succeed in
reclaiming his benighted countrymen was on the face of it exceedingly
remote.

On his return from the Spanish house, Cook found his protégé 'holding
forth to a large company'; and it was only with difficulty that the young
man was able to detach himself from the curious throng to make his
way back on board. That evening the commander held forth on his own
account to the ship's company assembled on the quarterdeck. He spoke
of the long and perilous voyage before them, pointed out the need to
conserve supplies, and suggested that they might forgo their usual ration
of spirits until they reached colder northern latitudes. To his satisfaction,
the gathering agreed to the proposal and Captain Clerke's crew followed their example the next day. So it was that during their stay in the
islands no more grog was served to the men, 'except', as Cook coyly
remarked, 'on Saturday nights when they had full allowance to drink to
their feemale friends in England, lest amongst the pretty girls of Otaheite
they should be wholy forgoten.' It seems probable that distant wives and
sweethearts were often lost sight of in the days and weeks that followed.
The women, noted Mr. Bayly, were thought friendlier than on former
voyages, a fact he put down to their great desire for red feathers. Many
would 'cohabit' for nothing else, he added, and as soon as they obtained
a small quantity vanished from sight.[8]

The self-denying resolution of his fellow travellers presumably had
little effect on Omai. As a regular guest at the captain's table he had
ample opportunity to indulge in his newly acquired taste for wine; and
in his role of returned voyager he would have had no trouble in satisfying

other needs and appetites — with or without the expenditure of red feathers. For most of the time he was at Vaitepiha Bay, on the authority of Rickman, he spent the nights ashore, occupying the Spanish house and sleeping in a bed 'put up after the English fashion'. He was so taken with the place that he 'offer'd largely for it', but the local people, fearing the Spaniards might return, would not part with the building. None the less they held him in high esteem not only because of his wealth and generosity but on account of his equestrian prowess. A couple of days after their arrival he and one of the officers exercised the two remaining horses amid scenes of 'Uproar & confusion' that Samwell found 'impossible to describe'. Making a valiant attempt (and probably embroidering on fact), Rickman pictured him riding with the officer (Cook in this version), 'dressed cap-a-pie in a suit of armour . . . mounted and caparisoned with his sword and pike, like St. George going to kill the dragon', while, somewhat out of saintly character, he fired a pistol over the crowd whenever it became 'clamorous, and troublesome'. The incident, as illustrated in Rickman's published journal, added a highly imaginative item to the iconography of Omai.[9]

The heavy rain that fell for some days failed to deter visitors from swarming in from neighbouring districts to dispose of their produce and pay their respects to the two captains. Ereti journeyed from Hitiaa and became a familiar figure on the ships. Nearly a decade had passed since he first regaled Bougainville with a simple repast that recalled the golden age. Now the chief enjoyed dining on board in European fashion and, it was observed, 'generally contrived to get drunk.' Among feminine callers the most distinguished was the absent Vehiatua's mother who allegedly 'became captain Clerke's taio, and exchanged names with him.' Both sexes entertained their guests with formal dances which in Samwell's opinion were far less graceful and diverting than those of the Friendly Islanders. The Oxford-educated Mr. King extended the comparison farther in a manner recalling the young Mr. Banks. The women here, he thought, were superior to their Tongan sisters — much more delicately formed, their features regular and beautiful, their outlines endowed with the softness and femininity so much wanting in Tonga. On the other hand he found the men in this island fell far short of his ideal in build, conduct, and manliness. 'On the whole', he summed up his impressions, 'as to figure if we want'd a Model for an Apollo or a Bachus we must look for it at Otaheite, & shall find it to perfection, but if for a Hercules or an Ajax at the friendly Isles.'[10]

Fortunately the weather cleared on the morning of the 17th when Cook was invited to call on the Vehiatua who had returned to the bay. Perhaps through an excessive desire to impress the gathering, Omai showed none of the sartorial good taste so often praised in England. With the help of his friends, Cook related, he arrayed himself 'not in English dress, nor in Otaheite, nor in Tongatabu nor in the dress of any Country upon earth, but in a strange medly of all he was possess'd of.' Reaching the shore, they joined the revered Etary and then seated them-

47
*Equestrian
exercise at
Vaitepiha Bay*

selves before a large house, first spreading their presents before them. When the Vehiatua appeared with his mother and their entourage, he proved to be a boy about ten years of age, cutting 'a very remarkable Figure' in a gold-laced Spanish hat and scarlet Spanish breeches reaching to his ankles. After Omai and Etary had both spoken, an orator on the other side informed the commander that, though 'the men of Rema' had forbidden them to do so, the people of Vaitepiha Bay now welcomed him and placed their possessions at his disposal. The young chief embraced him, exchanged names to ratify their 'treaty of Friendship', and was so pleased by his gift of a sword and a rich linen gown that he paraded about to display them. Omai entrusted him with an elaborate feather *maro* or girdle he had fashioned on the passage from Tonga. Much against Cook's advice and apparently to curry favour with both high chiefs, he asked the Vehiatua to dispatch the precious object to Otoo. When proceedings ended, the whole company adjourned to the *Resolution* for dinner. On the 19th the chief sent a handsome tribute of hogs, fruit, and cloth to Cook who responded that night with a display of fireworks as gratifying in its effects as earlier spectacles in Tonga.[11]

While addressing his men on the 13th, Cook had urged them not to be careless with their possessions and so put temptation in the way of the natives. Perhaps as a result of his warning, for the whole of their stay in this part of the island there were no complaints about theft and none of the customary 'incidents'. The Tahitians allowed their inquisitive guests to wander wherever they would, even assisting Cook in his impious inspection of the dead Vehiatua's remains hung round with mats and Spanish cloth. True, they showed great alarm at the removal of the memorial cross but were satisfied when it was replaced bearing an inscription to commemorate British exploits: *'Georgius tertius Rex Annis* 1767, 69, 73, 74 & 77.' His Majesty's loyal subjects were constantly reminded of their rivals, and both survivors of the first voyage to Peru appeared in person. One of them, who called on Clerke, 'had imbibed a good deal of that distant, formal deportment of the Spaniard' and 'so larded his Conversation with si Signior's as to render it unintelligible'. Nevertheless, the captain succeeded in drawing from him an opinion of 'Lima' which he thought a very poor country because 'there were no red Feathers there.' Further, 'when he saw the great Abundance of Omai's riches, he cursed the Signior's very heartily & lamented much, that his good fortune had not given him a Trip to England instead of Lima.' Though treated with great courtesy and rewarded with a present, the man did not come back. Cook had a similar experience with the second survivor who, on boarding the *Resolution*, was received with 'uncommon civility' but vanished before he could be questioned and failed to return. Cook suspected that during his own preoccupation with other matters the visitor had been hustled off the ship by Omai, 'despleased there was a traveler upon the island besides himself.'[12]

The jealous young man was a source of much anxiety to his friends on the *Resolution* and had given them cause for concern even before they reached Tahiti. As that sympathetic chronicler James King set out the position:

. . . Capt[n] Cook had taken a great deal of pains during the Voyage to prevail on Omai to agree to some certain arrangement by which his riches would be secur'd to him, & his own consequence rais'd & preserv'd, but he woud never listen to any plan, except that of destroying the bora bora chiefs & freeing his Native Island . . . from its present slavery to the King of that Island, & this C. Cook assur'd him he would not assist in doing, or even suffer him to do; not that he had any notion of its ever being in Omai's power, to whom he was invariably preaching the little weight & trifling consequence he woud find himself to possess among his Countrymen. Omai was not the less obstinate & it answerd a bad end, in making him rather fear than love the Captn.

Since their arrival the worried captain had found no reason to modify his opinion or take a more hopeful view of his protégé's future. With King he had been a witness of Omai's reception by mercenary relatives and self-proclaimed friends who, it was evident, were in love not with the man but his possessions and who, had it not been for his red feathers, would not have given him a single coconut. He had not expected anything else, Cook confessed, but he had hoped that with the property he now owned — a fortune compared to which Lord Clive's was 'a mere Mite', as another observer expressed it — Omai would have had the prudence to make himself 'respected and even courted by the first persons in the island'. Instead, during their stay at Vaitepiha Bay he had 'rejected the advice of those who wished him well and suffered himself to be duped by every designing knave.'[13]

At the end of ten days Cook decided to move on to his old anchorage at Matavai Bay where he hoped his troublesome charge might agree to settle. He had made the most of local resources — his reason for coming here in the first place — and Otoo clamoured for his presence. While the ships unmoored on the morning of 23 August, he and Omai went ashore to take leave of the Vehiatua. The visit was enlivened by the presence of another seer who, in the commander's opinion, had 'all the appearance of a man not in his right sences'. He was dressed only in plantain leaves wrapped round his waist and spoke 'in a low squeaking Voice' so that Cook found him almost incomprehensible, though Omai claimed to understand what he said. He advised the Vehiatua against leaving with the ships and foretold that they would not reach Matavai that day. The advice was unnecessary, objected the sceptical Cook, since no one had ever made such a proposal; as for the prophecy, he pointed out that there was not a breath of wind in any direction. Wondering at the credulity of his superstitious hosts, he bade them his last farewell and left with Omai.[14]

NO SOONER HAD THEY BOARDED THE SHIP than a breeze sprang up which carried the *Resolution* to Matavai Bay the same evening. But the *Discovery* did not arrive until the next day, so, as the fair-minded commander admitted, half the seer's prophecy proved true after all. Back in this historic place, endowed in the English imagination with a supreme ruler, a royal family, a Court, and other appurtenances of the monarchical system, Cook lost no time in meeting Otoo who had hurried from Pare on the morning of the 24th and was waiting near the anchorage. When the two captains disembarked, no effort was spared to impress the 'King' and his subjects. Rickman, with his eye for the picturesque, describes the party landing from pinnaces, decked out with 'silken streamers, embroidered ensigns, and other gorgeous decorations', after which they moved in procession to the air of a military march played by 'the whole band of music'. To the disappointment of the crowd, which had heard of his spectacular appearance at Vaitepiha Bay, Omai went on foot, dressed in uniform and almost indistinguishable from the English officers. On reaching the royal presence, Rickman continued, the returned traveller spoke in praise of the 'Great King of Pretanne', representing 'the splendour of his court by the brilliancy of the stars in the firmament; the extent of his dominions, by the vast expanse of heaven; the greatness of his power, by the thunder that shakes the earth.'[15]

In a more prosaic and probably more accurate description of the ceremony, Cook portrays his charge arrayed in 'his very best suit of clothes', kneeling to embrace Otoo's legs and generally acting with 'a great deal of respect and Modesty'. Just as the commander had feared, the Vehiatua had kept Omai's elaborate *maro* for himself, sending in its place a small tuft of feathers, not a twentieth part of its value. Now the suppliant tried to atone for his lapse by giving Otoo a large piece of gold cloth and more of the prized red feathers. None of the assembled dignitaries seemed to recognize him, and they paid him little attention — perhaps through envy, Cook surmised. He himself presented Otoo with a suit of fine linen, a gold-laced hat, some tools, and, most precious of all, feathers and a bonnet brought from the Friendly Isles. The monarch with his father, two brothers, and three sisters then left for the *Resolution*, followed by canoes laden with sufficient provisions to supply both ships for a week. Later in the morning Otoo's mother came on board with her own gifts of food and cloth which she divided between Cook and Omai; for the royal family had now learned of the lowly Raiatean's wealth and began to seek his friendship. Cook encouraged them to do so, he explained, because he hoped Omai would remain here and so be able to advise on the care and use of the remaining livestock. Moreover, it seemed that the farther he was from his native island the better he was likely to fare.[16]

Cook did not delay long before disposing of his precious cargo. After entertaining the guests at dinner, he took them back to Pare with a consignment of poultry — the peacock and hen he had received from Lord Bessborough, a turkey-cock and hen, a gander and three geese, a drake and four ducks. On reaching Otoo's domain, he found the Spanish bull of which he had heard at Vaitepiha Bay. It was owned by Etary, he now learned, and was awaiting transportation to Borabora. He had rarely seen a finer beast, Cook remarked in envious admiration; his fellow captain, on the other hand, was moved to cynical jest: 'poor Devil', exclaimed Clerke, 'he was the only Being I'll answer for it, throughout the Isle, that cou'd not now & then solace himself with a little amorous dalliance'. In fact there was another involuntary celibate in Otoo's keeping, a venerable gander, sole survivor of Captain Wallis's parting gift to Oberea ten years before. The next morning Cook relieved the bull's solitary plight by sending three cows to Pare. The rest of the livestock — a horse and mare, a young bull, some sheep and goats — he set ashore at Matavai. He now found himself relieved of a very heavy burden, Cook confessed; the trouble and vexation he had undergone during the voyage were hardly to be conceived. 'But', he comforted himself, 'the satisfaction I felt in having been so fortunate as to fulfill His Majesty's design in sending such usefull Animals to two worthy Nations sufficiently recompenced me for the many anxious hours I had on their account.'[17]

Other members of the expedition shared Cook's relief that their troublesome passengers had at last departed. 'Every person I am sure', wrote Mr. King, 'must have felt a singular pleasure in seeing them safely landed alive, after having been so long on board in such variety of climates . . . .' His own feeling was that the animals would provide some small compensation for 'the horrid disease' the voyagers had brought to these islands. King had been put in charge of the shore station and the observatories set up on the site of Fort Venus with a guard of marines. Here the *Discovery*'s mainmast was repaired, the stores examined, and other preparations made for the long voyage that lay ahead. Nearby, on 26 August, Cook had a piece of ground cleared for yet another of his gardens. Chastened by earlier experiences, he had little hope that the Tahitians would look after this latest venture. Nevertheless, he sowed melons, potatoes, pineapples and, collaborating with David Nelson in a new horticultural experiment, planted out citrus or shaddock seedlings brought from the Friendly Isles. He was confident these would flourish unless they suffered the same fate as the Spanish grape-vines at Vaitepiha Bay. Omai, he noted, had salvaged slips from the damaged plantation and brought them with him to stock his own garden once he was settled.[18]

That issue was still to be determined, but in the meantime Cook was fully occupied as he supervised his men or greeted old friends or entertained his many visitors. Ereti, still avid for European hospitality, had followed the ships from Vaitepiha to babble of Bougainville; Oamo, consort of the lamented Oberea, came from distant Papara; and Odiddy, Cook's companion on part of the previous voyage, lost no time in calling on his old patron. The Boraboran volunteer had been a great success on the *Resolution* and was much sought after at Tahiti when the ship returned there after parting with the *Adventure*. Indeed, in the course

48
Odiddy, Cook's favourite,
from a drawing by Hodges

of a short stay at Matavai he married a young woman, the daughter of a local chief; and, according to George Forster, soon after the nuptials became the bedfellow of Oberea (like her near-contemporary Catherine of Russia, a connoisseur of youthful lovers almost to the end). Of even greater moment for his future, he had won the favour of Otoo and received from him a pressing invitation to remain at Tahiti. Though attracted by the offer, Odiddy decided he should first farewell his relatives in the Society Islands and accordingly sailed on with the *Resolution.* Cook had been tempted to carry his attractive protégé back to England but seeing no prospect of His Majesty's ships ever returning (at this time he was, of course, unaware of Omai's travels) he abandoned the idea. So in June 1774 the sorrowing youth was left at Raiatea, 'universally belov'd by us all', as one of his shipmates testified.[19]

Somehow in the intervening years Odiddy had found his way back to Tahiti and when the latest expedition arrived was living with his wife at Matavai under Otoo's protection. In shipboard journals he was the subject of extensive comment, most of it uncomplimentary. Cook said surprisingly little about his favourite, merely recording that he had

given him the clothes sent out by the Admiralty together with a chest
of tools and 'a few other articles'. King dismissed him as 'a handsome
looking young man', 'quite an Otaheite Coxcomb', and 'the most stupid
foolish Youth I ever saw'. The last phrase was echoed in Samwell's more
elaborate account. They had been told by veterans of the last voyage,
he observed, that Odiddy was 'a fine sensible young fellow, much
superior to Omai in every respect'. What, then, was their disappointment to find him 'one of the most stupid Fellows on the Island, with a
clumsy awkward Person and a remarkable heavy look'; further, when
visiting the ship with his pretty wife, he was 'almost constantly drunk
with Kava'. As for his new clothes, after wearing them no longer than
two or three days, he disposed of them to the seamen for hatchets and
red feathers. In so doing, Samwell considered (lending support to the
views of Rousseau), 'he shewed some degree of Sense, as those articles
would be of much more Service to him than English cloaths which are
not half so well calculated for the Climate as their own'. His one champion was a German sailor on the *Discovery*, Heinrich Zimmermann,
who thought Odiddy knew how to deport himself better than Otoo and
spoke English as well as Omai, in spite of the latter's two years' sojourn
in the country. 'It would be more to the point', his admirer asserted, 'if
he could come to Europe for a time, since he possesses much natural
intelligence as well as a fine physique.' William Bayly advanced a quite
contrary opinion: 'It does not appear that he would have made any
figure in England if he had gone, for he appears to be one of the most
silly fillowes Among thim.'[20]

Shipboard tattle, emanating from Bayly and Samwell, links most of
the principal figures gathered at Matavai in a complicated plot worthy
of contemporary English — or Tahitian — farce. Otoo is not implausibly
said to have offered the services of his youngest sister to Cook for the
duration of his stay, but, observing his inflexible rule, the commander
declined the honour. He did, however, encourage a plan to marry the
same 'princess' to Omai, now living ashore with his own sister and
brother-in-law who had followed him from Vaitepiha Bay. The proposed
alliance with the royal family would have enhanced his status, secured
his safety, and kept him in Tahiti with the animals. Before the marriage
could be arranged, alas, the prospective bridegroom fell into the clutches
of the princess's lover and his cronies. Conspiring to alienate their
gullible victim from Otoo and seize his possessions, these 'raskels' 'provided
him with a very fine girl', their accomplice, and one night descended on
the couple as they slept. During the attack Omai fired his pistol, missing
the chief assailant, and (to follow Bayly), 'they all quarreled & the girl
left him but not till she had in a manner strip'd him of his most valuable
things, & to crown all she gave him the foul disease'. Bayly supplies a
further twist to this tangled skein of intrigue by claiming that the
unprincipled 'girl' was none other than Odiddy's pretty young wife. If
these sordid facts reached Cook, he failed to commit them to his journal.
There he merely complained that the wilful young man rejected his

advice, acted in such a way as to lose the friendship of Otoo and every other person of note, and consorted with 'none but refugees and strangers whose sole Views were to plunder him'.[21]

As the month of August drew to a close, the commander was beset by more urgent concerns than Omai's amours and indiscretions. On the morning of the 27th he was told that two Spanish vessels had anchored in Vaitepiha Bay. The report was so convincing that he sent a junior officer, John Williamson, to spy on the potential enemy and at the same time ordered guns to be brought on deck and had the ships cleared for action. This martial display greatly alarmed the local populace who, Samwell surmised, still remembered the destruction inflicted by the *Dolphin*. Amid universal panic, trading came to a stop, canoes vanished, and 'Sweethearts' fled ashore. With Williamson's return on the 29th, Cook learned that the story was a complete fabrication designed, he supposed, to lure him back to his first anchorage. Things had barely returned to normal when he discovered that the islanders, led by Otoo and his family, had again deserted the bay. He suspected that something had been stolen, and so it proved: a native guide had made off with four hatchets incautiously entrusted to him by one of the surgeons in quest of 'curiosities'. Catching up with the fugitives, Cook allayed their fears, assured them he had no thought of punishment, and brought them back to Matavai. His extreme solicitude for the chief's feelings is borne out by another incident not mentioned in his own journal. One night a man succeeded in evading the sentry and broke into the observatory. While he was moving about in the darkness, Mr. Bayly caught him by the hair but could not prevent his escape. The astronomer was convinced the thief was Otoo and told Cook whose only response was openly to absolve the royal marauder; the sentry, however, received 'a smart flogging' for his negligence.[22]

At this time Otoo himself was taken up with pressing affairs of state. During his previous visit to Tahiti (as William Watson testified), Cook had been deeply impressed by the great armada gathered to invade neighbouring Moorea. The attack had been unsuccessful, he was now

informed, and since then sporadic fighting had continued between opposing factions on the two islands. On 30 August, hearing that his Moorean allies had been driven to the mountains, the chief summoned a council at his house where Cook happened to be visiting. In the course of a heated debate, the commander was asked to take part in a new expedition against the enemy but declined on the grounds that he knew nothing of the dispute and could not make war on people who had never offended him. Otoo also seemed lukewarm about the enterprise, for he spoke only a word or two throughout the whole conference. Nevertheless, he was irretrievably committed to the new campaign and a couple of days later received a summons to attend a second gathering. The great warrior Towha (or Tahua) was offering up a human sacrifice to ensure the success of the invading fleet which he would command. Thinking it a good opportunity to witness 'this extraordinary and Barbarous custom', Cook set out with Otoo for the sacrificial *marae* some distance to the west, accompanied by Anderson, Webber, and Omai. While the protracted ceremony went on, the little European party restrained their feelings, but after it was over they voiced their

50
*Omai with Cook
and other officers:
detail of 49*

indignation in a stormy meeting with Towha, as Cook relates:

> Omai was our spokesman and entered into our arguments with so much Spirit
> that he put the Cheif out of all manner of patience, especially when he was told
> that if he a Cheif in England had put a Man to death as he had done this he
> would be hanged for it; on this he balled out 'Maeno maeno' (Vile vile) and
> would not here a nother word; so that we left him with as great a contempt of
> our customs as we could possibly have of theirs.[23]

On their way back to the ships Cook and his companions spent the
night of 3 September at Pare where they lodged in the 'palace' and
attended a dramatic performance staged by the three princesses aided
by a quartet of male comedians. From this point onwards the officers
were caught up in a whirl of engagements so that, as one of their number
remarked, 'We wanted no coffee-houses to kill time; nor Ranelaghs or
Vauxhalls for our evening entertainments.' The day they returned to
Matavai, Omai provided an excellent repast which included poultry
and puddings besides fish and pork. Otoo graciously attended, while
at this and later functions the host's English friends used their best efforts

to restore his damaged reputation and re-establish him in the eyes of influential islanders. Odiddy, too, was mindful of his social duties. Not unduly weighed down, it seems, by his own reputation as coxcomb and perhaps cuckold, he feasted his former patron and other English friends on those staples of Tahitian hospitality, fish, pork, and fruit. But Cook's protégés could not compete with their high-born rivals. The royal family were tireless in their attentions and continued to heap on Cook and Clerke lavish presents of food and 'prodigious' quantities of fine cloth ingeniously arranged on the persons of comely mannequins. The two captains in their turn bestowed their own gifts, staged their dinner-parties, or contrived more spectacular diversions. A display of fireworks on Sunday the 7th was more dramatic in its effects than any of its pre-decessors. Most of the vast concourse were 'terribly frightened', wrote Cook, and when a table rocket exploded, 'even the most resolute fled'. A week later he hit upon a further means of impressing the populace. After Omai had been thrown off a couple of times, the commander unkindly recorded, he and Captain Clerke rode the horses round the plain of Matavai, to the astonishment of the large train of spectators that followed. Henceforth the performance was repeated every day, and nothing, Cook felt, gave the Tahitians 'a better idea of the greatness of other Nations'.[24]

While ink and attention were profusely expended on the assembled dignitaries, English and Tahitian, one of the *Resolution*'s company spared a kindly glance for Omai's retainers. The New Zealand boys, wrote David Samwell, were delighted with the beauty of the island and spent much of their time on shore. The Tahitians treated them in a friendly manner, he said, though Coaa, the younger one, 'had a few Battles with the Otaheite Boys & was generally worsted by stripplings less than himself, which convinced him at last that it would be best to live in peace with them.' But he continued to bicker with the girls:

> Cocoa being what we call an unlucky Dog was fond of playing his Tricks, which now & then would bring him into Squabbles with the Girls. One of these being plagued by him reproached him with his Countrymen eating human flesh, at the same time making signs of biting her own Arm, the poor boy was much hurt at it and fell a crying; but presently recovering out of his Confusion and being still insulted by her, he put his fingers to his head as if searching for a louse & made signs of eating it, at the same time telling her that if his Country-men eat human flesh She eat lice which was almost as bad; by this quick stroke of retaliation our young Zealander got the laugh of his Side & the Girl was obliged to retreat & leave him master of the field.

Tiarooa, the older, quieter, and more dignified of the pair, was disposed of quite briefly: he 'always lived upon good terms' with the Tahitians and 'was esteemed for his friendly & modest disposition.'[25]

Cook had failed to mention the two exiles since their first days on the *Resolution* and continued to ignore their existence — at least in the copious entries of his journal. He himself, as the month of September slipped by, was often at Pare in the company of Otoo who, it was noted, had shed his timidity in the commander's presence and treated him with complete confidence. On the 16th the chief invited him to a function in honour of Etary, now settled near the palace after moving north from Vaitepiha Bay. Cook found the ceremony neither interesting nor curious but listened (presumably with Omai's help) while the Moorean war was considered and Etary's initial opposition overcome. The next evening news arrived that Towha and his fleet had already reached the island and launched an attack, with inconclusive results. On the morning of the 18th Cook set out once more for the royal seat, this time with Anderson, Omai, and the remaining sheep — an English ram and ewe, last survivors of King George's gift, and three Cape ewes — which he had decided to present to Otoo. Further, he hoped that Etary, who claimed the Spanish bull, might be persuaded to leave it at Pare; but the god-like Boraboran, having first given his consent, later withdrew it. Following fruitless arguments, Cook finally issued strict orders that all the animals must remain in Otoo's keeping until there was a stock of young ones to give away. His own account of the clash with Etary omits an incident recorded (evidently at second hand) in the lively pages of Samwell:

. . . Captain Cook finding there was nothing to be done with this stupid Block of Divinity by reasonable means, gave him to understand that all the Cattle must be the Property of Otoo, & then denounced Vengeance against him & all the people of Bolabola if any of them should ever offer to molest the Cattle or seperate them . . . . Omai was present at the transacting of this Business with the Eatooa, when Capt[n] Cook happening to say that 'instead of being a God he was the greatest Jackass he ever saw in his Life', Omai with much Simplicity made answer 'Ah Capt. Cook! he is a very goog Gog! a very goog gog Capt[n] Cook!'[26]

His removal of the animals to Pare was the first sign that Cook was preparing to leave. He would gladly have stayed on in Tahiti, for it was unlikely, he said, that they would be better or more cheaply supplied elsewhere. Furthermore, the people were friendlier than ever before and since his arrival there had been scarcely a theft worth mentioning. Only one thing prevented his remaining longer in this agreeable spot — the problem of Omai. That much discussed figure continued to draw comment from his usually censorious companions. His real name was Parridero, asserted Mr. Williamson of the *Resolution*, and he called himself Omai only because, as in Ireland, 'y[e] names of all the great Chiefs began wth an O.' In one of his infrequent references to his old friend, Lieutenant Burney deplored his 'Vanity' and drew attention to the 'tawdry' nature of his attire. Even the genial Samwell complained that he acted 'the part of a merry Andrew, parading about in ludicrous Masks & different Dresses'. But the main burden of criticism from these and other observers was on the score of his heedless extravagance and taste for low company. Such was his prodigality that to save him from destitution Cook felt compelled to impound most of his remaining possessions. As a result, he had nothing to trade with and was forced to beg for ship's victuals in order to feed the household he had set up ashore. Much of his erratic behaviour was put down to the influence of his brother-in-law who by his conduct at both anchorages had acquired a sinister reputation as petty thief and parasite. Omai, alas, chose to associate with this and other 'black guards' rather than with members of the royal family and, scorning the advice of his well-wishers, was resolute in his determination not to settle in Tahiti.[27]

So there was nothing for it but to sail on and, as the Lords of the Admiralty had decreed, carry Omai to the island of his choice. By 20 September the overhaul of both ships was completed, supplies of fresh water taken on board, and the shore station dismantled; but for a number of reasons their departure was delayed more than a week. In the first place Cook was an absorbed spectator of the martial and political drama that continued to unfold. Early on the morning of the 21st Otoo arrived to announce that the war canoes of Matavai were assembling before they joined his own fleet and left to assist Towha in Moorea. Hoping to pick up some details of Tahitian naval tactics, Cook persuaded the chief to arrange a mock battle between two canoes, one commanded by Omai, the other by Otoo and carrying Mr. King and himself as observers. Following complicated manoeuvres and 'a hundred Antick tricks' on the part of the opposing warriors, the vessels clashed head on and, after a struggle between the two crews, Omai's was judged the winner. Flushed with victory, the old campaigner was in reminiscent mood and spoke to Cook of adventures he had once related to Burney — of his capture by the Boraborans, his imprisonment on their island, and his escape by night on the very eve of execution. Finally, donning his suit of armour, he mounted a stage in one of the canoes to be paddled the length of the bay in full view of a disappointingly unresponsive crowd.[28]

Learning that Cook had decided to touch at Moorea on his way to the Society Islands, Otoo and his father called the next morning to ask whether they and their fleet might accompany him there. As long as he was not involved in the fighting, he saw no objection to the proposal and agreed to leave on the 24th. Before the plan could be carried out, however, news arrived that Towha had been compelled to arrange a truce with Maheine (or Mahine), leader of the opposing faction on Moorea, and had returned to Tahiti. In a further visit to Pare on the 23rd, Cook was present at a quarrelsome gathering where Otoo was blamed for the failure of the campaign through his dilatoriness in sending reinforcements and threatened with an attack by the forces of Towha and the young Vehiatua. Cook in his turn threatened retaliation if anyone dared to injure his friend, so putting a stop to all such violent talk. The debate had scarcely ended when a message came from Towha, who was not present on this occasion, summoning Otoo to a further conference to be held in his own territory. Cook was also invited but, feeling unwell, sent King in his place with Omai as interpreter. At this great assembly, attended by all the high chiefs including Oberea's son Teriirere (known to King as Terry Derry), the leaders patched up their differences and made peace with Maheine. Omai not only carried out his duties faithfully but won the favour of Towha who in return for some red feathers gave him a double sailing canoe completely manned and ready for sea. It was a pity, thought his shipmates, that he was not staying here to enjoy the patronage and protection of this great 'Admiral'.[29]

During the absence of King and Omai, Cook had reason to be grateful to his Tahitian friends. When they heard that he suffered acutely from 'a sort of Rheumatick pain', the princesses with their mother and their handmaidens visited the *Resolution* and subjected him to the same massaging and pummelling treatment Wallis had received from Oberea and her women. After three sessions under their practised hands, he found to his relief that he was completely cured. Nor were they less solicitous in attending to his material wants. On Otoo's return from the conference with Towha, the whole royal family visited the ship to bestow on Cook such a lavish gift of provisions that, for want of preserving salt, he had to refuse some of the hogs. In gratitude for their services he did everything possible for his hosts. At Otoo's request and following his specifications, he got the carpenters to construct a chest that would hold clothing and other European gifts. Not only was it fitted with locks and bolts but, as an additional safeguard against thieves, it was made large enough for two people to sleep on. The chief begged one last favour not mentioned by any diarist at the time but vividly recalled long afterwards by Midshipman John Watts of the *Resolution*. Having sat to Mr. Webber, Otoo asked if he might not have for himself a likeness of his friend and benefactor. Cook was pleased to comply, and the portrait, duly framed and placed in a box provided with lock and key, was handed to Otoo who promised to cherish the memento and show it to the commander of any ship that might visit the island.[30]

Everything was now ready for departure, but Cook lingered on for some days in this delectable place, detained, he said, by adverse winds. On the 27th he paid a visit to Pare to call on his friends and take a last look at the livestock. The whole collection, he found, was 'in a promising way'. Soon after they were transferred from the *Resolution*, the cows had taken the bull and in due course could be expected to calve; the small flock of sheep was settling into its new home; and the offspring of goats left by English and Spanish visitors were so numerous that Cook felt justified in carrying off four from Otoo's herd for distribution in other islands. The poultry also seemed in a flourishing condition: two geese and two ducks were already sitting and, though the peahen and the turkey had not yet begun to lay, there was no reason to suppose that they in their turn would not mate and multiply. In only one respect were the Englishmen disappointed. They had looked forward to witnessing the pleasure Oberea's gander would have in again meeting his own kind; but the venerable bird had been too long alone. He kept aloof from his 'brethren', merely 'making a Noise by himself', as the kindly Mr. King recorded.[31]

Omai had been perfectly satisfied to leave the bulk of the animals here, realizing that Otoo would be in a better position than himself to defend them from possible marauders. As his stay on the island drew to an end, he began to act more prudently and follow his patron's advice. The treasure brought from England was somewhat diminished, but he invested a portion of what was left in local cloth and coconut oil. These commodities were in great demand for trade and of finer quality than 'at any of the other Society islands', remarked Cook (extending the term to include Tahiti). Much of Omai's erratic behaviour, in the commander's opinion, had been due to the influence of his relatives and their shady hangers-on who had kept him to themselves with the sole aim of stripping him of all he possessed. By taking charge of what remained, Cook had frustrated their designs and now, to prevent further depredations, forbade Omai's sister and brother-in-law to follow him, as they intended. On the 29th he set out for Moorea in his sailing canoe, gaily hung with flags and pennants of his own fashioning and manned by its Tahitian crew and the two New Zealanders. The boys, Rickman noted, 'discovered no uneasiness at their present situation, nor any desire to return home.'[32]

The ships' departure the same afternoon was a more ceremonial affair, graced by the presence of Otoo. The chief was as assiduous as ever in his attentions and only the day before had brought to the *Resolution* a carved canoe which he asked Cook to carry to 'Pretane' and present on his behalf to the high chief of that country. The commander had been compelled to refuse this bulky tribute but was pleased to see that Otoo realized to whom he was indebted for his most valuable presents. Now he requested that King George should send by the next ship red feathers and the birds that produced them, axes, half a dozen muskets with powder and shot — and the great chief was 'by no means to forget horses'. Only one slight contretemps marred the proceedings. Otoo complained that Tahitian girls were being carried away and was disconcerted when they were bundled ashore; for, alleged Lieutenant Burney, he cared nothing for his subjects and merely wanted a handsome reward for allowing them to stay. Cook honoured him with a salute of seven guns and kept him on board until about five o'clock when he entered his canoe and left for Pare. After standing off the coast overnight, the ships followed Omai to Moorea.[33]

MEMBERS OF EARLIER EXPEDITIONS, notably Mr. Banks, had already landed on this island, lying less than ten miles from Tahiti, but Cook had not visited it before. His curiosity had doubtless been roused by its prominent part in the affairs of his Tahitian friends. Then, as always, he hoped to find here new subjects of interest and fresh sources of supply. Omai had arrived the previous night and when the ships appeared about midday on 30 September he was waiting in his canoe to guide them through the

reef into the more westerly of two harbours on the northern coast. Cook
thought it 'a little extraordinary' that no other visitor had mentioned
their existence; indeed, he had always supposed Moorea to be devoid of
such facilities. Now he found himself in a sheltered haven not inferior
to any in the South Seas. Running inland for more than two miles, it was
well provided with trees and fresh water, both easy of access, and was
so placed that a ship could use the prevailing wind to sail readily either
in or out. Thus it appeared to the professional sailor. Other more
imaginative observers were impressed by the 'romantic' vistas, 'delightful
beyond description', and by the background of volcanic mountains
suggesting 'the remains of some ancient & Noble Edifice' or, alternatively, 'old ruined castles or churches'.[34] Such was the setting for the
grim episode that followed.

As soon as they anchored, the ships were crowded with curious
islanders for whom Europeans and their prodigious canoes were a complete novelty. They brought nothing with them to exchange but returned
the next morning with breadfruit, coconuts, and a few hogs which they
traded for hatchets, nails, and beads. Red feathers were not in great
demand here and provisions seemed less plentiful than at Tahiti. It was
also agreed by authorities on the subject that the women were far inferior
to those they had just left. Even Cook, not much given to such comment,

51
The ships
approaching Moo
Omai's sailing
canoe marked A

remarked on their low stature, dark complexion, and generally forbidding demeanour. In a day or two, however, the disappointed voyagers where cheered by the arrival of former sweethearts who, after their unwilling disembarkation at Matavai Bay, had found other means of reaching this island. Soon familiar routines were re-established. Some men went to gather firewood, found in great abundance in the nearby forest; some filled water-barrels from the crystal-clear streams; others took the few remaining animals ashore to graze in the lush, tall grass; and others again, departing from routine, constructed rough gangways designed to lure a plague of rats from ships to land.[35]

Cook was eager to make the acquaintance of the redoubtable Maheine who had withstood superior forces in the recent war, proving himself at least their equal. Not surprisingly the chief was less anxious to meet the friends of his Tahitian adversaries and waited a couple of days before making a cautious approach to the *Resolution*; and even then he had to be coaxed on board. This 'Champion of Liberty' was as great a disappointment to some diarists as Opoony had been to members of the first expedition. Expecting a 'youthful Sprightly Active fellow', they found a man between forty and fifty years old, most unprepossessing in appearance. He was scarred with the wounds of many battles, had lost one eye, and was, besides, bald-headed — in these islands a rare affliction which he tried to conceal by wearing a turban. He brought with him a wife (or 'Mistress', Cook suspected), claiming to be Oamo's sister and therefore the sister-in-law of Oberea. Maheine gratefully accepted a flowered linen gown and some iron tools, professed his loyalty to Otoo, exchanged names with Cook, and at the end of half an hour left the ship. Soon he returned with his own gift of a hog and, after calling on Captain Clerke, departed with his consort (or paramour) for their home, some miles away.[36]

As the meagre journal entries indicate, little of note happened after this formal visit on 2 October. The same evening, Cook relates, he took a ride to the east accompanied by only a small 'train' of spectators, for Omai, his companion on the excursion, had forbidden the islanders to follow. After travelling some distance, they reached Maheine's district, there to witness the devastation wrought by Towha and his warriors. All the trees were stripped of their fruit and not a house was standing — every one had been pulled down or burned. Perhaps out of consideration for the unfortunate chief, they forbore to repay his call and, returning to the ships, resumed their usual occupations. The following day, Samwell observed, Omai with the help of his own people was busy raising a deck over his sailing canoe. By the 6th Cook had decided to make for the livelier and more fruitful Society Islands and, with the intention of leaving the next morning, ordered the ships to anchor in the stream. But he cancelled his plans on learning that one of the goats put on shore to graze had been stolen. In a vindication of his actions written some time later he explained: 'The loss of this Goat would have been nothing if it had not interfered with my views of Stocking other islands with these Animals but as it did it was necessary to get it again if possible.'[37]

Cook's suspicions immediately fell on Maheine who, he disclosed, had asked him for two goats only the day before. He had been compelled to refuse but in the hope that Otoo might supply a pair he had sent the request on to Tahiti together with full payment in red feathers. Now he consulted two local elders who said they would call on the chief to retrieve the missing animal. Glad to take advantage of the offer, he sent them in a boat to deliver a threatening message to Maheine. The diplomats carried out their mission with complete success. On the evening of the 7th they reached the ships bearing not only the goat but the thief who claimed that he stole it because 'Capt Cook's men had taken his bread fruit & Cocoa-nuts, & refused to pay him for them'. There the affair might have ended but for another unfortunate loss. Just before the goat was restored, a second one, a highly prized female big with kid, disappeared from the flock which had again been grazing ashore. At first Cook supposed it had merely strayed into the woods, but he began to think otherwise when natives he sent to find the animal failed to reappear. The next morning his fears that he had again been robbed were fully confirmed. Most of the local people had moved away and Maheine, he learned, had fled to the southernmost part of the island.[38]

In the next stage of what was becoming a major incident, Cook first moved circumspectly. Once more following the old men's advice, he sent a boat in charge of two midshipmen to the district where the goat was thought to have been carried. On the night of the 8th they returned empty-handed with reports that they had been treated with ill-concealed derision and fobbed off with empty promises. 'I was now very sorry I had proceeded so far,' Cook admitted, 'as I could not retreat with any tolerable credet, and without giving incouragement to the people of the other islands we had yet to visit to rob us with impunity.' In his perplexity he approached Omai and the two elders who told him to go with his men into the countryside and shoot every soul they met. This 'bloody advice' he could not follow, Cook commented, but he did resolve to lead an armed party across the island to reassert his damaged prestige and, if possible, reclaim the lost goat. With Omai and three or four of his people, thirty-five of his own men, and one of the elders to guide them, he set out at daybreak on the 9th.[39]

No sooner had they landed than the few remaining inhabitants fled in terror. When one man came within range, the zealous Omai, thinking his plan had been adopted, asked whether he should fire. Cook forbade him to do any such thing and, further, ordered him and their elderly guide to make it known that no one would be hurt, much less killed. The glad news soon spread, so that there were no more signs of fear and no opposition until the party reached the village suspected of harbouring the goat. Here armed warriors were seen to run into the woods and, on attempting to follow them, Omai was attacked with stones. At length Cook managed to pacify the villagers (by firing muskets over their heads, according to one report), but he could not get them to admit any knowledge of the stolen animal. Even his threats to their property, delivered through Omai, had no effect; whereupon he ordered some houses to be burned and several war canoes broken up. Once released, the flood of violence was not easily stemmed. For the rest of that day and most of the next Cook led his men through the island in an orgy of looting, burning, and destruction. On the evening of the 10th he had only just got back from a punitive foray into Maheine's territory when he learned that during his absence the precious goat had been restored. The spoils of the expedition added a quantity of fresh provisions to the ships' stores, but the person who profited most was Omai. He was as active as anyone in the rampage, noted Samwell, and returned with two more canoes and enough timber to build a European-style house.[40]

The episode released a spate of comment, ranging from bewildered post-mortem to downright condemnation. 'I doubt not but Captn Cook had good reasons for carrying His punishment of these people to so great a length, but what his reasons were are yet a secret', wrote Mr. Williamson, one of the officers directly involved. Except for Omai, 'who was very officious in this business', everyone carried out orders with the greatest reluctance, reported another eyewitness, George Gilbert of the *Resolution*. He could not, he confessed, account for Captain Cook's

52 A view of Moorea, after James Cleveley

53
*A view
of Huahine,
after Webber*

actions — 'they were so very different from his conduct in like cases in
former voyages'. The loyal Clerke, while deploring the damage inflicted
on 'these good people', said what he could on his colleague's behalf.
Every 'gentle method' was used to recover the goats, he claimed, but
nothing availed in the face of a 'perverseness' which he ascribed to the
workings of the Devil. Samwell assigned responsibility more directly to
the chiefs who had 'nobody but themselves to blame'; and he pointed
out on the credit side that 'during the whole of this disagreeable Business'
not one native had been hurt. But for the scrupulous Mr. King there
seemed no reason for the captain's 'precipitate proceedings' and nothing
to be said in mitigation. He doubted whether punishing so many
innocent people for the crimes of a few could be reconciled to any
principle of justice and took a gloomy view of the consequences. These
and other islanders, he thought, would give a decided preference to the
Spaniards and in future might 'fear, but never love us.'[41]

Cook himself seems to have felt some twinges of conscience as he reviewed the events of those few agitated days. Closing his journal entry for 10 October, he wrote: 'Thus this troublesome, and rather unfortunate affair ended, which could not be more regreted on the part of the Natives than it was on mine.' By the next day, he observed with relief, they were 'all good friends' again — the people were bringing their produce to barter 'with the same confidence as at first.' Evidently, however, there were none of the customary displays of sorrow when the ships set out the same morning, led by Omai in his sailing canoe. During the passage to Huahine the vanguard narrowly escaped misadventure. Before daylight the Englishmen heard firing which they supposed was Omai celebrating the first glimpse of land. Instead, they later discovered, his craft had nearly overturned in a squall and the shots were meant as a signal of distress. Somehow disaster was averted and, on reaching Fare Harbour at noon on the 12th, they found the canoe safely moored. Another inci-

dent in the crossing, recorded by King, concerned a native passenger
who was caught stealing just before the *Resolution* entered the harbour.
Cook 'in a Passion' immediately ordered the thief's head to be shaved
and his ears cut off, but 'an officer' (doubtless King himself) delayed the
more drastic part of the operation until the commander's anger had
cooled. Minus his hair and the lobe of one ear, the man was then cast
off the ship and made to swim ashore. While he failed to mention this
affair, Cook noted with satisfaction that other passengers were telling
the local people of his stern measures in Moorea, exaggerating the
destruction at least tenfold. His hope was that such reports would
improve the behaviour of these notoriously unruly islanders.[42]

AFTER AN ABSENCE OF MORE THAN FOUR YEARS, Omai had thus encircled
the earth and returned to his starting-point. On reaching Fare, Cook
found he had not yet landed but remained in his sailing canoe, surrounded
by a crowd of whom he seemed to take little notice. At this juncture,
confronted as he was by the urgent problem of his future, perhaps he
was in no mood for exchanging social pleasantries. The question of
finding a home for himself and his growing circle of dependants was still
undecided, though the choice had narrowed to one between Huahine
and Raiatea. In Tahiti the god-chief Etary had promised that his father's
land would be restored to him, and he now seemed to favour settling in
his native island. Nor was Cook opposed to the idea, thinking his own
influence there was sufficient to ensure that Etary's undertaking would
be honoured. On the afternoon of their arrival Omai boarded the
Resolution with three or four others, 'men of little consequence' judged
Bayly who happened to be present. He had come, it soon became
evident, not to seek advice but to announce that he and his companions
were going to attack the Boraborans living on Raiatea and wanted
Cook's help. He went on to say that, since his parents were both dead
and he had no property in Huahine, he could not stay here. Cook flatly
refused to have any part in the invasion, explaining that Orio and other
Boraborans were his friends. He then offered to reconcile Omai with
them, but the ardent young man was 'too great a Patriot' to listen to any
such proposal. So without more ado — and contrary to his instructions
— the commander took the decision into his own hands. 'Huaheine', he
resolved, 'was therefore the island to leave him at and no other.'[43]

While he was at Tahiti, Cook had already learned of political changes
in Huahine. He had always supposed the principal chief to be Oree, but
that venerable figure, it appeared, was only acting as regent for the
youthful Teriitaria and, having been overthrown since the previous
voyage, was now living in exile at Raiatea. His two sons were still on this
island, however, and even before the ship anchored, hastened to greet
their father's friend. The next day Cook got ready to pay his respects to
the young chief whose name he rendered as Tareederria. He hoped to
take advantage of the presence of other leaders, attracted from all parts
of the island by his arrival, to discuss arrangements for Omai's future.

That unpredictable person, Cook observed, dressed himself very properly for the meeting, prepared a number of handsome presents, and altogether, now he was clear of the 'gang' which had surrounded him in Tahiti, was behaving with such prudence as to win him respect. Followed by most of the ship's company, the two disembarked and made their way to a large house where the gathering was to be held. There was some delay before Tareederria appeared with his mother — he 'a very mean looking Boy' about the same age as the Vehiatua, she 'a fine jolly Dame . . . formerly a Tio of Mr Banks's'.[44]

As befitted the importance of the occasion, proceedings were conducted with great formality. Omai, standing with a friend apart from the rest of the company, first offered tributes to the gods which were placed before a priest to the accompaniment of what seemed to Cook speeches or prayers. These invocations apparently praised King George, Lord Sandwich, the two captains (Toote and Tate), and gave thanks for the voyager's safe return. The priest next took each object in the order in which it had been presented and, uttering incantations of his own, sent it off to a distant *marae*. The religious part of the ceremony was now at an end and Omai joined Cook who exchanged gifts with the boy chief and got down to business. Having warned his audience not to permit the abominable crime of theft, he pointed out with Omai's assistance

54 A view of Fare Harbour, Huahine, after J. Cleveley

that their countryman had been well treated in England and sent back
with many articles that would be very useful here. Were they prepared,
then, to give or sell him a piece of land where he could build a house
for his servants and himself? The alternative, Cook rather disingen-
uously suggested, was to carry him on to Raiatea. This last proposal
seemed to please the chiefs, rather to the commander's surprise until he
discovered that Omai was saying he would go there and with the help
of his European friends drive out the Boraborans. Cook soon quashed
the scheme, again insisting that he would not countenance any such
expedition. Thereupon, as he relates,

a Man rose up and told me that the whole island of Huaheine and every thing
in it was mine and therefore I might give what part I pleased of it to Omai.
Omai, who like the rest of his Country men seldom sees things beyond the
present moment, was greatly pleased with this declaration, thinking no doubt
that I should be very liberal and give him enough; but it was by far too general
for me; and [I] therefore desired they would not only point out the place, but
the quantity of land he was to have. On this some Chiefs who had left the
assembly were sent for, and after a short consultation amongst themselves my
request was granted by general consent and the ground immediately pointed
out, adjoining to the house in which we were assembled.

55 The ships' carpenters building Omai's house: detail of 54

Finally, in return for fifteen axes, some beads, and 'other Triffles', Omai was granted an area extending some two hundred yards along the shore and a little farther towards the hills.[45]

With this transaction completed, Cook was able to make plans for his stay on the island. He established a trading-station on shore, set up the observatories, and put the carpenters of both ships to work building a house from the timber pillaged in Moorea. By this means he hoped Omai would be able to safeguard his possessions and, to add further to his resources, the solicitous commander employed other hands to lay out a garden with shaddocks brought from Tonga and a variety of European fruits and vegetables. The landed proprietor himself was soon busy on the hillside at the back of his estate planting a small vineyard with the slips salvaged at Vaitepiha Bay. He was beginning to attend seriously to his affairs, Cook noted, and now repented his prodigality in Tahiti. A brother and a married sister were living here, but they did not plunder him as his other relatives had done. Nevertheless, they were powerless to protect either his person or his property, so, fearing he would be robbed when the ships left, Cook advised him to distribute some of his 'Move-ables' among the principal chiefs and in this way secure their favour and support. Omai adopted the suggestion which Cook followed up with threats that he would return and visit the full weight of his resentment on any who might injure his friend during his absence.[46]

Little occurred to disturb the harmony between visitors and hosts in the week or so that followed. Perhaps as a result of the warnings issued at the assembly of chiefs, only one theft was reported and the punish-ment was such as to dissuade others from following the criminal's example: half his head and one eyebrow were shaved and in addition he received a sound flogging. Cook was again indisposed but soon recovered sufficiently to accompany Omai on riding excursions when, asserted Samwell (surely in hyperbolical vein), 'they were followed by Thousands of Indians running & shouting like mad People.' Meanwhile normal tasks went forward and efforts were made to deal with another plague — not rats this time but cockroaches which devoured food, books, labels, stuffed birds, and soiled the bread with their excrement. For 'delicate feeders' put off ship's victuals by these pestilential creatures, there was an abundance of breadfruit and other fresh provisions readily purchased for ironware and red feathers, as highly prized here as in Tahiti. The precious commodities soon attracted local girls who flocked aboard to reinforce the contingent carried from Moorea. Rickman describes cosy shipboard *ménages* where 'the misses catered and cooked for their mates'. And to amplify the picture there is Bayly with his census of the sick — three or four men afflicted with yellow jaundice and twelve victims of 'the foul disease'.[47]

In the customary manner the islanders diverted their European friends with entertainments and on the night of 22 October arranged 'a grand Heivah' held by candlelight in a large house. The players were Raiateans, led by a young woman 'as beautiful as Venus'. Surfeited with such

experiences perhaps, Cook did not attend but later in the evening interrupted proceedings to demand the return of a sextant which had just
disappeared from Mr. Bayly's observatory. At first the assembled chiefs
were too absorbed in the performance to pay him much attention.
Whereupon he stopped the players and promised that if the instrument
was not found he would punish this island more severely than he had
Moorea. As a result, the thief was pointed out sitting unconcernedly in
the audience. Omai, who acted throughout as Cook's interpreter and
right-hand man, immediately drew his sword and arrested the felon, a
native of Borabora as it proved. Carried to the *Resolution*, he was put in
irons and, under Omai's insistent questioning, told his captors where he
had hidden the sextant. A search that night was unsuccessful, but it was
discovered the next morning hidden in some long grass, quite undamaged.
Meanwhile, alarmed by Cook's threats, the chiefs had fled from the
neighbourhood and were coaxed back only by assurances that neither
their persons nor their property would be harmed. Then, as Mr. King
reported, 'we once more liv'd on amicable & agreeable terms.'[48]

The incident, however, had by no means ended. As the thief appeared
to be 'a hardened Scounderal', Cook explained, 'I punished him with
greater severity than I had ever done any one before'. He omitted details
but they were supplied by other chroniclers. With hair shaved and both
ears cut off, the man was put ashore in a bleeding condition and, says
Rickman, 'exposed, as a spectacle to intimidate the people'. The sight
inspired horror and disgust among the islanders, asserted the same
informant, and even Omai was affected, though he tried to justify the
commander's actions by saying that in Britain the thief would have been
killed. The miscreant himself was certainly not intimidated. A couple of
nights later, probably helped by accomplices, he uprooted plants and
vines from the newly formed garden and openly threatened to kill Omai
and burn his house once the visitors had left. Cook again acted vigorously.
He had the man seized and imprisoned on the *Resolution*, with the
intention, he said, of carrying him elsewhere or, as others alleged, of
marooning him on a desert island. But after a few nights on board the
indomitable captive managed to free himself from his shackles, leaving
members of the watch to bear the full brunt of their commander's
displeasure. The petty officers were disrated and on three successive
days the sentry received a dozen lashes. A handsome reward of twenty
hatchets was offered for the prisoner's return but proved of no avail. He
remained at large, a threat to Omai's person and his future.[49]

By this time the carpenters had completed their work and the wooden
house was ready for occupation. According to Zimmermann, the
ungrateful Omai was dissatisfied with the result, saying that King
George had promised him a building with two storeys and this had only
one; moreover, he complained, it was a place 'such as was used for
housing pigs in England.' Whatever its limitations, it was a solid edifice,
eight yards long, six yards wide, and ten feet high, constructed with the
smallest possible number of nails to lessen the danger of its being dis-

mantled for the sake of the iron. And if it lacked a *piano nobile*, there was a loft above the main room and a magazine beneath. Omai furnished it with a bed and a few other articles, reported Samwell, and whenever he went out, unless Tiarooa was left in charge, was careful to lock the door and carry the key on his person. With the help of the local chiefs and his own men, his intention was to erect over the new house a large native building not only to protect it from the weather but to provide accommodation for his still growing 'family'. Besides the New Zealand boys there was the crew picked up in Tahiti, one of his brothers, and a few other followers, some ten persons in all — 'without ever a woman among them,' Cook remarked, 'nor did Omai seem attall desposed to take unto himself a Wife.'[50]

Now that they could be securely stored, the remnants of Omai's treasure were removed from the ship and unpacked before a large crowd, including the young Tareederria and lesser chiefs, gathered to witness the spectacle. If Mr. Bayly can be credited, when Omai came to examine the contents of his casks and boxes, he was 'very near going out of his Senses' from disappointment. He found that, apart from a few spikes, all his nails were 'small rubbish', most of his hatchets were of the very poorest quality, and among his glass beads there was not one that would purchase a coconut. The astronomer blamed Mr. Banks who professed to be the young man's friend and whose house was full of 'trade' he had collected for the last voyage. Yet he had not given Omai a single hatchet — in fact nothing 'except A Lectrifying Machine which could be of no service to him had he known how to use it.' Bayly was perhaps a little unfair. He himself mentioned a hand organ and 'two exceeding good Drums' included in the gift, while both he and Cook spoke of a box of toys which (as Mrs. Strange could have foretold) excited immense admiration in the gazing multitude. In contrast, hardly anyone so much as looked at the pots, kettles, dishes, plates, mugs, and glasses brought from England. Indeed, Cook noted, Omai began to think likewise: 'that a baked hog eat better than a boiled one, that a plantain leafe made as good a dish or plate as pewter and that a Cocoanut shell was as good to drink out of as a black-jack'. So, to augment his depleted fortune, he exchanged kitchen ware with members of the crew for hatchets or other iron tools. And to meet his future navigational needs he obtained from some nameless benefactor a compass, a globe, an abundance of charts and maps.[51]

Not all of Omai's possessions were so innocuous. His armoury included a musket with bayonet and cartouche box, a fowling-piece, a couple of pistols, and two or three swords and cutlasses. To these were now added cartridges, balls for musket and pistols, with some twenty pounds of gunpowder, securely stored in the magazine after Omai had been instructed how to preserve it and warned against fire. Then there were the famous suit of armour and a helmet, supplemented in some accounts by a coat of mail. Apparently Cook did not attempt to confiscate the weapons, as he had threatened in speaking to Boswell, though he

expressed some uneasiness. The supply of gunpowder, he said, made
Omai 'quite happy' and that, he added, was the only reason he left it,
'for I was always of Opinion he would have been better without fire
Arms'. On the other hand, he could have no doubts about the usefulness
of the livestock left on the island. Most precious in native eyes were the
two remaining horses and, since the stallion had covered the mare in
Tahiti, Cook had little fear but that in time they would be progenitors of
a breed. He also stocked the estate with an assortment of poultry — geese,
turkeys, ducks — and, as a parting gift, presented Omai with a boar
and sows 'of the English breed' and a goat 'big with kid'.[52]

As the ships prepared to leave, social compliments were exchanged on
all sides. The visitors again drew on their diminishing store of fireworks
and further entertained the islanders by arranging displays of music and
dancing 'according to the English fashion'. Omai in his turn diverted the
populace with fireworks or demonstrated the occult properties of his
hand organ and electrical machine, both of which, Mr. Bayly was forced
to concede, he operated 'tolerable well'. Two or three times he feasted
officers and chiefs, pressing them to 'drink out' his wine and supplying
delicacies cooked either in the island manner or the English. At such
functions his European friends did everything possible to instil into the
native mind a proper sense of his importance. Drums, trumpets, bagpipes, hautboys, flutes, violins played to the delight not only of guests
but of the spectators thronging the estate. But far from being elated by
his role as host to visiting and local dignitaries, Omai appeared despon-
dent. He seemed to realize, thought Rickman, that he inspired envy
rather than admiration in his countrymen who, for their part, regarded
him in the same light as Englishmen would on seeing a low-born citizen
suddenly rising from indigence to wealth. This, the writer continued,
was 'the real case with Omai':

while he was feasting the chiefs, and had nails to give to one, red feathers to
another, glass and china-ware to a third, and white shirts to the ladies; Who
but Omai? but, when he had expended in presents most of what he had brought
from abroad, and had but just enough left by the bounty of his friends, to
buy him a plantation and to stock it, the chiefs, while they partook of his
entertainments, paid him little or no respect, and, had it not been for their
deference to Captain Cook, would probably have treated him, amidst the
splendor of his banquets, with the utmost contempt — Such is the disposition
of mankind throughout the world. Men sprung from the dregs of the people
must have something more than accidental riches to recommend them to the
favour of their fellow citizens . . . .

Yet, contrary to the drift of this sententious piece of rhetoric, Rickman
concluded that Omai might rise superior to all the chiefs in the islands
round him 'and in time make himself lord over all.'[53]

Pondering in his own scrupulous fashion, Second Lieutenant King
was afflicted by serious misgivings. Although it was a great satisfaction
to have brought Omai safely home, he doubted whether they had added

to his future ease and happiness or ensured his well-being. Not that he agreed with a notion widely held in England concerning their charge — 'that his knowledge & enjoyment of a more comfortable & civilized way of life woud render his return to his former state unhappy.' If that was indeed his fate, in King's opinion, it would be through 'his want of some useful Knowledge that might have made him respect'd amongst his Countrymen, & woud have counterbalanced his defect in rank'. The most serious threat to his future, however, lay in his declared intention of driving out the Boraborans from Raiatea and winning back his father's estate by force — 'for quiet possession he might easily have had' through Etary's influence and Cook's. But he would not listen to any such proposal and, supposing his coat of mail and his weapons made him invincible, openly proclaimed his resolve 'to fight the Bora-Bora Chiefs the first Opportunity'. King agreed with Cook in regretting that Omai had not settled in Tahiti where the problems of his rank might have been overcome and he would have been farther removed from his enemies. As it was, the one hopeful sign was his more prudent conduct since reaching Huahine. This justified King in making a cautious prophecy: 'if he does not fall a sacrifice to his resentments against Bora-Bora he may yet be comfortable.'[54]

Cook, too, was in reflective mood as he reviewed Omai's past and speculated on his future. Whatever faults this 'Indian' had, they were, he thought, 'more than over ballanced by his great good Nature and docile disposition'. Very seldom during the time they were together had there been reason to find fault with his conduct. 'His gratifull heart always retained the highest sence of the favours he received in England', the commander went on in familiar strain, 'nor will he ever forget those who honoured him with their protection and friendship during his stay there.' He possessed 'a tolerable share of understanding, but wanted application and perseverance to exert it, so that his knowledge of things was very general and in many instances imperfect.' Indeed, Cook was forced to admit, Omai was not a man of much observation. He might have conveyed the arts and amusements of the Friendly Islands to his own people who would probably have adopted them, 'as being so much in their own way', but he made no attempt to master any of them. The seasoned explorer then proceeded to confirm from experience what the philosopher of primitive man had divined by intuition or deduced from books:

This kind of indifferency is the true Character of his Nation, Europeans have visited them at times for these ten years past, yet we find neither new arts nor improvements in the old, nor have they copied after us in any one thing. We are therefore not to expect that Omai will be able to interduce many of our arts and customs amongst them or much improve those they have got, I think however he will endeavour to bring to perfection the fruits & c[a] we planted which will be no small acquisition.

But the greatest benefit the islands were likely to receive from Omai's travels, he considered, were the animals which they would probably never have got had he not gone to England. When they multiplied (and Cook had little doubt they would), this would equal, if not exceed, 'any place in the known World for provisions.'[55]

So Cook's outlook was one of qualified optimism as he made final preparations for his departure from Huahine. Since there was no prospect of his returning (in spite of his earlier threats to the local chiefs), he rejected the volunteers who offered their services for the remainder of the voyage. And in case he should relent, there was the jealous Omai constantly at hand to remind him of Lord Sandwich's promise that no more of his countrymen would ever visit England. Still apprehensive of his protégé's fate once the ships had departed, Cook hit upon a device that would allay his anxiety in the immediate future. Before they left the next anchorage at Raiatea, Omai was to let them know how he fared and 'for want of Letters', Samwell explained (rather indicating the failure of Granville Sharp's tuition), 'he was to manage in the following Manner: If things turned out to his liking he was to send two white Beads, if indifferent two brown beads and if he was ill used or in distress two blue Beads were to be the Signal.' Before sailing, Cook ordered a latinized inscription to be carved on one wall of Omai's house: it commemorated the British sovereign, the date of their departure, 2 November 1777, and the two ships together with their captains.[56]

When entering up the events of his last day at Huahine, Cook referred to Omai's retainers for the only time since they boarded the *Resolution* and briefly recorded a mild crisis of conscience. 'If there had been the most distant probability of any Ship being sent again to New Zealand', he wrote, 'I would have brought the two youths of that Country home with me, as they were both desireous of coming'. Tiarooa, the elder of the two, he described as 'an exceeding well disposed young man with strong natural parts and capable of receiving any instructions'. Fully aware of the difference between his own barbarous homeland and these islands, he 'resigned himself very contentedly to end his days upon them'. But Coaa did not submit as willingly: 'the other was so strongly attached to us that he was taken out of the Ship and carried a shore by force'. He was 'a witty smart boy', Cook added, 'and on that account much noticed in the Ship.'[57]

Cook scarcely did justice to the popularity of the two exiles or to the circumstances of a parting recorded in detail by David Samwell. 'I was upon Deck & saw all this,' he related, 'and if ever I felt the full force of an honest Heart Ache it was at that time.' In his version, differing markedly from Cook's, Coaa was on Omai's large canoe and, seeing the *Resolution* spread its sails to leave, wept aloud, implored his friends to take him with them, and attempted to leap overboard in order to follow. Though held fast by the people in the canoe, after much struggling he managed to jump into the sea and swam with all his might after the ship. He was soon overtaken and brought back, only to free himself once more and make a further attempt to reach the *Resolution*. Too weak,

alas, to outstrip his pursuers, he was again captured and this time bound
with ropes; 'and now the poor little Fellow could do nothing but cry &
called to his old shipmates for Assistance which we were so inhuman as
to deny him.' Tiarooa followed them in another canoe, reported
Samwell, and although not less affected than Coaa, 'resigned himself to
his fate without murmuring & silently shed Tears.' The stoical youth
was 'a modest sensible young fellow' who 'always behaved with the
greatest Propriety during his Stay with us & was much esteemed by us
all'. His companion, who had obviously won Samwell's affection,
received a lengthier tribute:

Cocoa was very humorous & lively, by his many Drolleries he used to create
no small Diversion on board. He was a favourite with all, & every one of the
Jacks took a delight in teaching him something either in Speech or Gesture, at
which he himself was eminent, and as the sagacious New Zealander perceived
that he was caressed and applauded according to his proficiency in this kind of
Learning, he became a diligent Student and in a short time was a perfect adept
in Monkey-tricks & the witty Sayings of Wapping & St Giles.

'In short', the good-natured surgeon summed up his impressions, 'they
were both universally liked and we should have been much pleased to
have taken them with us to England.'[58]
    Other men of feeling on both vessels referred to the incident and
praised the unhappy victims. They showed 'the most violent & poignant
grief', remarked King who mentioned Tiarooa's 'mild & gentle turn, &
desire of improvement' while characterizing Coaa as 'a very lively,
quick, pert young boy, the favourite of the Boatswain & common
People'. 'They hoped to have gone along with the ships,' wrote Rickman,
'and they cried bitterly when they understood that they were to be left
behind.' In this questionable account of the departure it was not merely
Coaa but Tiarooa as well who had to be forcibly restrained from following their friends — 'no easy matter', observed Rickman, since the elder
was 'of prodigious strength' and the younger 'likewise a giant for his
age'. Their resolute and manly conduct he thought the very reverse of
that displayed by the islanders among whom 'they were destined to
abide, during the remainder of their lives'. 'We could never learn Capt.
Cook's real reason,' he complained, 'for refusing to take on board . . .
these gallant youths from New Zealand'. They were 'fine, well disposed
Youths,' echoed Clerke, 'with all the courage of their Countrymen', but
had lost their 'natural ferocity' since coming on board. European
example had erased their 'Cannibal Notions', he said, and they had
turned out 'very tractable good Lads'. The two 'Zealanders', Burney
noted in his turn, 'had quite shaken off that savage disposition so
inherent in their Countrymen'.[59]
    The two boys tended to steal the limelight on the afternoon of
2 November. Accounts of the parting with Omai are perfunctory by
comparison and certain particulars remain obscure. Apparently he first
visited the *Discovery* after it got under way to pay his respects to friends

on that vessel. James Burney, while betraying no emotion on his own part, spoke briefly of the 'Tears of real and unaffected sorrow' shed on this occasion by his old shipmate. Also briefly but with evident feeling, his other companion on the *Adventure*, Mr. Bayly, wrote that Omai was 'very much Afected so as to cry much as did most of us who were his Acquaintance he kiss'd us & bid us a long farewell.' Next he seems to have made his way to the *Resolution* where he remained until they were outside the reef. He took 'a very affectionate farewell of all the Officers', sustaining 'a manly resolution till he came to me', wrote Cook, 'then his utmost eforts to conceal his tears failed'. He continued to weep as he was carried ashore in a boat by Mr. King who confessed that he was moved by Omai's 'sensibility & gratitude to all who had been kind to him in England.' That he still cherished strong feelings for the country other chroniclers testified. He declared he would return 'by the first English ship which passed that way', asserted Zimmermann. Rickman implausibly depicted him begging Cook to let him stay on the *Resolution*, while the commander pointed out that now he had been restored 'at an immense expence to his royal master, it was childish to entertain a notion of being carried back.' Samwell merely said that Omai would willingly have remained with them but made no such proposal since he judged 'it would not have been agreeable to Capt[n] Cook'.[60]

Willingly or not, Omai and his New Zealanders were left behind while their sorrowing shipmates made for Raiatea to gather fresh supplies and prepare for the next phase of the expedition. They were surprised when the stealer of the sextant turned up and not a little relieved when he now claimed to be Omai's friend (won over, it was surmised, by a handsome present). Other visitors from Huahine soon brought news that Omai himself was in good health, living happily with his neighbours; when last seen he was trying to catch one of his horses which had broken loose. This favourable report was confirmed by the arrival of his sailing canoe with white beads signifying that all had gone well since the ships departed. The messengers spoke of only one misfortune, the death in kidding of the goat (perhaps the hapless creature bandied about on Moorea?), and brought from their master a request for two more axes. Cook sent these back together with a pair of goats, male and female, to replace the dead one. Relieved at last of Omai and his importunities, he continued his preparations for the voyage, complicated by difficulties with the islanders and the desertion of lovelorn members of his crew. After more than a month at Raiatea, he left for Borabora, hoping to obtain from Opoony the French anchor mentioned by Omai in his conversations with Burney on the *Adventure*. With a lavish expenditure of trade goods Cook purchased the battered relic which he wanted to convert into articles for barter before he ventured into the uncharted seas ahead. He stayed only a few hours on the island and on 8 December 1777 resumed his northward course.[61]

11. The End of Omai

MORE THAN TWO YEARS PASSED BEFORE WORD OF OMAI'S REPATRIATION reached his English friends. And then it was overshadowed by more sombre tidings: 'what is uppermost in our mind allways must come out first,' wrote Sandwich to Banks on 10 January 1780, 'poor captain Cooke is no more, he was massacred with four of his people by the Natives of an Island where he had been treated if possible with more hospitality than at Otaheite.' The melancholy news, he explained, came from Captain Clerke who, writing from Kamchatka, reported an otherwise prosperous voyage: they had lost only two men from sickness and one by drowning. 'Omai', the First Lord went on, 'arrived safe & was left at Huaheine but no particulars of his reception in Captain Cookes short letter which comes by the same conveyance.' Cook did, however, give some details of the animals he had landed at Tahiti and the Society Islands — a horse and mare, a bull and several cows, a ram and seven ewes. Sandwich ended by mentioning the changes which had followed Cook's death. Captain Clerke had taken over the *Resolution* and Captain Gore the *Discovery*. Clerke, now in charge of the expedition, would make one more effort to find a northern passage but did 'not seem to have much hopes of success.' The pessimistic forecast proved well founded. Like Cook before him, Clerke failed to penetrate through the polar ice to the Atlantic and did not long survive the attempt. He died in August 1779 and was buried in Kamchatka. Gore succeeded to the command of the *Resolution* while King was appointed to the *Discovery*. After taking a circuitous route to avoid the American colonists and their European allies (for Britain was again openly at war with its traditional enemies), the two ships anchored at Deptford early in October 1780.[1]

The interval since the *Resolution* set out from Plymouth in July 1776 had been an eventful one in the affairs of Omai's two English patrons. After the brief eclipse that followed his withdrawal from Cook's second expedition, Banks was again in the ascendant, both as private citizen and public figure. Seeking ampler space for his ever-growing collections, he moved from New Burlington Street in the autumn of 1776 to the roomy mansion in Soho Square that was to be his town house and the centre of his scientific activities for the rest of his life. Some two years later, in December 1778, he succeeded Sir John Pringle as President of the Royal

Society, a position he was to occupy for the next four decades; and in the same memorable month, sponsored by Sir Joshua Reynolds and Dr. Johnson, he joined the select company of the Literary Club. His marriage to an heiress, Miss Dorothea Hugessen, in March of the following year ended his bachelor state but did little to alter the ordered routine into which he had settled. The bride, 'a comely and modest Young Lady', as Sir John Cullum described her, joined Banks and his sister in a harmonious *ménage à trois* which, contrary to all probability, endured until Sarah Sophia's death in 1818.[2]

In marked contrast with his younger friend, Sandwich was nearing the end of his long career and was beset by misfortunes, both personal and public. In the month following Banks's marriage he lost the woman who had been his companion for the past two decades and the mother of his second family. One evening early in April 1779, when she was leaving Covent Garden Opera House to return to the Admiralty, Martha Ray was shot and killed by an obscure clergyman, James Hackman. The assassin, who had met her at Hinchingbrooke some years earlier, 'had been nourishing a hopeless passion for his victim' and intended to commit suicide but failed in the attempt and was later hanged. Sandwich was prostrated by Miss Ray's death and, though shunning society, could not ignore his pressing official duties. The blow fell while he was bearing the full brunt of criticism for repeated naval reverses in the unpopular war. By the time the *Resolution* and the *Discovery* reached the Thames, the danger of invasion was not entirely over and the divided country was on the brink of an election.[3]

With the expedition's arrival, the First Lord was faced by urgent, if relatively minor, problems and again turned to his friend. Writing from the Admiralty on 10 October 1780, he brought Banks up to date with recent events: according to that gentleman's desires, his gardener (David Nelson) had now been discharged from the ship; he himself with Captain King and Mr. Webber, the artist, had the previous Sunday visited Windsor where the drawings and charts of the voyage seemed to give His Majesty great satisfaction. The drawings were indeed very numerous, 'near 200 in number' and 'exceedingly curious & well executed', observed Sandwich, so he would like to consult Banks how to preserve them and select those that were suited for reproduction. 'I allso wish to have your opinion', he continued, 'about the Journals which are now in my possession, which I think should be made publick with as little delay as the nature of the business will allow; but I had so much trouble about the publication of the two last voyages, that I am counting or rather unwilling to take upon me to decide in what manner & for whose emolument the work shall be undertaken . . . .' Banks's advice on the matter would be of great use, Sandwich concluded, and he hoped it would not be long before he had the pleasure of seeing his friend in town.[4]

As a result of his consultations and profiting from past experience, the First Lord found a solution in a collective compromise. King, the best

educated and most cultivated officer of the expedition, was appointed
co-author with the dead Cook. Banks acted as consultant throughout
and Sandwich undertook the same office which he continued to perform
even after March 1782 when his old opponent Admiral Keppel replaced
him at the Admiralty. As the work progressed, a number of other people
were called in to advise and comment. Members of the Burney family
were asked to express their views on the esoteric subject of Polynesian
music (asserting in the course of a complicated correspondence: 'Omai
had a very bad ear, & could never *any where* have been a musician').
The astronomer William Wales was also a contributor and so was Henry
Roberts of the *Resolution* and so, among others, was Admiral John
Forbes who composed the closing tribute to the late commander. In the
matter of emoluments, it was finally decided that half the profits should
go to Cook's widow and family, a quarter to King, with smaller shares
to the heirs of Clerke and Anderson (another casualty of the voyage),
and to the *Resolution*'s master, William Bligh, presumably for the use
of his charts.[5]

Someone was obviously needed to co-ordinate the whole enterprise.
Sandwich's choice fell on Canon Douglas who had already displayed his
tact and proved his literary talent in revising Cook's narrative of the
second expedition and preparing it for the press. In the present instance
Douglas was in effect the unacknowledged general editor, performing
duties similar to those previously undertaken by the lamented Hawkesworth. He skilfully combined Cook's copious but incomplete records
with the journals of his fellow travellers. He imposed some unity on the
several contributions by rephrasing them in his own elegant Augustan
idiom. And, while taking fewer such liberties than Hawkesworth, he
reshaped his materials to emphasize dramatic incidents in the story or to
focus attention on its leading figures. The annals of this epic contained
no Banks to supply light relief for the heroic and now martyred Cook.
Nor was there an Oberea to divert the public with her antics and her
amours. But one personage could act both as foil to the commander and
centre of exotic attention. 'The history of Omai', remarked this exceptionally candid editor, 'will, perhaps, interest a very numerous class of
readers, more than any other occurrence of a voyage, the objects of
which do not, in general, promise much entertainment.'[6]

Following this cue, Douglas introduced into the narrative full details
of Omai's actions from the time of his embarkation at Sheerness until
he arrived at Huahine. The account usually kept fairly close to the
records of the voyage which were suitably emended or in some cases
expanded. At the climax, however, as the ships were on the point of
leaving the island, Douglas evidently thought some more elaborate passage was called for. Hence he placed in Cook's mouth a long rhetorical
set-piece for which there was little authority in his original journal
(though there were unmistakable echoes from King's). The commander
is shown soliloquizing as he prepares to farewell his charge. 'It was no
small satisfaction to reflect, that we had brought him safe back to the

very spot from which he was taken', the passage opens. 'And, yet, such is the strange nature of human affairs, that it is probable we left him in a less desirable situation, than he was in before his connexion with us.' For, through being much 'caressed' in England, Omai had lost sight of his original condition and forgotten the extreme difficulty he must experience in winning acceptance from his countrymen. Had he made proper use of the wealth and knowledge acquired during his travels, he could have formed the most profitable alliances. But with childish inattention he had neglected this obvious means of advancing his interests. There followed a catalogue of his repeated errors and indiscretions in the Friendly Islands and Tahiti. Then Cook-Douglas pondered on Omai's possible destiny:

Whether the remains of his European wealth, which, after all his improvident waste, was still considerable, will be more prudently administered by him, or whether the steps I took, as already explained, to insure him protection in Huaheine, shall have proved effectual, must be left to the decision of future navigators of this Ocean; with whom it cannot but be a principal object of curiosity to trace the future fortunes of our traveller.[7]

And so in the course of time it came about. Throughout the closing years of the eighteenth century a succession of navigators visited the group, leaving accounts not only of Omai's fate but of developments in a critical period of Pacific history. Much of what they learned from their informants was of necessity obscure or contradictory. More than a decade elapsed between the *Resolution*'s departure and the arrival of further visitors. During his last voyage, while trying to clear up the mystery of the Spanish settlers, Cook (in his own person) had expressed the conviction that most islanders were unable to recollect past events or tell when they happened, even after an interval of only ten or twenty months.[8] At a distance of ten years memories had inevitably grown dim, chronology become confused, many facts vanished beyond the possibility of recall.

THE FIRST EPISODE was indirectly linked with Banks who had grown in authority with the years, to become a kind of public oracle on a variety of topics. As early as 1779, on the strength of observations made during the voyage of the *Endeavour*, he had recommended to a parliamentary committee the establishment of a penal colony at Botany Bay. Nothing came of the proposal at the time but in due course, with the loss of the American possessions in the recent war, the scheme was revived. Sir Joseph Banks, as he was now known (he had been created a baronet in 1781), took an active part in organizing the expedition which set out in 1787 to found the settlement of New South Wales. One of the transports, the *Lady Penrhyn*, having discharged its human cargo on the inhospitable shores of the new colony, set out on the return voyage after a stay of only seven days. When it left Botany Bay the crew were already showing signs of scurvy and, as conditions worsened in the following weeks, Captain Sever, the commander, decided to make for Tahiti and procure fresh provisions. This course of action was probably influenced by the fact that the second in command, Lieutenant John Watts, had been one of the *Resolution's* midshipmen on its last voyage. Almost eleven years after his previous visit, he again entered Matavai Bay on 10 July 1788.[9]

The Tahitians were as friendly as ever. They flocked round the *Lady Penrhyn* while she anchored, shouting '"*Tayo Tayo*"' or '"*Pahi no Tutti,*" *Cook's ship*', and soon opened a brisk trade in foodstuffs which they disposed of 'on very moderate terms'. A chief who came on board that evening immediately recognized Watts and brought him up to date with local affairs. Otoo was still alive but at the time was absent from the district and would not be back for some days. He was now called '*Earee Tutti*' and had, it seemed, suffered for his namesake's actions. One night, in retaliation for Cook's destructive rampage through Moorea, Maheine had landed at Pare, destroying all Otoo's animals and forcing him to take refuge in the mountains. Towha, it was also suggested, had taken a hand in the business, and Watts remembered that chief threatening something of the kind in a quarrel with Otoo during his last visit to the island. The lieutenant picked up more news when Odiddy turned up the next morning. Cook's favourite rejoiced at seeing Englishmen again, made affectionate inquiries about his friends, and took much pleasure in recalling his travels on the *Resolution*. Since he was ignorant of Cook's death, Sever decided not to enlighten him and indeed gave him a present supposedly sent by the commander. Odiddy also mentioned the raid on Otoo and spoke briefly of Omai and the New Zealand boys. They had been dead 'a considerable time'; they had died through sickness; there was only one horse left on Huahine. Beyond that Watts could discover nothing.[10]

Early on the morning of the 14th the officers were summoned ashore to pay their respects to Otoo. They found him surrounded by 'an amazing concourse' and were pleased to see that he still possessed Webber's portrait of Cook, quite undamaged in its wooden box. It went with him everywhere, they were told, and was certainly placed in his canoe when he set out for the *Lady Penrhyn*. Watts thought the 'king' improved in person and much the best-made man they had seen. He was always accompanied by a woman of great authority but by no means handsome who seemed to be his wife. During his visit to the ship Otoo asked after his friends, Cook in particular, and on going below was astonished to find how few crewmen there were and what a number were sick. He in turn spoke of the revenge taken by his enemies from Moorea, asked why the *Lady Penrhyn* had not brought cattle, and added one or two details to the account Odiddy had given of Omai's end. After the event, he told Watts, there had been a skirmish between the people of Huahine and warriors from Raiatea. The invaders were victorious and carried off a great part of the dead man's property.[11]

They heard no more of Omai during the rest of the visit. Their situation in a small ship with a disabled crew seemed so precarious that Watts spent little time ashore and then was careful not to wander far. He did learn, however, that since his last visit great numbers of people had been carried off by venereal disease and that many women, especially in the lowest class, suffered from the 'terrible disorder'. Other signs of European influence were few. Apart from goats and cats, there seemed to be no imported animals and for want of attention Cook's vegetable gardens had gone to ruin. The islanders occasionally brought pumpkins, peppers, or cabbage leaves with their own produce, but they themselves refused to eat the pumpkins and said the peppers poisoned them. Except for the blade of one table-knife, they had used up all their iron and were so anxious to acquire fresh supplies that they sold their own commodities at very reasonable rates. Though the once prized red feathers were now worthless, hatchets, knives, nails, and similar objects were as much in demand as ever. One article of barter was of particular interest to Watts. It was a large ring which he immediately recognized as belonging to one of Bougainville's anchors — that very anchor which Cook had bought from Opoony in 1777 (and of which Omai had spoken in his talks with James Burney four years earlier). By some means the relic had come into the hands of Otoo who agreed to part with it for three hatchets.[12]

Otoo was assiduous in his attentions. He visited the ship daily and often acted as an intermediary in trade — not without profit to himself the visitors noted. He urged them to attack his enemies on Moorea, but to this suggestion they gave a positive refusal. Instead, after a fortnight in the bay, they set sail for the Society Islands. Their invalids had made a most astonishing recovery and, as they reflected with satisfaction, during the whole of their stay not one musket had been fired. Nevertheless, Captain Sever was careful not to announce his intentions and got under way before daylight. Despite these precautions, the *Lady Penrhyn* was soon boarded by a crowd of Tahitians led by Otoo who remained on the ship until it cleared the reef. He expressed great sorrow at their sudden departure, complained of the time which had elapsed since the British last visited the island, and urged them not to stay away so long again. He asked them to bring back some animals, especially horses, and finally requested that a few guns should be fired — a compliment Captain Sever was obliging enough to pay him. A pathetic note was introduced into the farewell by the presence of Odiddy. He, too, had visited the ship every day, always with a gift of ready-dressed provisions. Apparently things had not gone well with him in Tahiti, for he said he was very unhappy and begged to be taken to Raiatea. But Otoo forbade him to leave and Captain Sever was forced to put him into his canoe, shedding tears in abundance. Not once as the exile made for the shore did he look back at the *Lady Penrhyn*, now bound for Huahine.[13]

They sighted the island on 25 July but contrary winds prevented them from reaching Fare until the 29th, and then Captain Sever merely lay to off the coast. He intended staying only a day or two and did not think it worth the trouble to enter the harbour. The natives were again very friendly, swarming round the ship in their canoes while they offered the newcomers fresh produce and urged them to anchor inside. Sever resisted their importunities and as a result neither he nor his companions seem to have gone ashore. Fortunately, on the evening of their arrival they were visited by a local chief able and willing to answer their inquiries. He was an elderly man who went by the name of 'Tutti', and Lieutenant Watts remembered having often seen him in the company of Captain Cook. He confirmed earlier reports that Omai and the two boys were dead and spoke briefly of their life together. Cook's fears on his protégé's behalf were apparently quite justified. After he was settled, Tutti informed Mr. Watts, Omai was forced to purchase for himself and his family large quantities of cloth and other necessaries. Taking advantage of the situation, his neighbours made him pay extravagantly for every article. In addition, he often visited Raiatea and never went empty-handed. So by these means he expended much of his English treasure during his lifetime. The old chief assured Watts that Omai had died in his own house, as had the New Zealand boys, but in what order he was unable to say.[14]

Of the sequel Tutti was more positive. Warriors came over from Raiatea to seize the remnants of Omai's property which, they claimed, belonged to them by right since the dead man was a native of their island. The invaders carried away many articles but destroyed the muskets on the spot, breaking the stocks and burying the gunpowder in the sand. The fighting had been very fierce, Tutti added: great numbers were slain on both sides, and peace was not yet restored. Watts himself saw three men who had been terribly injured and learned (probably from Tutti) a few more facts about Omai's possessions. His house was standing but had been taken over by the high chief of Huahine and was now covered by a very large one 'built after the country fashion'. As for his horses, soon after foaling the mare had died together with the foal. The stallion was still living, 'though of no benefit'; 'thus', Watts concluded, 'were rendered fruitless the benevolent intentions of his Majesty, and all the pains and trouble Captain Cook had been at in preserving the cattle, during a tedious passage to the islands.'[15]

BENEVOLENT INTENTIONS again had some part in bringing the next British ship to Tahiti. Only three months after the Lady Penrhyn's departure, a second naval vessel entered Matavai Bay, sent out to gather seedlings of the breadfruit tree and transfer them to the West Indies. In the years since the Endeavour returned, some such project had been much discussed by members of the Banks circle, finding one ardent advocate in Solander (until his untimely death in 1782) and another in Ellis who published a pamphlet on the subject. Banks himself laboured tirelessly to put the scheme into effect. The American war brought his efforts to a temporary halt, but with the coming of peace he renewed his solicitations until the plan won acceptance among ministers of the government and high-placed officials. At first one of the Botany Bay transports was to be used for carrying the plants. This proposal was abandoned, however, and the *Bethia*, renamed the *Bounty*, was specially fitted out for the purpose under Banks's directions. He also recommended the appointment as commander of Lieutenant William Bligh who was well qualified for the post not only by his experience as master of the *Resolution* but by recent service in the West Indies. To undertake the delicate task of selecting and caring for the cargo went David Nelson, Banks's collector on Cook's last voyage, with an assistant. The expedition left England late in December 1787 and, after a trying passage by way of the Cape and Van Diemen's Land, reached Matavai Bay on 26 October 1788.[16]

The Tahitians were delighted at the arrival of another ship so soon after the *Lady Penrhyn* of whose visit they hastened to supply a few particulars in answer to Bligh's questions. Its captain was a man called Tonah, it had stayed a month, it had been gone four months or, as some held, only three. They in turn asked after Cook, Banks, Solander, and various members of the last British expedition. Despite Sever's precautions in his dealings with Odiddy, someone on the ship had evidently told them of Captain Cook's death. But they knew nothing of the circumstances, and these Bligh forbade his men to disclose. Three more fatalities the islanders announced quite positively: the 'famous Old Admiral Towah so often spoke of by Captn. Cook' was dead, and so were both Omai and the older New Zealand boy. Following Bligh's inquiries, he learned that his two shipboard companions had died not in war but of sickness — one from 'Epay no Etua', the other from 'Epay no Tettee', which he took to mean mortal diseases sent by two different gods. The younger boy's fate was not mentioned.[17]

Otoo, who was staying at another part of the island, sent a gift of hogs and plantains on the 27th with a message to say he would be at Matavai Bay the next day. Pending his arrival Bligh entertained the monarch's relations, called on old friends, and visited familiar places. He was received with touching courtesy wherever he went and, in contrast with Watts, found evidence that British efforts to civilize these people had not been wholly in vain. They now fashioned their implements on European models and were eager to acquire files, gimlets, combs, knives, and looking-glasses. The produce they supplied in return, he noted with satisfaction, included shaddocks, capsicums, and goats, but he could learn nothing definite about the cattle left behind in 1777. In one respect he saw a marked improvement. The only thing stolen during the first couple of days was a tin pot and when its loss was discovered, Otoo's brother flew into a violent rage and insisted that all thieves should be tied up and flogged. After this incident Webber's portrait of Cook was brought to the ship for repair. The painting had evidently suffered some mishap since the *Lady Penrhyn*'s visit, for Bligh observed that a little of the background was 'eat off' and the frame slightly damaged.[18]

Before beginning to gather breadfruit plants, Bligh thought it advisable

56 *Captain William Bligh,*
after J. Russell

to consult Otoo and the other chiefs, but early on the 28th he sent David Nelson ashore to spy out the land. About nine o'clock the same morning Fletcher Christian, the master's mate and acting lieutenant, escorted Otoo to the ship with his wife Iddeah (Itia) and a train of their relatives and attendants. On both sides there was perfect amity from the outset. The Tahitian visitors brought cloth and produce, while Bligh more than repaid them with lavish gifts which included two red flamingo wings acquired at the Cape. During the ritual of welcome he learned that the high chief was no longer called Otoo. That name had passed to his eldest son, who live at Pare, and the father was known to his own people as Tinah (Taina). Otoo or Tinah (as he was henceforth indifferently termed) spoke without shame of his defeat by the invaders from Moorea, the loss of his precious livestock, and his flight to the mountains. He was 'exceedingly frightned' by two shots from the guns, fired at his own request, and ate 'most voraciously' throughout the visit which lasted until the late afternoon. In the evening Nelson returned to report that breadfruit seedlings grew abundantly in the neighbourhood and that two shaddocks he had planted in 1777 were now fine large trees covered with fruit.[19]

The bonds with Otoo-Tinah were strengthened when, on 1 November, Bligh paid a return visit to Pare. Here he realized the full consequences of Cook's harsh policy in Moorea: there were no traces of the 'palace' or of the large chest fashioned by the *Resolution*'s carpenters; none of the substantial houses that once dotted the landscape; only two or three of the war canoes that formerly crowded the bay; and no signs of imported animals or poultry. Everything had been destroyed or carried off by the raiders who, Bligh was told, had joined forces with Towha to attack Otoo about five years after Cook's departure. By that time the cows had eight calves, the ewes had ten young ones, and the birds, except only for the turkeys and peacocks, had multiplied many times over. Now not a single one was left. 'Thus', Bligh lamented, 'all our fond hopes, that the trouble Captain Cook had taken to introduce so many valuable things among them, would by me have been found to be productive of every good, are entirely blasted.' He regretted that they had not left everything at Huahine where, he learned from different people, great care was taken of Omai's mare, though the stallion had died of natural causes. In spite of their misfortunes, Otoo and his family loaded their guest with gifts and entertained him at a *heiva*. He caught only a distant glimpse of the new 'King', a boy about six years old, who was carried on a man's shoulders and lived in surroundings so beautiful and picturesque as to defy Bligh's powers of description. He returned to Matavai in a mood recalling that of the bemused Bougainville. 'These two places', he exulted, 'are certainly the Paradise of the World, and if happiness could result from situation and convenience, here it is to be found in the highest perfection.'[20]

He soon felt confident enough to explain his mission to the chiefs with whose approval the gathering and potting of breadfruit seedlings began early in November. Since the work was largely delegated to the capable Nelson and his assistant, Bligh himself was free to follow his own manifold interests. Deeply imbued as he was with the dead commander's principles, his first concern was to continue Cook's horticultural experiments and, if possible, repair the damage inflicted by the Moorean invaders. With help from the crew, he and Nelson had already laid out two gardens and sown them with Indian corn and vegetables. Now almonds were distributed with instructions on their cultivation, while fruit stones and rose seeds were planted in suitable places. The almonds formed part of a gift sent to Omai by the daughters of Mr. Brand, the commandant at the Cape, and Bligh thought he could not put them to better use. He had no animals to restock the island, but after infinite trouble he did succeed in bringing to Matavai two isolated remnants of Cook's gift, a heifer and a bull, which quickly mated. On completing his arduous task, he expressed mingled feelings of loyalty and self-satisfaction:

Thus I have fixed in a fair way a Breed of Cattle in this Island, which after much trouble and care failed in the first instance and in all probability would never have taken place again, had it not been for this gracious Act of His Majesty our King to benefit his Subjects in the West Indies with the Breadfruit plant.

He was less fortunate with a sheep transported from Huahine by the chief Tareederia who told the sceptical Bligh there were ten more on the island. This one he identified as the English ewe left with Otoo in 1777, now reduced to mere skin and bone and afflicted with mange. Nevertheless, he bought the animal and in the hope of acquiring a ram offered a large reward if more sheep were retrieved. But before the poor creature could also be mated it was killed by a dog — or so the islanders reported. Bligh suspected they had made up the story for reasons of their own.[21]
   These people, he had long since decided, thought lying a real accomplishment — their whimsical and fabulous accounts were 'beyond every thing'. Yet this realization did not prevent him from recording fantastic travellers' tales or doubtful and sometimes inconsistent versions of past events. Particularly baffling were the meagre and often vague statements about Omai and his young companions. On that subject the chief authority was Odiddy whom Bligh first mentioned on 4 November. Cook's former protégé, now apparently reconciled to his lot, confirmed the earlier reports of Omai's death and supplied a few more details: his house had been accidentally burnt down; his stallion was dead; his muskets were taken care of. Odiddy told Bligh that Tiarooa was also dead but Coaa, he asserted, was alive and very well. A week later Bligh heard from some unnamed informant that Omai had lived only thirty months after Cook left him at Huahine and Tiarooa not much longer. 'Coah still remains there', he wrote in his log, 'and I have offered great rewards to any Cannoe that will go and fetch him, but as yet I have no hopes of seeing him.' He added a comforting observation, evidently picked up from the same source: 'Many enquiries were latterly made to Omai concerning England and it appears, poor fellow, that he impressed on their Minds not only our power and consequence, but our kindness and good will towards him.' The next day Bligh was again cheered to learn — this time from Odiddy — that the vines and other plants left at Huahine continued to grow and bear fruit. Even more reassuring was the news that there were cattle on Moorea and that European plants still flourished at Vaitepiha Bay.[22]
   If further reports were to be credited, Omai had long been outlived by the mortal enemy of his family and his people. On 13 November Bligh noted that Opoony, 'the famous Old Cheif of Bolabola', had died '30 Months since'. That day he made a determined effort to collect additional facts at a dinner attended, as usual, by members of the royal family and, on this occasion, by Odiddy. During the meal he steered the conversation to the subject of Omai, whereupon Odiddy spoke of the dead man's martial exploits:

Soon after Captn. Cook left Huaheine there were some disputes between the people of that Island and those of Ulieta, in which also the Natives of Bola-bola or Bora-bora took a part. Omai now became of consequence from the possession of three or four Muskets and some Ammunition, & he was consulted on the occasion. Whatever were the motives, such was Omai's opinion and Assurance of Success, that a War was determined on, and took place immediatly. Victory soon followed through the means of those few Arms and many of the Ulieta & Bora-bora men were killed. The Ammunition only lasted to end the contest, and they were in such want for flints that the Musquets were at last fired by a fire stick.[23]

Peace was again established, said Odiddy, ending his recital by repeating that both Omai and Tairooa had died natural deaths about thirty months after Cook's departure. 'I asked', wrote Bligh, 'if from this Victory Omai had gained any possessions or was of higher rank than we left him in.' The first question was ignored, but to the second the guests answered without hesitation: no, he remained in the same rank as before, and that was only one above the lowest. At this point Bligh inquired about the different orders of Tahitian society. Instead of the commonly recognized three (*arii, raatira, manahune*), this royal and aristocratic assembly named six, ranging from King to Servants and including Lords, Barons, and Esquires. Omai was placed in the class of 'Citizens' — 'Rateerah or Mana-hownee' (which tended, if anything, to confirm his middling status).[24]

A fortnight later, with the arrival of Tareederia from the Society Islands, Bligh renewed his inquiries. This man had been the boy chief of Huahine at the time of Cook's final visit and should have been well informed on Omai's history. His reports, however, did not differ materially from earlier ones. Nor, apparently, was he able to clear up the mystery surrounding the young New Zealander, for Bligh complained: '. . . I cannot get any person to bring Coah (who is alive and Well) to me, or acquaint him that I am here.' In the weeks and months that followed no more was said of the child (now, presumably, grown to manhood), while his master received only passing mention. On 8 December, when describing local manufactures, Bligh noted that since his previous visit there had been a vast improvement in the quality of cloth and mats. This he attributed to the attention which the Tahitian women had paid to the superior examples brought from the Friendly Islands by Cook and his men. Then, always ready to give credit where it was due, he added: 'They have received a great deal of information from Omai. They give him a very good Character and say he knew and showed them a great many things.' The banal tribute was Bligh's last reference to Omai until he was preparing to leave the island towards the end of March.[25]

Bligh spent more than five months in Tahiti. None of his English predecessors had been there so long and no one, not Banks himself, had surpassed him in the range and persistence of his inquiries. While the collection of breadfruit plants went on, he examined local habits and customs, observing, listening, noting, but rarely condemning. He praised the undemanding hospitality of these unspoiled people, their friendliness to strangers, and their parental virtues, scarcely equalled, he thought, in the most civilized society. The phallic contortions of the *arioi* were certainly not to his taste; nor could he share Iddeah's affection for her 'Mahoo' friend — boy in body, girl in manner — who, with others of the same kind, were 'equally respected and esteemed.' He inclined to the view that venereal diseases — or at least similar complaints — were endemic and not confined to the lower classes. The promiscuity of both sexes he regarded with an indulgent eye, and he even made light of petty thievery, more prevalent than he had first supposed. Where tolerance stopped short was in the treatment of his own countrymen. Early in the visit he introduced a practice, occasionally used by Cook, of penalizing not the native malefactor but the seaman through whose negligence the offence had been committed. These and similar measures understandably provoked the crew, and on 5 January three men made off with the ship's cutter. Recaptured with the help of Odiddy, the deserters were put in irons and severely punished. Later that month, for striking a Tahitian he suspected of theft, another sailor was ordered two dozen lashes — a sentence Bligh reduced following the intercession of Otoo and Iddeah.[26]

This humane couple were Bligh's constant companions. They paid frequent visits to the ship and late in November accompanied him to a great *heiva* where he shared the honours with Cook's portrait which was displayed as a kind of sacred image. Three weeks later they showed 'great attention and decency' at the funeral of the ship's surgeon who, having died from 'drunkeness and indolence' (Bligh's harsh verdict), was buried ashore in a grave marked by a cairn of stones. The friendship grew even closer when on Christmas Day he moved the *Bounty* to the more sheltered harbour of Pare to escape seasonal gales. Henceforth he was in Otoo's own district and entertained both the chief and his relatives almost daily. Through Odiddy, who served as his 'spy on all their Actions', he learned of intrigues in the royal family and of Iddeah's open infidelities. Tolerant as always, he remarked on her good sense, her cleverness, and the vast sway she exerted over her husband. She displayed great interest in European arms, he noted, and always came aboard to fire the sentinel's musket at sundown. Otoo, on the other hand, was 'one of the most timrous men existing', far surpassed in the martial arts by his youngest brother, renowned for having killed Maheine, the warrior chief of Moorea. Their mother, an aged lady of enormous corpulence, gave a long recital of the family's misfortunes and pledged their eternal friendship. Among other visitors was one of the travellers to Lima and a venerable figure who claimed to be Tupia's uncle. The patriarch still mourned the loss of his nephew and asked for the dead man's hair to be sent back. When Otoo talked of going to England, Bligh remarked, he made the same plea on his own account should he, too, die while absent from his native island.[27]

Otoo did not embark on the *Bounty*, though both he and Iddeah with many others begged to be taken. As Bligh observed on 21 March, '. . . Omai has impressed on their minds so much in favor of England, that I could, if I had occasion for it, man the Ship with Otaheiteans, and even with Cheifs.' One persistent volunteer was Odiddy, 'a very worthy good Creature', who was greatly attached to them, said Bligh, and anxious to accompany them, claiming it as his right 'because he was at Sea with Captain Cook.' Bligh fobbed off the suppliants with vague promises and excuses: before carrying them to his own country, he must get King George's permission; Iddeah would die of seasickness; he would come back with a larger ship properly fitted out for their accommodation. To console them further, he distributed lavish gifts of shirts, hatchets, saws, files, knives, and, as a replacement for Cook's stolen chest, he supplied Otoo with another, also large enough to serve as a bed. At the anxious chief's request, for protection against predatory rivals, he gave Iddeah and Odiddy two muskets and two pistols with a thousand rounds of ammunition. He left the firearms with considerable hesitation and only, he said, because his friends, through their long-continued association with the British, had incurred the envy and hostility of their neighbours. Once the *Bounty* was gone, he was convinced they would again be attacked; and he regretted that owing to the demands of his present mission he had been unable to punish Otoo's enemies for plundering him and taking his cattle. 'If therefore', he concluded, 'these good and friendly people are to be destroyed from our intercourse with them, unless they have timely assistance, I think it is the business of any of his Majesty's Ships that may come here to punish any such attempt.'[28]

In spite of some misgivings, Bligh could reflect that his visit had done something to advance Britain's civilizing mission. Iron tools had now replaced the old implements of stone and bamboo, he recorded with satisfaction, while the islanders had become 'immoderately fond' of European apparel — their habit of wearing a single shoe or stocking rendered them 'the most laughable Objects existing'. True, he must ruefully acknowledge, he had achieved little success with his gardens. The Indian corn had grown and ripened, but most of the vegetables had been destroyed by insect pests or trampled by marauding hogs. On the other hand, the two salvaged cattle promised to increase, and others, he was told, survived on Moorea. As for the official purpose of his voyage, it had succeeded beyond all expectations. When the *Bounty* left Pare on 4 April 1789, it was crammed to capacity with breadfruit seedlings. One of Bligh's last acts was to inscribe the total — more than a thousand — on the back of Cook's portrait and note other details of his stay. He restored the painting to his grief-stricken friends and sailed off. 'That I might get a farther knowledge concerning Omai', he explained, 'I steered for Huaheine.'[29]

The *Bounty* reached the island shortly after noon on the 6th, but Bligh had no intention of landing at Fare and kept well outside the reef. 'We could see every part of the Harbour very distinctly,' he emphasized, 'and my attention was drawn particularly to where Omais House stood, no part of which remained.' The natives waited on shore for some time, expecting the ship to sail in. At last, about three o'clock, a small craft arrived, followed by a large double canoe with a crew of ten. Among them was a handsome young man who immediately greeted Bligh by name and proved to be one of the people the *Resolution* had brought to Huahine to live with Omai. This was a very fortunate circumstance, Bligh remarked, for the weather was squally and both he and his visitors were anxious to get away as soon as they could. For that reason, he added, the man's account was very short but also very clear.[30]

What he related was indeed little enough, but he did settle the mystery of the younger New Zealander's fate. Omai died thirty months after Cook's departure, he told Bligh, and both Tiarooa and Coaa had died before their master, all three from natural causes. Of the animals only the mare still survived and nothing was said of the ten sheep reported by Tareederia. There lingered on, however, the memory of one small creature, now mentioned for the first time: 'Omai had a Monkey with him which created great mirth among the Natives, they called it Oroo Tata or Hairy Man. This Animal he described as did the People of Otaheite, to have fallen from a Cocoa Nutt Tree and was killed.' For the rest, the recital was one of almost unrelieved loss or neglect: Omai's house had been torn to pieces and stolen; his firearms were at Raiatea; his plants had been destroyed except for a tree which the young man was unable to name. He went on to say that they often rode together, Omai in boots — a detail that Bligh seized on as encouraging proof that 'he did not immediately after our leaving him, lay aside the Englishman.' Omai's influence was also evident in the tattooed horse and rider seen on the legs of several men and again in his companion's urgent plea to be taken to England. Bligh declined the request, gave the young man a small present, and at six o'clock bore away from Huahine, making for the Friendly Islands. Three weeks later, on 28 April 1789, he was seized by mutineers, led by Fletcher Christian, and with eighteen others set adrift in the ship's launch.[31]

THE UNCOMMUNICATIVE BLIGH apparently failed to pass on to his subordinates the details he had picked up concerning Omai. In his account of their five months at Tahiti, the boatswain's mate, James Morrison, wrote of the crowd who first greeted them: 'We also learnt by them that O'Mai was dead tho we could not learn by what means he died, but it was thought that he had been killd for the sake of his property'; 'however', he added, 'we were better informd afterwards as shall be shown in its proper place.' Again, in his reference to the call at Huahine on 6 April, he remarked: 'At Noon we hove too of[f] Farree Harbour to enquire for Omai; but could get no other information but that he was dead some time.' Morrison compiled his so-called journal while awaiting trial for his part in the mutiny and, since he denied all guilt, some bias in his own favour is only to be expected. Nevertheless, the journal (more accurately the narrative) was clearly based on diaries or notes and carries with it an air of authenticity. It remains, furthermore, the fullest record of the *Bounty*'s movements and the actions of its remaining men after Bligh's involuntary departure. Morrison relates how, on taking charge, Christian ordered the breadfruit plants to be thrown overboard and, for reasons he did not yet disclose, set off for Tubuai in the Austral Group, sighted by Cook during the third voyage. On 28 May they reached the hitherto untouched island where events took a familiar course. The inhabitants tried to drive off the newcomers with clubs and spears, blew conch shells in defiance or used their women as decoys, and finally on the 30th launched a concerted attack which the Europeans repelled with their muskets and four-pounders. In spite of this hostile reception, Christian thought the place would make a suitable refuge for the twenty-five men left on the ship but first decided to visit Tahiti to take on supplies and recruit companions who might solace them in their exile.[32]

They again reached Matavai Bay on 6 June, to the surprise of their old friends who were told that after leaving the island in April Mr. Bligh had met Captain Cook and joined the commander's ship with the breadfruit plants and some of his men. He himself had come back, Christian explained, to get animals for a settlement King George was forming in New Holland. The Tahitians appeared to accept the threadbare story of Cook's continued existence and while Christian remained aboard, plying the chiefs with wine and arrack, agents went ashore to exchange ironware for livestock and provisions. The results exceeded all expectations. In ten days they acquired more than four hundred hogs and fifty goats with fowls, dogs, cats, and, most precious of prizes, the bull and cow Bligh had succeeded in bringing together with so much difficulty. The natives set little store on the two animals, Morrison remarked, and sold them for a few red feathers. Having loaded the *Bounty*, Christian and his men set out for Tubuai. They carried some volunteers and when they were at sea stowaways appeared on deck. Among them was Odiddy who had seized this opportunity of ending his long thraldom to Otoo. Christian told the migrants, numbering twenty-eight in all, that they would never see Tahiti again; but neither then nor later, Morrison observed, did they show the least sign of regret. On the voyage back the weather was stormy, resulting in the loss of some livestock. One casualty was the bull which died as the result of repeated falls and was heaved overboard.[33]

Like islanders elsewhere in the Pacific, the people of Tubuai had learned the harsh lesson of British power. When the *Bounty* returned on 23 June, there was no sign of hostility and, to improve matters, the Tahitians made friends with the local inhabitants and, picking up a knowledge of their tongue, were soon able to act as interpreters. Under these favourable auspices Christian had no hesitation in landing the animals, some of which were transferred to small islands in the lagoon, while the cow and about two hundred hogs were put ashore and 'Sufferd to take their Chance'. Having disciplined two rebellious members of his crew, he sought a piece of land for the settlement he was planning. By playing off one group of natives against another (for this small island had its factions and its rival chiefs), he obtained a site where he intended building an elaborate stockade to be known as Fort George. On 18 July operations began with the turning of a turf, the hoisting of a union jack, and the drinking of a special allowance of grog. For the next month work went steadily forward.[34]

While Christian and his men toiled at Fort George, the latest visitors to Tahiti were picking up vague reports of their movements. On 12 August 1789 the brig *Mercury*, commanded by John Henry Cox, anchored in Matavai Bay. In explaining their presence in these remote waters, the historian of the voyage, Lieutenant George Mortimer of the Marines, was somewhat evasive. Though not wholly acquainted with Mr. Cox's motives, he remarked, he understood that gentleman was 'under an urgent necessity to go to China' and chose to sail rather in his own vessel than in an Indiaman, 'especially as he had a great desire to visit the Islands in the South Seas'. In fact the *Mercury*, also known as *Gustaf III* and employed by the King of Sweden in his war with Russia, was on its way to attack the enemy's trading posts in the North Pacific. These mercenaries had no patience with the natives who crowded the ship on its arrival and no success in satisfying their curiosity about one renowned islander of whom they had probably read in accounts of Cook's third expedition. 'Our first enquiries', wrote Mortimer, 'were directed after Omai, the man whom Captain Cook brought to England, and who returned with him in his last voyage; but, notwithstanding we used our utmost diligence to gain any information concerning him, we could learn little else than he died a natural death, some time since, at the Island of Ulietea, his native place.'[35]

On landing, they found unmistakable signs of their predecessors — details of the *Bounty*'s visit on the back of Cook's portrait brought to them by a local chief, the dead surgeon's grave, and an English pointer which singled them out, showing its joy 'by every action the poor animal was capable of'. As they walked on, they noticed vegetables 'choked up with weeds, and totally neglected by the natives, who set no kind of value upon them.' There were no signs of Cook's livestock, but on a later excursion Mortimer heard that some of the cattle were on the island of Moorea. One afternoon he saw a strange-looking club in the hands of a man who told him it had been brought from a place called Tootate by Titreano, Mr. Bligh's chief officer. His informant went on to say that Titreano returned in the *Bounty* about two months after she first sailed, leaving Mr. Bligh behind at Tootate. Others confirmed the story and added that Titreano had left again only fifteen days before the *Mercury*'s arrival, carrying away several Tahitian families. At the time Mortimer had no idea who Titreano was or where Tootate could be; but 'the principal part of this strange relation', he later decided, 'was true'.[36]

Iddeah soon paid her respects to Mr. Cox but Otoo, 'the present king', did not appear until the 16th, after which he was a constant visitor to the *Mercury*, often spending the night on board. He excelled his subjects not only in size, Mortimer noted, but also in appetite, for he ate enormously and quaffed wine very freely in honour of King George, a custom he had acquired on the *Bounty*. Like Bligh before him, the lieutenant compared the monarch most unfavourably with his consort, 'a clever sensible woman' and an excellent shot, as she proved by firing at a distant buoy which she hit at the first attempt. Other members of the royal family were frequent callers — Otoo's equally bibulous brothers and their mother, one of the largest women Mortimer had ever seen but 'a good motherly sort' and 'of a lively chearful disposition'. Otoo, who was undertaking a tour of the island, could not wait to farewell his guests when they finally sailed and, to their relief, left on the 23rd, entrusting them with a message to King George. His fellow monarch was asked to send a large ship that would remain at Matavai Bay and bring plenty of guns. He had already taken his presents away in a chest made for the purpose and this time carried off a living trophy. He was a sailor named Brown who a week before had 'in a terrible manner' slashed a crony with a razor and been put in irons. The man now told Cox he wanted to stay on the island and, as Otoo promised to care for him, the captain gladly let him go. When Brown left, he showed not the least sign of regret, nor did he take leave of a single person. The next day he wrote to say he was well treated, adding a request for a bible and tools to build a boat. Cox supplied the articles together with a letter of advice on Brown's future conduct towards his protectors.[37]

Late in August, while the crew busied themselves getting the ship ready for sea, the officers crossed over to Moorea to see Captain Cook's cattle (or their descendants). The Tahitians had warned them they would be killed, but they landed without opposition and while the excited islanders summoned their 'king', the visitors inspected a bull and two cows, all in good condition but very wild. The natives took little notice of the animals and set no value on them, Mortimer reported; indeed, he thought they must be an encumbrance rather than a benefit since there were no fences to keep them out of gardens and plantations. On his arrival, Maheine's successor had little to say and seemed to be 'of a timid disposition'. His wife, however, was an 'agreeable, insinuating woman' — so agreeable that she made her person available that night, as did another royal lady, claiming to have been the 'Tayo' of Sir Joseph Banks (presumably twenty years earlier when he came to observe the transit of Venus). Before they returned to Tahiti the sightseers rowed to Cook's anchorage, 'a most beautiful spot', and by the 29th were back in Matavai Bay making final preparations for the coming voyage. On 2 September 1789 the ship set out on the next stage of its sinister mission, leaving behind Tahiti's first British settler. As Mortimer reported in his introduction, he returned to England in time to tell Captain Edwards of the *Pandora* what he knew of the mutineers. His hope was that 'these daring offenders' would suffer 'that condign punishment' they so justly merited.[38]

At about this time the daring offenders and their companions were in some disarray on their island refuge. The people of Tubuai had shown themselves less docile than the Tahitians, and their women were far less accessible. So it was decided to abandon Fort George and split into two groups: one would return to Tahiti while the other, led by Fletcher Christian, would seek some even more remote hiding-place elsewhere in the Pacific. Before they could put the plan into effect, however, they ran into serious trouble. While rounding up their livestock they clashed with the islanders who were finally worsted after losing at least sixty of their men in battle. Morrison paid a tribute to the martial prowess of their Tahitian followers, especially Odiddy, 'an excellent Shot'; and he recorded a farewell feast provided by Bligh's treasured cow which, he laconically observed, 'proved excellent meat'. On 22 September, three weeks after the *Mercury's* departure, they were again anchored in Matavai Bay. Christian waited only long enough to land the dissident party with their possessions before taking on board a further complement of Tahitians and sailing off to his unknown destination.[39]

The men who had elected to stay behind, sixteen in all, first visited Pare to offer 'the Young King' gifts of red feathers and curiosities brought from Tubuai and the Friendly Islands. Odiddy had also left the *Bounty* and acted as their spokesman both at this and later functions when they were feasted and given a piece of land for their use. Otoo, or Matte (Mate) as Morrison called him, was absent in the southern part of the island, occupied with some mysterious business of his own, but sent each man a hog and a piece of cloth. They in turn dispatched their own presents by a delegation which returned with Brown, the razor-slashing sailor from the *Mercury*. He spoke openly of this and similar exploits, going on to complain that, while Captain Cox had given Otoo a musket and pistols, he had been left with neither arms nor tools. He 'appeard to be a dangerous kind of a Man', Morrison decided, and was relieved when he again left to rejoin Otoo. After a month or so the members of the ill-assorted group gradually went their separate ways. Some established themselves at Pare with their old sweethearts; several followed Brown to the south where they became involved in the intrigues of Otoo and other chiefs; the remainder stayed on at Matavai, living either independently or with their Tahitian friends. Once they had settled down, Morrison and his companions, none of them active conspirators in the mutiny, agreed to build a small schooner. They announced that it was intended for cruising among the islands; in reality, they hoped it would take them to Batavia and thence home to England.[40]

The work began early in November and went steadily on throughout the ensuing months. On Sundays and sacred holidays the men hoisted the ensign and held a service, often attended by the local people who behaved 'with much decency' and inquired into the mysteries of the Christian religion. The Europeans in their turn took part in Tahitian festivities, watching with interest when at a great *heiva* early in February the celebrants paid homage to Captain Cook's portrait by stripping to the waist before the precious relic. As reports of dissension reached them from every quarter, it became evident that affairs on the island were in a dangerously unsettled state. On 9 March the young king, fearing an attack from hostile neighbours, summoned them to Pare to help him. This proved a false alarm, but some weeks later Otoo sent a messenger to ask their advice about settling scores with a recalcitrant chief on Moorea. Morrison and his party refused to be drawn into the quarrel, though they did clean and repair firearms for a punitive expedition sent over in charge of Odiddy. That redoubtable fighter carried out his mission with complete success, killing one leader and forcing the rebel chief to seek refuge with his relatives at Papara. Scarcely had this incident ended when news reached Matavai that, following the death of the Vehiatua, two mutineers settled in the south had both been murdered, one by his companion, the other by a native in retaliation.[41]

The boat-builders, in contrast, remained on good terms with their neighbours and resolutely persisted with their laborious enterprise. Early in July they finished the hull which was launched with the help of their Tahitian hosts and given the historic name *Resolution*. For the next few weeks they occupied themselves in completing the schooner and salting pork for the voyage to Batavia until they, too, were drawn into the factional struggle. As Bligh had predicted, the enemies of Otoo's family combined to crush their rivals and, just as he had hoped, British mariners rallied to support his friends. On 12 September Morrison and his men again received a plea from the young king for help to repel invading warriors. This they succeeded in doing without much trouble, but later in the month a full-scale war broke out in which the contingent from Matavai joined other members of the *Bounty* crew together with Brown and Odiddy to crush the opposing forces. By the end of the month European tactics combined with European firearms had prevailed and at a gathering to ratify peace all the chiefs of Tahiti Nui promised 'they would always honor the Young King as their Sovereign'. Proceedings were accompanied by volleys from the victorious muskets and ended with a great feast where conquerors and conquered mingled in seeming amity.[42]

Following this martial interlude, Morrison and his party returned to Matavai to put the finishing touches to the *Resolution*. By the beginning of November, just a year after they had begun work, the schooner was fitted out with masts, rigging, and temporary sails made of local cloth. They now felt they could venture from the bay to other harbours in Tahiti or to nearby islands. During a visit to Moorea they sought out the cattle, increased to seven since Mortimer's census and, as Morrison remarked, 'quite wild, being only kept as curiositys'. The chief purpose of the excursion was to procure woven matting for sails, but neither here nor in Tahiti could they find anything strong enough to withstand the stress of a long voyage as far as Batavia or even beyond. Some of the men, moreover, had grown lukewarm about that perilous venture. So, on their return to the bay early in December, they abandoned the idea

IV Head of Omai (detail) by Sir Joshua Reynolds, c. 1775

of leaving their agreeable asylum. Since they expected the rainy season
to set in shortly, they hauled the schooner ashore and built a shelter to
protect her from the weather.[43]

Storms and squalls failed to deter the Society Islanders from traversing
the miles of open ocean that separated them from Tahiti. There were
many visitors 'from different parts', Morrison reported early in January
1791, noting in particular 'the Ryeatea people, who made much inquirey
about Captain Cook, Sir Joseph Banks &c. &c.' Then came the long-
promised revelations concerning Omai:

— and as we were also Visited by several people of note from Hooa-heine, the
Island where Captain Cook had left Omai, we learnt of them that he died (of
the Hotatte, a disorder not much different from the Fever & Ague) about four
years after he had landed, and the New Zealand boys both died soon after,
they greived much for Poenammoo their Native Country, and after OMai died,
they gave over all hopes & having now lost their chief friend, they pined
themselves to Death.[44]

In addition, the visitors supplied details (some of them clearly
inaccurate) of Omai's travels and his treatment by the islanders after
Cook left Huahine:

— They also inform'd us that Omai was one of the Lowest Class (Calld
Mannahownee) and had been condem'd to be sacraficed for Blasphemy against
one of the Chiefs, but his Brother getting wind of it sent him out of the way,
and the Adventure arriving at Taheite at the Time, he got on board her and
came to England, and his Friendship with Captain Cook afterwards, made
him more respected then his riches, and the meaness of his birth made him
gain very little credit with his countrymen tho he kept them in awe by his arms.

Both the persons of note from Huahine and 'a very intelligent man who
lived with Omai some time as a servant' spoke of the reputation he had
achieved as a warrior:

. . . His Arms and the Manner in which he used them made him Great in War,
as he bore down all before him, and all who had timely notice fled at his
Approach and when accouterd with his Helmet & Breastplate, & Mounted on
Horse back they thought it impossible to hurt him, and for that reason never
attempted it, and Victory always attended him and his Party. Nor was he of
less consequence at sea, for the enemy would never attempt to come near the
Canoe which he was in.[45]

To questions about Omai's property the islanders replied in contradictory terms. Some reported that he had been very careful of it during
his lifetime, while others held that he scattered it widely. According to
these informants, he had lost the stallion soon after landing in rather
bizarre circumstances: the animal had been gored in the belly by a goat
and, as he knew no remedy, Omai could do nothing but take revenge

by killing the goat. The mare survived on the island and part of the house built by Captain Cook still remained. After Omai's death, they said, his goods were distributed among his friends; one of them (Taree-deria's brother) had inherited the muskets, but they were of no use, 'being both disabled'. For the rest, Morrison heard the familiar story of loss and neglect: Omai's garden, 'having no body to look after it', had been destroyed by hogs and goats; except for one goose, his poultry were dead, 'being devided and kept in different parts of the Island as Curiositys after His Death' or taken elsewhere in the group.[46]

Morrison wrote nothing more about Omai and his possessions. On 10 January he reported the arrival of Iddeah, full of gratitude for the Englishmen's services in the recent war. She had come, it soon appeared, to prepare for her son's investiture with 'the Royal Marro', a momentous event which had no doubt also brought the visitors from the Society Islands. A month later, with elaborate ritual accompanied by thirty human sacrifices, the assembled chiefs acknowledged the young Otoo's authority. At the ceremony the British nation, through whose influence a comparatively obscure family had risen to supreme power, was not unworthily represented by James Morrison. Late in March he was at Papara consorting with Oamo ('the same mentioned by Captain Cook') and his son when a messenger came from Odiddy to say that a ship had reached Matavai Bay. It was the *Pandora*, sent out to capture the *Bounty*'s crew and bring them to trial. Aided by Brown, the new arrivals rounded up the Tahitian contingent and on 19 May set forth again in search of Christian and his followers. They carried away both Brown and Odiddy who was left at the Society Islands, so passing out of recorded history nearly two decades after he first joined the *Resolution*.[47]

VETERANS OF COOK'S VOYAGES were serving at this period not only in the tropical Pacific but also in the ocean's northern reaches where, with the coming of peace, they had found an occupation in the profitable fur trade between China and the north-west coast of America. While Bligh was engaged in his charitable mission, James Colnett, once a midshipman on the *Resolution*, had been employed to set up a trading post at Nootka Sound in what is now British Columbia. Arriving there in the *Argonaut* at the end of June 1789, he was confronted by a party of Spaniards sent to assert His Catholic Majesty's rights and establish a colony. In the dispute that followed, the *Argonaut* was seized and its commander taken to Mexico, a prisoner in his own ship. After 'Twelve Months and four days' Cruelty, Robbery, and Oppressive treatment', as he expressed it, Colnett was freed, but early in April 1791 he again clashed with a Spanish officer, Manuel Quimper, off the island of Hawaii. When reporting the incident in his journal, he wrote:

Manuel Quimper was in the Ship that Visited Oteihitee, when so much pains were taken to depreciate the English nation, which is taken notice of in Captain Cook's Voyages; and this Quimper has been there since. When I was in Mexico

I was inform'd from good authority that the Spaniards kill'd Omia, Destroy'd his dwelling, stock, and every other present, made him by the English, that they could come at, in the following manner: While the Ship lay at Huhana, they frequently Visited Omia at his house, and constantly lavish of their own praises, and no ways sparing of their abuse of the English. Omia, warm with Gratitude for the many favours he had receiv'd, hastily took up a Fowling piece, and Shot the Officer which was the second Captain, and a Frenchman, thro' the head for which they retaliated.

On being charged with complicity in the murder, Quimper dismissed the whole story, but his denial did nothing to satisfy Colnett. In the Englishman's view a nation which had thought it no crime to slaughter tens of thousands during a recent insurrection in Peru would not have hesitated to kill one individual.[48]

Colnett occupies a small niche in Pacific history not merely as recorder — or perhaps author — of the most sensational and obviously least authentic legend of Omai's death. As a result of his misadventures, the Admiralty sent out a further expedition comparable with its predecessors and led by another officer who had served under Cook. Though Colnett had no official status when the *Argonaut* was seized, the British Government took up his cause and by mobilizing the Fleet compelled the Spanish authorities to restore the confiscated property and, even more important, acknowledge for the first time Britain's right to trade and explore in the Pacific. Following this forced concession, the *Discovery* and a smaller supply ship the *Chatham* were commissioned to reclaim the Nootka Sound station and chart the west coast of America to the north of existing Spanish settlements. The command was entrusted to George Vancouver who had sailed as a midshipman on Cook's second and third voyages. He was an able navigator and a highly intelligent man but apparently shared his old commander's prejudice against specialized supernumeraries. He took no official artist, dispensed at first with the services of an astronomer, and raised objections to the appointment of Banks's nominee, Archibald Menzies, as naturalist. Sir Joseph ultimately had his way and also secured a passage home for one more Polynesian wanderer, a Hawaiian youth from the Sandwich Islands known as Towraro or Towereroo (perhaps Kaualelu in modern transcription). Brought to England by traders in July 1789, he had since lived in great obscurity, Vancouver explained, 'and did not seem in the least to have benefited by his residence in this country.' They left Falmouth at the beginning of April 1791 and, sailing by the Cape of Good Hope route, reached Matavai Bay at the close of December.[49]

On arriving in the *Discovery*, Vancouver was relieved to find the *Chatham* already at anchor. The two ships had lost touch in a storm off the New Zealand coast, but William Broughton, the lieutenant in command, had succeeded in bringing his vessel to the appointed rendezvous and was already *au fait* with affairs on the island. Otoo was living on Moorea, it seemed, and was now called '*Pomurrey*' (Pomare) by his own people. Though he still retained authority as regent, he had handed over sovereign power together with his former name to his eldest son who had invited Mr. Broughton to meet him that day at Matavai. Assured by native advisers that his presence would be 'esteemed a civility', Vancouver accompanied his colleague ashore where they paid their respects to 'his Otaheitean majesty'. The monarch, a boy of about nine or ten carried everywhere on a man's shoulders, at first treated the visitors with extreme reserve but later shook them by the hand and urged that a boat should be sent for his father. Vancouver agreed to the request and, encouraged by the warm reception he received from lesser chiefs and the common people, decided to prolong his stay, originally intended as a brief call to replenish supplies. He chose the site for a shore station and on the back of Cook's portrait which, he remarked, had 'become the public register' saw that the *Pandora* had quitted the island in May. Improving on the words of his revered commander, he wrote of New Year's Day: 'lest in the voluptuous gratifications of Otaheite, we might forget our friends in old England, all hands were served a double allowance of grog to drink the health of their sweethearts and friends at home.'[50]

The next day Otoo-Pomurrey reached the bay, remarking as he saluted Vancouver that his English friend had grown much since they parted and 'looked very old'. He brought with him a chief called Mahow (Mahau), 'the reigning prince' of Moorea, who seemed in the final stages of a decline, and they were followed by Iddeah and a younger sister with other members of the royal family. The captain treated the whole party to dinner, noting with surprise that the women sat at table with the men, though he believed the practice was not general. Both sexes, he observed, were anxious to adopt European customs and sought spirituous liquors avidly. In the course of the meal Otoo drank a whole bottle of brandy and in consequence suffered such violent convulsions that four strong men were required to hold him down. He learned the lesson of moderation, however, and by the end of the week restricted himself to a few glasses of wine. More notabilities soon arrived to greet the visitors — a kinsman of Otoo who after Opoony's death had assumed power in Raiatea and Tahaa; the high chief of Huahine, also related to Otoo; and the latter's two sons, the young king and his brother, recently created Vehiatua. As Vancouver perceived, 'all the sovereigns of this group of islands', save only Opoony's daughter, were assembled at Matavai. To honour the distinguished gathering, on Saturday the 7th he entertained them at dinner and later with martial exercises followed by a display of fireworks. Hitherto Otoo had given Vancouver only trifling presents, but he now brought a truly regal tribute which included three specimens of the mourning dress, most precious of all Tahitian mementoes. On the 9th he left for Moorea, promising to return before the ships finally sailed.[51]

Throughout the Moorean party's visit Mahow had been a pathetic figure, eager to inspect all things English but too feeble to walk and carried everywhere on a litter. On the 14th Otoo sent a messenger to say that the chief had died and mourning ceremonies would begin at Pare on the 17th. To ensure the Englishmen's presence, early on the appointed day an escort reached the ships, but before he set out Vancouver saw fit to dispense justice to two natives. They had been caught stealing a hat from the *Discovery* and, in the hope that this might cure an epidemic of petty theft, he ordered their heads to be shaved and 'slight manual correction' administered. With that duty performed, he left to attend Mahow's affecting and malodorous obsequies. The mourners soon recovered, for they arrived the next morning 'in high spirits' and were overjoyed when he promised them a second fireworks display to be held later in the week on the eve of his departure. All was amity for some days until thieves, undeterred by the captain's harsh measures, stole a bag of linen; as a further complication, Towereroo, who had succumbed to the charms of a Tahitian girl, deserted and took to the hills. The Hawaiian youth was recaptured but all efforts to recover the linen failed and, to show his displeasure, Vancouver cancelled a *heiva* arranged in his honour together with the promised exhibition of fireworks. By the time he finally got away on the 24th, a reconciliation had been patched up and Otoo received the customary salute from the *Discovery*'s guns as the ships sailed on to the north.[52]

With becoming diffidence Vancouver apologized for shortcomings in his remarks on 'a people whose situation and condition have been long the subject of curious investigation'. His stay on the island was short, he explained, his knowledge of the language limited, and his problems increased by 'the difficulty of obtaining the truth from a race who have a constant desire to avoid, in the slightest degree, giving offence'. Certainly what he learned of Omai from Matuarro (Matuaro), the visiting chief of Huahine (doubtless Tareederia under a new name) added little to existing knowledge; and what he did record smacked somewhat of the official obituary:

Omai having died without children, the house which Captain Cook had built for him, the lands that were purchased, and the horse which was still alive; together with such European commodities as remained at his death, all descended to *Matuarro*, as king of the island; and when his majesty is at home, *Omai*'s house is his constant residence. From *Matuarro* we learned, that *Omai* was much respected, and that he frequently afforded great entertainment to him, and the other chiefs, with the accounts of his travels, and in describing the various countries, objects, &c. that had fallen under his observation; and that he died universally regretted and lamented.

Both he and the New Zealand boys had died of 'a disorder . . . attended by a large swelling in the throat'. Most of its victims suffered a slow lingering death, they were told, and the fatal malady had been brought by a Spanish vessel which had anchored near the southern part of Tahiti.[53]

Omai and his retainers were gradually fading into the legendary past.

Vancouver was more informative when he wrote of recent events in
Tahitian history since he could still meet and question the chief actors.
From Otoo and his brothers he heard of their defeat at the hands of
Maheine and Towha, their temporary eclipse, and their gradual return
to power. The ultimate victory he attributed to a number of causes —
the help they received from the *Bounty*'s people, their possession of arms
procured from visiting ships, and the combined and also complementary
qualities of Otoo and Iddeah. Once peace was made, their elder son was
firmly established at Pare, while his brother had lately been created
Vehiatua. Through the authority vested in these children the family had
gained control of all Tahiti and on the grounds of conquest or kinship
claimed to be overlords of Moorea, Huahine, and Raiatea. Now they
planned an attack on the territory which Opoony's daughter had
inherited from her father, insisting 'it was highly essential to the comfort
and happiness of the people at large, that over the whole group of these
islands there should be only one sovereign.' To achieve this end they
asked Vancouver to supply them with more firearms and, when he was
unwilling to comply, suggested he should conquer the islands on their
behalf. He again refused, whereupon Otoo urged that on his return to
England he should solicit King George to send out another ship for that
purpose. He frequently made the plea, Vancouver related, and did not
fail to repeat it in the most pressing manner as they finally parted.[54]

Thus Vancouver was a witness to the acceptance and triumph of the
monarchical principle unknown in Tahiti when Wallis arrived in 1767.
He was also at pains to record other changes — mostly for the worse —
which had come about through European influence in the previous
quarter-century. He observed a marked decline in the appearance of the
women, once so highly praised for their beauty. This alteration, he said,
the natives themselves freely admitted, attributing it to the 'lamentable
diseases' introduced by visiting seamen. Indeed, on meeting the 'wives'
of the *Bounty*'s crew and the mothers of their children, he had been
astonished that through their infatuation with people so lacking in
personal attractions Englishmen could have sacrificed country, honour,
and even their lives. It was partly at least through the mutineers' example
that the Tahitians had modified their mode of warfare, chiefly maritime
in character when Wallis discovered the island. Now they fought on
land, so that during his stay, Vancouver asserted, not one war canoe
had been seen by his men or himself. Many of the old crafts, in fact,
had vanished or were falling into disrepute. The few bone or stone tools
and utensils brought for sale were of inferior workmanship, while the
manufacture of local fabrics was being neglected through the widespread
use of foreign cloth. Such was the present demand for axes, files, knives,
fish-hooks, and red cloth or linen that the price of provisions had fallen
at least 200 per cent since Cook's time — and this notwithstanding the
Pandora's recent visit. By 'all the laws of humanity', Vancouver urged,
Europeans were bound to continue supplying those wants which they
alone had created.[55]

If his predecessors had destroyed much of the old culture, they had been singularly unsuccessful in introducing elements of their own. Vancouver was as eager as Bligh to observe the fate of his former commander's experiments and even more distressed by the results. 'Most of the animals, plants, and herbs, which had caused Captain Cook so much anxiety and trouble to deposit here,' he wrote, 'have fallen a sacrifice to the ravages of war.' The cattle had been carried to Moorea and, though some goats remained, they had become scarce because the Tahitians found no use for their milk and considered them not fat enough for eating. As for the many vegetable exotics brought to the island from time to time, he saw nothing but some few indifferent shaddocks, a little tolerably good maize, a few pods of the capsicum, and some very coarse radishes. His concern at the situation, he said, was the greater since he was able to do so little to remedy it. All he could add to 'the race of animals' were two Cape geese and a gander. Besides this, he and his men had planted orange and lemon trees, vine cuttings, and an assortment of seeds. But nature had been so bountiful in what she had bestowed on the island, Vancouver acknowledged, that the natives seemed to have little desire for any addition; and, judging by the deplorable state of the gardens sown by previous visitors, he had small reason to be sanguine about the success of their own. 'Nor', he added, 'do I believe such attempts will ever succeed until some Europeans shall remain on the island, and, by the force of their example, excite in the inhabitants a desire of cultivating the soil . . . .'[56]

IN THE TWELVE MONTHS that followed Vancouver's departure in January 1792, a succession of ships — whalers, traders, naval vessels — visited Matavai Bay, leaving behind a handful of castaways and deserters. But it was not until March 1797 when the *Duff* arrived with Protestant missionaries that Tahiti became the home of Europeans dedicated to the agricultural virtues; and even then many years passed before the benefits became visible in salvaged souls and ordered cultivations. At first the newcomers were caught up in the rivalry between Otoo and his eldest son, known to posterity as Pomare I and Pomare II. This unsettling episode ended with the father's death in 1803, only to be succeeded by Pomare II's protracted wars with his rivals. For, contrary to Vancouver's assumptions, Otoo had subdued, not vanquished, his traditional enemies. That struggle, too, came to a close when the monarch finally triumphed in 1815, three years after his conversion to Christianity. At one critical point in the conflict, towards the end of 1808, the missionaries were forced to abandon their buildings, animals, and gardens at Matavai to seek refuge in Huahine. Under the patronage of Iddeah, now married to a local chief, they established a new settlement near the site of Omai's house. And there a decade later came William Ellis who was at pains to gather all he could about the fate of that now legendary figure.[57]

Writing half a century after the events he recorded, Ellis thought it necessary to supply the background to his account of the Raiatean exile who had left Huahine with Captain Furneaux. 'The name of this individual', he explained, 'was *Mai*, usually called *Omai*, from the circumstance of the *o* being prefixed in the native language to nouns in the nominative case.' By birth Mai or Omai was apparently not connected with the regal or sacerdotal class. He was tall and thin in person, easy and engaging in his manners, polite in address, but in expression, features, and complexion inferior to the majority of his countrymen. The first South Sea Islander to do so, he reached England when interest in Captain Cook's voyages was universal and created unprecedented excitement. Considered a sort of prodigy, he was introduced to fashionable parties in London, conducted to the entertainments of the highest classes, and presented at Court amidst a brilliant assemblage. The ease with which he comported himself in these exalted circles Ellis ascribed not to early training but, like Dr. Johnson, to the example of his highborn acquaintance combined with his own mimic skill:

The Tahitians in general are good imitators of others; this talent he possessed in an eminent degree, and adopted that polite, elegant, and unembarrassed address, whereby the class with which he associated has ever been distinguished. Naturally quick in his perceptions, and lively in his conversation, although the structure and idiom of his own language effectually prevented his speaking English with ease or fluency, he was soon able to make himself understood; and the embarrassment he occasionally felt, in giving utterance to his thoughts, perhaps added to the interest of those who were watching the effect which every object in a world so new to him must naturally occasion.[58]

Omai (again to summarize Ellis's diffuse and censorious narrative) repeatedly visited every place of public amusement and every exhibition designed for pleasure. The multiplicity of spectacles presented in rapid succession kept his mind in a state of perpetual excitement and prevented him from paying particular regard to any one thing. He had been afforded the most favourable opportunity of acquiring a knowledge of British agriculture, arts, manufactures, and institutions — knowledge that would have enabled him to introduce salutary improvements among his countrymen. 'Thus', Ellis moralized, 'he might have become a father to his nation; and his visit to England might have been rendered a blessing to its latest generations.' As it was, with one exception (here followed a tribute to the efforts of Granville Sharp), no one attempted to impart to him useful information or the principles of revealed religion. True, on his return Captain Cook built him a house in the European style, planted a garden with many valuable seeds and roots, and left him a breed of horses, goats, and other animals. On the other hand, most of his presents were comparatively useless, 'though he landed with a coat of mail, a suit of armour, musket, pistols, cartouch-box, cutlasses, powder, and ball!' And in addition he was furnished with a portable organ, an electrical machine, fireworks, and numerous trinkets.[59]

The account Ellis gives of Omai's conduct after his return is of particular interest. Of all the witnesses hitherto cited he alone lived on Huahine

57 Fare Harbour, Huahine, showing the mission buildings on Omai's estate

and questioned his informants in their own language. It must be remembered, however, that he arrived there in 1818, forty years after Cook's
departure. Moreover, as his testimony discloses, he had little sympathy
for Omai or indeed for any of the islanders in their unregenerate state.
The voyager, he reported, 'soon threw off his European dress, and
adopted the costume, uncivilized manners, and indolent life, of his
countrymen. Weakness and vanity, together with savage pride, appear
to have been the most conspicuous traits of character he developed in
subsequent life.' As one instance of his vainglory, Ellis mentioned the
use of his horses which Omai seemed to regard as 'mere objects of
curiosity'; when he occasionally rode them it was 'to inspire terror or
excite admiration in the minds of the inhabitants.'[60]

In the missionary's version of Omai's martial career there are faint
echoes of the tributes picked up by Bligh and Morrison. But the supposed facts are given with no suggestion of praise and supplied with
romantic and melodramatic additions peculiar to Ellis:

His implements of war, and especially the fire-arms, rendered his aid and
co-operation a desideratum with the king of the island, who, in order more
effectually to secure the advantage of his influence and arms, gave him one of
his daughters in marriage, and honoured him with the name of *Paari*, (wise or
instructed,) by which name he is now always spoken of among the natives;
several of whom still remember him. He appears to have passed the remainder
of his life in inglorious indolence or wanton crime, to have become the mere
instrument of the caprice or cruelty of the king of the island, who not only
availed himself of the effects of his fire-arms in periods of war, but frequently
ordered him to shoot at a man at a certain distance, in order to see how far the
musket would do execution; or to despatch with his pistol, in the presence of
the king, the ill-fated objects of his deadly anger.[61]

Ellis failed to identify the 'king', but he could hardly have been
Tareederia who, as everyone testified, was a boy at the time of Omai's
repatriation. Nor does the honorific title Paari altogether square with
the monster conjured up later in the paragraph. Throughout the narrative, in fact, Ellis seems to be presenting two separate and not easily
reconciled pictures of Omai: on the one hand, the good-natured, sociable
but somewhat feckless figure who also appeared in the journals of his
fellow-voyagers; on the other, the ruthless warrior consumed with self-
pride and impelled by a wanton delight in violence. There may, of
course, have been some deterioration in his character, foreshadowed
perhaps by his conduct on Moorea. Possibly, however, the missionary
was misled by informants who out of politeness — or, as Vancouver put
it, from a desire to avoid giving offence — told Ellis what they suspected
he wished to hear. He himself noted differences of opinion together with
certain discrepancies between oral and published sources when continuing
his observations:

The majority of those whom I have heard speak of him, generally mentioned his name with execration rather than respect; and though some of the chiefs consider him as a man who had seen much of the world, and who possessed, according to their ideas, an amazing mass of information, his memory is certainly very lightly esteemed by his countrymen. As he does not, however, seem to have evinced, either on board the vessels in which he sailed, or among the company with which he mingled while in England, any latent malignity of character, or cruelty of disposition, he might perhaps have returned with very different sentiments and principles, had he fallen into other hands during his visit here [i.e. in Britain].[62]

When he drew not on the memories of unreliable witnesses but on his own observations Ellis was more convincing. 'The spot where Mai's house stood', he wrote, 'is still called Beritani, or Britain, by the inhabitants of Huahine.' In what was once part of his garden there grew a shaddock tree which the natives said was planted by Captain Cook himself while the vessels lay at anchor. With the exception of goats and pigs, his animals had all died, and so 'the benevolent intentions of the British government, in sending out horses, cattle, &c. proved abortive.' Furthermore:

The helmet, and some other parts of his armour, with several cutlasses, are still preserved, and, when we arrived in Huahine, were displayed on the sides of the house standing on the spot where Mai's dwelling was erected by Captain Cook. A few of the trinkets, such as a jack-in-a-box, a kind of serpent that darts out of a cylindrical case when the lid is removed, were preserved with care by one of the principal chiefs, who, when we first saw them, considered them great curiosities, and exhibited them, as a mark of his condescension, to particular favourites.

Ellis could not discover what had become of the organ and the electrical machine, but among the curiosities owned by the young chief of Tahaa there was one he was very glad to see — a large quarto bible with numerous coloured engravings. This, he was told, belonged to Paari or Mai, 'although no mention whatever is made of a Bible, or any other book, among the various articles enumerated by those who conveyed him to his native shores.'[63]

There Ellis's testimony ended, leaving most of the obscurities and contradictions in earlier reports still unresolved. How long Omai survived Cook's departure (whether four years or only thirty months), when and how the New Zealanders died, the sex of the remaining horse — these and other details were as uncertain as before. What did emerge clearly from his account was the missionary's disapproval of the whole enterprise. As Ellis viewed it, Omai's visit to Britain was an experiment in which 'the effect of refinement, civilization, and philosophy, upon the ignorant and uncivilized' had been tested under the most favourable circumstances. And, he concluded, 'the result was affecting':

The individual who had been brought from the ends of the earth, and shewn whatever England could furnish, suited to impress his wondering mind,

returned, and became as rude and indolent a barbarian as before. With one
solitary exception, the humanizing and elevating principles of the Bible do not
appear to have been presented to his notice, and he seemed to have derived no
benefit from his voyage.[64]

If that experiment in civilization had ended in failure, the next one
was more encouraging. After their expulsion from Tahiti in 1808, Ellis
recalled, the missionaries re-established themselves on the land formerly
granted to Omai. Only a few yards from where his house once stood
and near the glossy-leaved shaddock planted by Captain Cook, 'the
first building for the worship of Jehovah was erected; and on the same
spot the first school in Huahine was opened'. When he was last there in
1824, Ellis went on, he found in the same neighbourhood one of the
most neat, substantial, and convenient modern homes in the settlement.
The surrounding district, uncultivated when the missionaries arrived
and overrun with brushwood, had now been cleared, while Omai's
garden had again been enclosed and planted with many useful vegetables. Within these precincts the native proprietors, who there was
every reason to hope were Christians, had built a rustic summer-house
called 'a *fare bure huna*, or house for hidden prayer'. Visiting the place
almost daily, Ellis related, he often compared the condition of Beritani's
present inhabitants with that of its former proprietor, the 'gentle savage'
invoked in the 'beautiful and pathetic' lines of Cowper.[65]

12. Omai in Europe —
the Literary Aftermath

WHILE THE MEMORY OF OMAI GREW DIMMER IN THE TRADITIONS OF HIS OWN scriptless islands, his name lived on in European literature. Not only did he become the 'gentle savage' of William Cowper but also the central figure of an elaborate stage spectacle and the hero of a prose work epic in its scope and proportions. Duly described and labelled, he made his début as a natural history specimen, the representative of a new race. He continued to supply satirists with a pretext for their attacks on a decadent social order and remained the subject of debate between high-minded moralists and their more worldly opponents. Indeed, he was still sailing in mid-Pacific when he sparked off a controversy involving veterans of the second expedition and his former patrons. In March 1777 George Forster issued the two volumes of his *Voyage round the World*, a narrative of his experiences on the *Resolution*. In origin the work was partly at least a means of evading the Admiralty's restraints on the elder Forster after the collapse of the scheme for joint authorship with Cook. Since John Reinhold was forbidden to publish until after the appearance of the official account, George took the enterprise in hand and, using his father's material as well as his own, succeeded in anticipating by six weeks Cook's *Voyage towards the South Pole*.[1]

As already related, Forster had been prejudiced against Omai from the outset, stigmatizing him as ill-favoured and dark-complexioned; furthermore, he alleged, the man's low birth was clearly evident from the fact that on the *Adventure* he associated not with the captain but with the armourer and the common sailors. Yet, Forster conceded, Omai possessed some of the better qualities of his countrymen: 'he was not an extraordinary genius like Tupaia, but he was warm in his affections, grateful, and humane; he was polite, intelligent, lively, and volatile.' The last impressions were probably formed in England, for occasional references in Forster's volumes make it clear that after his own return he had sought out Omai and consulted him on a variety of topics. According to his testimony, the Tahitians used no fewer than fourteen different plants for making perfumes, 'which shews how remarkably fond these people are of fine smells.' He again asserted 'in the strongest terms' that a race of cannibals, now extinct, had once lived in Tahiti and assured Forster that among the *arioi* it was the fathers, not the mothers, who were guilty of infanticide. From their conversation there also emerged a hitherto unrecorded (and perhaps apocryphal) incident in Omai's history — that he had been among the attendants of Oberea and her husband when they were forced to flee to the mountains from their enemies.[2]

Forster was chiefly concerned, however, with Omai's sojourn abroad, on which subject his comments were again scattered and his views often implied rather than stated. Both Omai and Tupia, he asserted, had left their homes in order to acquire firearms and so rescue their native island from its servitude to Borabora. Tupia, in Forster's view, might have succeeded had he lived, 'but O-Mai's understanding was not sufficiently penetrative, to acquire a competent idea of our wars, or to adapt it afterwards to the situation of his countrymen.' Nevertheless, he was obsessed with the idea of freeing Raiatea, his detractor continued, and before he returned often said that if Cook did not assist with his plan he would take care the captain received no supplies from his fellow-islanders. As for his stay in Britain, Forster hinted, it had been spent in frivolous pursuits or worse. When criticizing Cook's refusal to allow the elder Forster to bring home a youth called Noona, the loyal son explained:

As it was intended to teach him the rudiments of the arts of the carpenter and smith, he would have returned to his country at least as valuable a member of society as O-Mai, who, after a stay of two years in England, will be able to amuse his countrymen with the music of a hand-organ, and with the exhibition of a puppet-show.

In a similar context Forster reflected that in view of Omai's fate it was perhaps fortunate that Odiddy chose to remain in the South Seas: 'The splendour of England remains unknown to him; but at the same time he has no idea of those enormities which disgrace the opulent capitals of the world.' Here he failed to specify the enormities but, after claiming that prostitution was not universal in Tahiti, he went on: 'It would be singularly absurd, if o-Maï were to report to his countrymen, that chastity is not known in England, because he did not find the ladies cruel in the Strand.'[3]

Having glanced obliquely at the subject in the course of the narrative, Forster returned to it in his preface. There he undertook to summarize the experiences in England of the native 'vulgarly called Omiah', though their substance would, he claimed, 'furnish an entertaining volume.' With a judicial air he began: 'O-Maï has been considered either as remarkably stupid, or very intelligent, according to the different allowances which were made by those who judged of his abilities.' His difficulties with the new language, for instance, had too often been misconstrued and were due to the fact that his native tongue with its profusion of vowels 'had so little exercised his organs of speech, that they were wholly unfit to pronounce the more complicated English sounds'.

In Forster's opinion Omai was deficient not so much in intellect as in judgement. Introduced into genteel company on his arrival, led to the most splendid entertainments, and presented at Court, he adopted the manners and occupations of his companions, giving many proofs of a quick perception: 'Among the instances of his intelligence, I need only mention his knowledge of the game of chess, in which he had made an amazing proficiency.' On the debit side, the multiplicity of objects crowding upon him prevented his paying due attention to what would have been beneficial to himself and his countrymen on his return. Moreover, the continued round of enjoyments left him no time to think of his future; 'and being destitute of the genius of Tupaïa, whose superior abilities would have enabled him to form a plan for his own conduct, his understanding remained unimproved.'[4]

For that failure Forster, like earlier critics, blamed not Omai but his patrons. It could hardly be supposed, he asserted, that the visitor never expressed a wish to obtain some knowledge of English agriculture, arts, and manufactures; 'but no friendly Mentor ever attempted to cherish and to gratify this wish, much less to improve his moral character, to teach him our exalted ideas of virtue, and the sublime principles of revealed religion.' Yet the scenes of debauchery almost unavoidable in the civilized world had not corrupted the 'natural good qualities' of Omai's heart. At parting from his friends his tears flowed plentifully and his behaviour proved him deeply affected. On the other hand, he was not entirely uncorrupted since he carried with him 'an infinite variety of dresses, ornaments, and other trifles, which are daily invented in order to supply our artificial wants.' For, as Forster went on to explain,

His judgment was in its infant state, and therefore, like a child, he coveted almost every thing he saw, and particularly that which had amused him by some unexpected effect. To gratify his childish inclinations, as it should seem, rather than from any other motive, he was indulged with a portable organ, an electrical machine, a coat of mail, and a suit of armour. Perhaps my readers expect to be told of his taking on board some articles of real use to his country; I expected it likewise, but was disappointed. However, though his country will not receive a citizen from us much improved, or fraught with valuable acquisitions, which might have made him the benefactor, and perhaps the lawgiver of his people, still I am happy to reflect, that the ships which are once more sent out upon discovery, are destined to carry the harmless natives of Taheitee a present of new domestic animals.

Unconsciously supporting Cook and extending optimism even farther, Forster thought the introduction of cattle and sheep to that island would increase the happiness of its people and, 'by many intermediate causes', improve their intellectual faculties.[5]

Though by no means novel, Forster's views were expressed fully and with exceptional force and would be drawn on by a succession of writers, including the missionary Ellis. The immediate response was a pamphlet by the *Resolution*'s astronomer, William Wales, who, there is little doubt, had the support of Banks and Sandwich. Having quoted the contemptuous reference to Omai's organ, electrical machine, and armour, he asked why Forster had not specified what articles would have been 'of *real use*' to the returning voyager. 'Omai', he continued, 'carried out, or was furnished at the Cape of Good Hope, with horned cattle, sheep, geese, turkies, &c. and also with a horse and two mares, for whose reception, he gave up, with cheerfulness, his cabbin, and betook himself to the more inglorious accommodation of a common hammock.' Since the last particulars could have come only from Cook's private letters to the First Lord and Banks, it is fair to assume that Wales had consulted one or both of the two men. His remarks on Omai may thus be taken as in some measure a defence of their much criticized treatment of the visitor during the two years he spent under their protection.[6]

In this section of his pamphlet Wales attacked Forster for his suppression or distortion of facts as well as for the falsity and superficiality of his reasoning. Omai, he pointed out, had been given not only musical instruments and toys but animals, poultry, axes, saws, ironwork — indeed every article whatsoever that was valuable in the islands. What else, then, would Forster have put on board? True, he was not furnished with a profusion of things for which he had not the least inclination or which only 'the merest speculative reasoner' could suppose to be of use to his people. Similarly, it was thought unnecessary to 'teaze' him with a knowledge of English agriculture, arts, and manufactures. These were by no means so well adapted to his surroundings as his own pursuits and, furthermore, could not have been carried on unless ships were sent there every year with raw materials. Even then Forster's proposals would have answered no other purpose than to gratify the curiosity of Europeans and demonstrate the clumsy manner in which natives imitated them. For (to continue the summary of Wales's verbiage) it was the work of many years for a man to master but one single art or manufacture, assisted though he was by all the skill and experience of ages. In the case of poor Omai it would have been necessary for both him and his teachers to learn a new language, nay to create a new set of ideas. With a body never inured to labour, a mind little used to reason, he was in the compass of a year or two to acquire a knowledge of English arts and manufactures; afterwards he was to put them into practice under many disadvantages amongst a people who, because they could not possibly foresee their use, would deride rather than assist him. If Forster and others who had been pleased to express themselves very freely had but considered all this, urged Wales, they would surely have written with more diffidence and less asperity.[7]

Wales passed lightly over the charge that Omai's patrons had failed in their duty by not introducing him to the beliefs and ethics of Christianity. 'To as little purpose', he asserted, 'would it have been to teach him "our exalted ideas of virtue, and the sublime principles of revealed religion," in order "to improve his *moral* character" . . . .' Every reasonable man, he held, must foresee that once Omai had gone from amongst us he would never again think of such matters. Or, if he did, was it to be expected that they would have more influence on him than they did on some of ourselves? And Wales instanced those of his fellows who with moral principles continually in their mouths were at the same time endeavouring to hack to pieces the reputation of a neighbour or 'trying, by every piece of artful chicanery, to undermine his property.' With that innuendo, possibly directed at John Reinhold, he left the subject of Omai to criticize other views put forward by the unpopular pair.[8]

By no means quelled by the astronomer's onslaught, Forster returned to the attack. If, he retorted, Mr. Wales failed to see that during his stay Omai could have more usefully employed his time than at Court or in the theatres, the Pantheon, the taverns, and other scenes of dissipation, then any attempt to enlighten his own intellect and mend his morals might prove unsuccessful. Mr. Wales, he exclaimed incredulously, thought that a man with a good heart — and Omai really possessed such — after being taught to form a rational idea of virtue, to comprehend the importance of religion, and to believe its divine origin, would forget these glorious truths and never think of them again after he departed! Would not every virtuous reader, the pious young naturalist inquired, think that this doctrine, which placed in a contemptuous light all that was sacred and respectable amongst men, most unerringly betrayed its secret author?[9]

After delivering this dark shaft (perhaps aimed at his father's enemy, the adulterous Sandwich), Forster dwelt on more mundane matters. Mr. Wales, he went on, asserted that our arts and manufactures were not so well adapted to the climate of Tahiti as to our own. But did it follow that *none* of our arts deserved to be transplanted thither? And would there have been no benefit if the returning voyager could have taught his countrymen to perform in a day what now cost them weeks and months of tedious labour? More explicit than his predecessors, Forster supplied practical reasons for introducing European amenities to the islanders:

The more their labour is abridged, the more time remains for reflection, and for the improvement of social and moral felicity. O-Mai might have been taught to fabricate iron into tools, to make pots and other vessels of clay, to prepare from cotton, and from grass, more lasting garments than the bark of a tree, and to improve the knowledge of agriculture among his countrymen. A ship load of raw materials would not only have served him, but made happy many generations of Taheiteans, particularly if hints had been given him to search for some of these articles, such as iron, clay, and cotton in his own country. It is next to a certainty, that the chiefs of the country will strip him of all his riches, the moment after Captain Cook is sailed from thence; he then returns to his first insignificance; whereas, had he been taught a trade, his knowledge would always have been real riches to him, and paved his road to honour and opulence among his countrymen.

A

VOYAGE

TOWARDS THE

SOUTH POLE,

AND

ROUND THE WORLD.

PERFORMED IN

His Majefty's Ships the RESOLUTION and ADVENTURE,
In the Years 1772, 1773, 1774, and 1775.

WRITTEN

By JAMES COOK, Commander of the RESOLUTION.

In which is included,

CAPTAIN FURNEAUX's NARRATIVE of his
Proceedings in the ADVENTURE during the Separation of the Ships.

IN TWO VOLUMES.

Illuftrated with MAPS and CHARTS, and a Variety of PORTRAITS of
PERSONS and VIEWS of PLACES, drawn during the Voyage by
Mr. HODGES, and engraved by the moft eminent Mafters.

VOL. I.

LONDON:
Printed for W. STRAHAN; and T. CADELL in the Strand.
MDCCLXXVII.

Before leaving the subject of Omai to take up different issues with his antagonist, Forster corrected one of that gentleman's misconceptions: 'Mr. Wales insists much on the utility of introducing cattle at Taheitee; and if he hath carefully examined my preface, he must have perceived, that I am far from censuring this step; but I cannot help smiling when he talks so pompously of "poor O-Mai's" horses.' The *'real use'* of those animals on a small island could, he held, be only the gratification of the owner's vanity. By displaying feats of horsemanship he would 'become an object of wonder and amazement to the inhabitants, and give the poets of his country an opportunity to revive the fable of the Centaurs.'[10]

WHILE GEORGE FORSTER CARRIED ON HIS DEBATE WITH WALES, *A Voyage towards the South Pole* had made its triumphant appearance. Cook's own narrative of perhaps the most romantic of his expeditions was immensely popular from the outset, soon ran into three editions, was quickly translated into other European languages, and won the captain novel acclaim as author with renewed praise for his feats as explorer. He had expressed himself 'with a plain natural strength and clearness, and an unaffected modesty which schools cannot teach' was the opinion of an unnamed writer in the *Gentleman's Magazine* who claimed that in the role of navigator Cook undoubtedly ranked as 'the first of this or any age or nation'. The reviewer touched on outstanding incidents in the voyage — the 'transmutation' of sea ice into fresh water, the assembling of the great fleet of war canoes at Tahiti, the supposed sale of children at Queen Charlotte Sound — but refrained from retelling the 'horrid tale' of the *Adventure*'s boat crew, an episode that confirmed beyond doubt the New Zealanders' custom of eating human flesh. Much more pleasing, he said, were Cook's remarks on Omai. These he quoted in full while expressing the hope that the islander was now 'alive and merry among his countrymen'. He lavished praise on the admirable engravings after Mr. Hodges and ended with a brief reference to George Forster's book: though undoubtedly of merit it was not only superseded by the present work but was 'invidious and interested'.[11]

Of the highly miscellaneous offspring — or putative offspring — of Cook, Forster, and lesser accounts of the expedition, the earliest was a satire published anonymously but now ascribed to an Irish poet-dramatist, William Preston. *Seventeen Hundred and Seventy-Seven*, further diffuse addition to the Oberea cycle, is grandiosely entitled a 'Picture of the Manners and Character of the Age' and described as 'An Epistle from a Lady of Quality, in England, to Omiah, at Otaheite'. The picture displayed is that of folly and corruption common to works of this kind, and neither correspondent nor recipient becomes more than a shadowy counter. With Banks and the other stock figure of Tahitian satire the returned voyager is invoked in the opening lines:

> If yet thy land preserves Opano's name,
> And Oberea pines with am'rous flame;
>
> .   .   .
>
> If joys remember'd rapture can impart,
> And London lives within Omiah's heart;
> Dear shall this greeting from thy Britain prove,
> And dear these wishes of eternal love.

In a reference to Sandwich, lightly disguised as Rufo, Omiah is presented not as his lordship's cherished protégé but in terms that would have won Forster's approval, as the victim of that supposedly licentious nobleman:

> For British navies own his forming hand,
> And, lur'd by him — Omiah blest the land.
> His gentle mind with polish'd arts he stor'd,
> And stews, and palace, with his guest explor'd.
> And say, Omiah! does thy heart complain
> Of fates, which call'd thee to the British plain?[12]

In the face of this sinister precedent, the Lady of Quality makes no attempt to deter other southern visitors; quite the reverse in fact. In so far as her purpose may be discerned through her indiscriminate condemnation of French novels, Italian fashions, and English morals, it is to persuade Omiah's compatriots to follow his example:

> These faithful lines shall tell thy native train,
> What honours court them to the British plain.
> Oh, may the picture tempt the youths to rove,
> And bring their pleasures, and their arts of love!
> Let sooty throngs the cream-fac'd courtiers shame,
> And southern lovers glad the curious dame . . . .

These virile immigrants will bring to 'Britannia's shore' the arts and diversions of Tahiti, such as (in allusion to Banks and Oberea),

> Luxurious feasts by blest Opano seen,
> Instructive pageants of an am'rous queen.

They will establish the *arioi* society described by Hawkesworth and introduce the custom of infanticide, so that

> Intruding babes shall bleed as soon as born,
> And pleasure bloom divested of its thorn . . . .

The flow of migrants, however, need not be confined to Tahitian youth: in her final rousing address, while renewing her invitation to nature's children, the Lady of Quality foresees a two-way traffic between north and south, with a visit to Oberea and her kingdom replacing the conventional tour of Europe:

> Our silken youths for you shall cross the line,
> To dress your females and your boards refine;
> Each travell'd peer shall bless you in his tour
> With arts of play, and secrets of amour.
>
> Then shall perfection crown each noble heart,
> When southern passions mix with northern art;
> Like oil and acid blent in social strife,
> The poignant sauce to season modish life.[13]

But would northern visitors still find the tropical paradise uncovered by their predecessors more than a decade before? Another Irish writer, identified as the Revd. Gerald Fitzgerald, thought otherwise and presented his conclusions in *The Injured Islanders; or, The Influence of Art upon the Happiness of Nature*, published anonymously in 1779. Citing in his support a passage from George Forster, he asserted in a preface that, whatever the benefits to commerce and science, Pacific exploration had brought only suffering to 'the innocent Natives'. The false value they placed on European trifles together with the ravages of 'a particular Disorder' had, he held, undermined their morals and destroyed their peace. Explicitly rejecting the satiric mode, he placed his versified sermon in the mouth of Oberea (or 'OBRA') who, in a further breach

THE

INJURED ISLANDERS;

OR,

THE INFLUENCE OF ART

UPON

THE HAPPINESS OF NATURE.

New wonder rose, when ranged around for Thee,
Attendant Virgins danc'd the TIMRODEE.

L O N D O N,

PRINTED FOR J. MURRAY, No. 32, OPPOSITE ST. DUNSTAN'S CHURCH,
FLEET-STREET.

MDCCLXXIX.

with tradition, addresses not Banks but Wallis. She recalls the happy state of her kingdom before his arrival,

> When kindred Love connected ev'ry Shore,
> When mutual Interest, spreading unconfin'd,
> Parental Care and Filial Duty join'd . . . .

Now, since 'Europe's Crimes with Europe's Commerce spread', all is changed:

> Discord and War in dread Confusion rise,
> With Widow's Wailings, and with Orphan's Cries . . . .

Social life is poisoned at the source by the dread contagion introduced by some 'vagrant' of 'ever-hateful Name':

> Thro' ev'ry Nerve th' infectious Terrors rove,
> Sap the shrunk Frame, and taint each Source of Love . . . .

Oberea herself, 'Remov'd from Power' by her rivals, looks for salvation in the return of Wallis and, at the rumoured approach of a ship, hurries to the shore; but 'In vain I haste, — no WALLIS meets me there . . . .' In her extremity she dispatches a trusted envoy to summon the captain:

> Hope flies to Thee; thy Guidance to implore
> I send TUPIA to the British Shore —
> Send, but in vain, alas, his hapless End!
> Lost was my statesman, Counsellor, and Friend . . . .

Omai now makes his appearance in a novel guise, as Tupia's successor and Oberea's messenger to Wallis:

> Lo! next OMIAH dares the task pursue
> And bears this fond Commission to thy View,
> Asks, and entreats in OBRA'S injur'd Name,
> Thy wish'd for Presence to restore her fame . . . .

This mission, she is convinced, will be successful. Wallis will revisit Tahiti and replace her on the throne:

> Thy faithful OBRA, aided by thy Hand,
> Again shall rise, the Empress of the Land,
>
> Her Wrongs redress, her Regal Rights restore;
> Till, smiling Peace thro' every Region seen,
> She rules triumphant, and expires — a Queen.[14]

After attracting a succession of versifiers since the publication of Hawkesworth, the Oberea cycle was showing signs of exhaustion and soon came to an ignominious end. In the same year, 1779, appeared the anonymous *Mimosa: or the Sensitive Plant*, since traced to the pen of another witling, James Perry. Dedicated to Banks, addressed to 'Kitt Frederick, Dutchess of Queensberry, elect', the poem is supplied with the same mock-scholastic apparatus as most of its forerunners and abounds in references to obscure personages and forgotten scandals. In his dedication the writer pays a tribute to Banks 'whose desire of acquiring knowledge has led him to climates, most happily adapted to the nourishment and the cultivation of that wonderful *lusus naturae.*' The 'plains of *Otaheité*', he continues, rear this plant to an amazing height, 'and Queen Oberea, as well as her enamoured subjects, feel the most sensible delight in *handling, exercising,* and proving its virtues.' Furthermore, 'Your friend *Omiah*, hath confessed . . . that the true and native *soil* of England, is exquisitely *prepared* for the reception of the *plant*; will raise it to very *vigorous extent*; feed it with the most vegetative *juices*; and promote its *articulations*, with as much *kindness* and animating warmth, as the sultry soil of *Otaheité.*' Italicized innuendoes in profusion, both here and in the body of the work, make it clear that the sensitive plant was a hitherto uncelebrated part of the Polynesian anatomy, the penis.[15]

While poetasters of the Pacific pursued their titillating themes, prose writers followed a more sober course. In 1778 an anonymous and still unidentified author had opened up new imaginative territory with a work bearing an elaborate title-page that also summarized the contents: *The Travels of Hildebrand Bowman, Esquire, Into Carnovirria, Taupiniera, Olfactaria, and Auditante, in New-Zealand; in the Island of Bonhommica, and in the powerful Kingdom of Luxo-volupto, on the Great Southern Continent. Written by Himself; Who went on shore in the Adventure's large Cutter, at Queen Charlotte's Sound New-Zealand, the fatal 17th of December 1773; and escaped being cut off, and devoured, with the rest of the Boat's crew, by happening to be a-shooting in the woods; where he was afterwards unfortunately left behind by the Adventure.* An epigraph ran:

> An Ape, and Savage (cavil all you can),
> Differ not more, than Man compared with Man.

In a facetious letter to Banks and Solander, the writer requested permission to dedicate the book to them: as his friend Omai was indebted to their protection which they gave in grateful remembrance of favours received in his native country, he flattered himself they would not refuse him their patronage merely because he was born in England. At one point in the narrative Bowman mentioned Omai's arrival on the *Adventure* and claimed to have acquired from him 'in a tolerable degree' his own knowledge of the Tahitian language.[16] But apart from such incidental references, Bowman's celebrated friend had no part in the proto-novel. It was concerned in fact not with one islander but with a wide range of Pacific denizens in all their imagined diversity.

The sole survivor of the *Adventure*'s cutter tells how he made his way back to the ship's anchorage, only to find it had sailed. Crossing Cook Strait to escape the Carnovirrians (as the inhabitants of Queen Charlotte Sound are termed), he enters the country of the Taupinierans, a people even more primitive than their cannibalistic neighbours. Pygmies in stature, they have porcine faces and are equipped with rudimentary tails. Their vision is mole-like so that they sleep in caves by day and emerge at night to fish in the sea and gather shellfish on the beaches. They communicate in grunts and possess no form of government nor any religion beyond 'a kind of veneration for the moon'. Bowman next crosses the lofty range of mountains enclosing Taupiniera and reaches the land of Olfactaria inhabited by a race endowed with superhuman powers of scent, a gift they employ in continual hunting. They speak the Tahitian language, worship the sun and moon, and though experienced warriors are not cannibals. Indeed, their inveterate enemies are the Carnovirrians who attack them in force and are vanquished through the the hero's skill in military tactics. So Hildebrand avenges his murdered companions, but his martial prowess provokes the jealousy of rivals and he moves on to Auditante. This fourth division of New Zealand is populated by tribes who wander about with their flocks and herds and their trains of slaves and wives. They are polygamous and idolators, use a form of script resembling Hebrew or Arabic, and are so idle that they make no attempt to manufacture wool or other products of their animals. Gifted with the most acute hearing, they spend their abundant leisure in listening to music or recitals of poetry and in al fresco feasting. The disapproving and somewhat dour Bowman (a Yorkshireman like Cook) finds such pleasures cloying and leaves the country with a party of visiting merchants for the island of Bonhommica. This proves to be the true earthly paradise, no licentious Cythera but a nation of modest, industrious citizens, ruled over by a benign monarch and united in the practice of their austere religion. Thence Hildebrand travels to one of the kingdoms of the Great Southern Continent, Luxo-volupto, where he finds a large population living in magnificent surroundings but given up to vice and self-indulgence. They have numerous priests and ostentatious temples, but these do nothing to curb the 'universal profligacy' that confronts the censorious but ruttish Bowman. The adventurer finally returns to Britain in March 1777, concluding that the manners of his countrymen resemble those of the Luxo-voluptans more closely than the sober ways of the Bonhommicans.[17]

Hildebrand Bowman seems to have been the work of a Grub Street journeyman, familiar with the gossip of learned London, who set out to exploit the speculative interests roused as well as appeased by Cook's discoveries. The book is no *Gulliver* and no *Rasselas*, but it belongs to the same order of imaginary travels and embodies in a crude form current theories about human society and the South Seas. The Taupinierans, it has been convincingly shown, illustrate Lord Monboddo's views that man in his primitive state retained many characteristics of the animal and led an isolated, brutish existence.[18] To follow up this clue, the Carnovirrians may be seen to embody the second step in the evolutionary scale, while at the next level are the Olfactarians who, though retaining some savage characteristics, no longer devour their own kind. Then come the Auditantines, pastoral nomads living, as Hildebrand remarks, in a state resembling that of the biblical patriarchs. Bonhommica, to which he later transfers himself, marks the peak of human felicity — an eighteenth-century state shorn of its defects. Lastly there is Luxo-volupto which represents civilization in its decline and supplies the author with opportunities for scourging the vices of his age and his country. The physical peculiarities shown by certain of these people — the mole-like sight of the Taupinierans, the acute sense of smell displayed by the Olfactarians — may illustrate the idea of adaptation or, possibly, some notion of antipodean reversal, a variation on Othello's 'men whose heads do grow beneath their shoulders'. On the other hand, they may be nothing more than the pointless inventions of a hack who in this way supplemented the mildly salacious details he sprinkled throughout the text.

Bowman's creator thought it necessary to touch on the religious condition of Pacific peoples, a subject to which a nameless satirist later applied his meagre talents. Some time in the early seventeen-eighties there appeared *A Letter from Omai to the Right Honourable the Earl of ********, Late ——— Lord of the ———. Translated from the Ulaietean Tongue.* The crowded title-page claimed to expound 'The Nature of Original Sin' and to outline 'A Proposal for Planting Christianity in the Islands of the Pacific Ocean.' Addressed from Raiatea, where the author evidently supposed Omai to have settled, the letter is dated 2 October 1780; but the pamphlet itself must have been published after March 1782 when Sandwich, obviously referred to in the title, left office. Presented in tract form, the letter opened with disarming politeness: 'My Dear Lord, I take this opportunity, the last perhaps I may ever have, of inquiring after your Lordship's health; as also of thanking you again for the many favours I received at the hands of yourself, and your friends.' The writer's real intention becomes clear in the next sentence with its echoes of Forster and other critics of Omai's patrons: 'And after thanking you for the powder, shot, gun, crackers, sword, feathers, and watch, let me thank you also for my conversion to Christianity . . . .'[19]

This sarcastic attack on the discredited Sandwich for his failure to concern himself with the voyager's spiritual welfare leads to the promised examination of the doctrine of original sin. As a result of visiting Britain and hearing Christ's message, Omai asserts, he has, according to Methodist beliefs, rescued himself from eternal damnation. But what, he inquires, is the situation of his unregenerate countrymen who have not enjoyed the same advantages? Here he considers the plight of his pagan cousin Twainoonoo:

. . . Twainoonoo is under the general condemnation of original sin. — I ask, may he not also be included in the general atonement made by the death of Christ? — A Methodist will say no, because Twainoonoo never having heard of Christ, and consequently not believing in him, cannot be benefited by his intercession. — But, God help him, what, in such a situation, is to condemn him? Original sin. That is original condemnation; or, in other words, Twainoonoo is damned to all eternity for being born.

The Established Church fares no better than Methodism at the hands of this sceptical convert who suggests that one ambitious ecclesiastic might become 'archbishop of the Great Southern Ocean' and recommends lesser clerics made redundant by the decline of faith in Britain to volunteer as missionaries. In passing he criticizes the conduct of the American war and aims his final shaft at one of the unlikeliest of targets: 'I cannot conclude my letter, without saying how much real concern I feel for the unfortunate fate of poor Captain Cook, who was certainly very cruelly and inhumanly butchered, for nothing more than ordering his crew to fire on a banditti of naked savages, who seemed to look as if they had a right to the country in which he found them.'[20]

THE GRATUITOUS GIBE must have struck a uniquely discordant note at a time when adulation of the dead navigator was universal and the public

clamoured for printing after printing of Anna Seward's *Elegy on
Captain Cook* with its invocation to Tahiti and the island's notabilities:

> Gay Eden of the south, thy tribute pay,
> And raise, in pomp of woe, thy Cook's Morai!
> Bid mild Omiah bring his choicest stores,
> The juicy fruits, and the luxuriant flow'rs;
>
> Come, Oberea, hapless fair-one! come,
> With piercing shrieks bewail thy hero's doom![21]

Miss Seward's banal tribute, first issued in 1780, was followed by works
from members of the expedition who in defiance of Admiralty orders
had retained their papers. Early on the market, in 1781, was the anonymous *Journal of Captain Cook's Last Voyage*, attributed to John
Rickman, second lieutenant on the *Discovery*. With its melodramatic
frontispiece depicting Cook's death, the small octavo volume was calculated to appeal to readers eager for details of the hero's end and met
with instant success. Quickly running into a second edition, it was translated in France, pirated in Ireland, and plagiarized in America. The briefer
account by Heinrich Zimmermann, able seaman on the *Discovery*,
came out in the same year as Rickman's. The author attached his name
to the modest book but escaped any official consequences by writing in
his native tongue and publishing in Germany. William Ellis, who had
acted as surgeon's mate on both ships and for his services won the dying
gratitude of Captain Clerke, boldly acknowledged authorship of his
two-volume *Authentic Narrative* which appeared early in 1782 and
was reprinted the next year. Ellis, however, lived to regret his transgression. He earned the displeasure of Sir Joseph Banks and, as that
gentleman informed him, by 'so imprudent a business', forfeited all
hope of preferment with the Admiralty.[22]

As occasional consultant and minor collaborator, Banks of course had
a proprietary interest in the official *Voyage to the Pacific Ocean* which
after many delays at last made its appearance in June 1784. Rival
publications proved to have whetted rather than appeased the popular
appetite. Priced at four and a half guineas, the three volumes sold out
in a few days, were immediately reprinted, and soon found translators
in the major European countries. Of all the accounts of Cook's travels
this was perhaps the most widely read and acclaimed for reasons that
are not far to seek. When editing the manuscript, Canon Douglas had
ventured to assert that readers would be chiefly interested in the story of
Omai; here he overlooked the one episode that loomed largest in contemporary eyes. The work, proclaimed a reviewer in the *Gentleman's
Magazine*, did honour to the English nation: to the King and his ministers
who had planned the expedition; to the officers who undertook it; to the
authors and illustrators; 'but, above all, to the memory of that unparalleled navigator whose name it bears, a name *semper honoratum,
semper acerbum*, and whom all succeeding ages will ever revere and

lament.' Since the magazine had already summarized the events of the voyage (in Rickman's version), the writer merely added two lengthy extracts, the first being Captain King's description of Cook's death in Hawaii. Yet Douglas was not wholly wide of the mark, for in two further issues subscribers were entertained with a detailed narrative of Omai's doings based on 'all those passages which relate to the celebrated native'.[23]

Within a short time of publication Cook and King's quarto volumes were to be found in genteel libraries, sometimes competing for attention with more sophisticated literature, as Fanny Burney testifies. Late in 1784 she was in the country, seeking solace among her new friends the Lockes for the rupture of her intimacy with the widowed Mrs. Thrale who, to the consternation of the Streatham circle, had recently married the Italian singer Gabriel Piozzi. Writing to her sister Susan, Fanny mentioned that on wet days she read extracts from 'Cook's last voyage' while Mrs. Locke in her turn diverted the company with the *Letters* of Madame de Sévigné. They went on but slowly with Captain Cook, she wrote a week later, for 'this syren' de Sévigné had seduced them from other authors. The same year another rural household gathered for a similar purpose, but more seriously and single-mindedly, around the person of William Cowper. As the readings continued throughout the summer and autumn, the poet sometimes passed on his impressions to

A

V O Y A G E

TO THE

P A C I F I C   O C E A N.

UNDERTAKEN,

BY THE COMMAND OF HIS MAJESTY,

FOR MAKING

Difcoveries in the Northern Hemifphere.

TO DETERMINE

The POSITION and EXTENT of the WEST SIDE of NORTH AMERICA; its DISTANCE from ASIA; and the PRACTICABILITY of a NORTHERN PASSAGE to EUROPE.

PERFORMED UNDER THE DIRECTION OF

Captains C O O K, C L E R K E, and G O R E,

In his MAJESTY'S Ships the RESOLUTION and DISCOVERY.

In the Years 1776, 1777, 1778, 1779, and 1780.

IN THREE VOLUMES.

VOL. I. and II. written by Captain JAMES COOK, F.R.S.
VOL. III. by Captain JAMES KING, LL.D. and F.R.S.

Illuftrated with MAPS and CHARTS, from the Original Drawings made by Lieut. HENRY ROBERTS, under the Direction of Captain COOK; and with a great Variety of Portraits of Perfons, Views of Places, and Hiftorical Reprefentations of Remarkable Incidents, drawn by Mr. WEBBER during the Voyage, and engraved by the moft eminent Artifts.

Publifhed by Order of the Lords Commiffioners of the Admiralty.

V O L. I.

L O N D O N:

PRINTED BY W. AND A. STRAHAN;
FOR G. NICOL, BOOKSELLER TO HIS MAJESTY, IN THE STRAND;
AND T. CADELL, IN THE STRAND.
MDCCLXXXIV.

clerical acquaintances: the pleasure he derived from the descriptions of tropical scenes; his interest in the 'exquisite' dancing of the Friendly Islanders, unsurpassed, he thought, on the European stage; his sombre conviction that Cook's death was a judgement on the navigator's impiety, the verdict of a jealous Providence. The volumes, Cowper informed one correspondent, furnished him not only with entertainment but with 'much matter of philosophical speculation'. And, as it proved, they supplied him with material for the 'new production' on which he was then working, his long reflective poem *The Task*.[24]

In Book I Cowper presents in succinct terms the debate between 'nature' and 'civilization' which, in one form or another, runs through so much of the literature inspired by Pacific discovery. His own sympathies, dictated both by temperament and belief, lay not with some supposedly idyllic state conjured up by deluded theorists but with the ordered and established society he knew,

> Where man, by nature fierce, has laid aside
> His fierceness, having learnt, though slow to learn,
> The manners and the arts of civil life.

Against this civilized standard he measures the plight of men living in 'remote / And barb'rous climes' — not only the 'shiv'ring natives of the north' and the 'rangers of the western world' where it thrusts 'Towards th'Antarctic' but also the denizens of happier regions:

> Ev'n the favor'd isles
> So lately found, although the constant sun
> Cheer all their seasons with a grateful smile,
> Can boast but little virtue; and inert
> Through plenty, lose in morals, what they gain
> In manners, victims of luxurious ease.

In words that hardly square with the sentiments expressed in his correspondence Cowper deplores the cultural poverty of the Pacific islanders, cut off in their isolation from everything that gives civilized life its motive force and meaning:

> These therefore I can pity, placed remote
> From all that science traces, art invents,
> Or inspiration teaches; and inclosed
> In boundless oceans . . . .[25]

Ceasing to generalize, Cowper turns to address the islander who has figured so largely in the narrative of Cook's last expedition and the readings of his own small circle:

> But far beyond the rest, and with most cause
> Thee, gentle savage! whom no love of thee

> Or thine, but curiosity perhaps,
> Or else vain glory, prompted us to draw
> Forth from thy native bow'rs . . . .

That episode is over, the 'dream is past', and Omai has returned to his native surroundings but perhaps, the poet speculates (echoing the valedictory reflections of Mr. King), he is no longer content with his former companions and old manner of life:

> And having seen our state,
> Our palaces, our ladies, and our pomp
> Of equipage, our gardens, and our sports,
> And heard our music; are thy simple friends,
> Thy simple fare, and all thy plain delights
> As dear to thee as once? And have thy joys
> Lost nothing by comparison with ours?

The questions are rhetorical; Cowper supplies an answer which ranges him with Forster rather than Wales in the debate on Omai's treatment by his English patrons:

> Rude as thou art (for we return'd thee rude
> And ignorant, except of outward show)
> I cannot think thee yet so dull of heart
> And spiritless, as never to regret
> Sweets tasted here, and left as soon as known.

Expanding this theme, Cowper pictures the sorrowing native as he strays on the beach, asking the 'surge' if it has washed the distant shore of England. Next he sees the young patriot weeping 'honest tears', saddened because no power of his can raise his country from its 'forlorn and abject state'. Fancy finally discloses Omai on a mountain top,

> with eager eye
> Exploring far and wide the wat'ry waste
> For sight of ship from England. Ev'ry speck
> Seen in the dim horizon, turns thee pale
> With conflict of contending hopes and fears.[26]

With his melancholy musings and moralizings Cowper had created an enduring literary portrait of Omai but not the one most widely translated and read. That distinction must probably go to a small work first issued by an Oxford printer in the same year as *The Task* and attributed to a German refugee Rudolf Erich Raspe. In full flight from his creditors, this harassed and somewhat disreputable man of letters reached England in the autumn of 1775 when Omai was still in the country and, as a result of Cook's return from his second voyage, again figured in the news. So a decade later when putting together a catch-penny trifle, *Baron Munchausen's Narrative of his Marvellous Travels*, it was not

wholly surprising that he should introduce a passing reference to 'the
Island of Otaheité, mentioned by Captain Cook as the place from
whence they brought Omai'. Those names were again topical in 1785
and served to fill a line or so in a hurried compilation.[27]

Omai's part in the unexpectedly popular concoction of tall stories was
slightly enlarged when some unknown hack was commissioned to prepare a second collection in 1792. The so-called *Sequel to the Adventures
of Baron Munchausen* was a more pretentious work than the original,
drawing heavily on literary sources and facetiously dedicated to James
Bruce of Abyssinian fame. In one episode Munchausen, accompanied by
Gog and Magog, Lord Whittington, Don Quixote, and other members
of his entourage, flies to the South Seas in pursuit of Wauwau, the
mythical bird from the kingdom of Prester John. He reaches Tahiti
where he meets 'his old acquaintance Omai, who had been in England
with the great navigator, Cook'. Omai, he is glad to find, has 'established
Sunday schools over all the islands'. Questioned about Europe and his
voyage to England, the unhappy man replies with a flat rendering of
the mournful sentiments expressed by Cowper:

'Ah!' he said, most emphatically, 'the English, the cruel English, to murder me
with goodness, and refine upon my torture — took me to Europe, and showed
me the court of England, the delicacy of exquisite life: they showed me gods,
and showed me heaven, as if on purpose to make me feel the loss of them.'

Omai, commanding 'the chiefest warriors of the islands', now joins forces
with the Baron and his party. He and his fleet of canoes equipped with
fighting stages are last seen making for the Isthmus of Darien.[28]

In the interval between the two editions of *Baron Munchausen* the
putative founder of Polynesian Sunday schools had again served the
purposes of social satire. The anonymous author-editor of *The Loiterer*,
an Oxford periodical, announced in July 1789 the discovery of 'a very
great literary Curiosity', the journal kept by Omai during his visit to
Europe. The original, a vast work in three volumes, he promised to
deposit in the archives of the Royal Society but before doing so wished
to entertain his readers with specimens of the islander's observations.
First in scientific importance is Omai's theory that many ages ago a large
war canoe of his country with some fishing boats were forced out to sea
and so peopled the rest of the world. The difference in colour between
Europeans and himself he explains by the coldness of their climate which
has caused the human species to degenerate, making them less vigorous
and 'of a pale, meagre, sickly, disagreeable complexion'. As proof of his
claim for the Polynesian origin of mankind, he cites the similarity
between certain words in his own language and others in English. He
has learned, for example, that the chiefs or great men of *'Pretane'*
were formerly (though very seldom now) called *'Heroes'* which is of
course the term *'Erys'* applied to chiefs in Tahiti. There follows a gibe at
the expense of Sandwich. Another variant of *'Ery'*, Omai discovers, is

'*Earl*', a title borne by 'the King of the Ships' who, being asked by the visitor to show his scars as proof of valour, had to admit that 'he had never received any Wounds, but in the Wars of Venus.'[29]

Some British customs, Omai notes, resemble those of the South Seas while others are unique. The inhabitants are often '*tataowed*', and he himself had to submit to the operation at the hands of 'the most famous *Tataower* in the Country' (i.e. Baron Dimsdale). From the highest to the lowest they are also addicted to thieving, for the doors and windows of their houses are fastened every night with locks, bolts, and bars of the most intricate construction. These are to prevent external robbers entering, but in addition every room, closet, and box inside a house must be locked; which goes to show that husbands hardly dare to trust their wives and children, masters their servants, or servants their masters. Not only are they 'downright Thieves' but also 'absolute Cannibals', a fact Omai never suspected until one day, while passing through a crowded market, he saw nearly twenty men slaughtered and a woman first strangled and then roasted, 'much after the same manner as they do Pigs in Otaheite.' Following the body of one man, he saw it taken to a large house where it was stripped naked, laid on a table before a great crowd, and cut up by a cook dressed in apron and sleeves. He himself was so shocked by the sight that he ran off, leaving the others to finish their 'horrid Banquet'. Despite such barbarity, Omai acknowledges one virtue — 'the wonderful Love and Affection, which these people enter-tain for their King; far exceeding any thing in his own Country.' It is usual, he says, for everyone to collect little round pieces of metal bearing the King's image, particularly the yellow ones. Veneration for these images is so great that at first he thought they must be gods but later discovered that an even greater value was placed on slips of paper marked with a female likeness, apparently the Queen's. As the editor reports:

He was unable to find out what use this thin paper could possibly be of; and what was to him still more astonishing, notwithstanding the great value which every Body put upon it, yet they strangled, without mercy or exception, almost every person that was ingenious enough to make it. In short, he adds, in many things it is absolutely impossible to assign any reason whatever for the actions of this extraordinary People . . . .[30]

Meanwhile, in belated fulfilment of a proposal once aired by David Garrick, Omai had made his début on the English stage. It was not, however, as Garrick had suggested, in the guise of an '*Arlequin Sauvage*' to ridicule the follies and fashions of the time, but as a figure second only in heroic stature to his martyred commander. Some time in 1785 the proprietors of the Theatre Royal, Covent Garden, casting about for a subject on which to base their annual pantomime, hit upon a highly topical theme, Cook's last voyage, of which the official account had been published in the previous year. Once the decision was made, tried

At the Theatre Royal, Covent Garden,
This prefent TUESDAY, December 20, 1785,
Will be prefented the TRAGEDY of

JANE SHORE.

Haftings by Mr. HOLMAN,
Being his SECOND Appearance in THAT Character.
Glofter by Mr. AICKIN,
Belmour by Mr. HULL,
Catefby by Mr. PALMER,
Ratcliffe by Mr. GARDNER,
Derby by Mr. THOMPSON,
And Shore by Mr. FARREN,
Alicia by Mrs. BATES,
And Jane Shore by Mrs. WELLS.

To which will be added, for the FIRST Time, a NEW PANTOMIME, called

OMAI:

Or, A Trip Round the World.

The PANTOMIME, and the Whole of the Scenery,
Machinery, Dreffes, &c. &c.
Defigned and Invented by Mr. LOUTHERBOURG,
And Executed under his Superintendance and Direction by
Meffrs. RICHARDS, CARVER, and HODGINGS,
Mr. CATTON, jun. Mr. TURNER,
ASSISTED BY TWO OTHER CELEBRATED ARTISTS.
The Mufic entirely New, compofed by Mr. SHIELD.

. BOOKS containing a fhort Account of the Pantomime, as well as the Recitatives,
Airs, Duets, Trios, and Chorufes, and a Defcription of the Proceffion, to be had at the
Theatre.

Nothing under Full Price will be taken.

To-morrow, will be prefented the Tragedy of PERCY.

61
Playbill for first
performance of Omai

theatrical journeymen were entrusted with the production. The play-wright John O'Keeffe received £100 to write the book and it was he, apparently, who chose to centre the piece on Cook's exotic companion. For the same fee the continental-born Philippe Jacques de Louther-bourg R.A., long domiciled in England, designed costumes and scenery, while the theatre's resident composer, William Shield, was responsible for the music. All three men necessarily worked in collaboration and in their efforts to secure verisimilitude O'Keeffe and de Loutherbourg consulted veterans of the expedition, James Webber in particular. As preparations went forward, interest mounted in artistic and theatrical circles. It was rumoured that both Gainsborough and Cipriani might contribute their talents to the spectacle, but in the end de Loutherbourg's designs were carried out by a group of lesser artists led by the Revd. William Peters R.A., Chaplain to the Royal Academy. On 20 December 1785 the first performance of 'OMAI; Or, A Trip Round the World' was advertised for that night, following 'the Tragedy of Jane Shore'. There was no mention of the author's name, but Mr. Shield was billed as composer and Mr. Loutherbourg given full credit for designing and inventing 'The Pantomime, and the whole of the Scenery, Machinery,

Otoo King of Otahaite

Toha. Chief of Otahaite oediee

A Man of New Zealand

62-65 *De Loutherbourg's drawings for the costumes of Omai: Otoo; Oberea; Towha; Man of New Zealand*

The APOTHEOSIS of CAPTAIN COOK.

From a Design of P.J.De Loutherbourg, R.A. The View of KARAKAKOOA BAY
Is from a Drawing by John Webber, R.A (the last he made) in the Collection of Mr. G. Baker.

London, Pubd. Jany. 20. 1794, by J. Thane, Spur Street, Leicester Square.

Dresses, &c. &c.' In anticipation of a heavy demand for places, patrons
were warned: 'Nothing under Full Price will be taken.'[31]

Garrick had not lived to see his original idea shorn of its satirical
purpose and presented with all the resources of his old theatre. Predeceasing
both Cook and Omai, he had been interred in Westminster Abbey nearly
seven years before. But Sir Joshua Reynolds was in the crowded house,
prominently seated in the orchestra, perhaps in deference to his fame,
perhaps on account of his defective sight and hearing. A memorable
evening opened with *Jane Shore* which, the *Morning Chronicle* reported
the next day in a lengthy review, was tolerated rather than enjoyed:

> Though the Play was upon the whole far from ill-performed, the audience
> during its representation expressed great impatience for the Pantomime, of
> which vague report had said enough, to raise very great expectation. At length
> the curtain drew up, and before it dropped, all present were convinced, that
> not a syllable too much had been said in favour of *Omai*. A spectacle abounding
> with such a variety of uncommonly beautiful scenery never before was seen
> from the stage of a theatre; nor was there ever, considered altogether, a more
> rich treat for the lovers of musick, Mr. Shield having been remarkably success-
> ful in the composition of the airs, recitatives, and accompanyments.

Amid a further welter of superlatives the only hints of adverse criticism
were directed at the plot where the 'business' was rather slender and the
incidents few. But in the first part, the writer conceded, they were 'light
and laughable' and in the second merely 'calculated to serve as a necessary connection of the changes of scenery; for the exhibition of which
the whole of the piece has been obviously imagined and contrived'. It
should, he summed up, 'be considered as the stage edition of Captain
Cook's voyage to Otaheite, Kamschatka the Friendly Islands, &c. &c.
and a most beautiful edition it is.'[32]

The pantomime, or at least O'Keeffe's contribution, seems in reality
to have had closer affinities with Munchausen's *Marvellous Travels* than
with Cook and King's sober narrative. The plot, as recorded in newspaper summaries, was a fanciful *mélange* in which stock figures of
European comedy mingle with fictitious characters, patriotic abstrac-
tions with personages drawn from the official volumes and freely
adapted to histrionic requirements. Omai, elevated to regal status as the
son of Otoo, is transported from his ancestral domain by Britannia and
reaches England. There he worsts his Spanish rival Don Struttolando,
wins the hand of Londina, and carries her back to the South Seas,
touching at many places visited by Cook and so supplying pretexts for
the display of de Loutherbourg's scenic invention. The minor characters
include Harlequin, Colombine, and Clown who are servants of the three
principals; Towha is described as 'the Guardian Genius of Omai's
ancestors'; Odiddy (here termed Oediddee) is another of Omai's rivals,
'Pretender to the throne' of Tahiti; and in a further sinister metamor-
phosis Oberea becomes 'Regent and Protectress of Oediddee, an enchant-
ress'. Proceedings reach their triumphant conclusion in the scene of

Omai's coronation and marriage which takes place 'in the great bay of Otaheite',

with a view of ships at anchor, and a royal palace in front, and the people ready to receive and crown their King. A fine view offers itself of all the boats of the islands entering the bay with Ambassadors from all the foreign powers bringing presents, and a procession ensues, and salutes Omai, as the ally of Britain, and compliments him with an English sword. This is succeeded by dancing, wrestling, boxing, &c. The Clown wins one of the dancers by the present of a nail. Harlequin and Colombine, Omai and Londina, are united, and the entertainment concludes with an *apotheosis* of Captain Cook, crowned by Fame and Britannia . . . .

Reynolds was said to have expressed the utmost satisfaction with the landscape scenes but was less complimentary about the apotheosis, painted by Mr. Peters from de Loutherbourg's design. Perhaps, it was surmised, he disapproved of the Academy's chaplain lending himself to an enterprise of this kind.[33]

Whatever the nature of Sir Joshua's reservations, they do not seem to have troubled many patrons of Covent Garden. The tribute to Cook was one of the most celebrated features of the performance, sharing in the applause that nightly greeted scenic effects and music. If there was any weakness it was in the 'comick business', but efforts were soon made to improve this part of the production and by Christmas Eve it was reported that the humorous scenes now excited 'the most extravagant testimonies of delight'. Special mention was made of a new character, introduced the previous night (and evidently based on the historical Omai), who had accompanied the hero on his travels and 'most whimsically and pantomimicaly dressed himself in a piece of the habit of each country he had met with'. This and similar measures ensured the success of the spectacle which in its first season ran for fifty performances, one by royal command, and held the stage until 1788. In one of his earlier manifestations, as the scourge of English society, perhaps Omai himself made the appropriate comment:

> The stage, once rich in stores of genuine wit,
> When Nature dictated what SHAKESPEARE writ;
> When GARRICK's pow'rs that Nature could improve,
> And rouse the soul to rage, or melt to love;
> Now in vile farce and pantomime displays
> The vicious taste of these refining days . . . .[34]

SOME SUCH VIEW was indeed expressed by a critical observer of contemporary England. In the autumn of 1785 the young French poet Louis de Fontanes reached London on an extended visit. He had come with the idea of publishing a series of letters that would bring English society up to date with the latest intellectual movements in his own country but, receiving no encouragement, soon abandoned the plan. Instead, he contented himself with sending back to his friend Joseph Joubert impressions of life in the capital with any information he could pick up about Cook for use in the panegyric Joubert, a devoted student of the explorer, was then writing. What he learned was little enough and that often far from complimentary. People who had known the great man in private life spoke of his forbidding manner, an opinion confirmed by stories of his disputes with the Forsters during the second expedition. Cook was accused of obstinacy, even of jealousy; on the other hand, de Fontanes conceded, the younger Forster had shown bitterness and vanity in his own conduct. The 'respectable' Banks was out of town when the Frenchman arrived and on his return disclosed nothing of importance concerning Cook. Nor would he comment on the Forsters, though it was apparent from his silence that he took the captain's side in the controversy. Altogether, the poet assured his friend, Forster had put into his narrative everything about the voyage that could interest anyone of sensibility and imagination. As for Joubert's hero, he enjoyed far less renown among his own people than he did in France, for the English ranked Cook no higher than their other leading navigators. They had not yet raised a monument to him and the only tributes to his memory were mementoes of his voyages and a portrait displayed in the 'Sandwich room' of Sir Ashton Levert's museum.[35]

De Fontanes had some pretensions as a connoisseur and critic of art. Early in his stay he called on Sir Joshua Reynolds at his studio and saw the 'original' portrait of Omai, apparently known to him before through an engraved copy. At the time he expressed no opinion of the work but later, while acknowledging some merit in the 'chevalier's' portraiture, found it much inferior to Romney's. On the subject of Reynolds's history painting he was extremely scathing: 'The Death of Dido' he thought unworthy of the most mediocre dauber. The more he saw of England, he confessed, the more he became convinced that it was a nation given up to trade and money rather than to pleasure or the fine arts. The age of Charles II and Queen Anne had polished Court manners a little, but that was now past, leaving the mass of people as barbarous as ever. It was their ferocity and stupidity, de Fontanes held, that set the tone for public shows and entertainments. What did they applaud at the theatre? Not those pieces by Shakespeare worthy of esteem but usually the most tasteless and ridiculous — and he instanced the much applauded *Measure for Measure*, a play that could only have been written for the London taverns. So he was hardly in a receptive mood when late in January 1786 he went to see *Omai* still playing to great crowds at Covent Garden. The subject was charming, he remarked, and the genius of Cook should have inspired those responsible. As it proved:

Ah well! they have made Harlequin Omai's servant. They portray the Tahitian disembarking at Portsmouth, chased by customs officers and policemen in a large carriage. The scene changes. The young islander is returning to his homeland. They are waiting for something: it is a sailor who, intending to pick up his coat from the coach where he left it, finds there a huge crab which devours his entire head, etc.

The scenery, he added, was taken from designs by the famous Loutherbourg. It was very beautiful but only made one realize more strongly the absurdity of the rest.[36] How much better they ordered such matters in France was the implied comment.

Not only better but on a suitably monumental scale, as Guillaume-André-René Baston, professor of theology at Rouen and a canon of its cathedral, was soon to demonstrate. The abbé had succeeded in combining his professorial and clerical duties with a close study of the South Seas and in 1790 published the results of his wide-ranging research. Had he rendered them in conventional expository form, he would probably have joined de Brosses and Prévost in the distinguished line of French Pacific scholars. As it was, he chose to present his conclusions in fictional guise and, not altogether deservedly, they passed into oblivion. Issued anonymously in four bulky volumes, the novel was entitled *Narrations d'Omaï, Insulaire de la Mer du Sud, Ami et Compagnon de Voyage du Capitaine Cook*. A frontispiece displayed an oval portrait of Omai, based on the engraving after Hodges and ornamented by symbolic objects — a cornucopia, a quiver of arrows, quills, paper, a pile of books. Beneath it was a crude landscape, apparently of a tropical beach, showing the prow of a ship and grazing horses. The work purported to be Omai's autobiography, written in his native tongue and entrusted to its translator, Monsieur K***, who on his death-bed at the Cape of Good Hope handed the manuscript over to his old schoolfellow and shipmate Captain L.A.B. The memoirs were divided into twenty-five 'Narrations', each dedicated to a leading character and arranged in chronological sequence.[37]

Throughout his recorded career, observers of Omai had speculated on the possibilities that lay open to him when he again reached home. Would he become the Czar Peter the Great of his nation? To Lichtenberg it seemed unlikely. Rickman, on the other hand, thought he might rise superior to all the chiefs in the surrounding islands and in time become lord of them all. Cook pitched his expectations lower but was fairly confident his protégé would tend

NARRATIONS
D'O M A Ï,
INSULAIRE DE LA MER DU SUD,

AMI ET COMPAGNON DE VOYAGE

DU CAPITAINE COOK.

Ouvrage traduit de l'O-Taitien, par M.K***, & publié par le Capitaine L. A. B.

TOME PREMIER.

A ROUEN,

Chez LE BOUCHER le jeune, Libraire, rue Ganterie,

& A PARIS,

Chez BUISSON, Libraire, rue Haute-Feuille.

M. DCC. XC.

the plants and livestock left with him and so transform Huahine into a storehouse of European supplies. Paradoxically it was his sternest critic who saw in Omai's travels the greatest potentialities for good. If only he had fallen into the right hands, Forster lamented, he might have become the law-giver and benefactor of his people. He might have taught them new crafts and industries, helped them to explore and use their resources, introduced them to the ethics and beliefs of Christianity. Suppose, then, the returned voyager had done all these things and more. Suppose he had preserved what was best in island life while abolishing its evils. Suppose he had been wise, industrious, modest, humane, far-seeing. Suppose, in short, he had possessed all the qualities he so conspicuously lacked in the eyes of his detractors. Such was Omai as Baston conceived him, such the hero he lovingly evoked in the course of his elaborate fantasy.

The early pages skilfully blend biographical details with an outline of recent Pacific history. The narrator summarizes each expedition and, with a noticeable bias in favour of the French, characterizes their leaders — the cruel Wallis, the well-beloved Bougainville, the brave but not wholly blameless Cook. There is passing mention of 'Aoutourou' who had the 'incredible audacity' to embark with Bougainville but who, alas,

OMAI, amené en angletere par le Cap.^ne Furneaux

did not survive. Omai himself, as he relates the story, appears in a highly sympathetic light. He is of superior but not royal birth, the son of a Raiatean landowner slain with his own hands by 'Opoony', the tyrant of Borabora. While languishing in exile, he loses his mother and is saved from despair only by the hope of joining 'Tupia' to redress their wrongs and destroy the usurper. During his countryman's absence on the *Endeavour* the hapless youth figures in a familiar tableau as he paces the shore, transforming detached clouds into imaginary ships. At length two vessels do appear but without Tupia who, Omai learns, is also dead. 'Ah!' he exclaims, 'who then will free my native land? Who will take revenge on Opoony?' None other than Omai himself. In pursuance of his sacred mission he joins the *Adventure* and so begins the travels that fill most of the first volume. His opening narration he inscribes to Furneaux but for whose 'noble obstinacy' (in opposing Cook's prejudices), he gratefully acknowledges, he would have ended his life poor and ignorant or clubbed to death in battle.[38]

As he boards the ship at Huahine, Omai breaks off the story to consider the charges brought against him by Cook and Forster, first quoting the captain's references to his lowly status and dark colour. It is hardly surprising, he retorts, that a man who was exiled from his country, deprived of possessions, and saved from death by a miracle should not hold a high social position. Going on to refute the suggestion that his dusky countenance implies low birth, he points out that in England he met noble lords whose appearance was far from inviting, whereas in the lowest classes he saw complexions as fair as the rose, as white as the lily. General rules, he observes, are not without exceptions. Furthermore, his wanderings, his misfortunes, the constant necessity to earn a subsistence by fishing accentuated the natural darkness of his skin. Even Cook's compliments are not entirely to the young democrat's taste. The captain, he remarks, has commended him for his pride in avoiding the society of the low-born while he lived in England; but he scarcely knows whether to take this as praise or blame. He cultivated people of quality, he explains, not through 'pride' but simply because they could give him more help than their social inferiors in carrying out his plans.[39]

From Cook he turns to a less generous chronicler, George Forster. This critic again casts doubt on his status by asserting that on the *Adventure* he preferred the company of armourer and sailors to the captain's. True, Omai admits, at that time he considered the humblest European superior to his own chiefs. In addition, he courted the armourer because European weapons were among the things that interested him most; and he mixed with the men because he could question them freely and found their replies within his comprehension. As for the charges that he was stupid, that his tastes were childish, that his time in England was spent in frivolous pursuits — these calumnies he indignantly denies. Could a stupid man, he asks, have mingled with ease in the highest social circles or mastered the game of chess? Forster again derides his acquisition of a portable organ, an electrical machine, a suit of armour; but in his country, Omai points out, such things were worth more than all the guineas in the three kingdoms. Even more wounding are the comparisons Forster makes with Tupia's genius and superior talents. Omai freely acknowledges his compatriot's merit but does not concede that it infinitely surpasses his own. The proof, he asserts, will be found in the course of his narrative, and he goes on to deny Forster's monstrous charge that he threatened to cut off Cook's supplies unless the captain helped with his plans for revenge. In sum, he concludes, Forster has treated him far less kindly than Cook. And the reason? Merely because the naturalist resented the fact that while Omai was taken to England his own nominee was refused a passage.[40]

After this self-justifying digression, Omai returns to the account of his voyage on the *Adventure*, first recording his chagrin when another islander — a Boraboran and kinsman of Opoony at that! — joins the expedition at Raiatea. To his relief it appears that Odiddy is to voyage only in the Pacific and will not therefore be his rival in the quest for

British wealth and weapons. He briefly describes subsequent events — the visit to the Friendly Isles, the disappearance of the *Resolution*, the tragic episode in Queen Charlotte Sound, and the passage to England. Though his appearance in London created a sensation, it was, he asserts, nothing to what he felt: 'Ye gods! how many things astonished me! What a host of oddities, of inconsistencies, of contradictions!' He acknowledges the graciousness of the King in granting him a private audience and pays his respects to his zealous protectors and honoured friends, Mr. Banks, Dr. Solander, and 'Mylord' Sandwich (who is accorded the special tribute of a dedication). Two years passed, he writes, during which, in spite of Forster, he did not neglect to gather useful knowledge. Pleasure also occupied part of his time, for he was young and often tempted. But, again in reply to his detractor, he never resorted to the ladies in the Strand; he was too well warned, had too much self-regard, too much respect for his friends to degrade himself with such infamous creatures. He left on the *Resolution* in July 1776.[41]

The return voyage, largely based on published sources, may be quickly summarized, for it is not here that Baston displayed his originality. Omai tells of the passage to New Zealand where the two boys enter his service; he modestly plays down his own part in the perilous day spent on Atiu; and he dwells at length on their adventures in the Friendly Isles, giving a sympathetic picture of his patron Feenough. Of their weeks in Tahiti he says little and of his recorded indiscretions nothing. At Vaitepiha Bay he greets his relatives while Cook learns that the 'celebrated' Oberea is dead and listens incredulously as the prophet Etary foretells that he is to die at the hands of men who will pay him divine honours. Reaching Matavai, Omai relates, he does obeisance to Otoo and again meets Odiddy of whom he is no longer jealous since his former rival's travels have been so limited compared with his own. He is mildly critical of the commander's actions on Moorea but conceives a dislike for the ill-favoured Maheine and continues with an account of subsequent events at Huahine: Cook's decision that he must settle here and not at Raiatea; his meeting with Tareederia, the young King's widowed mother (known as 'Nowa'), and the assembly of local chiefs; then the granting of his estate, followed by the building of a house and the transfer of animals and treasure to his property. On the eve of sailing, Cook in a Polonius-like oration counsels prudence in his charge's dealings with Opoony and advises him to marry: a good wife, he says, will make him cherish life more than vengeance. As for himself, the captain ends, he is overcome with forebodings and feels it unlikely they will again meet. At the moment of parting, Omai recalls, he bathed his protector's face with 'a torrent of tears' and returned to the shore overcome by 'a frenzy of suffering'.[42]

With Cook's departure towards the end of Volume I, Baston was wholly released from the trammels of recorded fact to develop his heroic theme as he pleased. In spite of his grief, the fictional Omai loses no time before organizing his domestic affairs and instituting reforms. One

of his sisters, 'Zée' by name, having joined the household, he insists that
she sit with the menfolk at table, for the 'ridiculous' custom of women
eating separately is, he holds, injurious to 'the comelier half of human
kind'. Guided by an engraving in his collection and aided by his retainers,
he now lays out his estate, designs formal gardens, digs irrigation channels,
and extends the vegetable plots sown by Cook. The products, popularly
known as 'manger de Cook' or 'manger d'Omaï', surpass all expectations,
transforming Huahine into a cornucopia of supplies. Encouraged by
this success, Omai ventures on a bolder experiment. Using one of his toys
as a model, he sets out to fashion a plough with the help of the New
Zealander Tiarooa who shows some inventive talent. The result, he
admits, is faulty but, given their limited means and lack of experience,
a masterpiece. At a great gathering attended by the King, his mother
Nowa, with other notabilities from this and the neighbouring islands,
he yokes his horses to the plough and demonstrates its use. Others follow
his example and the men of Huahine soon become expert tillers of the
soil. With his eye on their womenfolk, he persuades Otoo to transfer
Cook's cattle to his own care, whereupon he teaches Nowa, Zée, and
their humbler sisters how to make butter and cheese, domestic arts they
quickly master. His next achievement is designed to add to the amenities
of island life. He builds a carriage — not, he again acknowledges, as
elegant as that of an English 'Mylord' but well enough fashioned and
embellished. As a token of regard, he presents the vehicle to Nowa.[43]

His civilizing mission thus begun, Omai proceeds to discharge the
sacred obligations he owes to his dead father and oppressed countrymen.
A chance meeting with the exiled King of Raiatea spurs him on to dis-
lodge the Boraborans from his native island. He throws down the
gauntlet with a daring raid on Borabora itself where by a ruse of the
quick-witted Coaa he captures Opoony's small flock of sheep, thus
ensuring Huahine's monopoly of the precious animals. Next, leading a
force equipped with English weapons and drilled in English tactics, he
invades Raiatea and defeats the usurpers. Coaa, alas, is one of the
casualties, but Tiarooa proves his heroic mettle and soon holds the post
of Omai's chief lieutenant. Opoony marshals his subjects to crush the
impudent upstart, only to be overcome in a great naval battle and
carried off to Huahine. After a series of military triumphs, Omai controls
the whole of the Society Group, while his friend King Otoo is firmly
established at Tahiti. In a final campaign he joins with his allies to crush
the villainous Maheine and restore the rightful monarch to the throne of
Moorea. His victories are won, however, without recourse to traditional
savagery. Omai forbids unnecessary bloodshed, frees his prisoners, and,
despite opposition from his vengeful countrymen, refuses to execute
Opoony, sentencing him instead to honourable exile. Nor will he himself
assume the deposed tyrant's mantle. The grateful inhabitants repeatedly
offer him the crown of some liberated territory, but each time he declines
the honour, preferring to nominate such trusted favourites as Tiarooa.
He chooses to remain at Huahine with Nowa, 'the best of women',

whom he has admired from the first and whom after a chaste courtship he has married.[44]

Omai the Civilizer, the Conqueror, the King-maker, now assumes the role of Law-giver. Summoning the rulers of neighbouring kingdoms, he persuades them to adopt a constitution for a new state to be known as the Confederation of the United Islands. It will have two chambers, one of sovereigns and chiefs, the other of deputies representing the lower orders. In addition, there will be the Supreme Council, a sort of cabinet in permanent session, led by a president who will also be viceroy of the capital and commander of its garrison. To avoid jealousy among rival candidates and ensure the president's impartiality, a foreigner is chosen to hold the high office, the New Zealander Tiarooa. Under these auspices and profiting by his European experience, Omai introduces reforms covering every aspect of island life. As a beginning he persuades the members of the Supreme Council, on behalf of their people, to join together with indissoluble ties of brotherhood and abolish war. All quarrels will in future be submitted to the Supreme Council for arbitration. They then proceed to forbid such practices as public prostitution in honour of the gods, human sacrifice, and infanticide. The ancient custom of circumcision, which Omai now considers unnecessary, is discouraged but not forbidden.[45]

Omai and his colleagues devote special attention to the affairs and status of women. Like Zée, they will no longer be segregated at table and, following the English fashion, will occupy the place of honour at festivals and all entertainments. At the time of marriage the possessions of wife and husband will be pooled and, should one partner die, the survivor will retain half the estate and their offspring the remainder. Children will inherit the property of their parents equally, with no distinction between boys and girls, older and younger, legitimate progeny and those born out of wedlock. But Omai is far from encouraging sexual licence and introduces measures designed to curb the notorious immorality of his native islands. Prostitutes must declare their occupation to the Chief Magistrate and wear a special dress distinguishing them from 'honest' women. Any chief resorting to a prostitute will forfeit all his inherited rights which can be restored only by a decree of the Supreme Council. The problem of venereal disease, introduced by Europeans, is disposed of summarily. Those suffering from the malady will be transported to uninhabited islands, men and women separately, to undergo treatment until certified as cured. Further, to prevent a recurrence of the disease, any women who allow themselves to be seduced by visiting mariners will be banished. Other evils are dealt with in a penal code of the utmost simplicity. Little distinction is made between sins and social crimes which are reduced to four — impiety, homicide, adultery, theft. Penalties range from death by clubbing (for murder and adultery) to banishment and the bastinado. 'Be warned, Europeans,' Omai advises future navigators, 'if henceforth you take without permission our grass, our wood, our water, our cloth, you will not carry your ears back to Europe. It is from you we have learned this punishment for theft.'[46]

His travels have convinced Omai of the importance of education but have not removed all his aristocratic prejudices. At his prompting a Master of Reading and Writing is appointed on each island to set up schools. The chiefly class are obliged to send their children to these academies, parents of the next class are permitted but not compelled to, while those of the lowest order may do so only with leave from their betters. When the legislators go on to consider the arts, more especially the art of literature, they are guided by the advice of Monsieur K***. This French visitor informs the assembly that a philosopher of his country has composed a magnificent discourse to show that letters have enervated mankind, corrupted their morals, and destroyed their natural taste for beauty, truth, and goodness. As a safeguard against such dangers, a strict system of censorship is introduced. To practise authorship a man must secure official permission, first proving himself a person of mature years, good repute, and sound education. He will be expected to support belief in God and the after life, obedience to the law, love of human kind, and unquestioning loyalty to the Federation. Before issuing a work he must submit it for approval to three commissioners. Once it is passed he will be absolved from all further responsibility; but should he publish or circulate it surreptitiously, even if it is the greatest masterpiece in the world, he with any accomplices will be banished.[47]

The story of Omai's rise to supreme eminence and the creation of his not wholly benign theocracy occupies three volumes crammed with incident. Narration succeeds narration as Baston develops his labyrinthine plot and deploys his immense array of characters, some drawn from Cook, others (such as Nowa) mentioned but not named in the official account, others again wholly imagined. The fictitious Monsieur K***, for example, accompanied by the historical Feenough, reaches Huahine bearing tragic news of Cook, slain, as Etary had prophesied, by people who thought him a god. The Frenchman temporarily settles with Omai and furthers that leader's designs. Among many services, he assists in the invasion of Moorea, discovers iron on an outlying island, teaches his hosts to forge implements, advises the constitutional assembly, and, as a one-man Academy, purges the native language of error. Feenough, if less versatile, proves himself Omai's staunch ally, to be rewarded in due time with the throne of Tahaa and the hand of Opoony's daughter, the beautiful 'Eman-Hué'. Throughout the narrative royal nuptials proliferate, battle scenes abound, rhetoric flows in turgid profusion, envoys perpetually speed with their felicitations, their edicts, and their ultimatums. Omai, eruditely citing Homer whom he read in London, likens his companions to warriors from the *Iliad*.[48]. In fact, his campaigners, puppet kings, and princelings resemble figures of the Napoleonic era, Omai himself prophetically filling the role of a modest Bonaparte.

Baston's generalissimo-statesman had a more exact counterpart closer to home. On the authority of Vancouver, soon after the abbé published his fantasy Otoo-Pomare was planning to unite Tahiti and the surrounding islands under one supreme ruler. Similarly, the final episode of the novel foreshadows events in the Pacific future, though not their historical outcome. Reports reach Huahine that strangers, evidently of Spanish origin, have landed on one of the islands and begun to build a fort. Omai confronts the leader to demand what justification he has for his actions. Because he is stronger, the Spaniard replies, adding that he has taken possession of the place in the name of his sovereign. 'What right has your sovereign to seize a country which already has inhabitants and a king?' Omai retorts. Observing strict legal procedure, he leaves to report to the Supreme Council which authorizes him to repel the intruders. By a series of clever stratagems he seizes the Spanish vessel, overwhelms the fort, and captures the would-be colonists. The Council orders the prisoners to return to Europe in their own ship under the command of Monsieur K*** but magnanimously allows anyone to stay provided he observes local customs and laws. Among those who elect to settle is a Christian missionary of proven gentleness and piety. Even before the Spanish ship sails, Omai declares that he has learned to admire the beauty and sublimity of the new religion which is fast winning converts. On the morrow, he says, he will for the last time embrace Monsieur K*** who is to carry off his narrations. 'May they instruct!' he exclaims, 'or if that is to aspire too high, may they amuse!'[49]

It is to be feared that Baston's own novel met with little success on either score. Outside Germany, where versions were published in Dresden and Leipzig, the supreme literary tribute to Omai seems to have been received with indifference. In England it found no translator and in France failed to reach a second edition. The abbé's *longueurs*, his bulk, his peculiar blend of liberalism and reaction were evidently not to the taste of French readers. In the seventeen-nineties, furthermore, they were too preoccupied with their own affairs of state to spare much thought for the founder of an imaginary federation at the far ends of the earth. More than a decade passed before Omai was again presented to the French public and then it was as one figure in another grandiose compilation, the three volumes of *Voyages chez Les Peuples Sauvages, ou L'Homme de la Nature, Histoire morale des peuples sauvages des deux Continens, et des naturels des Isles de la mer du Sud*. Published in 1801, the book had been conceived and partly written much earlier. In an introduction the nominal author, François Babié, told how he received the manuscript, the product of continuous reading and arduous research, from an aged cleric and man of letters, Citizen R***, who had been imprisoned during the Terror. On his release the venerable Citizen, realizing he was too weighed down by years and his recent ordeal to complete the task, handed it over to Babié. This preamble, so similar to the framing device used by Baston, represented actual facts. Citizen R*** was a priest, Jérôme Richard, who died two years before the appearance of his much edited and mutilated collection. Babié brazenly explained that he had found it necessary to abridge the original, purge it of dry metaphysical passages or opinions that might offend republicans, and embellish it with anecdotes drawn from modern navigators. In a dedicatory epistle to Bonaparte he announced his aim: to vindicate civilized man, traduced by pseudo-philosophers with their unworthy preference for savages. The work, he repeatedly emphasized, was not a novel but the true account of natural man as he really was.[50]

In the circumstances it is impossible to separate one contributor's share from the other's. Perhaps Richard was responsible for the curious fragments of erudition culled from classical sources. Babié, as he claims, probably drew on the writings of recent explorers and was almost certainly the spokesman for a jealous nationalism voiced in the closing sections. Whatever the exact nature of the partnership, it resulted in an untidy anthology of travellers' tales bulked out with romantic additions and spiced with semi-salacious details. The story of 'Pocahunta' is related and so is the similar idyll, taken from Rickman, of the British sailor and his New Zealand lover. The suggestion is that savage women are irresistibly drawn to Europeans; and on the authority of English seamen it is claimed that the stratagems of London prostitutes are nothing compared with those employed by their Tahitian sisters. Amid a profusion of anecdote and assertion the lineaments of the 'Man of Nature' become more indefinite than ever. Nor does it seem at all certain, even to the authors themselves, that he is in any way inferior to civilized man. In the traditional manner the Society Islanders (a term embracing the Tahitians) are compared with the ancient Greeks; they are praised for their good nature and their humanity; and their lot is favourably compared with that of Europeans, so often condemned to unremitting toil.[51]

Where the authors of *Voyages chez Les Peuples Sauvages* differed markedly from such predecessors as Monboddo was in the emphasis they placed on so-called savage man in his southern habitat. They devoted the whole of their second volume to the South Seas and introduced many references to the same region elsewhere. Writing after the great period of Pacific discovery, they drew not only on the major accounts from Hawkesworth to Forster but also on lesser works. The anonymous *Endeavour* journal, published in France as *Supplément au Voyage de M. de Bougainville,* yielded colourful details including the picture of Borabora as a nest of pirates ruled over by the tyrant 'Opuna'. Another favourite source was Rickman who was particularly useful because of the often unflattering picture he presented of his commander. For the Cook of Richard and Babié (or perhaps only of Babié) is not the heroic leader and faithful friend of their countryman Baston but 'le terrible *Cook*' — a man whose naturally severe and melancholy disposition had been accentuated by the fatigue of his voyages and the decline of his health; who adopted the loftiest tone in dealing with all those people he regarded as savages; who treated them with the utmost severity (notably on Moorea); who exacted vengeance for every small transgression, every petty theft committed on his ships; who did all this to advance his schemes for English domination; and who on the island of Hawaii was the victim of his own presumption.[52]

   This conspiratorial view of the English navigator adds an original touch to a lengthy sketch of Omai based on the official narratives of the last two expeditions liberally supplemented by Forster and Rickman. How, it is asked, can the captain's flattering account of his charge during the return voyage be reconciled with his first unfavourable impressions? An explanation follows:

It is probable that Cook thought he saw in Omai the seed of those talents which had raised him from utter obscurity to a distinguished rank in the English Navy. He hoped that, after re-education, Omai would be qualified to further the plans he himself had been making for the Society Islands — plans that would redound to the glory and profit of his own nation. His experience of living with the islander, the care he took in training him, taught him to see the man in a totally different light from that in which he had appeared when he first embarked.

Omai was a British agent, according to this theory, his wooden house an outpost of empire. But the scheme met with a fate the patriotic Frenchmen also predicted for the recently founded colony at Botany Bay. On obscure authority they asserted that the English ships had scarcely set sail from Huahine when Omai's countrymen descended on him during the night, overturned his house, destroyed his plantations, and 'probably' killed his animals. Perhaps, they commented, referring to Rousseau's *Discourse on Inequality*, the educated Hottentot was wiser and better ensured his future happiness by discarding European ways and returning to the customs of his forefathers.[53]

THE OLD DEBATE pursued its inconclusive course, the quest for 'natural man' still went on among theorists of an older generation. While the Abbé Richard compiled the eclectic annals of savage life, his near-contemporary Lord Monboddo continued his investigations into the origin of language and the nature of primitive society. Writing to Sir Joseph Banks in July 1782, the sponsor of Mademoiselle Le Blanc announced an even more momentous discovery. On a recent journey back to Scotland he had seen 'one of the greatest curiosities in England' — none other than a semi-human creature mentioned by Rousseau himself, the Hanoverian child befriended by the English royal family and known as Peter the Wild Boy. Now a venerable greybeard, this legendary figure had dwelt since childhood in Hertfordshire. One aged woman in the neighbourhood, a Mrs. Callop, remembered his arrival when he 'fed upon raw Vegetables, such as Leaves of Cabbage and even of Trees.' Since his return to Edinburgh, Monboddo went on, he had learned that the child was brought from Hanover, 'where he was said to have been catched, running upon all four in the woods', and presented to George I in 1726. Perhaps, he suggested, Sir Joseph might send him further information concerning the wild man and if it could not be got in England extend his inquiries to Hanover. 'For', the antiquarian emphasized, 'he is in my opinion a greater Phenomenon than the new Planet that has appeared.' As an afterthought, he mentioned hearing of someone in London who had travelled in Africa and seen such men as Peter — in other words the orang-outangs. Would Banks also look into this? He made no apology for his requests, Monboddo concluded, as he knew his friend desired to promote knowledge of every kind.[54]

Knowledge certainly, Banks might have replied, but not credulous superstition. He was already well informed about Peter by the first-hand report of another correspondent, Arnold Mello. From this and other sources he had apparently concluded that the famous Wild Boy was nothing but an idiot, an opinion he did not hesitate to pass on to Monboddo together with his view that it was absurd to suppose a race of orang-outangs inhabited Germany. His lordship hastened to agree with the second assertion but in this and a further letter vehemently denied that Peter was in any way defective. At the time of the child's arrival in England, he said, the newspapers had made no such insinuation. Moreover, what he had seen himself combined with the remarks of the woman of the house and the testimony of an officer quartered in the neighbourhood all convinced him that Peter possessed human intelligence, though admittedly it was childish and uncultivated. Nor, in answer to another of Banks's quibbles, did he think it very strange that a human creature should be able to subsist on herbage and the products of trees, a fact well attested by ancient as well as modern authors. Captain Cook, to go no farther, related that the inhabitants of New Caledonia ate the bark of a certain tree which his crew had tasted and found palatable. He again urged that a search for authentic information on Peter should be undertaken in Hanover and in his final letter was gratified to learn that Banks was following his advice.[55]

With Solander's death in the previous May, Banks seems to have given up all idea of publishing the account of their Pacific voyage, the long-promised 'grand *Natural History Work*'. His authorial ambitions laid aside, he would henceforth fill the role of intermediary and oracle on matters scientific not only in Britain but in the learned circles of Europe and North America. At the time of Monboddo's epoch-making discovery he was already in touch with a rising scholar, Johann Friedrich Blumenbach of Göttingen, who, probably at his request, undertook a searching study of the Wild Boy's history. What the German investigator eventually disclosed did nothing to support popular legend. From his examination of original documents he proved that, far from being a naked child of nature, Peter wore torn fragments of a shirt at the time of his capture and showed by the whiteness of his thighs that he had been clad in breeches. He was in fact the dumb offspring of a man called Krüger and after being shut out of their home by his stepmother had merely sought shelter in the woods. So, as Blumenbach announced with evident relish, the *Juvenis Hannoveranus* of Linnaeus, celebrated by Buffon, Rousseau, and more recently Monboddo, was an impostor — 'a striking example of the uncertainty of human testimony and historical credulity'. For good measure this sceptic cast doubts on the authenticity of all other reports of so-called wild children — Mademoiselle Le Blanc, the infant suckled by wolves, the Lithuanian bear-child, etc. — and asserted elsewhere that no trustworthy witness had established the existence of men with tails. Fortunately for Monboddo's peace of mind, he died in 1799, long before the publication of this onslaught on his cherished theories.[56]

Blumenbach, who has been termed the founder of modern anthropology by at least one authority, adopted a more systematic approach to the study of primitive man than most of his predecessors. His *De Generis Humani Varietate Nativa*, first published in 1776, made a somewhat dubious contribution to scholarship by dividing mankind into four races. Revising the monograph in 1781, he extended the number to five — Caucasian, Mongolian, Ethiopian, American, Malay (the last category including the people now termed Polynesian). He intended bringing out a new and very much improved edition, he informed Banks in January 1794. To illustrate the little book, might he have the Tahitian skull Sir Joseph had 'destined' for his collection? And could his friend recommend a *'particular striking characteristical likeness'* of some member of the same nation, perhaps one of the published prints of

69
*Omai as an
anthropological specimen*

Omai? The work duly appeared in the following year with a dedication
to 'Virum Perillustrem Josephum Banks' and a plate of the Tahitian
cranium but no illustration of a living native. As a result of further
correspondence, in 1798 Blumenbach was rewarded by Lady Banks
with the 'precious miniature' of Omai he had admired when he first met
that gracious gentlewoman in England seven years before. The 'inestimable present' was immediately shown to colleagues and friends.
'Prof. Lichtenberg who had Seen Omai at London was Struck with the
Likeness of that masterly little picture', Blumenbach reported in December 1798. The following month he wrote to say that an appreciative
'conoisseur' thought it done by Meyer, 'a German painter in that line',
who was also in London at the time of Omai's visit.[57]

When Blumenbach introduced Omai to the scientific world it was in
successive editions of a popular miscellany, *Objects of Natural History
Illustrated*. Lady Banks's miniature apparently came too late to be
included and the illustration was an oval head taken from Jacobi's
engraving of the portrait by Reynolds. There followed a brief account of
the 'widely-known man from *Otaheite* (or more properly from *Ulietea*)'
containing one or two novel facts, others that were familiar, and some
conspicuous errors in chronology. Formerly 'a sort of page-boy to Queen
Oberea', Omai had been brought to London by Captain Furneaux in
1773 and in 1779 restored by Captain Cook to his native land 'where he
died some years afterwards.' That he had become proficient at the game
of chess in a short time (not so short by this reckoning) seemed to
Blumenbach less a proof of the man's capacity for learning than of his
ability to acquire the tone of refined London society. He had done this
so rapidly and so well, the writer continued, that once, when seated at
dinner opposite Lord Mulgrave and the visitor, the 'celebrated' Dr. Johnson
was 'so impressed by the elegance of O-MAI'S manners that he was
unable for a time to distinguish between him and the Lord.' The article
ended with a paragraph in Blumenbach's relaxed literary manner:

> Much though the worthy man from Otaheite felt himself at home in London,
> he nevertheless longed to be back under his own happy skies and to tread the
> *dulce natale solum* of his much-lauded island. Concerning this he said to an
> English lady shortly before his departure: 'At home, it is true, I shall have no
> horses, no French fruit, and no tea-tables; — oh, Miss, I am leaving all that
> behind, and — *yet* there I shall be happy.'[58]

Blumenbach might have read the Johnson story in Boswell's *Life*, published in May 1791. Or he could have picked up this and other particulars
when he visited Sir Joseph and Lady Banks in December of the same
year. By that time — and probably much earlier — Omai's stature had
dwindled in the small circle which had once courted his company and
sung his praises. Little now survived but memories of his proficiency at
chess, his quaint sayings, and the skill he displayed in aping his betters.
These had become topics of condescending reminiscence or jocular

badinage, sometimes with unfortunate results, as a further anecdote illustrates. In his memoirs Giuseppi Baretti described his last meeting with Johnson at some unspecified time before the doctor's death in December 1784. He had expected to find the sage very ill but instead he was in high spirits and, Baretti relates, 'the conversation happening to turn about Otaheite, he recalled that Omiah had once conquered me at Chess; a subject on which, whenever chance brought it about, he never failed to rally me most unmercifully . . . .' On this occasion Johnson pushed matters so far that Baretti, unable to stem the stream of banter, snatched hat and stick, quitting the room 'in a most choleric mood'. Miss Reynolds, Sir Joshua's sister, gave a different account of the quarrel which she had from an eye-witness. In this version Baretti claimed to have beaten Omai both times they played chess at Sir Joshua's home. When Johnson questioned his veracity, the Italian asked: '"Do you think I should be conquered at chess by a savage?"' '"I know you were,"' retorted the doctor. Since Baretti still persisted in his assertion, Johnson 'rose from his seat in a violent rage, shouting, "I'll hear no more."' Thereupon the visitor fled the house, never to return. The point of the incident, explains Baretti's biographer, was that Johnson, with his strict regard for truth, would not countenance 'even an exaggeration by his dear mistress', much less a downright lie.[59]

As she neared the end of her life, Johnson's 'dear mistress' in her turn recalled the exotic guest she and Henry Thrale had once entertained at Streatham. In the summer of 1819 the twice widowed Mrs. Piozzi had withdrawn from the exhausting pleasures of Bath to rusticate in the small town of Weston-super-Mare. Gradually she had grown accustomed to the rigours of this social desert, devoid of books, diversions, even a market, and found herself positively enjoying the pleasures yielded by primitive nature. When expressing these sentiments to her friend Sir John Fellowes on 27 August, she summoned up figures from the remote past — Fanny Burney, Omai, and Reynolds's model, the beautiful Mary Horneck:

When Miss Burney asked Omiah, the savage, if he should like to go back to Otaheite, 'Yes, Miss,' said he; 'no mutton there, no coach, no dish of tea, no pretty Miss Horneck; good air, good sea, and *very good dog*. I happy at Otaheite.' My tastes and his are similar.

Fanny, here identified as Blumenbach's anonymous 'English lady', had recently lost her *émigré* husband, General d'Arblay. In their common plight the two widows, estranged since Mrs. Thrale's second marriage, had become reconciled and carried on a guarded correspondence. Seeking health and novelty, the aged but indomitable Mrs. Piozzi, now in her eighty-first year, had settled briefly at Penzance in Cornwall and journeyed on to Clifton, the fashionable resort near Bristol. On 15 March 1821, a few weeks before her death, she began what proved to be the farewell letter to her old friend, again referring, with more obscure intent, to Omai's legendary remarks:

I feel quite happy in being able to reply to dear Madame d'Arblay's good-natured inquiries, from this, the living world. Such we cannot term Penzance — not with propriety — much like Omai, who said to you, 'No mutton there, missee, no fine coach, no clock upon the stairs,' etc.; but *en revanche* here is no Land's End, no submarine mine of Botallock![60]

This, however, was not the final reference to Omai by one of his former admirers. Just as Fanny, in the rapturous letter to Susan Burney, had been among the first to write of the 'Stranger's' arrival from the South Seas, so the last word was hers. It was her fate to survive most of her contemporaries and all Omai's English hosts and patrons. In one year, 1792, Banks mourned the loss of three close friends — Lord Mulgrave, Lord Sandwich, and Sir Joshua Reynolds. He himself continued to enjoy fame and honours for nearly three more decades, ending his long career in 1820. Under the patronage of Banks, James Burney had won modest fame as historian of the Pacific and fleeting honour as vice-admiral; but he too died in 1821, six months after Mrs. Piozzi. Madame d'Arblay alone lived on, labouring for years to impose order on an immense mass of family papers and her vast store of somewhat uncertain recollections. At length in 1832, at the age of eighty, she published the compilation entitled *Memoirs of Doctor Burney.*[61]

Omiah, as he was termed throughout, formed the subject of one of the lengthy character sketches in which the *Memoirs* abound. But he was no longer the Omai of Fanny's youthful journal nor of the excited letter sent to Mr. Crisp. These sources had clearly been drawn on but their simple language had been inflated and generalized, the colloquialisms expunged or rephrased, and some fresh facts introduced — whether from Madame d'Arblay's memory, from her imagination, or from documents since destroyed it is impossible to decide. She praised the behaviour of 'this young Otaheitean, who it would be an abuse of all the meaning annexed to the word, to call a savage'; she described his complexion, 'swarthy and dingy' but 'by no means black'; she mentioned his features, partaking 'far more of the African than of the European cast'; and in discussing his limited command of English she made some entirely novel remarks, perhaps based on her youthful impressions but more probably inspired by a comic figure of stage or fiction:

Omiah understood a little English, when addressed in it slowly and distinctly; but could speak it as yet very ill; and with the peculiarity, whether adopted from the idiom of his own tongue, or from the apprehension of not being clearly comprehended, of uttering first affirmatively, and next negatively, all the little sentences that he attempted to pronounce.

Thus, when asked how he did, he answered 'Ver well; not ver ill.' Or how he liked any thing, 'Ver nice, not ver nasty.' Or what he thought of such a one, 'Ver dood; not ver bad.'

The revised version of Omiah's first visit to the Burneys ends with the familiar comparison between Mr. Stanhope (no longer a *pedantic Booby*' but a 'heavy, ungainly, unpleasing character') and the islander, endowed with all those graces 'the most elaborately accomplished of noblemen had vainly endeavoured to make the ornament of his son.'[62]

Omiah's newly disclosed eccentricities of expression were again illustrated in an account of his second call at Newton House. To Dr. Burney's inquiry concerning the King, '"Yes," he answered, "Yes. King George bid me, 'Omy, you go home.' O! dood man, King George! ver dood man! — not ver bad!"' Similarly, in passing on to the company his experiences at a school, 'He then described the master giving the boy a rap on the shoulder with the book. "Ha! ha! — Boy like ver bad! not ver well. Boy do so;" making wry faces. "Poor boy! not ver dood. Boy ver bad."' The effect of this gibberish is to conjure up not the gracious stranger of Fanny's earlier impressions but some Black Sambo of the popular boards. (Could he have been modelled on Omai in the Covent Garden spectacle?) Even when her intentions were altogether praiseworthy, Madame d'Arblay could not avoid a note of amused condescension. As in her earlier narrative, at Dr. Burney's suggestion the guest consented to entertain the gathering with one of his songs. This he did with reluctance, blushing 'alike at his own performance, and at the barbarity of his South Sea Islands' harmony'. Nevertheless, he took pains 'to Englishize the meaning of his ditty', the tale of an 'ancient enamorata' who by her 'languishing grimaces' attempts to lure a young man away from his lover. The item, commented the ancient memorialist, 'afforded great amusement, of the risible kind, to the Doctor and his family' who farewelled Omiah with regret, 'so gentle, so ingenuous, so artless, and so pleasing had been his conduct and conversation in his frequent visits to the house; nor did he, in return, finally quit them without strong symptoms even of sadness.' With habitual inaccuracy in dates and matters of detail the authoress concluded this episode: 'In the February of the ensuing year, 1776, Captain Burney set sail, with Captain Cooke and Omiah, on their watery tour.'[63]

Madame d'Arblay's last years were saddened by personal losses and embittered by a scathing attack on the *Memoirs* in the *Quarterly Review*. She died on 6 January 1840, a month before the 'savage' country of New Zealand, as she had once denounced it, became a British colony.[64] Her life had spanned the great period of southern exploration; and she was a witness to the rise and decline of the obscure figure who through an accident of history became for a time the most celebrated of all Pacific denizens.

Postscript

ONE OF MY AIMS IN COMPILING THIS BOOK WAS TO PUT ON RECORD ALL THE extant material, written or pictorial, concerning Omai. On completing the typescript early in 1976 I reflected with a certain satisfaction that, for once, I had achieved my objective. That complacent mood soon ended. Shortly afterwards Michael Gill of the B.B.C. pointed out Omai's part in a collection of letters between Martha Ray and her murderer, James Hackman (p. 262 above). Thus prompted, I traced three publications brought out soon after the sensational affair. Two were anonymous pamphlets, the first defending Hackman's cause, the second Miss Ray's, both alleging they had been lovers whose 'familiarities' Omai had observed and reported to 'his friend and benefactor', Sandwich.[1] In the roles of voyeur and informer he again appeared in a more elaborate work, *Love and Madness*. This purported to be the love letters of the guilty pair but was in fact from the pen of a shady journalist, Herbert Croft. Rather implausibly Miss Ray is endowed with the author's literary and philosophical interests. 'Come then', she urges Hackman, '. . . and surely Omiah will not murder love! . . . But, is a child of nature to nip in the bud that favourite passion which his mother Nature planted and still tends? — What will Oberea and her coterie say to this . . . ? . . . . What would Rousseau say to it . . . ?'[2]

Three more Grub Street trophies were perhaps of small moment. Not so a document that came to my notice while checking page proofs. I then learned that an eye-witness report of Omai's presentation at Court (p. 96 above) was held not in some remote repository but among the family papers of Mr. Peter G. Markham of Tauranga. It was a letter (perhaps a copy) from George III's second son Prince Frederick to his former tutor, Bishop Markham (later Archbishop of York and Mr. Markham's ancestor). Writing on 18 July 1774, the prince gave his impressions of the 'man from Ulatea': he was 'about five foot ten inches high, of a very swarthy complexion, the nose flat, and his upper lip turned up, and quite purple'; he was 'tattooed upon the arms and other parts'; he wore native dress, 'like the ancient toga', but Mr. Banks 'thought it would not be proper for him to come without stockings and shoes.' When summoned to prayers the first Sunday on board, the letter continued, 'he was much afraid, thinking that they were going to sacrifice him.' As to the killing and eating of Captain Furneaux's men, the prince remarked, it was 'perfectly true'; the New Zealanders had been found 'actually feasting upon the flesh of these men'.[3]

What other documents, I now wonder, still lurk in some unseen collection, perhaps in the city of Auckland?

Sources

MANUSCRIPTS

Letters and other manuscript material are included in References to Sources, pp. 341-52 below. They have been drawn from the following collections in England, Australia, New Zealand, and the United States:

BRITISH MUSEUM, LONDON. J. F. Blumenbach to J. Banks, 8 Jan. 1794, 20 Dec. 1798, 30 Jan. 1799; Charlotte Burney to Frances Burney, 10 Apr. 1780; Frances Burney to S. Crisp, 1 Dec. 1774, 14, c. 24 Apr. 1775, 5 Apr. 1776; R. D. Cumberland to G. Cumberland, 10 Oct. 1774, c. 6 Nov. 1775; G. Cumberland to R. D. Cumberland, 18 Oct. 1774; J. Elliott, 'Memoirs'; D. C. Solander to Lord Hardwicke, 5 Aug. 1774; R. Stevens to Banks and Solander, 26 Sept. 1774.

BRITISH MUSEUM (NATURAL HISTORY), LONDON. Banks, 'Journal of a Voyage Made in the Augusta Yatch', typescript copy of original at Mapperton House, Dorset. Dawson Turner Copies as follows: J. Lind to Banks, 2 Mar. 1775; Lind to N. Maskelyne, 30 Jan. 1775; A. Mello to Banks, 16 July 1776; Lord Monboddo to Banks, 9 July, 29 Aug. 1782, 30 Jan. 1783; C. Phipps to Banks, 17 Sept. 1774; W. Robertson to Banks, 18 Feb. 1773; Lord Sandwich to Banks, 29 Dec. 1774.

COUNTY ARCHIVES. Kent Archives Office, Maidstone: Notebook of the Revd. J. E. Gambier, 11 Aug. 1774. County Record Office, Stafford: Sir Harry Trelawny to the Revd. Mr. Broughton, 14 Jan. 1776. Suffolk Record Office, Bury St. Edmunds: the Revd. Sir John Cullum to the Revd. Michael Tyson, 2 Jan., 13 Dec. 1775; Tyson to Cullum, 27 Dec. 1774, 4 Jan. 1775.

ROYAL SOCIETY, LONDON. Banks to C. Blagden, 12 Aug., c. Sept. 1774.

DIXSON LIBRARY, LIBRARY OF NEW SOUTH WALES, SYDNEY. Banks, 'Journal . . . of a tour in Holland 1773; C. Burney to Lind, 12 Aug. 1775; Sandwich to Banks, 14 Aug. 1774; Solander to Banks, 10 Nov. 1774; Solander to Lind, 27 July 1774; W. Watson to E. W. Montagu, 19 Sept. 1775.

MITCHELL LIBRARY, LIBRARY OF NEW SOUTH WALES, SYDNEY. Banks to Sarah S. Banks, 21 July 1774; J. Burney, 'Journal of . . . the Discovery', photocopy of original in Public Record Office; Phipps to Banks, c. 6 Aug. 1774, photocopy of original in Webster Collection; Sandwich to Banks, 10 Oct. 1780; Solander to Banks, 28 June 1775.

NATIONAL LIBRARY OF AUSTRALIA, CANBERRA. Banks papers, including 'Account of Presents Sent out with Omai', 'Account of the Bills for Oediddee', 'Expenses on account of Omai', 1774, 1775, 1776, 'Things intended for Omai'; Banks, 'On the Manners of the Women of Otaheite'; Sarah S. Banks, 'Memorandums'; J. Hawkesworth to C. Burney, 6 Oct. 1771; J. Burney, Private Journal, recently published as *With Captain James Cook in the Antarctic and Pacific: the Private Journal of James Burney*, ed.

Beverley Hooper (Canberra, 1975); page references below are to the manuscript version.

ALEXANDER TURNBULL LIBRARY, WELLINGTON. Banks to Sandwich, 29 July 1774, photocopy of original at Mapperton House, Dorset; W. Bayly, 'Journal . . . in His Majesty's Ship Adventure', 'Journal of Cook's Third voyage', Supplementary Journal of Third Voyage; Susan Burney (Phillips) to C. Burney, c. Feb. 1784, photocopy of original at Mapperton House, Dorset; Solander to Lind, 19 Aug. 1774; S. Wallis, 'Log book of H.M.S. "Dolphin" . . . 1766-68'.

PIERPONT MORGAN LIBRARY, NEW YORK. Frances Burney to Susan Burney, c. 15 July 1774.

PUBLICATIONS

This select bibliography is primarily intended as a key to References to Sources, pp. 341-52 below. The titles of newspapers and periodicals are not included, nor those of publications referred to only in passing.

ANDERSON, B. *Surveyor of the Sea: The Life and Voyages of Captain George Vancouver*, Seattle, 1960.

ANGELO, H. *Reminiscences of Henry Angelo*, 2 vols., London, 1828-30.

ARMSTRONG, W. *Sir Joshua Reynolds*, London, 1900.

BANKS, J. *The 'Endeavour' Journal of Joseph Banks 1768-1771*, ed. J. C. Beaglehole, 2 vols., Sydney, 1962.

BASTON, G.-A.-R. *Narrations d'Omaï, Insulaire de la Mer du Sud, Ami et Compagnon de Voyage du Capitaine Cook*, 4 vols., Rouen and Paris, 1790.

BEAGLEHOLE, J. C. *The Exploration of the Pacific*, 3rd ed., London, 1966.

BEAGLEHOLE, J. C. *The Life of Captain James Cook*, London, 1974.

BEDDIE, M. K., ed. *Bibliography of Captain James Cook*, 2nd ed., Sydney, 1970.

BLIGH, W. *The Log of the Bounty*, ed. O. Rutter, 2 vols., London, 1936.

BLUMENBACH, J. F. *Abbildungen naturhistorischer Gegenstände*, 2nd ed., Göttingen, 1810.

BLUMENBACH, J. F. *The Anthropological Treatises of Johan Friedrich Blumenbach*, ed. T. Bendyshe, London, 1865.

BLUMENBACH, J. F. *De Generis Humani Varitate Nativa*, 3rd ed., Göttingen, 1795.

BOSWELL, J. *Boswell for the Defence*, ed. W. K. Wimsatt and F. A. Pottle, London, etc., 1960.

BOSWELL, J. *Boswell: the Ominous Years*, ed. C. Ryskamp and F. A. Pottle, London, etc., 1963.

BOSWELL, J. *Boswell's Life of Johnson*, ed. G. B. Hill, rev. L. F. Powell, 6 vols., Oxford, 1934-50.

BOUGAINVILLE, L.-A. DE. *Voyage autour du Monde*, 2nd ed., 2 vols., Paris, 1772.

BOUGAINVILLE, L.-A. DE. *A Voyage round the World*, trans. J. R. Forster, London, 1772.

BROSSES, C. DE. *Histoires des Navigations aux Terres Australes*, 2 vols., Paris, 1756.

BURNEY, FRANCES (D'ARBLAY). *Diary and Letters of Madame d'Arblay*, ed. A. Dobson, 6 vols., London, 1904-5.

BURNEY, FRANCES (D'ARBLAY). *The Early Diary of Frances Burney*, ed. Annie Raine Ellis, Bohn's ed., 2 vols., London, 1907.

BURNEY, FRANCES (D'ARBLAY). *Memoirs of Doctor Burney*, 3 vols., London, 1832.

CAMERON, H. C. *Sir Joseph Banks*, London, 1952.

CARTWRIGHT, G. *A Journal of Transactions and Events . . . on the Coast of Labrador*, 3 vols., Newark, 1792.

CLOYD, E. L. *James Burnett*, Oxford, 1972.

COLLISON-MORLEY, L. *Giuseppi Baretti*, London, 1909.

COLMAN, G. *Random Records*, 3 vols., London, 1830.

COLNETT, J. *The Journal of Captain James Colnett aboard the 'Argonaut'*, ed. F. W. Howay, Toronto, 1940.

COOK, J. *The Journals of Captain James Cook on his Voyages of Discovery*, ed. J. C. Beaglehole, 3 vols., Cambridge, 1955-67.

COOK, J. *A Voyage towards the South Pole*, 2 vols., London, 1777.

COOK, J. AND J. KING. *A Voyage to the Pacific Ocean*, 3 vols., London, 1784.

CORNEY, B. G. *The Quest and Occupation of Tahiti by Emissaries of Spain*, 3 vols., London, 1913-19.

COURTENAY, J. *An Epistle (Moral and Philosophical) from an Officer at Otaheite*, London, 1774.

COWPER, W. *The Correspondence of William Cowper*, ed. T. Wright, 4 vols., London, 1904.

COWPER, W. *The Task*, London, 1785.

CRADOCK, J. *Literary and Miscellaneous Memoirs*, 4 vols., London, 1828.

DALRYMPLE, A. *Discoveries made in the South Pacifick Ocean*, London, 1767.

DALRYMPLE, A. *A Letter from Mr. Dalrymple to Dr. Hawkesworth*, London, 1773.

DALRYMPLE, A. *Scheme of a Voyage . . . to New Zealand*, London, 1771.

DAVIES, J. *The History of the Tahitian Mission 1799-1830*, ed. C. W. Newbury, London, 1961.

DAWSON, W. R., ed. *The Banks Letters*, London, 1958.

DUNMORE, J. *French Explorers in the Pacific*, 2 vols., Oxford, 1965.

ELLIS, W. *An Authentic Narrative of a Voyage performed by Captain Cook and Captain Clerke*, 2 vols., London, 1782.

ELLIS, THE REVD. W. *Polynesian Researches*, new ed., 4 vols., London, 1853.

An Epistle from Mr. Banks . . . to Oberea, Queen of Otaheite, London, 1774?

FARINGTON, J. *The Farington Diary*, ed. J. Greig, 8 vols., London, 1922-8.

FITZGERALD, G. *The Injured Islanders; or The Influence of Art upon the Happiness of Nature*, London, 1779.

FONTANES, L. DE AND J. JOUBERT. *Correspondance de Louis de Fontanes et de Joseph Joubert*, ed. R. Tessoneau, Paris, 1943.

FORSTER, G. *Reply to Mr. Wales's Remarks*, London, 1778.

FORSTER, G. *A Voyage round the World*, 2 vols., London, 1777.

GARDINER, W. *Music and Friends*, 2 vols., London, 1838.

HALKETT, S. AND J. LAING, eds. *Dictionary of Anonymous and Pseudonymous English Literature*, new ed., 7 vols., Edinburgh, 1926-34.

HANDY, E. S. C. *History and Culture in the Society Islands*, Honolulu, 1930.

HAWKESWORTH, J. *An Account of the Voyages . . . in the Southern Hemisphere*, 2nd ed., 3 vols., London, 1773.

HEMLOW, JOYCE. *The History of Fanny Burney*, Oxford, 1958.

An Historic Epistle, from Omiah, to the Queen of Otaheite, London, 1775.

HOARE, P. *Memoirs of Granville Sharp*, 2 vols., London, 1828.

HUDSON, D. *Sir Joshua Reynolds*, London, 1958.

JOHNSON, S. *The Letters of Samuel Johnson*, ed. R. W. Chapman, 3 vols., Oxford, 1952.

A Journal of a Voyage round the World, in His Majesty's Ship 'Endeavour', London, 1771.

LESLIE, C. R. AND T. TAYLOR. *Life and Times of Sir Joshua Reynolds*, 2 vols., London, 1865.

*A Letter from Omai to the Right Honourable the Earl of ********, London, 1782?

LICHTENBERG, G. C. *Vermischte Schriften*, 9 vols., Göttingen, 1800-6, facsimile reprint, Berne, 1972.

LONSDALE, R. *Dr. Charles Burney*, Oxford, 1965.

LYSAGHT, AVERIL M. *Joseph Banks in Newfoundland and Labrador, 1766*, London, 1971.

MARTELLI, G. *Jemmy Twitcher*, London, 1962.

MARTIN-ALLANIC, J.-E. *Bougainville Navigateur et les Découvertes de son Temps*, 2 vols., Paris, 1964.

MONBODDO, LORD (JAMES BURNETT). *Of the Origin and Progress of Language*, 6 vols., Edinburgh, 1773-92.

MORRISON, J. *The Journal of James Morrison*, ed. O. Rutter, London, 1935.

MORTIMER, G. *Observations and Remarks made during a Voyage to the Islands*, London, 1791.

O'KEEFFE, J. *Recollections of the Life of John O'Keeffe*, 2 vols., London, 1826.

OLIVER, D. L. *Ancient Tahitian Society*, 3 vols., Honolulu, 1974.

Omiah's Farewell; inscribed to the Ladies of London, London, 1776.

O'REILLY, P. AND E. REITMAN, eds. *Bibliographie de Tahiti et de la Polynésie Française*, Paris, 1967.

Otaheite: A Poem, London, 1774.

PARKINSON, S. *Journal of a Voyage to the South Seas*, London, 1773.

PEAKE, R. B. *Memoirs of the Colman Family*, 2 vols., London, 1841.

PERRY, J. *Mimosa: or the Sensitive Plant*, London, 1779.

PRESTON, W. *Seventeen Hundred and Seventy-Seven*, London, 1777.

RASPE, R. E. AND OTHERS. *Singular Travels, Campaigns and Adventures of Baron Munchausen*, introd. J. Carswell, London, 1948.

RICHARD, J. AND F. BABIÉ. *Voyages chez Les Peuples Sauvages, ou L'Homme de la Nature, Histoire morale des peuples sauvages des deux Continens, et des naturels des Isles de la Mer du Sud*, 3 vols., Paris, 1801.

RICKMAN, J. *Journal of Captain Cook's Last Voyage to the Pacific Ocean*, London, 1781.

ROBERTSON, G. *The Discovery of Tahiti*, ed. H. Carrington, London, 1948.

ROUSSEAU, J.-J. *A Discourse upon the Origin and Foundation of the Inequality among Mankind*, London, 1761.

SCOTT, J. ? *An Epistle from Oberea, Queen of Otaheite, to Joseph Banks, Esq.*, London, 1774 [1773].

SCOTT, J. ? *A Second Letter from Oberea, Queen of Otaheite, to Joseph Banks, Esq.*, London, 1774.

SHARP, G. *An English Alphabet for the Use of Foreigners*, London, 1786.

SMITH, B. *European Vision and the South Pacific*, Oxford, 1960.

SMITH, E. *The Life of Sir Joseph Banks*, London, 1911.

SMITH, J. E. *A Selection from the Correspondence of Linnaeus and other Naturalists*, 2 vols., London, 1821.

SPARRMAN, A. *A Voyage round the World*, London, 1944.

THRALE, HESTER L. (PIOZZI). *Autobiography, Letters and Literary Remains of Mrs. Piozzi (Thrale)*, ed. A. Hayward, 2 vols., London, 1861.

THRALE, HESTER L. (PIOZZI), *Thraliana*, ed. Katharine C. Balderston, 2nd ed., 2 vols., Oxford, 1951.

The Travels of Hildebrand Bowman, London, 1778.

VANCOUVER, G. *A Voyage of Discovery to the North Pacific Ocean, and round the World*, 3 vols., London, 1798.

The Voyage of Governor Phillip to Botany Bay, 2nd ed., London, 1790.

WALES, W. *Remarks on Mr. Forster's Account of Captain Cook's Last Voyage*, London, 1778.

WALPOLE, H. *The Letters of Horace Walpole*, ed. Mrs. Paget Toynbee, 16 vols., Oxford, 1903-5.

WATERHOUSE, E. K. *Reynolds*, London, 1941.

WATERHOUSE, E. K. *Reynolds*, London, 1973.

WHITLEY, W. T. *Artists and their Friends in England 1700-1799*, 2 vols., London and Boston, 1928.

ZIMMERMANN, H. *Zimmermann's Account of the Third Voyage of Captain Cook*, trans. Miss U. Tewsley, Wellington, 1926.

ZIMMERMANN, H. *Zimmermann's Captain Cook*, ed. F. W. Howay, Toronto, 1930.

REFERENCES TO SOURCES

ABBREVIATIONS

ATL   Alexander Turnbull Library, Wellington.
BJ   *The 'Endeavour' Journal of Joseph Banks 1768-1771*, ed. J. C.
              Beaglehole, 2 vols., Sydney, 1962.
BM   British Museum (now British Library), London.
CJ   *The Journals of Captain James Cook on his Voyages of Discovery*,
              ed. J. C. Beaglehole, 3 vols., Cambridge, 1955-67.
DL   Dixson Library, Library of New South Wales, Sydney.
D.T.C. BM(NH) Dawson Turner Copies of Banks Correspondence, British Museum
              (Natural History), London.
ED   *The Early Diaries of Frances Burney*, ed. Annie Raine Ellis, Bohn's
              ed., 2 vols., London, 1907.
ML   Mitchell Library, Library of New South Wales, Sydney.
NLA   National Library of Australia, Canberra.

1. Mai and the European Discovery of Tahiti

1. D. C. Solander to J. Lind, 19 Aug. 1774, ATL.
2. The necessarily simplified account that follows is drawn mainly from: the Revd. W. Ellis, *Polynesian Researches* (new ed., 4 vols., London, 1853), Teuira Henry, *Ancient Tahiti* (Honolulu, 1928), E. S. C. Handy, *History and Culture in the Society Islands* (Honolulu, 1930), and I. Goldman, *Ancient Polynesian Society* (Chicago, 1970).
3. This and the following precepts have been adapted from Handy, p. 47.
4. Solander, 19 Aug. 1774.
5. ibid.
6. J.-J. Rousseau, *A Discourse upon the Origin and Foundation of the Inequality among Mankind* (London, 1761), p. xlv; A. O. Lovejoy, 'The Supposed Primitivism of Rousseau's *Discourse on Inequality*', *Modern Philology*, xxi (1923), 165-86.
7. Rousseau, *Discourse upon . . . Inequality*, pp. 115-20, 231.
8. ibid., pp. 188-9.
9. ibid., pp. 20, 33-34, 197-200.
10. ibid., pp. 252-7.
11. ibid., pp. 219-22, 229-30, 234.
12. C. de Brosses, *Histoire des Navigations aux Terres Australes* (2 vols., Paris, 1756), i. 80.
13. ibid., i. 5, 13-17, 45, ii. 386-7, 390-3.
14. A. Dalrymple, *Discoveries made in the South Pacifick Ocean* (London, 1767), pp. ii-vii, x-xi, xiv, 89-90.
15. ibid., p. xi; J. C. Beaglehole, *The Exploration of the Pacific* (3rd ed., London, 1966), pp. 194-202.
16. S. Wallis, 'Log book of H.M.S. "Dolphin" . . . 1766-68', ATL, 19-23 June 1767; G. Robertson, *The Discovery of Tahiti*, ed., H. Carrington (London, 1948), p. 137.
17. Wallis, 24-25 June 1767.
18. ibid., 26 June 1767; Solander, 19 Aug. 1774.
19. Wallis, 26 June-13 July 1767.
20. ibid., 13-27 July 1767.
21. ibid., 'Remarks' following 27 July 1767.
22. Wallis, 22, 27 July 1767; Robertson, pp. 189, 193.
23. J.-E. Martin-Allanic, *Bougainville Navigateur et les Découvertes de son Temps* (2 vols., Paris, 1964), i. 647-8; J. Dunmore, *French Explorers in the Pacific* (2 vols., Oxford, 1965), i. 57-78.
24. Martin-Allanic, i. 652-63.
25. ibid., 663-78.
26. ibid., 677-83.
27. ibid., 683-5.
28. ibid., 692, n. 191 and 194, 696, 704, 706.
29. ibid., i. 696, 699, 704, 742, 756, 791, ii. 823, 835.
30. ibid., ii. 885-6, 964-70.
31. ibid., ii. 889, 969-71; D. Diderot, *Supplément au Voyage de Bougainville*, ed. G. Chinard (Paris, etc., 1935), p. 112.

32. Martin-Allanic, ii. 981-5.
33. *The Journals of Captain James Cook on his Voyages of Discovery* (henceforth cited as *CJ*), ed. J. C. Beaglehole (3 vols., Cambridge, 1955-67), i. cvii, cix, cxxxiii-vi, 76.
34. ibid., cxxxiv-vii, clx.
35. *The 'Endeavour' Journal of Joseph Banks 1768-1771* (henceforth cited as *BJ*), ed. J. C. Beaglehole (2 vols., Sydney, 1962), i. 252-60.
36. ibid., 258, 266-7, 270-1, 274 and n. 2; *CJ*, i. cxli.
37. *BJ*, i. 267, 270, 271, 275, 276, 279, 282, 283-4; *CJ*, i. 93 and n. 2, 94 and n. 1, 97-98.
38. *BJ*, i. 288-90, 292-5, 300, 303-5, 351; *CJ*, i. 108 and n. 1 and 2, 564.
39. *BJ*, i. 305-13, 316.
40. Solander, 19 Aug. 1774; *BJ*, i. 275.
41. *CJ*, i. 141, 144, 146, 151, 153, 157; *BJ*, i. 314-18, 321-5, 327, 329.
42. *CJ*, i. 121, 155-7; *BJ*, i. 333 ff., 341, 374-5, 379-80, 384-6, 388-9.
43. *CJ*, i. 167 ff., 240, 242-3, 273; *BJ*, i. 399, 401, 403, 412-13, 420, 434, 437, 455, ii. 54, 58, 74, 77-82, 105-8, 184, 186; Dunmore, i. 149-56.
44. *CJ*, i. 432-3, 441-2; *BJ*, ii. 185-91.
45. S. Parkinson, *Journal of a Voyage to the South Seas* (London, 1773), p. 182 n.
46. *CJ*, i. 440 ff., 477 and n. 2; *BJ*, ii. 248-9.

2. Between Voyages

1. *BJ*, i. 4, 7, 9, 13; 'Memorandums', NLA, p. [2].
2. *CJ*, i. 642-9 *passim*.
3. ibid., 651-5 *passim*.
4. ibid., 637-8.
5. *BJ*, i. 52-53; J. E. Smith, *A Selection from the Correspondence of Linnaeus and other Naturalists* (2 vols., London, 1821), i. 263.
6. *BJ*, i. 56-61.
7. ibid., 54-56; Averil M. Lysaght, *Joseph Banks in Newfoundland and Labrador, 1766* (London, 1971), p. 49.
8. *BJ*, i. 7-8, 105; *General Evening Post*, 29 Nov.-1 Dec. 1774, p. [3]; G. Martelli, *Jemmy Twitcher* (London, 1962), pp. 38, 40.
9. *The Early Diary of Frances Burney 1768-1778* (henceforth cited as *ED*), ed. Annie Raine Ellis (Bohn's ed., 2 vols., London, 1907), i. 138-9.
10. ibid., 139-40; J. Hawkesworth to C. Burney, 6 Oct. 1771 (transcript of MS. in NLA supplied by W. H. Pearson).
11. *The Letters of Horace Walpole*, ed. Mrs. Paget Toynbee (16 vols., Oxford, 1903-5), vii. 277.
12. Martin-Allanic, ii. 1251-2, 1268 n. 8.
13. *A Journal of a Voyage round the World in His Majesty's Ship 'Endeavour'* (London, 1771), pp. i-ii.
14. *Gentleman's Magazine*, xli (1771), 509; see also *CJ*, i. cclxvi and M. Holmes, *Captain James Cook: A Bibliographical Excursion* (London, 1952), pp. 20-21.
15. *Gentleman's Magazine*, xli (1771), 509-12; *Journal* (1771), pp. 45, 47-49, 61-64, 67 n., 105.
16. *Bibliography of Captain James Cook*, ed. M. K. Beddie (2nd ed., Sydney, 1970), pp. 132-3; *CJ*, i. cclxiv; Martin-Allanic, ii. 1330.
17. A. Dalrymple, *Scheme of a Voyage... to New Zealand* (London, 1771), pp. [3]-5.
18. Lewis de Bougainville, *A Voyage round the World*, trans. J. R. Forster (London, 1772), pp. xix n., 221 n.
19. L.-A. de Bougainville, *Voyage autour du Monde* (2nd ed., 2 vols., Paris, 1772), i. xiv-xv; Bougainville, trans. Forster, pp. xxvi, 220-3, 228, 245 and n., 249, 253, 258-61, 269, 285-6.
20. Bougainville, trans. Forster, pp. 255, 262-3, 267, 272 and n.
21. *Gentleman's Magazine*, xlii (1772), 57-59, 105-10, 320-1.
22. *Monthly Review*, xlvi (1772), 204-12.
23. *BJ*, i. 52 and n. 5, 6, 53 and n. 1, 5; J. E. Smith, i. 272; *The Letters of Samuel Johnson*, ed. R. W. Chapman (3 vols., Oxford, 1952), i. 274-5; *Boswell for the Defence*, ed. W. K. Wimsatt and F. A. Pottle (London, etc., 1960), p. 56.
24. *CJ*, i. xxiv-xxv, clxvii-clxx.
25. ibid., xxvi-xxvii, 901-3; *Gentleman's Magazine*, xli (1771), 565.
26. *BJ*, i. 69, 72-73.
27. ibid., 73; *CJ*, i. 5, 6 and n. 1.
28. *CJ*, ii. 6-8, 934.
29. ibid, 704-7, 937-8.
30. *BJ*, i. 81-86.
31. *CJ*, ii. 11, 12, 877, 878, 880, 885-7, 892-3, 943.

32. G. E. Manwaring, *My Friend the Admiral* (London, 1931), p. 13; Frances Burney (d'Arblay), *Memoirs of Doctor Burney* (3 vols., London, 1832), i. 270; *ED*, i. 180.

3. *The Voyage of H.M.S.* Adventure

1. J. Burney, Private Journal, NLA, p. [1]; *CJ*, ii. 6-8, 685.
2. *CJ*, ii. 26-31, 30 n. 2, 32 and n. 1, 33, 34 n. 1, 37 and n. 2, 40, 43 n. 3, 45; Burney, Private Journal, p. [4].
3. *CJ*, ii. 49-50; Martin-Allanic, ii. 1324-5.
4. *CJ*, ii. 49, 51, 877, 883, 887.
5. ibid., 686-9.
6. ibid., clxvii, 53, 56, 57, 59 n. 1, 60 ff., 71-72, 729.
7. ibid., 73, 74 and n. 3, 76, 80 ff., 86, 87 n. 3, 89 n. 3.
8. ibid., 143-4, 731-6; Burney, Private Journal, p. [11].
9. *CJ*, ii. 157 and n. 1, 2, 737-40; Burney, Private Journal, p. [20].
10. *CJ*, ii. 165-9, 740-1; Burney, Private Journal, pp. [24]-[25].
11. *CJ*, ii. 170-5.
12. ibid., 175 ff., 185 and n. 2, 4, 186 and n. 4, 187, 189-90, 189 n. 2, 193 ff., 198-200.
13. ibid., 197, 200-2; Burney, Private Journal, p. [31].
14. *CJ*, ii. 200 and n. 4, 201-2, 204 n. 4, 205, 792-3.
15. ibid., 203, 204 and n. 1, 205 and n. 3.
16. ibid., 205-6.
17. ibid., 207-10, 209 n. 5.
18. ibid., 210-15; Burney, Private Journal, p. [36].
19. *CJ*, ii. 233-5.
20. ibid., 215-18, 217 n. 4.
21. ibid., 218-20, 221 n. 5.
22. ibid., 220-1; G. Forster, *A Voyage round the World* (2 vols., London, 1777), i. 388-9.
23. *CJ*, ii. 222, 428 n. 2; J. Cook, *A Voyage towards the South Pole* (2 vols., London, 1777), i. pl. LVII; J. Elliott, 'Memoirs', BM, f. 19 (generously supplied by the late J. C. Beaglehole).
24. *CJ*, ii. 892.
25. ibid., 222-7, 233.
26. ibid., 223 and n. 6, 224, 227-8; Burney, Private Journal, p. [42]; Forster, *Voyage*, i. 394.
27. Burney, Private Journal, pp. [42]-[43].
28. *CJ*, ii. 230 and n. 3, 239, 887; Forster, i. 311.
29. *CJ*, ii. 233, 236, 239.
30. W. Bayly, 'Journal . . . in His Majesty's *Ship Adventure*' (henceforth cited as *Adventure* Journal), ATL, p. 92; Burney, Private Journal, p. [49].
31. Burney, Private Journal, pp. [32], [36], [37], [49].
32. ibid., p. [35].
33. ibid., p. [37].
34. ibid., p. [38].
35. ibid.
36. ibid., pp. [38]-[39], [45].
37. ibid., pp. [39], [45].
38. ibid., pp. [39]-[41].
39. ibid., pp. [47]-[48].
40. *CJ*, ii. 243-8; Burney, Private Journal, p. [51].
41. *CJ*, ii. 248, 249 and n. 5, 251, n. 2, 275.
42. ibid., 249 ff., 254-5, 257, 259-60, 262 and n. 7, 274, 275-6.
43. ibid., 252, 271 and n. 1, 275-6, 449 and n. 3; Burney, Private Journal, p. [55].
44. *CJ*, ii. 275 ff., 278-9, 283; Bayly, *Adventure* Journal, p. 101.
45. *CJ*, ii. 741-2; Bayly, *Adventure* Journal, pp. 102, 103.
46. *CJ*, ii. 742; Bayly, *Adventure* Journal, p. 104.
47. *CJ*, ii. 742-3; Bayly, *Adventure* Journal, pp. 104-6.
48. *CJ*, ii. 297 n. 2, 743.
49. ibid., 743, 888; Burney, Private Journal, pp. [62]-[64].
50. Burney, Private Journal, p. [63].
51. *CJ*, ii. 743; Burney, Private Journal, pp. [65]-[67]; Bayly, *Adventure* Journal, pp. 107-10.
52. *CJ*, ii. 743-4, 749.
53. ibid., 744 and n. 4, 745, 892.
54. Cook, *Voyage towards the South Pole*, i. 169; Forster, *Voyage*, i. 388.

4. *Mr. Banks, Lord Monboddo, Dr. Hawkesworth, and Others*

1. *BJ*, i. 90-93.
2. ibid., 93 and n. 1; *Boswell for the Defence*, p. 146.
3. *An Account of a Savage Girl* (Edinburgh, 1768), Banks's copy, BM, pp.

iii-vi, viii-ix, xi-xii, xviii, 2, 8-9.

4. *BJ*, i. 93-94, 95 and n. 6, 98-100; Lysaght, pp. 48-49.
5. *BJ*, i. 94-96.
6. ibid., 96; J. Banks, 'Journal . . . of a tour in Holland 1773', DL, p. 45.
7. 'On the Manners of the Women of *Otaheite*', NLA, *passim*.
8. *BJ*, i. 95 and n. 3, 6, 97; Lysaght, pp. 257-9; *Gentleman's Magazine*, xliii (1773), 297.
9. *Gentleman's Magazine*, xlii (1772), 596; G. Cartwright, *A Journal of Transactions and Events . . . on the Coast of Labrador* (3 vols., Newark, 1792), i. 262, 266-72, 266, i.e. [274]; Lysaght, p. 86.
10. Cartwright, i. 266-9.
11. Lysaght, pp. 86-87.
12. ibid., pp. 87-88, 260; Cartwright, i. 265-72, i.e. [273]-[280].
13. 18 Feb. 1773, D.T.C. BM(NH).
14. ibid.
15. *Gentleman's Magazine*, xliii (1773), 242; *Monthly Review*, xlix (1773), 166 ff., 321 ff., 332.
16. *Of the Origin and Progress of Language* (6 vols., Edinburgh, 1773-92), i. 141 and n., 172 n., 174 ff., 180 and n., 206 n., 220 ff., 227 ff., 231-2, 315 ff., 316 n.
17. ibid., 220 n., 232-8.
18. ibid., 206-7, 206 n., 208 n., 234, 346-7.
19. J. Hawkesworth, *An Account of the Voyages . . . in the Southern Hemisphere* (2nd ed., 3 vols., London, 1773), i. A2 ff., vi; ii. xiii and *passim*; W. H. Pearson, 'Hawkesworth's Voyages', *Studies in the Eighteenth Century*, ed. R. F. Brissenden (Canberra, 1973), p. 239.
20. Hawkesworth, i. iv, [A][3]; in this and the following paragraphs I am deeply indebted to W. H. Pearson's 'Hawkesworth's Alterations', *Journal of Pacific History*, vii (1972), 45-72.
21. Hawkesworth, i. 433-90, ii. 79-248 and *passim*.
22. ibid., 83-85, 100, 107, 124-5, 128, 147-8, 168-9, 207-8.
23. ibid., ii. xiii, 146.
24. ibid., 186-7.
25. ibid., pl. iii-vii.
26. *Monthly Review*, xlix (1773), 136-7, 497-8.
27. ibid., 296, 298 ff., 301-2, 484-5.
28. ibid., 302, 479, 483-4, 486-7, 489-90, 491 ff.
29. *Gentleman's Magazine*, xliii (1773), 286-90, 321-4, 541, 590, 652.
30. Beddie, pp. 121-4.
31. *Boswell's Life of Johnson*, ed. G. B. Hill, rev. L. F. Powell (6 vols., Oxford, 1934-50), ii. 247-8; Walpole, ed. Paget Toynbee, viii. 277, 292-3.
32. *Gentleman's Magazine*, xliii (1773), 330-2, 505-7.
33. *A Letter from Mr. Dalrymple to Dr. Hawkesworth* (London, 1773), pp. 1-2, 24-25, 26, 32.
34. Hawkesworth, i. [A]1; *CJ*, i. cclii; *ED*, i. 272, 273.
35. *An Epistle from Oberea* (London, 1774, i.e. 1773), pp. [2]-[3], 5; *Monthly Review*, xlix (1773), 503-4; *Dictionary of Anonymous and Pseudonymous English Literature*, ed. S. Halkett and J. Laing (new ed., 7 vols., Edinburgh, 1926-34), ii. 179; Beddie, p. 672.
36. *An Epistle from Mr. Banks* (London, 1773), pp. 11-13; Beddie, p. 671.
37. *Westminster Magazine*, ii (1774), 42-43; I first learned of this work in Colin Roderick's 'Sir Joseph Banks, Queen Oberea and the Satirists', *Captain James Cook: Image and Impact*, ed. W. Veit (Melbourne, 1972), pp. 79-81.
38. *Otaheite* (London, 1774), pp. 3, 5, 12, 13, 14; *Monthly Review*, l (1774), 310-11.
39. *Otaheite*, pp. 14-15, 16.
40. *Gentleman's Magazine*, xliii (1773), 342.
41. *BJ*, i. 101 and n. 1, 102.
42. 5 Aug. 1774 (transcript of MS. in BM kindly supplied by Averil M. Lysaght).
43. *BJ*, i. 97, 100; J. E. Smith, ii. 13-14; Walpole, ed. Paget Toynbee, ix. 16.

5. *The Advent of Omai*

1. *General Evening Post*, 14-16 July 1774, p. [4].
2. To J. Lind, 19 Aug. 1774.
3. n.d. (c. 15 July 1774), fragment, Pierpont Morgan Library, New York.
4. *Gentleman's Magazine*, xliv (1774), 330; J. Banks, 21 July 1774, ML.

5. 'Memorandums', p. [10].
6. *Daily Advertiser*, 16 July 1774, p. [1]; *London Chronicle*, 16-19 July 1774, p. 62.
7. *General Evening Post*, 14-16 July 1774, p. [4]; *London Chronicle*, 14-16 July 1774, p. 56.
8. *General Evening Post*, 14-16 July 1774, p. [4]; *London Chronicle*, 19-21 July 1774, p. 66.
9. *General Evening Post*, 19-21 July 1774, p. [3]; *Daily Advertiser*, 21 July 1774, p. [1].
10. *London Chronicle*, 14-16 July 1774, pp. 54, 56; *General Evening Post*, 16-19 July 1774, p. [4].
11. p. [1].
12. 21-23 July 1774, pp. 78, 80.
13. 21-23 July 1774, pp. [3], [4], 23-26 July, p. [4], 26-28 July, pp. [1], [4].
14. *London Chronicle*, 28-30 July 1774, p. 102.
15. ibid., p. 101.
16. *London Chronicle*, 4-6 Aug. 1774, p. 127; *St. James's Chronicle*, 4-6 Aug. 1774, p. [1].
17. ibid.
18. *General Evening Post*, 6-9 Aug. 1774, p. [4]; *London Chronicle*, 9-11 Aug. 1774, pp. 143-4.
19. ibid.
20. C. W. Dixon, *Smallpox* (London, 1962), pp. 221, 244.
21. J. E. Smith, ii. 14-18.
22. 27 July 1774, DL.
23. Notebook of the Revd. J. E. Gambier, 11 Aug. 1774, Kent Archives Office, Maidstone.
24. ibid.
25. *London Magazine*, xliii (1774), 363-4; *London Chronicle*, 1-3 Sept. 1774, p. 221; *Annual Register . . . for the Year 1774* (London, 1775), 'Characters', pp. 61-3, etc.
26. photocopy, ATL.
27. 'Memorandums', pp. [11]-[12], [14].
28. c. 6 Aug. 1774, photocopy of MS. in Webster Collection, ML.
29. 5 Aug. 1774, BM.
30. J. E. Smith, ii. 18-19.
31. 'Memorandums', p. [14].
32. 12 Aug. 1774, Royal Society, London.
33. 14 Aug. 1774, DL.
34. 19 Aug. 1774, ATL.
35. ibid.
36. ibid.

6. Omai in Society

1. 23-25 Aug. 1774, p. [3].
2. *London Chronicle*, 25-27 Aug. 1774, p. 194, 27-30 Aug., p. 203.
3. *General Evening Post*, 27-30 Aug. 1774, p. [4].
4. *ED*, i. 321-2. Square brackets have been omitted from this and other quotations from *ED*.
5. 3-6 Sept. 1774, p. [1].
6. 'Memorandums', p. [14].
7. J. Cradock, *Literary and Miscellaneous Memoirs* (4 vols., London, 1828), i. 127-8.
8. 'Memorandums', pp. [15]-[17].
9. n.d. (early Sept. 1774?), Royal Society, London.
10. 17 Sept. 1774, D.T.C. BM(NH).
11. 24-27 Sept. 1774, p. [4].
12. Cradock, i. 121; W. Gardiner, *Music and Friends; or Pleasant Recollections of a Dilettante* (2 vols., London, 1838), i. 4-5.
13. Cradock, i. 122, 125-6, iv. 179.
14. 26 Sept. 1774, BM.
15. *General Evening Post*, 5-8 Nov. 1774, p. [4].
16. R. D. Cumberland to G. Cumberland, 10 Oct. 1774, c. 6 Nov. 1775; G. Cumberland to R. D. Cumberland, 18 Oct. 1774, BM.
17. 'Memorandums', pp. [18]-[19].
18. J. E. Smith, ii. 20.
19. 'Memorandums', pp. [19]-[21].
20. ibid., pp. [19], [21].
21. 10 Nov. 1774, DL.
22. *An Epistle (Moral and Philosophical) from an Officer at Otaheite* (London, 1774), pp. [1], 2, 4, 5, 6, 7, 10, 19, 20, 27, 28, 29-30; Beddie, p. 671; *Gentleman's Magazine*, xlii (1772), 90; *Monthly Review*, lii (1775), 188.
23. *A Second Letter from Oberea* (London, 1774), pp. 3-4; Halkett and Laing, v. 201; *Monthly Review*, li (1774), 394.
24. *A Second Letter*, pp. 5, 14-15.
25. *General Evening Post*, 29 Nov.-1 Dec. 1774, p. [3].
26. *ED*, i. 313-14, 328, 332, 333 n. 2.
27. 1 Dec. 1774, BM.
28. ibid.
29. ibid.
30. ibid.
31. ibid.

32. ibid.
33. Tyson to Cullum, 27 Dec. 1774, Cullum to Tyson, 2 Jan. 1775, Suffolk Record Office, Bury St. Edmunds; E. Smith, *The Life of Sir Joseph Banks* (London, 1911), pp. 41-43.
34. Cullum to Tyson, 2 Jan. 1775.
35. ibid.
36. ibid.
37. Tyson to Cullum, 4 Jan. 1775.
38. *General Evening Post*, 29 Nov.-1 Dec. 1774, p. [3], 7-10 Jan. 1775, p. [3]; Lysaght, pp. 44, 51; J. E. Smith, ii. 20.
39. 29 Dec. 1774, D.T.C. BM(NH).
40. ibid.
41. 'Expenses on account of Omai in 1774', NLA.

7. *Omai and the Return of the* Resolution

1. *CJ*, ii. 953; 'Expences incurrd . . . in . . . 1775', 'Expences incurrd . . . in . . . 1776', NLA; *ED*, ii. 134.
2. *General Evening Post*, 19-21 Jan. 1775, p. [4].
3. *CJ*, iii. lxxxiv n. 2, 1483-4.
4. D.T.C. BM(NH).
5. 'Memorandums', pp. [4]-[5].
6. D.T.C. BM(NH).
7. *ED*, ii. 24-25.
8. 14, c. 24 Apr. 1775, BM.
9. *Gentleman's Magazine*, xlv (1775), 132, 166-7.
10. G. C. Lichtenberg, *Vermischte Schriften* (9 vols., Göttingen, 1800-6, facsimile reprint, Berne, 1972), iii. 391-2. The translation is by R. A. Lochore.
11. Lichtenberg, iii. 391-3.
12. ibid., 390, 393-6.
13. ibid., 393-4, 396.
14. *General Evening Post*, 18-20 Apr. 1775, p. [4]; Cradock, i. 127.
15. 20-22 Apr. 1775, p. 382.
16. H. Angelo, *Reminiscences of Henry Angelo* (2 vols., London, 1828-30), ii. 56; (new ed., 2 vols., New York and London, 1969), ii. ix, 42-43.
17. *London Magazine*, xliv (1775), 74-76.
18. *An Historic Epistle, from Omiah* (London, 1775), pp. [iii], 2, 31-32, 34, 35, 39.
19. ibid., pp. 3, 11.
20. ibid., pp. 5 ff., 8 ff., 11 ff., 14, 16 and n., 18, 19 n., 21 ff., 28, 30.
21. ibid., pp. 35 and n., 37, 38, 42-44.

22. *London Chronicle*, 30 May-1 June 1775, p. 514, 22-24 June, p. 589; *General Evening Post*, 8-10 June, p. [1], 10-13 June, p. [1], 13-15 July, p. [3].
23. 'Journal of a Voyage Made in the Augusta Yatch', typescript copy of original at Mapperton House, Dorset, BM(NH), pp. 1-2. I am indebted to Averil M. Lysaght for obtaining a photocopy of the document and to A. B. Hooper for the interpretation and translation of Omai's remarks.
24. *Augusta* journal, pp. [3]-5.
25. ibid., pp. 6, 9, 10, 11, 12, 13, 14, 15, 19.
26. 24-27 June 1775, p. [1], 27-29 June, p. [1].
27. 22 March 1775, *CJ*, ii. 691-3.
28. 28 June 1775, ML; *CJ*, ii. 952-3; *BJ*, i. 105 and n. 3.
29. *Augusta* journal, pp. 19-25.
30. *General Evening Post*, 13-15 July 1775, pp. [3], [4], 18-20 July, p. [1]; *Augusta* journal, p. 10.
31. E. Smith, pp. 43-44; H. C. Cameron, *Sir Joseph Banks* (London, 1952), p. 108; *BJ*, i. 105.
32. J. E. Smith, ii. 23.
33. *CJ*, ii. 957.
34. *General Evening Post*, 27-29 July 1775, p. [4], 8-10 Aug., p. [3]; *London Chronicle*, 29 July-1 Aug., p. 111, 8-10 Aug., p. 142.
35. 12 Aug. 1775, DL; *General Evening Post*, 18-20 July 1775, p. [1], 8-12 Aug., p. [4].
36. 17-19 Aug. 1775, p. [3].
37. *CJ*, ii. 960.
38. ibid., 958-9.
39. *London Magazine*, xliv (1775), 441.
40. 14 Sept. 1775, *CJ*, ii. 699; 6 Sept. 1775, *CJ*, ii. 695.
41. *CJ*, ii. 656-8; A. Sparrman, *A Voyage round the World* (London, 1944), pp. 187-8.
42. *London Magazine*, xliv (1775), 496-7.
43. G. Colman, *Random Records* (3 vols., London, 1830), i. 152-6, 175. J. C. Beaglehole (*BJ*, i. 103 and n. 2) places the episode in the early summer or late spring of 1775, but Colman himself mentions August and September (i. 183, 184).
44. Colman, i. 157-61.
45. ibid., 162-6.
46. ibid., 182-5.

47. ibid., 187-9, 191, 193-5, 196-7.
48. R. B. Peake, *Memoirs of the Colman Family* (2 vols. in 1, London, 1841), i. 387-9.
49. ibid., 389.
50. 19 Sept. 1775, DL.
51. *ED*, ii. 130-1.
52. ibid., 131.
53. ibid., 131-2.
54. ibid., 132.
55. ibid., 131, 132-3.
56. *Philosophical Transactions*, lxv (1775), 28-29; R. Lonsdale, *Dr. Charles Burney* (Oxford, 1965), pp. 158, 173, 250.
57. *ED*, ii. 133-4.
58. 'Expences incurrd . . . in . . . 1775', NLA; *ED*, ii. 131.

8. Omai's Farewell

1. *Gentleman's Magazine*, xlvi (1776), 44, 46.
2. *General Evening Post*, 16-18 Jan. 1776, p. [1], 23-25 Jan., p. [1], 25-27 Jan., p. [3]; *London Chronicle*, 23-25 Jan., p. 86.
3. Walpole, ed. Paget Toynbee, ix. 320-2.
4. ibid., i. 28 n. 15; L. G. Crocker, *Jean-Jacques Rousseau* (2 vols., New York and London, 1968-73), ii. 276; G. de Beer, *Jean-Jacques Rousseau* (London, 1972), p. 85.
5. *General Evening Post*, 25-27 Jan. 1776, p. [3].
6. *CJ*, iii. liv-lv, 1485, ii. 700-3.
7. Cullum to Tyson, 13 Dec. 1775, Suffolk Record Office, Bury St. Edmunds.
8. County Record Office, Stafford.
9. P. Hoare, *Memoirs of Granville Sharp* (2 vols., London, 1828), i. 220-1.
10. ibid., 221-2.
11. G. Sharp, *An English Alphabet* (London, 1786), pp. 14, 56.
12. Hoare, i. 223, 225-6.
13. ibid., 226-7.
14. 5 Apr. 1776, BM; *ED*, ii. 138-9.
15. *Boswell's Life of Johnson*, iii. 8.
16. *ED*, i. 337 n.; *Autobiography, Letters and Literary Remains of Mrs. Piozzi (Thrale)*, ed. A. Hayward (2 vols., London, 1861), i. 48; *Thraliana*, ed. Katharine C. Balderston (2nd ed., 2 vols., Oxford, 1951), i. 48.
17. *Boswell: the Ominous Years*, ed. C. Ryskamp and F. A. Pottle (London, etc., 1963), pp. 308-9.

18. ibid., pp. 309, 310-11.
19. ibid., p. 310.
20. ibid., p. 341.
21. ibid., p. 344; *Boswell's Life of Johnson*, iii. 49-50.
22. E. K. Waterhouse, *Reynolds* (London, 1941), pp. 66-67; C. R. Leslie and T. Taylor, *Life and Times of Sir Joshua Reynolds* (2 vols., London, 1865), ii. 106, 146; D. Hudson, *Sir Joshua Reynolds* (London, 1958), p. 76; 'Sir Joshua Reynolds Loan Exhibition . . . At 45 Park Lane [London] February 9th to March 23rd . . . 1937', No. 15, 'WANG-Y-TONG'; Lord Sackville to the writer, 7 Apr. 1975.
23. E. K. Waterhouse, *Reynolds* (London, 1973), pp. 37, 39; Hudson, pp. 248-50; Charlotte Burney to Frances Burney, 10 Apr. [1780], BM; *The Farington Diary*, ed. J. Greig (8 vols., London, 1922-28), ii. 158-9.
24. Waterhouse (1941), p. 66; Librarian, Royal Academy of Arts, London, to the writer, 1 Nov. 1967.
25. W. Armstrong, *Sir Joshua Reynolds* (London, 1900), p. 222; A. Graves and W. V. Cronin, *A History of the Works of Sir Joshua Reynolds* (4 vols., London, 1899-1901), ii. 107-8, iv. 1380; W. Hazlitt, *Conversations of James Northcote* (London, 1830), Northcote's annotated copy, BM, pp. 170-1; Sir Ellis K. Waterhouse to the writer, 21 Aug. 1976.
26. *CJ*, ii. cxlviii-ix; J. C. Beaglehole, *The Life of Captain James Cook* (London, 1974), pp. 461-5.
27. *CJ*, iii. 1485, 1489, 1491-2, 1494, 1496-7, 1499.
28. ibid., 1460-3, 1465-7, 1471-3.
29. *Zimmermann's Account of the Third Voyage of Captain Cook*, trans. Miss U. Tewsley (Wellington, 1926), p. 48.
30. *CJ*, iii. lxxxiv, 1507.
31. J. E. Smith, ii. 24-25.
32. *CJ*, iii. lxxxiv, 1478.
33. ibid., 4, 193-4.
34. 'Account of Presents Sent out with Omai', etc., NLA.
35. 'An Account of the Bills for Oediddee', 'Things intended for Omai', NLA.
36. *BJ*, i. pl. v, facing p. 116.
37. Cradock, i. 128-9.
38. *General Evening Post*, 25-28 May 1776, p. [1], 8-11 June, p. [4].
39. ibid., 15-18 June 1776, p. [4]; *London*

Chronicle, 15-18 June, p. 582.
40. *CJ*, iii. lxxii, 4-5, 1506.
41. Beaglehole, *Life*, pp. 468-9.
42. *CJ*, ii. 428 n. 2; Cook, i. 169-70.
43. Cook, i. 170.
44. ibid., 170-1.
45. *Omiah's Farewell* (London, 1776), pp. [i]-ii; *Monthly Review*, lv (1776), 159; *Gentleman's Magazine*, xlvi (1776), 426.
46. *Omiah's Farewell*, pp. ii-iii.
47. ibid., pp. iii-iv.
48. ibid., pp. [1]-3.
49. ibid., pp. 4-11.
50. 'Omiah: an Ode', *The New Foundling Hospital for Wit* (6 vols., London, 1784), ii. 132-6; P. O'Reilly and E. Reitman, *Bibliographie de Tahiti et de la Polynésie Française* (Paris, 1967), p. 872.
51. 'Omiah: an Ode', 133 and n. 3, 134 and n. 1, 137.
52. 'Expences incurrd . . . in . . . 1776', NLA.

9. *Omai on the* Resolution

1. *CJ*, iii. lxxxv, 4-6.
2. ibid., ccxx-xxiv, 6-7.
3. ibid., 1511-12.
4. ibid., 7; *Gentleman's Magazine*, xlvi (1776), 257, 258, 262.
5. *CJ*, iii. 9-12, 730-2, 734.
6. ibid., 12 and n. 3, 13, 14 and n. 3, 15 and n. 1, 17, 741, 754.
7. ibid., 1514-15.
8. ibid., 17-18, 1515.
9. ibid., 18-20.
10. 'A Cape Link with Omai', *Africana Notes and News*, xl (1954), 169-70.
11. *CJ*, iii. 756-8, 1518-20.
12. ibid., 1520-21.
13. ibid., 24, 759-60, 1520, 1523-4.
14. ibid., 24-25, 25 n. 5, 26 and n. 2, 762-6; J. Rickman, *Journal of Captain Cook's Last Voyage to the Pacific Ocean* (London, 1781), pp. 33-34.
15. *CJ*, iii. 29-32, 33 n. 1, 42-43, 48 and n. 1, 769, 777, 990.
16. ibid., 48-52, 58 n. 2, 991.
17. ibid., 50-52, 54-55, 54 n. 2, 786-7, 993; J. Burney, 'Journal of . . . the Discovery' (henceforth cited as

Journal), photocopy, ML, 28 Jan. 1777.
18. *CJ*, iii. 53, 55-56, 56 n. 3, 58-59, 785, 993, 994; Rickman, pp. 42-43.
19. *CJ*, iii. 59-62, 70 and n. 1, 994-5, 998.
20. ibid., 59-61, 60 n. 3, 995.
21. ibid., 62-63, 66-67, 66 n. 2, 996, 1001.
22. ibid., 62-64, 68, 73, 814; Rickman, p. 55.
23. *CJ*, iii. 67-68, 813, 815, 818, 1000; Burney, Journal, 24 Feb. 1777.
24. Rickman, pp. 47, 50-51, 56-57, 59, 69-75.
25. *CJ*, iii. 69-71; W. Ellis, *An Authentic Narrative of a Voyage performed by Captain Cook and Captain Clerke* (2 vols., London, 1782), i. 27.
26. *CJ*, iii. 70, 1001; Rickman, pp. 54, 70.
27. *CJ*, iii. 76, 818, 1001-2; Rickman, p. 76.
28. *CJ*, iii. 71, 73-75.
29. ibid., 1002.
30. ibid., 75, 76 n. 3, 77 and n. 1, 78 and n. 1, 823 and n. 1, 1003; Rickman, pp. 78, 80.
31. *CJ*, iii. 78-80, 826-7.
32. ibid., 81-84, 81 n. 4, 833-4.
33. ibid., 86, 834-40, 843, 1006-7; Burney, Journal, 3 Apr. 1777.
34. *CJ*, iii. 86-87, 836, 839-40.
35. ibid., 88-89, 844-5.
36. ibid., 89-90, 89 n. 3 and 4, 846-7, 1010.
37. ibid., 91.
38. ibid., 91-93, 94 n. 3, 854-5, 1011-12; Ellis, i. 53; Burney, Journal, 16 Apr. 1777.
39. *CJ*, iii. 96-97; Rickman, p. 96.
40. *CJ*, iii. 1014; Rickman, pp. 96-102.
41. *CJ*, iii. 98-99, 99 n. 1, 1014; Burney, Journal, 7 May 1777.
42. *CJ*, iii. 99 n. 1, 100-2, 120, 865; Rickman, p. 104; Burney, Journal, 7 May 1777.
43. *CJ*, iii. 102-10, 107 n. 1, 1019, 1021-2, 1361-2.
44. ibid., ciii-iv, 111-12; Rickman, pp. 109-11.
45. *CJ*, iii. 111 and n. 1, 113, 115-16, 116 n. 2.
46. ibid., 113 n. 5, 118.
47. ibid., 118-23, 121 n. 1.
48. ibid., 124-5, 1024, 1031, 1045.
49. ibid., 125, 131, 136, 140-1, 145 and n. 1, 146-7, 158.
50. ibid., 1032; Burney, Journal, 11, 12 June 1777.

51. *CJ*, iii. 132 and n. 1, 134, 136-7, 1029; Rickman, p. 121; Burney, Journal, 18 June 1777.
52. *CJ*, iii. 133-4, 133 n. 2, 144, 155.
53. ibid., 158; Burney, Journal, 11 June 1777.
54. *CJ*, iii. 156-60, 158 n. 2.
55. ibid., 928-9.
56. ibid., 160, 170.
57. ibid., cvii-viii, 162-3, 163 n. 3, 182-5, 1051-2; W. Bayly, 'Journal of Cook's Third voyage', ATL, p. 120.

10. Omai's Homecoming

1. *CJ*, iii. 1052, 1368-9.
2. ibid., 186-7, 1052-3, 1369.
3. ibid., 187, 1053, 1370.
4. ibid., 188 and n. 1, 2, 1057, 1313.
5. ibid., 188, 972, 1054, 1314, 1371; W. Ellis, i. 125-6.
6. *CJ*, iii. 222; B. G. Corney, *The Quest and Occupation of Tahiti by Emissaries of Spain* (3 vols., London, 1913-19), i. xxxiv, 10-15, 254, ii. 172-3, 224, 357.
7. *CJ*, iii. 223, 1314; Corney, ii. 93, iii. 266, 269.
8. *CJ*, iii. 187 n. 3, 189, 974.
9. ibid., 1056, 1372; Rickman, pp. 133-4, pl. facing p. 136.
10. *CJ*, iii. 189, 1057, 1373; W. Ellis, i. 127-8.
11. *CJ*, iii. 189-90, 974-5, 1056, 1372.
12. ibid., 188, 190-1, 224, 1315, 1371-2.
13. ibid., cx, 186, 1368-9.
14. ibid., 185, 191-2, 1372.
15. ibid., 192; Rickman, pp. 137-9.
16. *CJ*, iii. 192-3.
17. ibid., 193-4, 1314.
18. ibid., 194-5, 1374-5.
19. W. Ellis, i. 137; G. Forster, ii. 89-90, 103; *CJ*, ii. 399-400, 426 and n. 2, iii. 195, 1063.
20. *CJ*, iii. 195 and n. 1, 1058-9, 1375; *Zimmermann's Captain Cook*, ed. F. W. Howay (Toronto, 1930), pp. 54-55.
21. *CJ*, iii. 193 and n. 2, 195 n. 1, 1059.
22. ibid., 196-7, 196 n. 2, 1060-2, 1345, 1375.
23. ibid., 197-9, 198 n. 4, 205-6.
24. ibid., 206-10, 985-6, 1062, 1375; Rickman, pp. 137, 142, 149.
25. *CJ*, iii. 1062-3.
26. ibid., 208-11, 1066, 1376.
27. ibid., 186 n. 2, 220, 221, 1062, 1343, 1387; W. Ellis, i. 135-6; Burney, Journal, 14 Aug. 1777.
28. *CJ*, iii. 212-13.
29. ibid., 213-19, 216 n. 1, 1066, 1381, 1387.
30. ibid., 214-15, 218, 222; 'Lieutenant Watts's Narrative', *The Voyage of Governor Phillip to Botany Bay* (2nd ed., London, 1790), pp. 244-5.
31. *CJ*, iii. 211, 218-20, 1066, 1374.
32. ibid., 219-21, 1066-7; Rickman, p. 161.
33. *CJ*, iii. 220-1, 224 n. 2, 1381.
34. ibid., 224-6, 225 n. 7; W. Ellis, i. 146.
35. *CJ*, iii. 226 and n. 2, 232, 1067, 1382; Zimmermann, pp. 56-57.
36. *CJ*, iii. 226 and n. 3, 227 and n. 1, 2. 1067, 1382; W. Ellis, i. 144.
37. *CJ*, 227-8, 1067.
38. ibid., 228-9, 229 n. 1.
39. ibid., 229.
40. ibid., 230-1, 1069.
41. ibid., 231 n. 5, 232 n. 1, 1069, 1383.
42. ibid., 232-3, 1069, 1383.
43. ibid., 223, 1387; Bayly, 'Journal of Cook's Third voyage', pp. 131-2.
44. *CJ*, iii. 233-4, 233 n. 2.
45. ibid., 234-5, 235 n. 1.
46. ibid., 235-6, 1070.
47. ibid., 236 and n. 1, 1070, 1384; Rickman, pp. 170-1, 175; J. Cook and J. King, *A Voyage to the Pacific Ocean* (3 vols., London, 1784), ii. 98-99; Bayly, Supplementary Journal of Third Voyage, ATL, p. 23.
48. *CJ*, iii. 236, 1070-1, 1384-5.
49. ibid., 236-8, 238 n. 2, 1071-2; Rickman, pp. 174, 182.
50. *CJ*, iii. 239, 1070; Zimmermann, p. 59.
51. *CJ*, iii. 193 n. 2, 237 and n. 2, 1386; Bayly, Supplementary Journal, p. 26.
52. *CJ*, iii. 238-9, 1387; Zimmermann, p. 59.
53. *CJ*, iii. 239-40, 1386; Rickman, pp. 177-8, 180-1, 186.
54. *CJ*, iii. 1386-7.
55. ibid., 240-1.
56. ibid., 240, 241, 1072.
57. ibid., 241-2.
58. ibid., 1072-3.
59. ibid., 242 n. 1, 1387-8; Rickman, pp. 184-5; Burney, Journal, 2 Nov. 1777.
60. *CJ*, iii. 240 and n. 4, 1073, 1386; Burney, Journal, 2 Nov. 1777; Zimmermann, p. 59; Rickman, pp. 183-4.
61. *CJ*, iii. 242, 244-5, 244 n. 6, 252-3,

1074, 1079; Burney, Journal, 12 Nov. 1777.

11. The End of Omai

1. *CJ*, iii. 698, 700-3, 717, 1552-3.
2. *BJ*, i. 114, 118-19; Cameron, pp. 254-5, 273; E. Smith, p. 62 and n. 1.
3. Martelli, pp. 165, 176, 224, 234-5.
4. ML.
5. *CJ*, iii. cxcviii-cciv, cc n. 1; Martelli, p. 268; Susan Phillips to C. Burney, n.d. (Feb. 1784), photocopy, ATL.
6. *CJ*, iii. cxcviii; Cook and King, ii. 103.
7. Cook and King, ii. 105-8.
8. *CJ*, iii. 222.
9. Cameron, pp. 179, 271; E. Smith, 213-16; *CJ*, iii. 1466-7; 'Watts's Narrative', *The Voyage of Governor Phillip*, pp. 10, 233, 241, 257.
10. 'Watts's Narrative', pp. 241-2.
11. ibid., pp. 243, 245-6.
12. ibid., pp. 247-9.
13. ibid., pp. 246-7, 249-51.
14. ibid., pp. 251-2.
15. ibid., pp. 252-3.
16. Cameron, pp. 77-78; D. Mackay, 'Banks, Bligh and Breadfruit', *New Zealand Journal of History*, viii (1974), 61-73; *The Log of the 'Bounty'*, ed. O. Rutter (2 vols., London, 1936), i. 370.
17. *'Bounty' Log*, i. 371-2.
18. ibid., 371-3.
19. ibid., 373-5; H. B. Adams, *Tahiti* (3rd ed., Ridgewood, 1968), p. 99.
20. *'Bounty' Log*, i. 378-81, 401.
21. ibid., i. 375-6, 384-6, 407, ii. 14-15, 19-21.
22. ibid., i. 385, 393, 394.
23. ibid., 394.
24. ibid.
25. ibid., 408, 417.
26. ibid., i. 384, ii. 17, 21-22, 27, 35, 45, 51, 58-60.
27. ibid., i. 388, 399, 403, 406, 407, 411, 418-19, 427, ii, 25, 48, 57.
28. ibid., i, 4, 26-27, ii. 28, 49, 61, 68, 70.
29. ibid., ii. 27-28, 40, 58, 63-64, 67, 69, 70.
30. ibid., 82-83.
31. ibid., 82-84, 118-20.
32. *The Journal of James Morrison*, ed. O. Rutter (London, 1935), pp. 6, 12, 31, 36, 47-51.
33. ibid., pp. 51-53.
34. ibid., pp. 53-57.

35. G. Mortimer, *Observations and Remarks made during a Voyage to the Islands* (London, 1791), pp. v-vi, 22-25; J. Cottez, 'Histoire d'une Expédition Militaire Suédoise dans le Pacifique à la fin du xviiime Siècle', *Bulletin de la Société d'Études Océaniennes*, viii (1950-2), 425-53.
36. Mortimer, pp. 25-26, 33, 36.
37. ibid,, pp. 26-28, 30-32, 34-35, 45.
38. ibid., pp. vii, 36-42, 44-48.
39. Morrison, pp. 60-64, 74-76.
40. ibid., pp. 76-81.
41. ibid., pp. 81, 83-85, 89, 92-94.
42. ibid., pp. 97-106.
43. ibid., pp. 107-8, 111.
44. ibid., p. 112.
45. ibid., pp. 112-13.
46. ibid.
47. ibid., pp. 107, 113, 116-17, 119, 121, 124.
48. *The Journal of Captain James Colnett aboard the 'Argonaut'*, ed. F. W. Howay (Toronto, 1940), pp. xiii, xvii, xxi-xxv, 211, 213-14, 217-18; B. Anderson, *Surveyor of the Sea: The Life and Voyages of Captain George Vancouver* (Seattle, 1960), pp. 32-35; *CJ*, ii. 876.
49. Anderson, pp. 35-47, 234-7; G. Vancouver, *A Voyage of Discovery to the North Pacific Ocean, and round the World* (3 vols., London, 1798), i. 2, 4, 79; *CJ*, ii. 880, iii. 1472; A. B. Hooper to the writer, 5 Nov. 1975.
50. Vancouver, i. 70, 96, 98-100, 102, 104.
51. ibid., 102-5, 110-11, 113.
52. ibid., 103, 114-15, 123-9, 133-4.
53. ibid., 135-6, 141.
54. ibid., 137-40, 142-4.
55. ibid., 145-8.
56. ibid., 137, 148-9.
57. D. L. Oliver, *Ancient Tahitian Society* (3 vols., Honolulu, 1974), iii. 1272-3, 1294-5, 1298, 1339, 1349; J. Davies, *The History of the Tahitian Mission 1799-1830*, ed. C. W. Newbury (London, 1961), pp. 63-64, 125, 127, 221.
58. The Revd. W. Ellis, ii. 365-6.
59. ibid., 366-8.
60. ibid., 369.
61. ibid.
62. ibid., 369-70.
63. ibid., 370-1.
64. ibid., 375.
65. ibid., 371-4.

12. *Omai in Europe — the Literary Aftermath*

1. *CJ*, ii. cxlviii-ix.
2. Forster, *Voyage*, i. 388-9, ii. 83, 92, 134.
3. ibid., i. 392, ii, 54, 90-91, 143.
4. ibid., i. xiv-xvi.
5. ibid., xvi-xvii.
6. W. Wales, *Remarks on Mr. Forster's Account of Captain Cook's Last Voyage* (London, 1778), p. 15.
7. ibid., pp. 15-16.
8. ibid., pp. 16-17.
9. G. Forster, *Reply to Mr. Wales's Remarks* (London, 1778), pp. 21-22.
10. ibid., pp. 22-23.
11. *CJ*, ii. cxlviii; Beddie, 221-5; *Gentleman's Magazine*, xlvii (1777), 491-4.
12. W. Preston, *Seventeen Hundred and Seventy-Seven* (London, 1777), pp. 1, 2; Halkett and Laing, v. 237.
13. Preston, pp. 3, 16, 18, 21, 25.
14. *The Injured Islanders* (London, 1779), pp. [5] and n., [6]-[7], 1, 4, 7, 13-14, 24-25; B. Smith, *European Vision and the South Pacific* (Oxford, 1960), p. 62.
15. J. Perry, *Mimosa* (London, 1779), pp. iii-v; Halkett and Laing, iv. 80.
16. *The Travels of Hildebrand Bowman* (London, 1778), pp. iii-iv, 13, 79.
17. *Hildebrand Bowman*, pp. 26-398 *passim*.
18. B. Smith, pp. 72-73.
19. *A Letter from Omai* (London, 1782?), p. 1.
20. ibid., pp. 4-5, 15, 24.
21. *Elegy on Captain Cook* (London, 1780), pp. 15-16; *Gentleman's Magazine*, l (1780), 432; Beddie, 453-4.
22. *CJ*, iii. ccv-vii; Beddie, 311-17; E. Smith, pp. 52-53.
23. *CJ*, iii. cciv; Beddie, 298-306; *Gentleman's Magazine*, liv (1784), 449, 683.
24. *Diary and Letters of Madame d'Arblay*, ed. A. Dobson (6 vols., London, 1904-5), ii. 256, 266; *The Correspondence of William Cowper*, ed. T. Wright (4 vols., London, 1904), ii. 236, 238, 249.
25. W. Cowper, *The Task* (London, 1785), pp. 32-34.
26. ibid., pp. 34-35.
27. R. E. Raspe and others, *Singular Travels, Campaigns and Adventures of Baron Munchausen*, introd. J. Carswell (London, 1948), pp. xxi-xxii,

xxviii, 60, 168-9.
28. ibid., pp. xxviii-xxix, 152-3, 176-7.
29. *The Loiterer*, No. xxxv (Oxford, 18 July 1789), pp. [3]-5, 8.
30. ibid., pp. 7, 9, 10-11, 12-13.
31. W. Huse, 'A Noble Savage on the Stage', *Modern Philology*, xxxiii (1936), 303-16; J. O'Keeffe, *Recollections of the Life of John O'Keeffe* (2 vols., London, 1826), ii. 113-14; W. T. Whitley, *Artists and their Friends in England 1700-1799* (2 vols., London and Boston, 1928), ii. 353; *Morning Chronicle, and London Advertiser*, 20 Dec. 1785, p. [1].
32. *Gentleman's Magazine*, xlix (1779), 98; Whitley, ii. 354; *Morning Chronicle*, 21 Dec. 1785, p. [3].
33. *London Chronicle*, 20-22 Dec. 1785, pp. 595, 596; Whitley, ii. 354.
34. Whitley, ii. 354; *Morning Chronicle*, 22 Dec. 1785, p. [2], 24 Dec., p. [2]; Huse, 303; *An Historic Epistle*, p. 21.
35. *Correspondance de Louis de Fontanes et de Joseph Joubert*, ed. R. Tessoneau (Paris, 1943), pp. iii-iv, xi, 1, 11-12, 14, 20, 28-29.
36. ibid., pp. 11, 19, 26-28.
37. J. Gautier, 'Abbé Baston', *Journal de la Société des Océanistes*, iii (1947), 52; G.-A.-R. Baston, *Narrations d'Omaï* (4 vols., Rouen and Paris, 1790), i. [v]-[viii].
38. Baston, i. 3, 9-10, 13, 14, 26, 28-29, 31, 36.
39. ibid., 37-41.
40. ibid., 43-50.
41. ibid., 50-52, 54, 56-64, 68.
42. ibid., 111, 126-8, 172, 253-4, 257, 259, 262, 298, 304, 323-6, 332-3.
43. ibid., i. 336-7, 339, 342, 344, 405, 423-5, ii. 27-34.
44. ibid., i. 427, ii. 232-3, 237, 269 ff., 275-80, 284-5, 394-5, 401, 424-6, iii. 26 ff., 46, 81, 126, 293 ff., 350-4, iv. 216.
45. ibid., iv. 243, 289-90, 301, 305, 309-10, 318, 360, 363-4.
46. ibid., 323-4, 327-30, 332-3, 335, 337-40.
47. ibid., 350-1, 353-4.
48. ibid., ii. 359, iii. 181, 264, 285-7, 339, iv. 183-4, 238, 332, 381.
49. ibid., iv. 384-5, 397-9, 404-6, 409, 445-6, 451, 457, 462.
50. O'Reilly and Reitman, pp. 819, 820-1; J. Richard, *Voyages chez Les Peuples*

Sauvages (3 vols., Paris, 1801), vol. i, 'Epitre Dedicatoire', pp. i-ii, 'Avis de l'Editeur', pp. i-iv.

51. Richard, ii. 178-9, 197-8, 359, iii. 250-60, 262-6.

52. ibid., ii. 135-6, 384-9, 394-5.

53. ibid., ii. 446-8, iii. 270-1, 475-6.

54. Monboddo to Banks, 9 July 1782, D.T.C. BM(NH).

55. A. Mello to Banks, 16 July 1776, Monboddo to Banks, 29 Aug. 1782, 30 Jan. 1783, D.T.C. BM(NH); *The Banks Letters*, ed. W. R. Dawson (London, 1958), p. 603.

56. Cameron, pp. 77-8; Dawson, p. 110; *The Anthropological Treatises of Johann Friedrich Blumenbach*, ed. T. Bendyshe (London, 1865), pp. 259, 331-2, 334, 336-8; E. L. Cloyd, *James Burnett* (Oxford, 1972), p. 190.

57. Blumenbach, ed. Bendyshe, pp. vii-ix; Blumenbach to Banks, 8 Jan. 1794, 20 Dec. 1798, 30 Jan. 1799, BM; J. F. Blumenbach, *De Generis Humani Varietate Nativa* (3rd ed., Göttingen, 1795), table II. 4.

58. J. F. Blumenbach, *Abbildungen naturhistorischer Gegenstände* (2nd ed., Göttingen, 1810), sect. 4. The translation is by R. A. Lochore.

59. *Boswell's Life of Johnson*, i. 9 n. 3; Blumenbach to Banks, 20 Dec. 1798, BM; L. Collison-Morley, *Giuseppi Baretti* (London, 1909), pp. 330-3.

60. Hester L. Thrale (Piozzi), ed. Hayward, ii. 294; Hudson, p. 142; Frances Burney (d'Arblay), ed. Dobson, vi. 397.

61. Lysaght, p. 59; Martelli, pp. 286-7; Lonsdale, p. 361; E. Smith, p. 326; Joyce Hemlow, *The History of Fanny Burney* (Oxford, 1958), pp. 428, 456.

62. Frances Burney (d'Arblay), *Memoirs of Dr. Burney*, i. 283-7.

63. ibid., ii. 4-8.

64. Hemlow, p. 491.

Postscript

1. *The Case and Memoirs of the Late Rev. Mr. James Hackman* (2nd ed., London, 1779), p. 2; *The Case and Memoirs of Miss Martha Ray* (London, 1779), p. 28.

2. H. Croft, *Love and Madness: A Story too True in a Series of Letters* (new ed., London, 1780), p. 6.

3. I am indebted to Mr. T. Wilsted, Manuscript Librarian of the Alexander Turnbull Library, for drawing my attention to the letter and to Mr. Peter G. Markham for allowing me to reproduce it. By a coincidence in my edition of Edward Markham's *New Zealand or Recollections of it* (Wellington, 1963) both Mr. Markham and the Archbishop are mentioned, the latter as 'preceptor' to George III's two elder sons (pp. 13, 16).

Index

Page references to illustrations and maps are in *italic* type. Where necessary, references to the two voyages of the *Resolution* (1772-5 and 1776-80) are distinguished as *Resolution* (1) and *Resolution* (2).

Abyssinia, 93, 96, 97, 111, 312
Acclimatization, of animals, etc.: 30-31, 40, 42, 179, 298; Huahine, 256, 271, 275, 283-4, 290, 293; Moorea, 274, 277, 278, 280, 289; N.Z., 44, 64, 67-68, 201-2; *Resolution* (2), 191, 193, 194, 195, 198, 206, 210; Tahiti, 50, 225, 226, 232-3, 240, 242-3, 261, 265-6, 268, 270-1, 274, 276, 289, 297, 300; Tonga, 64, 213, 220-1, 222; Tubuai, 276, 279; Van Diemen's Land, 200; of plants, etc.: 30-31, 40; Huahine, 253, 271, 275, 284, 290, 293; N.Z., 43, 44, 64, 68, 201; Tahiti, 226, 233, 266, 268, 269, 270, 271, 274, 277, 289; Tonga, 62, 64, 213, 217-18, 221-2; Van Diemen's Land, 200
Adventure, purchased and named, 34; leaves Plymouth, 38; passage to Cape of Good Hope, 39-40; in Antarctic, 41-42, 151; at Van Diemen's Land, 43; in N.Z., 43-44; in Pacific, 44, 46; at Tahiti, 47-51, 283; in Society Is., 51-57; picks up Omai, 53, 305; in Tonga, 62-64; returns to N.Z., 64-70, 202, 301; reaches England, 71, 94-96, 98; other references: 101, 102, 106, 109, 134, 135, 146, 150, 200, 205, 233, 260, 321; map, *45*; *41*, *68-69*, *70*
Adventure Bay, 43, 198
Ahutoru, *see* Aoutourou
American War of Independence, 96, 124, 135, 141, 149, 163, 186, 187, 261, 264, 267
Amo, *see* Oamo
Amsterdam I., *see* Tongatapu
Anderson, William, joins *Resolution* (2), 178; passage to Cape of Good Hope, 191-2; mentions Omai, 192; at Cape, 194-5; reports on Omai, 194; lists animals, 195; at Kerguelen I., 198; in Van Diemen's Land, 199; in N.Z., 202; on Omai as interpreter, 202; on New Zealanders, 202; benefits from Omai, 206; on Mangaians, 206; visits Atiu 207-8; refers to Omai, 208, 209; lands on Palmerston, 210; praises Omai, 210; tribute to Tongans,

222; at Tahitian human sacrifice, 237; visits Pare, 240; and narrative of 3rd expedition, 263; death, 263
Andrews, Thomas, 96, 102, 109, 117, 121, 135, 160, 161, 163, 187
Angelo, Domenick, 140-1
Angelo, Henry, 140-1
Antarctic, 34, 40, 42, 57, 64, 67
Aoutourou, boards *Étoile*, 14, 20; on *Boudeuse*, 15-17, 24; in Paris, 17-18; at Mauritius, 16-17, 24, 138; Bougainville discusses, 32; death, 40, 48, 100, 101, 113, 138, 151; and Marion du Fresne, 40, 93, 151, 195; and Monboddo, 80; in Baston, 321
Apyrexia, 104, 139
Arblay, Madame d', *see* Burney, Frances
Argonaut, 284, 285
Ataongo, *see* Otago
Atiu, 207-8, 209, 323
Attuiock, 76-77
Augusta, 144-7, 161, 182
Australia, *see* New Holland

Babié, François, 327-9
Banks, Dorothea (*née* Hugessen), 262, 332
Banks, Joseph, on *Endeavour*, 18-24, 46, 48, 56, 100, 103, 133, 141, 219, 251, 264, 278, 283; returns to England, 25-34; projected natural history, 30, 33, 92, 93, 133, 330; prepares for 2nd expedition, 34-37, 39; withdraws from expedition, 37, 39, 88, 133, 156; breach with Sandwich, 37-38; proposed Pacific voyage, 38, 41, 73, 74, 78, 80; visits Iceland, 38, 73; visits Scotland, 73-74, 77; returns to England, 74; proposed Arctic expedition, 74-76, 93; visits Holland, 74-75; in Wales, 75; and Eskimos, 76-78; in Hawkesworth, 80, 82-83, 170, 263; satirized, 89-90, 92, 122-4, 142, 143, 186, 301-2, 304; meets Omai, 94-97, 106, 109, 139, 183; during Omai's inoculation, 98, 101-10; reconciled with Sandwich, 106, 110, 133; at

extends term, 243; *Resolution* (2) and *Discovery* visit, 249-60; *Lady Penrhyn* calls at, 266-7; *Bounty* calls at, 274-5; other references: 93, 132, 206, 234, 245, 261, 283, 284; map, *54*
See also Borabora, Huahine, Raiatea, Tahaa
Society Islanders, *see* Tahitians and Society Islanders
Solander, Daniel Carl, on *Endeavour*, 18-24, 80, 100, 103, 141; returns to England, 24, 25-34; projected natural history, 30, 33, 92, 93, 133; Boswell meets, 34; prepares for 2nd expedition, 34-37, 156; visits Iceland, 73; in Edinburgh, 73; in Wales, 75; meets Eskimos, 77; in Hawkesworth, 83; satirized, 90, 143, 186; criticizes Hawkesworth, 92; discusses Furneaux, 101, 102; meets Omai, 94, 99, 105, 139, 183; discusses Omai, 94, 101-2, 106, 109-10, 113, 117, 121; escorts Omai, 97, 105, 112, 125, 127, 138, 140; during Omai's inoculation, 98, 101-10; at Hinchingbrooke, 112, 113; in London, 113, 118, 121, 138, 148; elected to council, Royal Society, 130; reports on voyage of *Resolution* (1), 146-7, 148-9; advocates transfer of breadfruit, 179, 267; in painting by Parry, 180; Omai greets, 195; death, 267, 330; in *Hildebrand Bowman*, 305; in Baston, 323; other references: 115, 170, 178, 268; *107*
Southern Continent, de Brosses on, 8; Dalrymple discusses, 9, 88; Wallis seeks, 9; Cook seeks, 21, 22; Tupia ignorant of, 22; Cook renews search for, 34, 41-42; Hawkesworth uninterested in, 82, 88; Solander on, 101; Cook discusses, 146, 151, 156; and Kerguelen, 198; in *Hildebrand Bowman*, 306
Spaniards in Tahiti, 48, 50-51, 224-5, 226-7, 230, 236, 248, 264, 273, 284-5, 287, 327
Sparrman, Anders, 40, 51-52
Stanhope, Philip, 128, 335
Steele, Joshua, 160
Stevens, Richard, 115
Strange, Mrs. Isabella, 136-7, 180, 255
Strange, Isabella Katherina, 111
Strange, Robert, 124, 125, 127
Sunninghill, 95
Surville, Jean- François-Marie de, 22, 151, 206
Sweden, 277
Swift, Jonathan, 141
Syren, 191

Table Bay, 40, 41, 71, 192, 195
Table Cape, 64
Tahaa, 21, 53, 60, 286, 293; map, *54*
Tahiti, Omai escapes to, 3; Omai lives in, 3-4; *Dolphin* visits, 9-12; Wallis names King George III's Island, 11; Bougainville visits, 12-15; Bougainville names New Cythera, 15; *Endeavour* visits, 18-21, 132; Cook names Otaheite, 19; *Resolution* (1) and *Adventure* visit, 46-51; *Resolution* (1) returns to, 146, 156; Spaniards visit, 48, 50-51, 226-7; Hawkesworth on, 82-83, 87; breadfruit

flourishes in, 179; *Resolution* (2) and *Discovery* visit, 223-43; *Lady Penrhyn* visits, 265-6; *Bounty* visits, 267-74, 275, 276, 279; European influence on, 268, 274, 286, 288, 299; *Mercury* visits, 277-8; mutineers settle in, 279; *Pandora* visits, 284; Vancouver visits, 285-9; *Chatham* visits, 285; missionaries settle in, 289; other references *passim*; maps, *15, 54*; *2, 3, 10, 46-47*
Tahitians and Society Islanders, social and religious customs, 1-4; Wallis describes, 12; Bougainville describes, 15-16, 32; Banks describes, 22, 75, 228; newspapers mention, 25-26; in unauthorized *Journal* of *Endeavour*, 30; *Monthly Review* discusses, 33, 85-86; Cook discusses, 51, 57; Omai discloses, 60-61; Hawkesworth on, 82; satirists on, 89-90; in *Otaheite*, 91-92; compared with Tongans, 64, 228; Hodges praises, 148; compared with Cook Islanders, 207; in Baston, 324-6; attributes, customs, institutions, etc.: *arioi*, 4, 20, 82, 133, 273, 295, 302; astronomical lore, 4, 16, 30, 61; ceremonies, 1, 3, 21, 228-30, 232, 250-3, 279-80, 284; entertainments, 4, 16, 22, 50, 55, 60, 228, 238, 253-4; food, 1, 2-3, 14, 20, 33; human sacrifice, 1, 16, 32, 51, 60-61, 237-8, 284, 325; *236-7*; infanticide, 20, 60, 75, 82, 91, 122, 141, 296, 302, 325; music, 14, 159-60, 263; religious observances, 1, 2, 4, 20, 21, 26, 30, 32, 33, 60-61; sexual customs, 4, 14, 16, 20, 26, 30, 33, 75, 82, 85, 89, 91, 122, 170, 325; social classes, 1, 4, 58, 99, 122, 272; supercision, 4, 30, 133, 325; tattooing, 3, 12, 14, 21, 26, 89, 90, 122, 133, 275; thievery, 11, 14, 19, 20, 26, 47, 82, 268, 273, 287; warfare, 20, 32, 47, 50, 59-60, 82, 85, 156, 236-7, 241-2, 245, 265, 270, 271-2, 280, 283, 288, 292, 324
Tahiti Iti, 20, 46, 47; map, *15*
Tahiti Nui, 3, 20, 47, 49, 280; map, *15*
Tahua, *see* Towha
Taina, *see* Otoo
Takutea, 209
Tamar River, 147
Taputapuatea, 2
Tareederria, 250, 251, 255, 271, 272, 284, 287, 292, 323, 324
Tasman, Abel Janszoon, 22, 42, 62
Tasmania, *see* Van Diemen's Land
Tayeto, 21, 23, 24, 25, 40, 113; *23*
Tenerife, 191
Teriitaria, *see* Tareederria
Tereroa, 59, 60
Teriire, *see* Terry Derry
Terra Australis, *see* Southern Continent
Terry Derry, 20, 242, 284
Te Weherua, *see* Tiarooa
Thrale, Henry, 162, 169, 173, 333
Thrale, Mrs. Hester Lynch (Piozzi), 169, 173, 309, 333-4
Tiarooa, N.Z. youth, 200; recruited by Omai, 204; on *Resolution* (2), 204-6; at Hervey Is.,